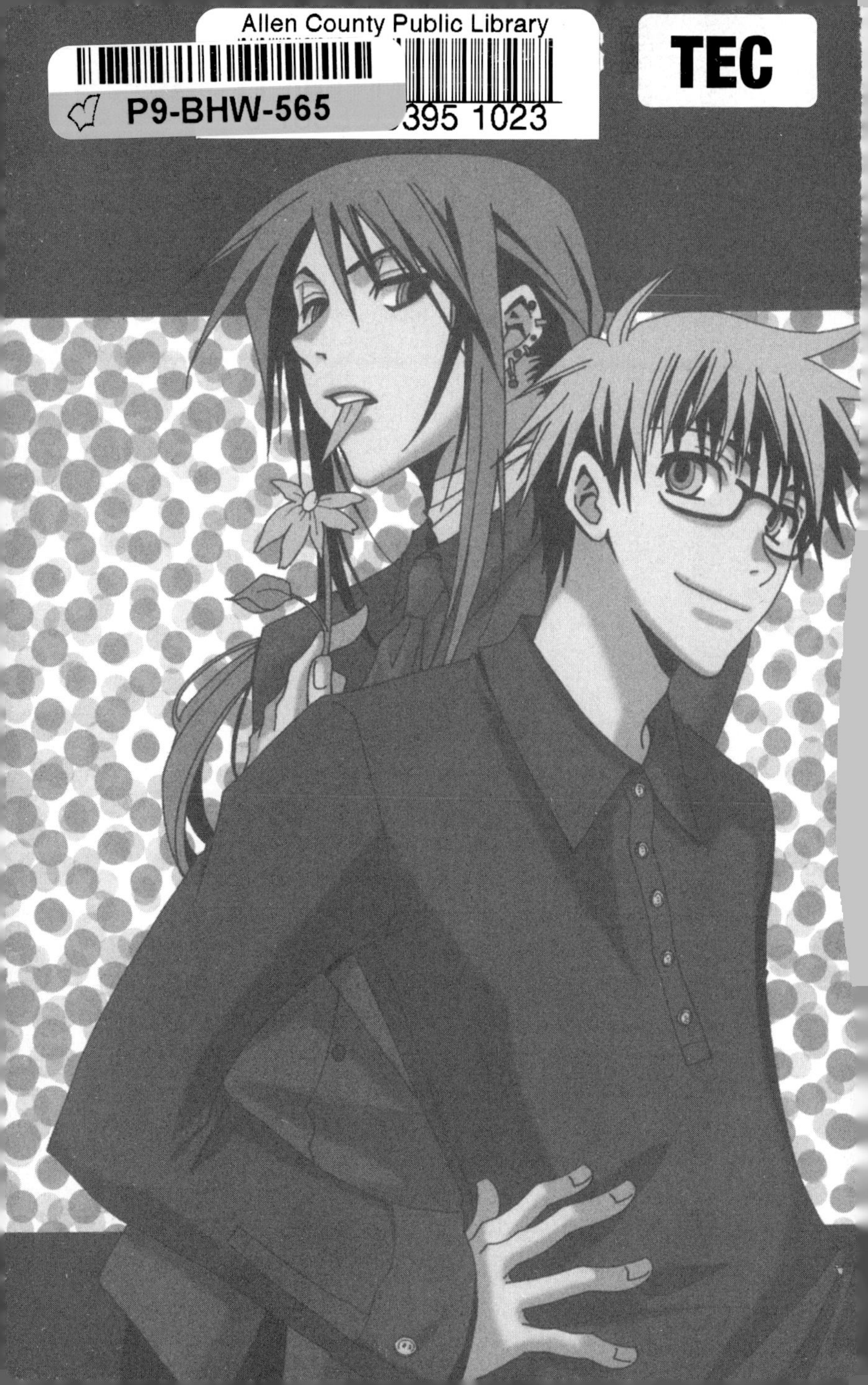

Shinshoku Kiss Volume 1
Created by Kazuko Higashiyama

Translation - Monica Seya Chin
English Adaptation - Jay Antani
Copy Editor - Stephanie Duchin
Retouch and Lettering - Star Print Brokers
Production Artist - Skooter
Cover Design - James Lee

Editor - Hope Donovan
Digital Imaging Manager - Chris Buford
Pre-Production Supervisor - Erika Terriquez
Production Manager - Elisabeth Brizzi
Managing Editor - Vy Nguyen
Creative Director - Anne Marie Horne
Editor-in-Chief - Rob Tokar
Publisher - Mike Kiley
President and C.O.O. - John Parker
C.E.O. and Chief Creative Officer - Stuart Levy

A  **TOKYOPOP**® Manga

TOKYOPOP and are trademarks or registered trademarks of TOKYOPOP Inc.

TOKYOPOP Inc.
5900 Wilshire Blvd. Suite 2000
Los Angeles, CA 90036

E-mail: info@TOKYOPOP.com
Come visit us online at www.TOKYOPOP.com

ISBN: 978-1-4278-0307-8

First TOKYOPOP printing: October 2007
10 9 8 7 6 5 4 3 2 1
Printed in the USA

KAZUKO HIGASHIYAMA

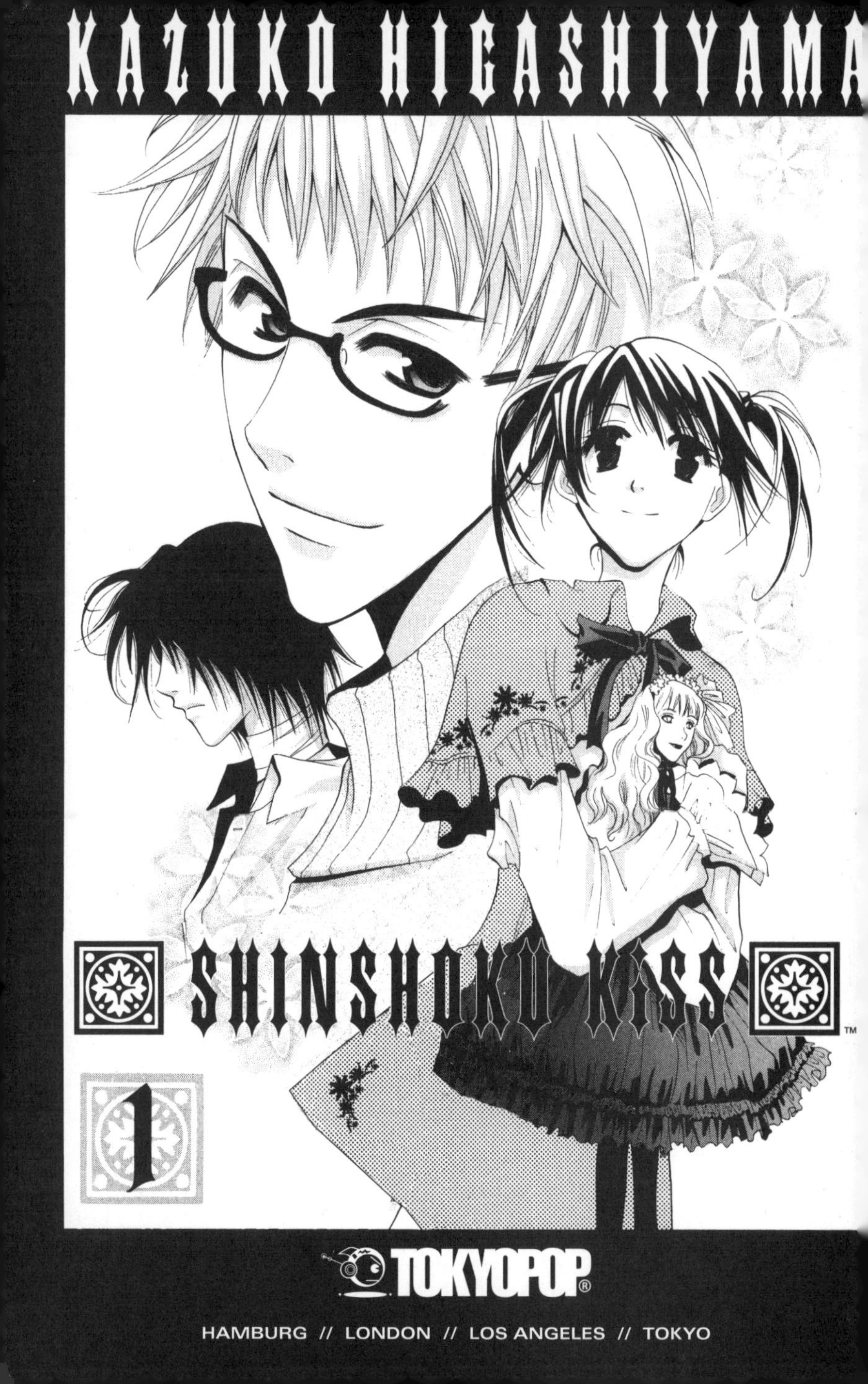

SHINSHOKU KISS™

1

TOKYOPOP®

HAMBURG // LONDON // LOS ANGELES // TOKYO

Kazuko Higashiyama
SHINSHOKU KiSS

CONTENTS

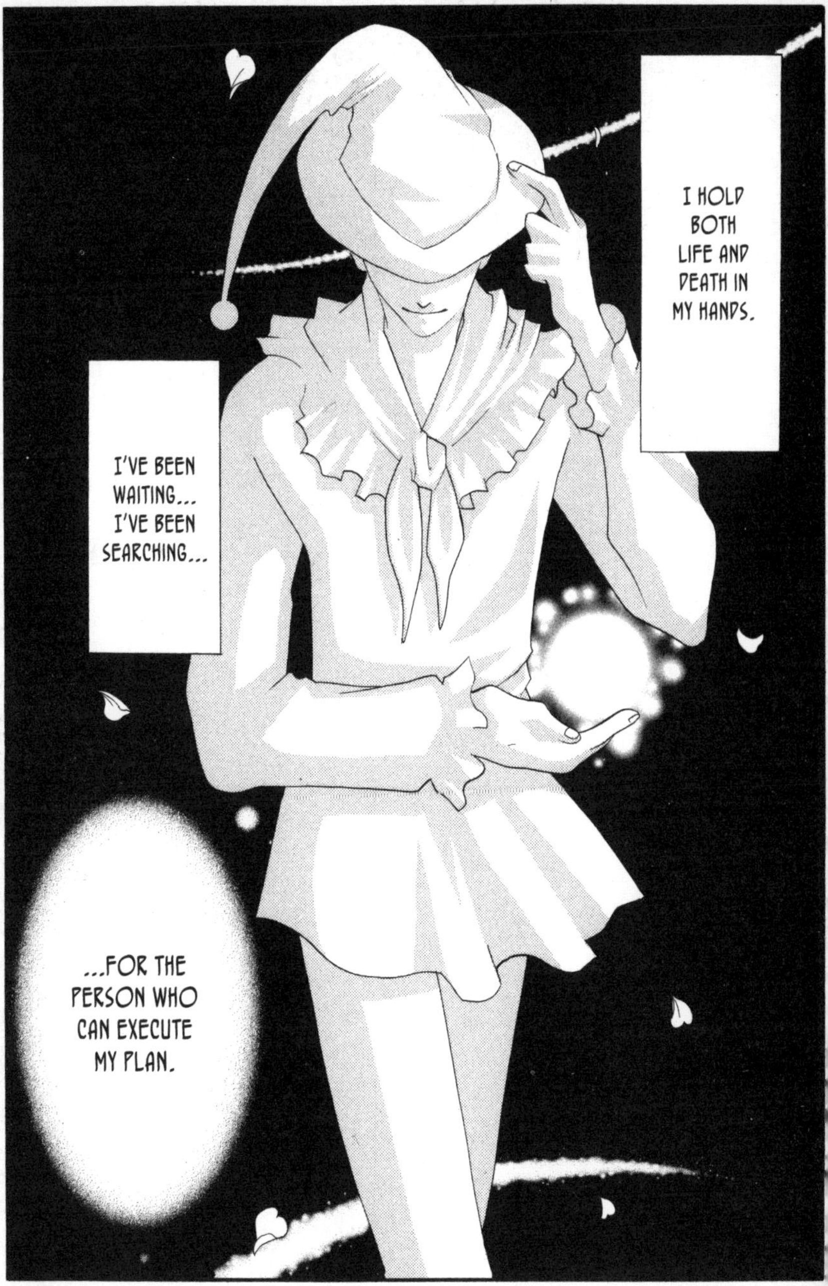
I HOLD BOTH LIFE AND DEATH IN MY HANDS.
I'VE BEEN WAITING... I'VE BEEN SEARCHING...
...FOR THE PERSON WHO CAN EXECUTE MY PLAN.

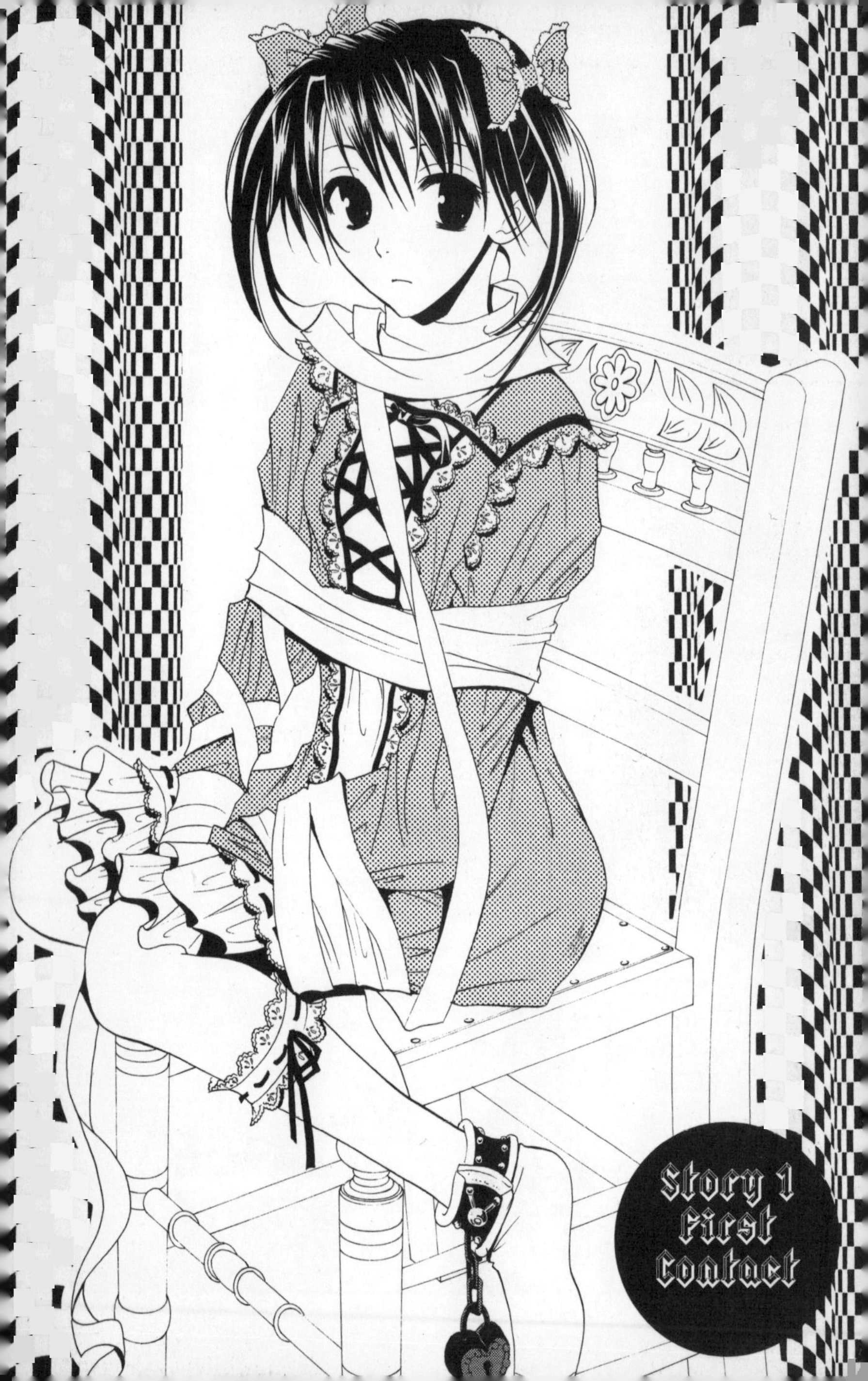
Story 1
First
Contact

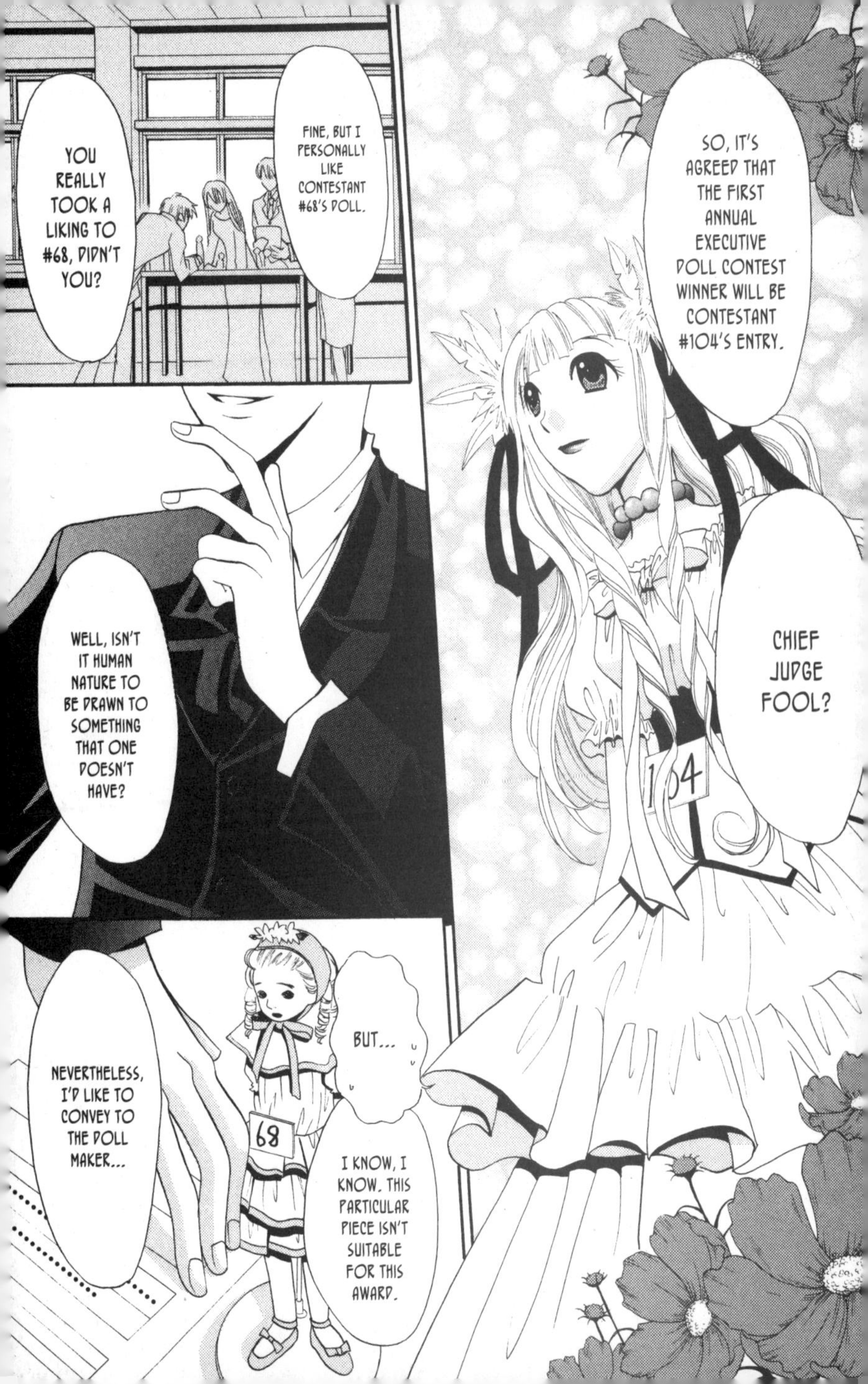
SO, IT'S AGREED THAT THE FIRST ANNUAL EXECUTIVE DOLL CONTEST WINNER WILL BE CONTESTANT #104'S ENTRY.
CHIEF JUDGE FOOL?
104
FINE, BUT I PERSONALLY LIKE CONTESTANT #68'S DOLL.
YOU REALLY TOOK A LIKING TO #68, DIDN'T YOU?
WELL, ISN'T IT HUMAN NATURE TO BE DRAWN TO SOMETHING THAT ONE DOESN'T HAVE?
BUT...
68
I KNOW, I KNOW. THIS PARTICULAR PIECE ISN'T SUITABLE FOR THIS AWARD.
NEVERTHELESS, I'D LIKE TO CONVEY TO THE DOLL MAKER...

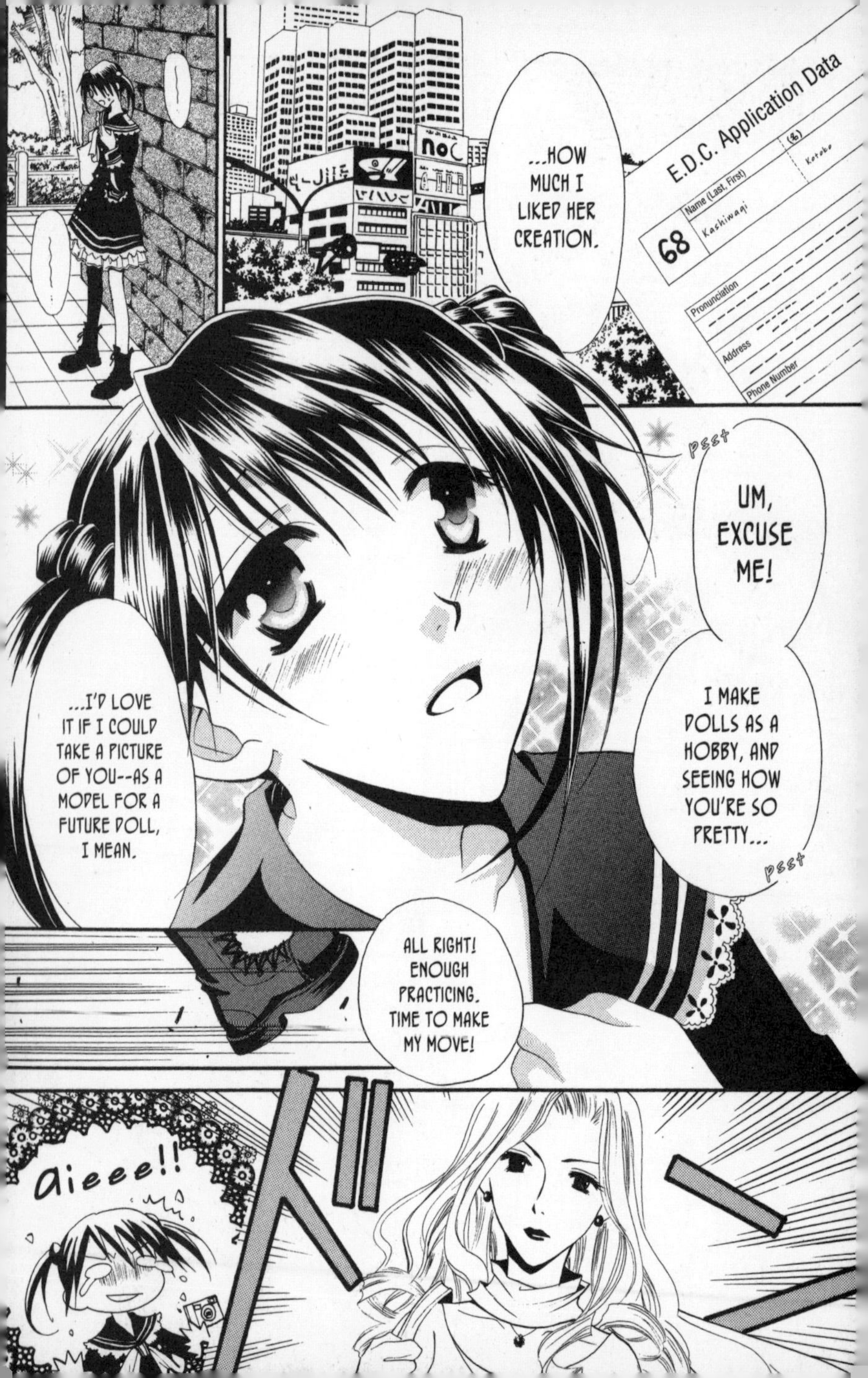
E.D.C. Application Data
68
Name (Last, First)
Kashiwagi
Kotoko
Pronunciation
Address
Phone Number
...HOW MUCH I LIKED HER CREATION.
psst
UM, EXCUSE ME!
I MAKE DOLLS AS A HOBBY, AND SEEING HOW YOU'RE SO PRETTY...
...I'D LOVE IT IF I COULD TAKE A PICTURE OF YOU--AS A MODEL FOR A FUTURE DOLL, I MEAN.
psst
ALL RIGHT! ENOUGH PRACTICING. TIME TO MAKE MY MOVE!
aieee!!

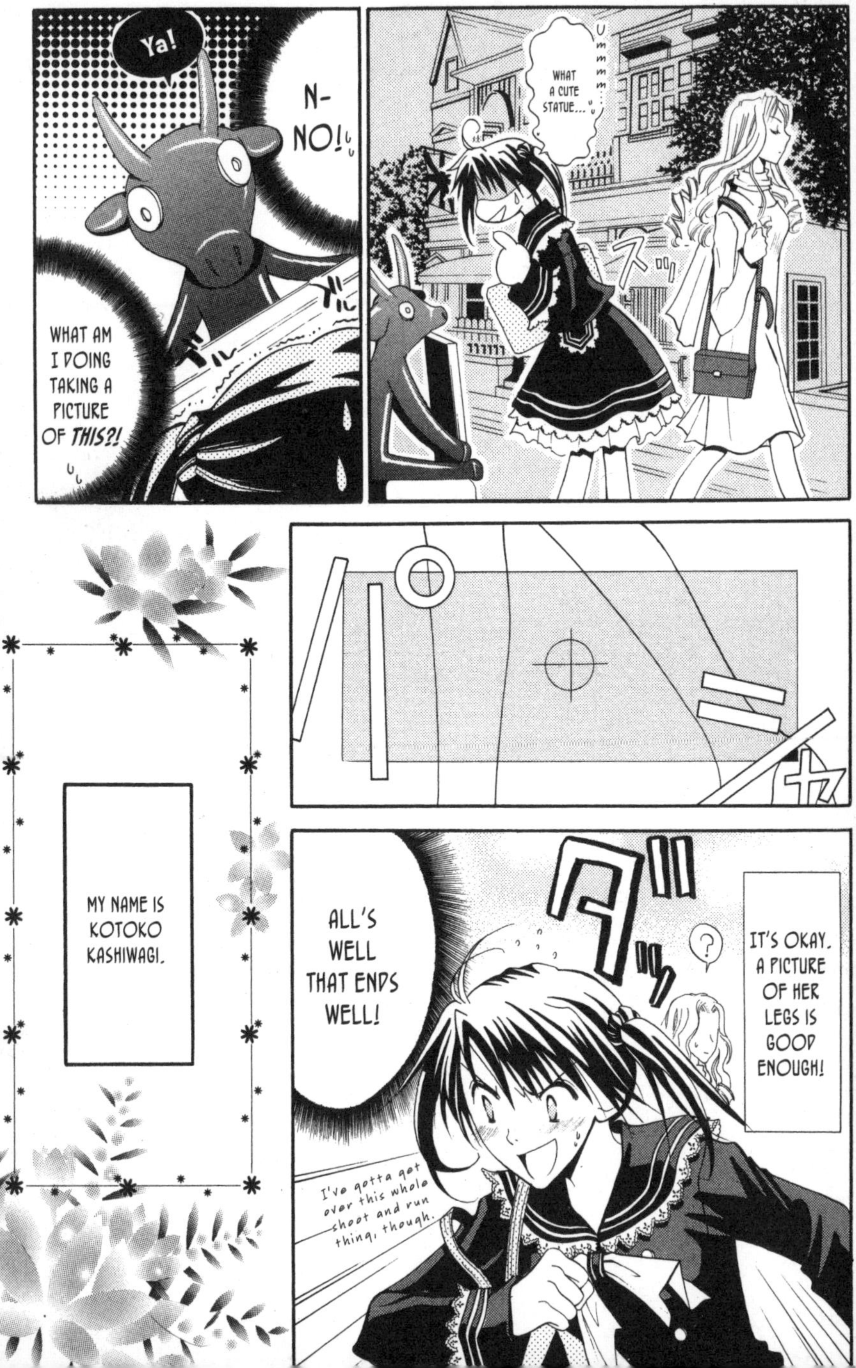
Ummmm...
What a cute statue...
Ya!
N-NO!
What am I doing taking a picture of THIS?!
It's okay. A picture of her legs is good enough!
?
All's well that ends well!
I've gotta get over this whole shoot and run thing, though.
My name is Kotoko Kashiwagi.

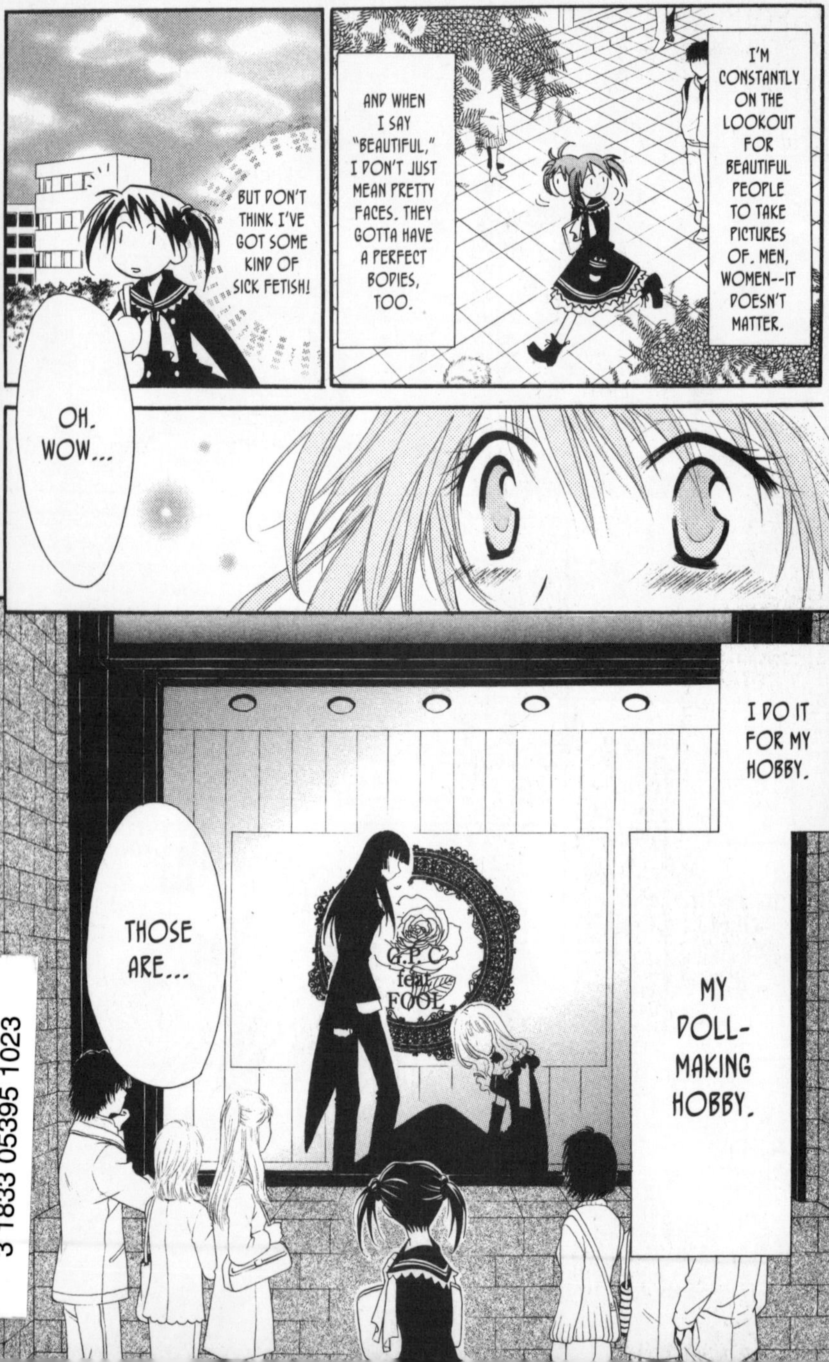
I'M CONSTANTLY ON THE LOOKOUT FOR BEAUTIFUL PEOPLE TO TAKE PICTURES OF. MEN, WOMEN--IT DOESN'T MATTER.
AND WHEN I SAY "BEAUTIFUL," I DON'T JUST MEAN PRETTY FACES. THEY GOTTA HAVE A PERFECT BODIES, TOO.
BUT DON'T THINK I'VE GOT SOME KIND OF SICK FETISH!
OH. WOW...
I DO IT FOR MY HOBBY.
MY DOLL-MAKING HOBBY.
G.P.C feat FOOL
THOSE ARE...

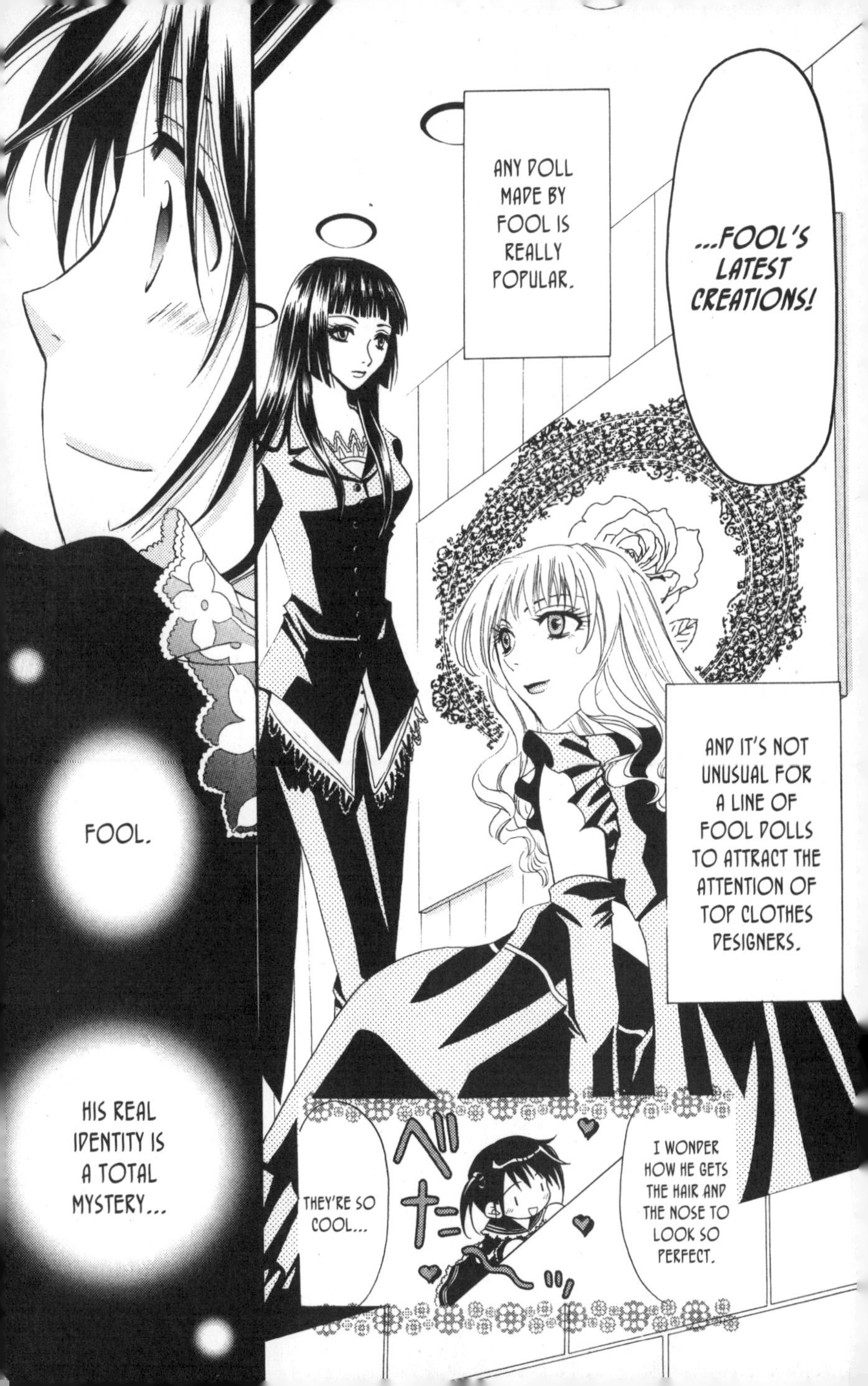
...FOOL'S LATEST CREATIONS!
ANY DOLL MADE BY FOOL IS REALLY POPULAR.
AND IT'S NOT UNUSUAL FOR A LINE OF FOOL DOLLS TO ATTRACT THE ATTENTION OF TOP CLOTHES DESIGNERS.
I WONDER HOW HE GETS THE HAIR AND THE NOSE TO LOOK SO PERFECT.
べた
THEY'RE SO COOL...
FOOL.
HIS REAL IDENTITY IS A TOTAL MYSTERY...

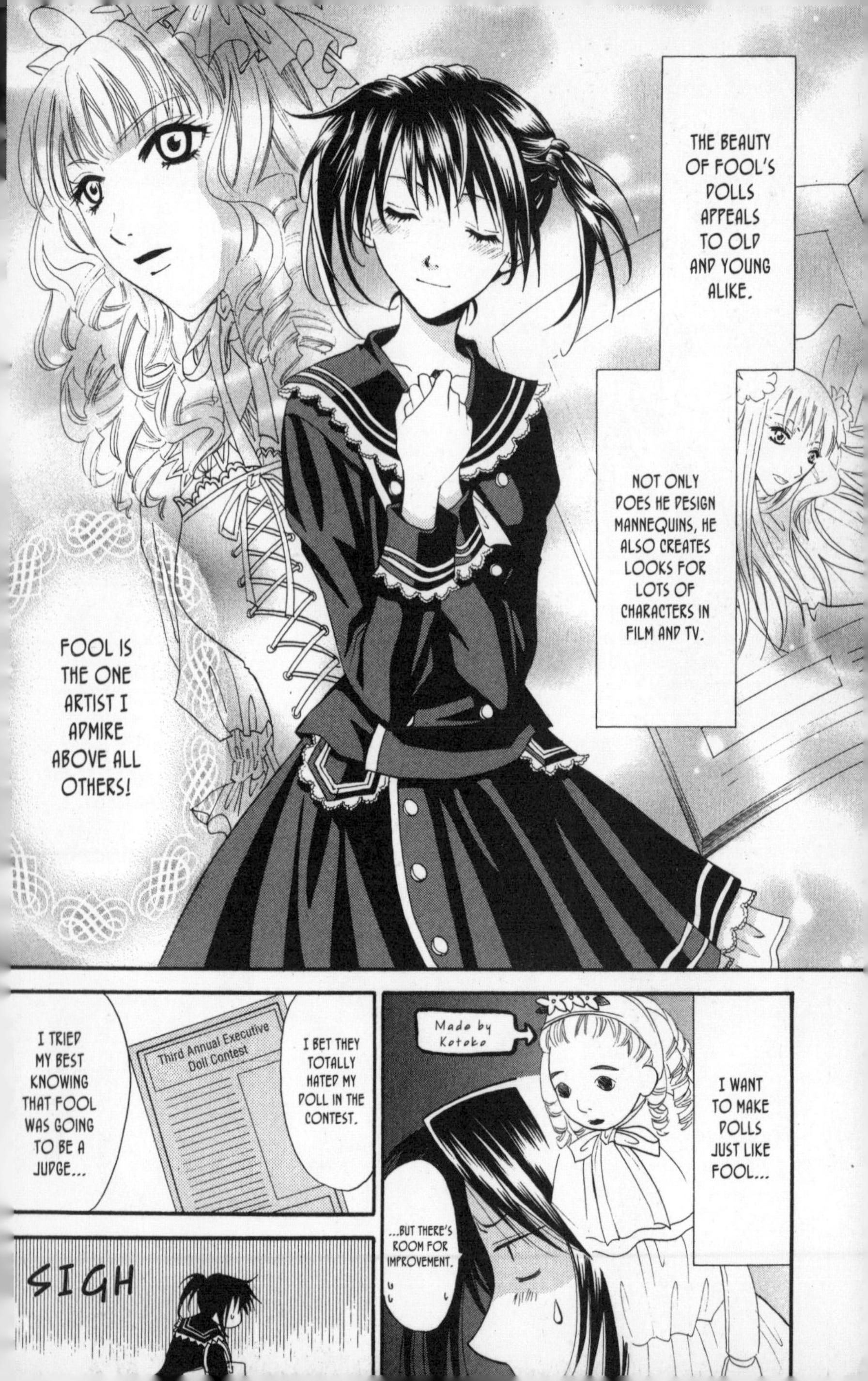
THE BEAUTY OF FOOL'S DOLLS APPEALS TO OLD AND YOUNG ALIKE.
NOT ONLY DOES HE DESIGN MANNEQUINS, HE ALSO CREATES LOOKS FOR LOTS OF CHARACTERS IN FILM AND TV.
FOOL IS THE ONE ARTIST I ADMIRE ABOVE ALL OTHERS!
Made by Kotoko
I WANT TO MAKE DOLLS JUST LIKE FOOL...
...BUT THERE'S ROOM FOR IMPROVEMENT.
I BET THEY TOTALLY HATED MY DOLL IN THE CONTEST.
Third Annual Executive Doll Contest
I TRIED MY BEST KNOWING THAT FOOL WAS GOING TO BE A JUDGE...
SIGH

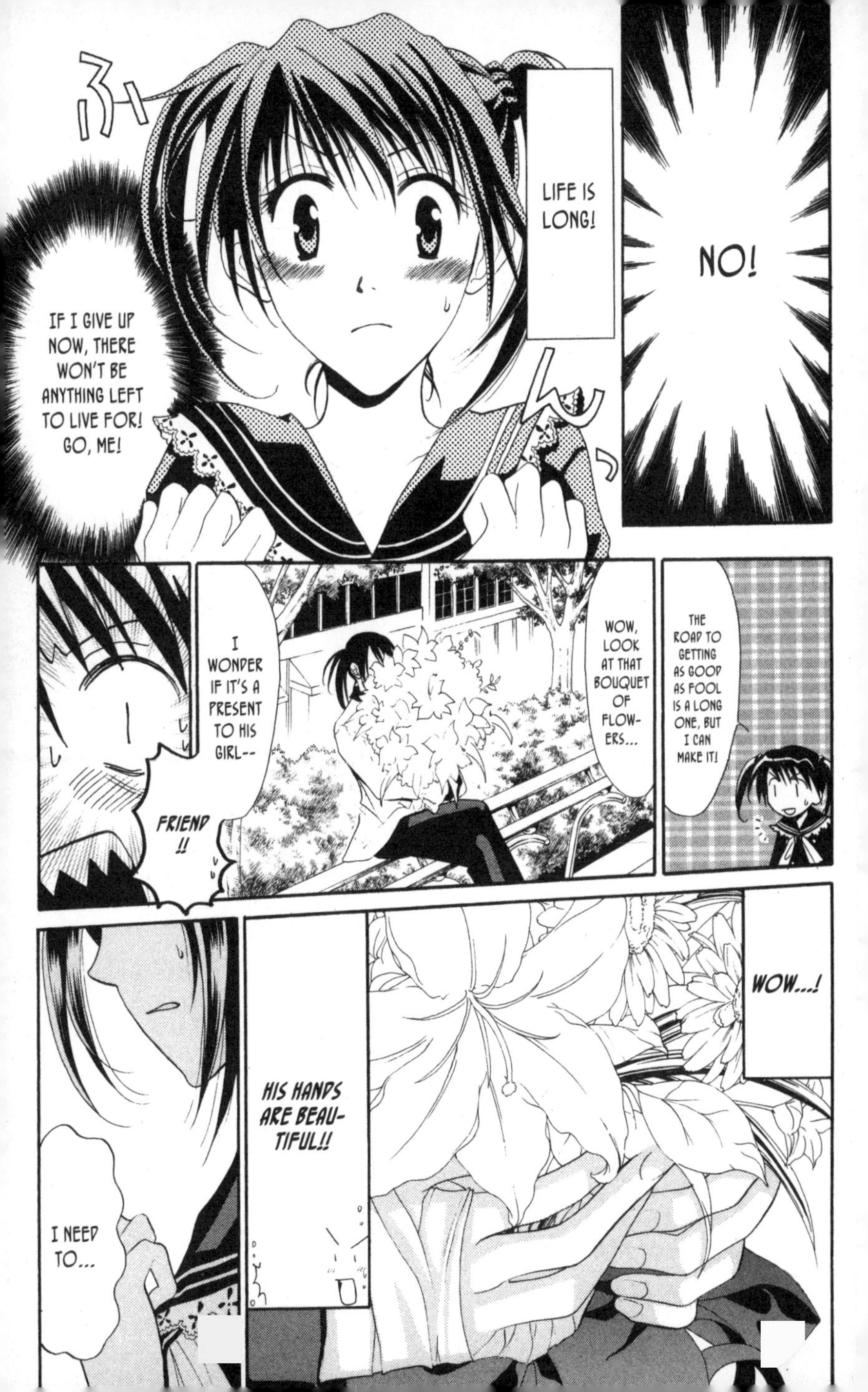
NO!
LIFE IS LONG!
IF I GIVE UP NOW, THERE WON'T BE ANYTHING LEFT TO LIVE FOR! GO, ME!
THE ROAD TO GETTING AS GOOD AS FOOL IS A LONG ONE, BUT I CAN MAKE IT!
WOW, LOOK AT THAT BOUQUET OF FLOWERS...
I WONDER IF IT'S A PRESENT TO HIS GIRL--
FRIEND !!
WOW...!
HIS HANDS ARE BEAUTIFUL!!
I NEED TO...

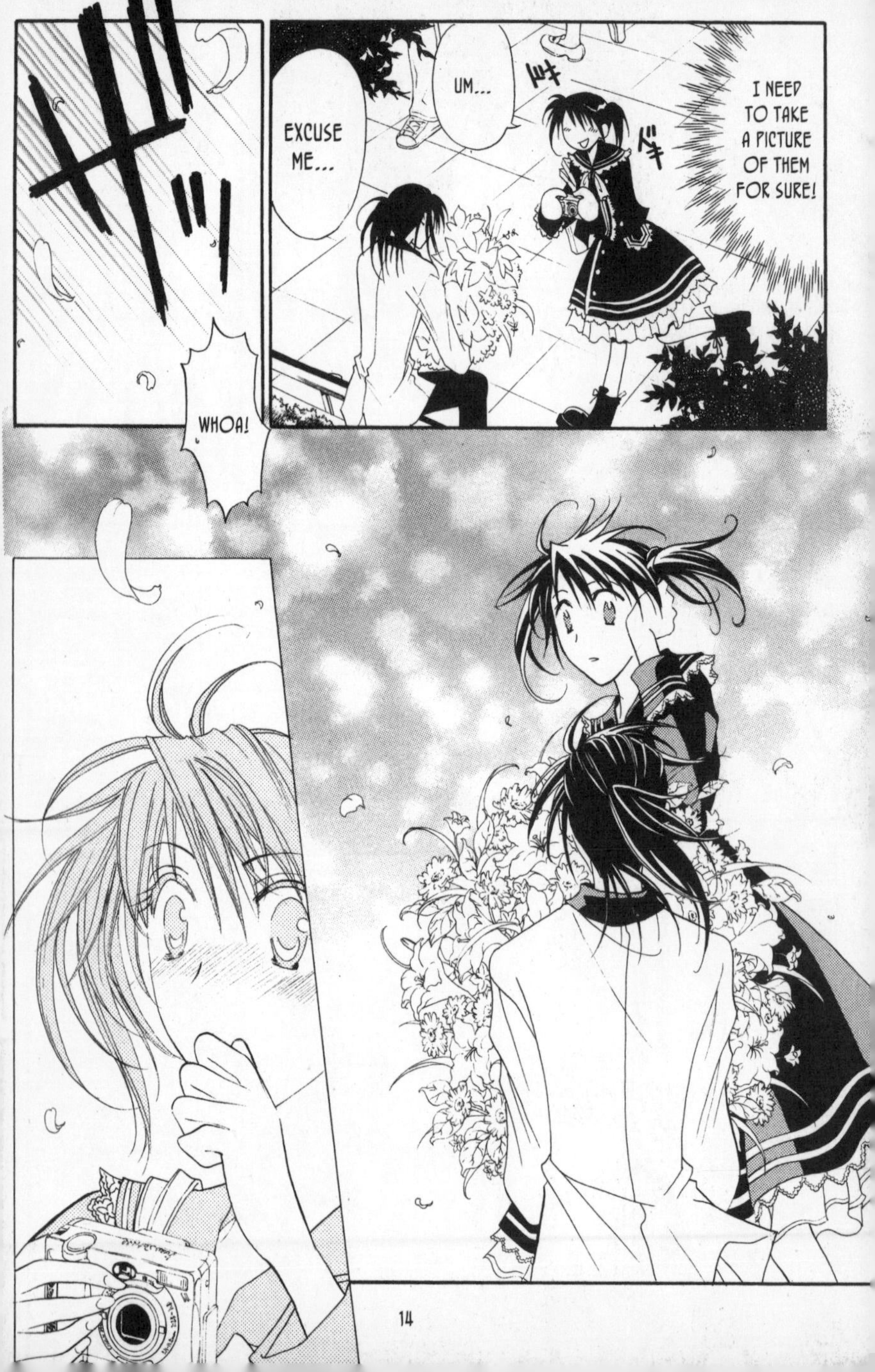
I NEED TO TAKE A PICTURE OF THEM FOR SURE!
ドキ
ドキ
UM...
EXCUSE ME...
WHOA!

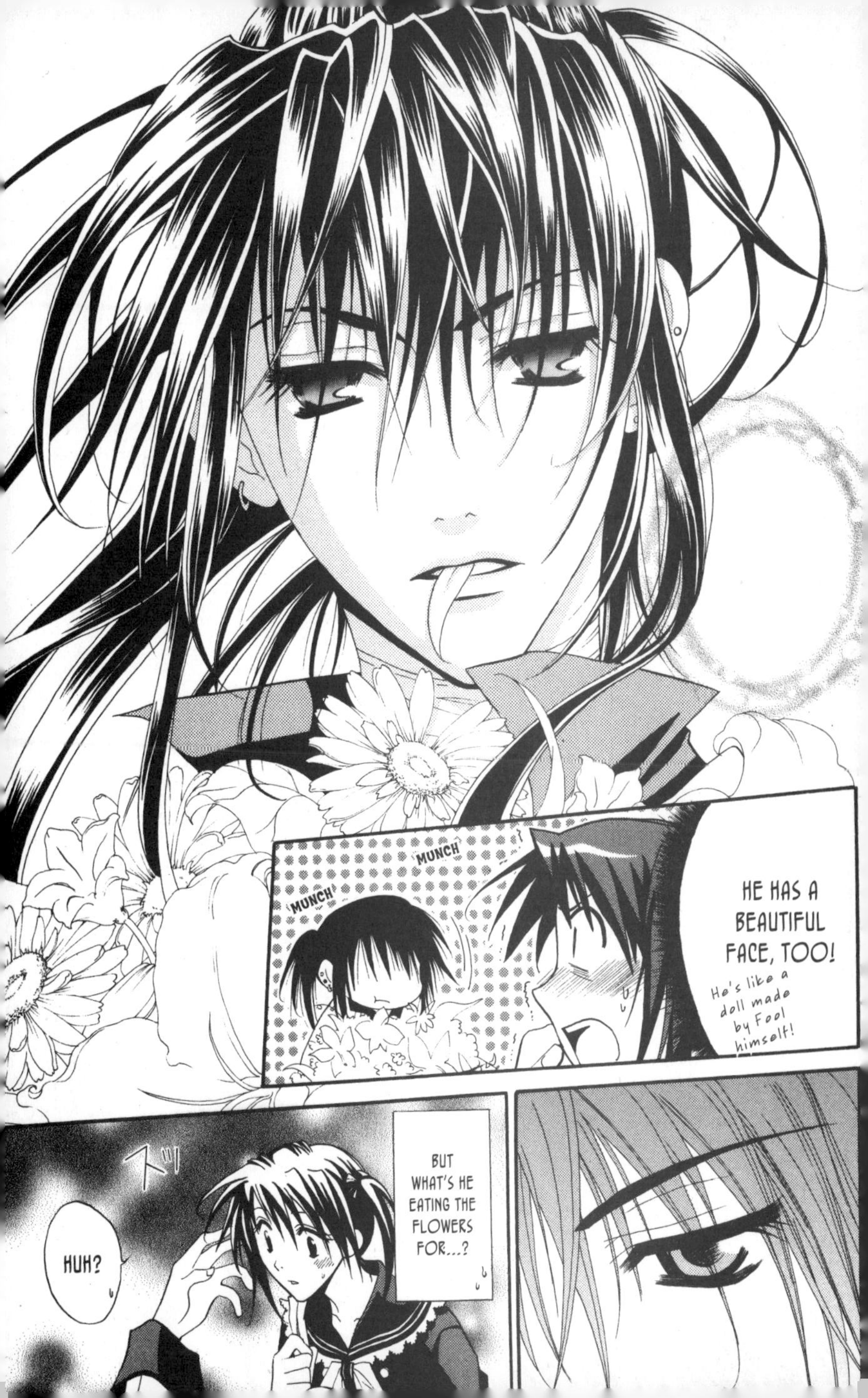
HE HAS A BEAUTIFUL FACE, TOO!
He's like a doll made by Fool himself!
MUNCH
MUNCH
BUT WHAT'S HE EATING THE FLOWERS FOR...?
HUH?

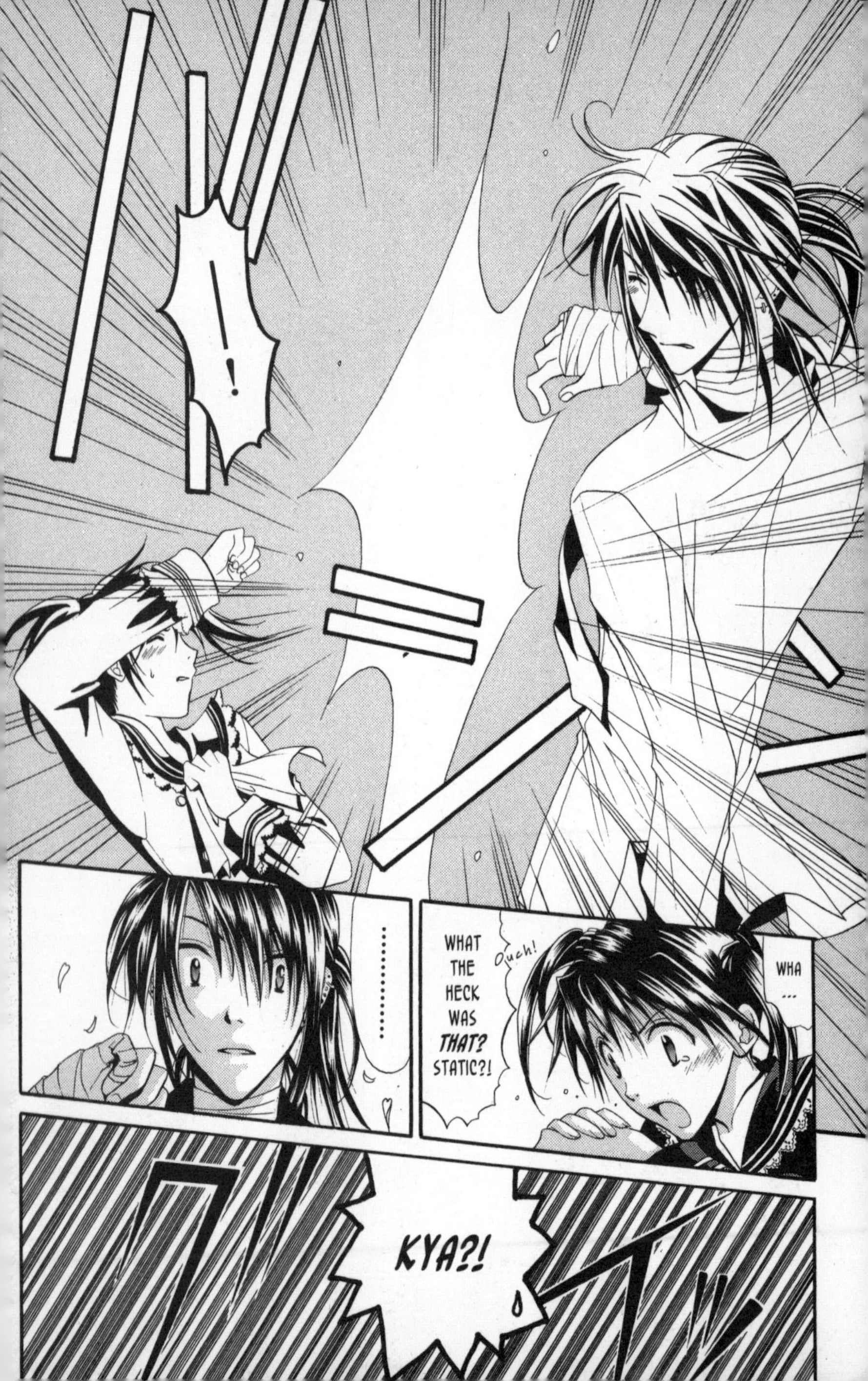
!
WHA ...
Ouch!
WHAT THE HECK WAS *THAT?* STATIC?!
......
KYA?!

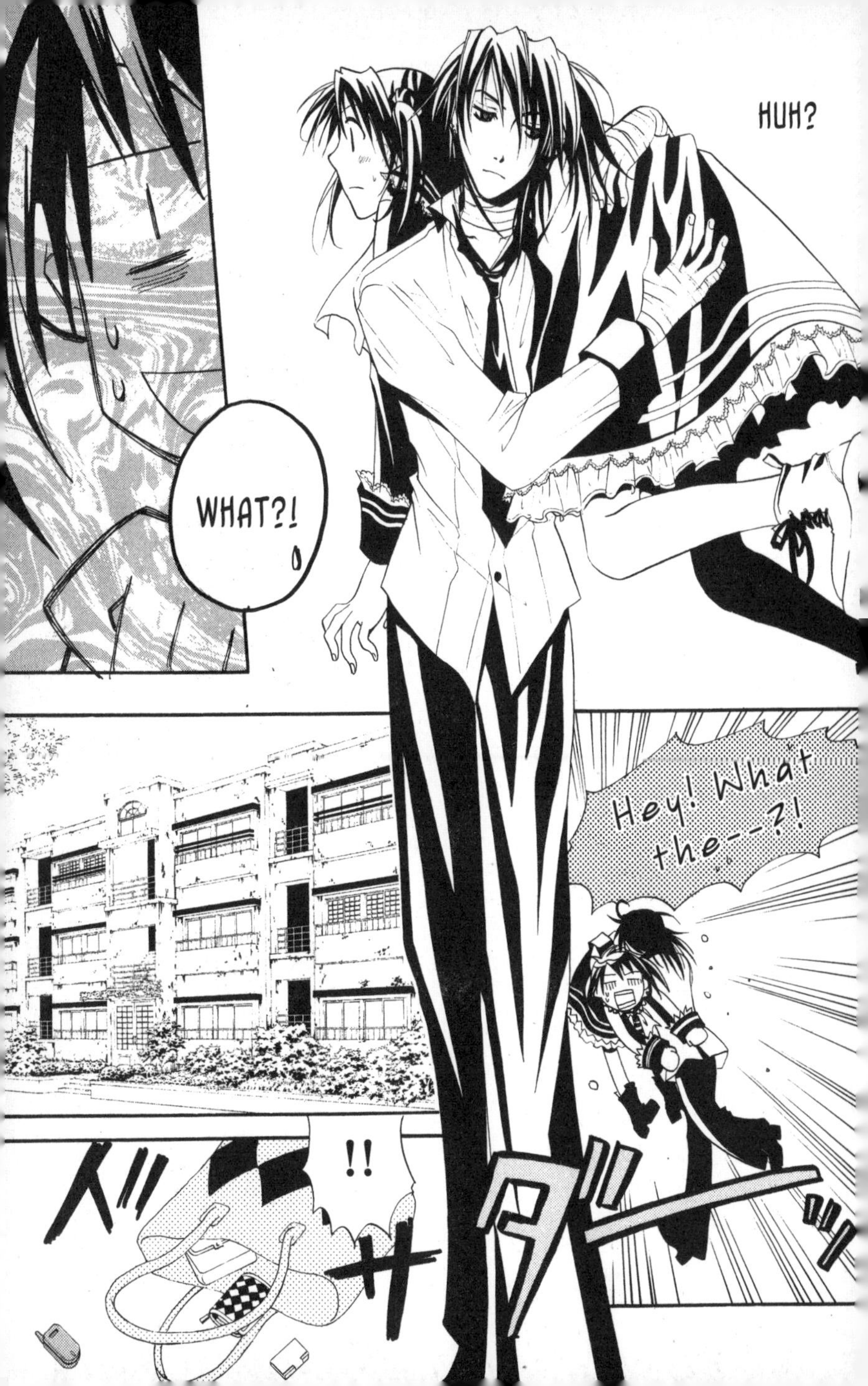
HUH?
WHAT?!
Hey! What the--?!
!!

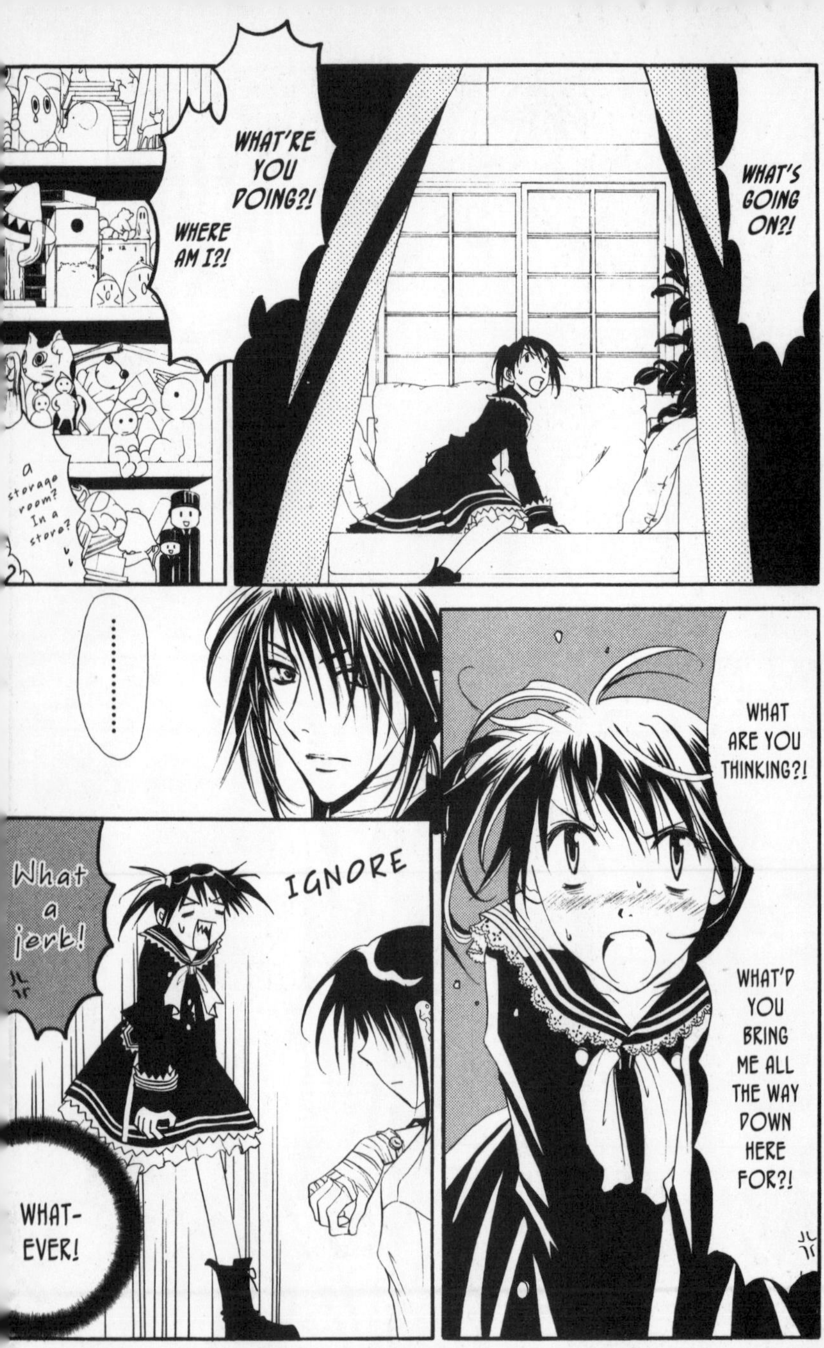
WHAT'S GOING ON?!
WHAT'RE YOU DOING?!
WHERE AM I?!
a storage room? In a store?
WHAT ARE YOU THINKING?!
WHAT'D YOU BRING ME ALL THE WAY DOWN HERE FOR?!
......
IGNORE
What a jerk!
WHAT-EVER!

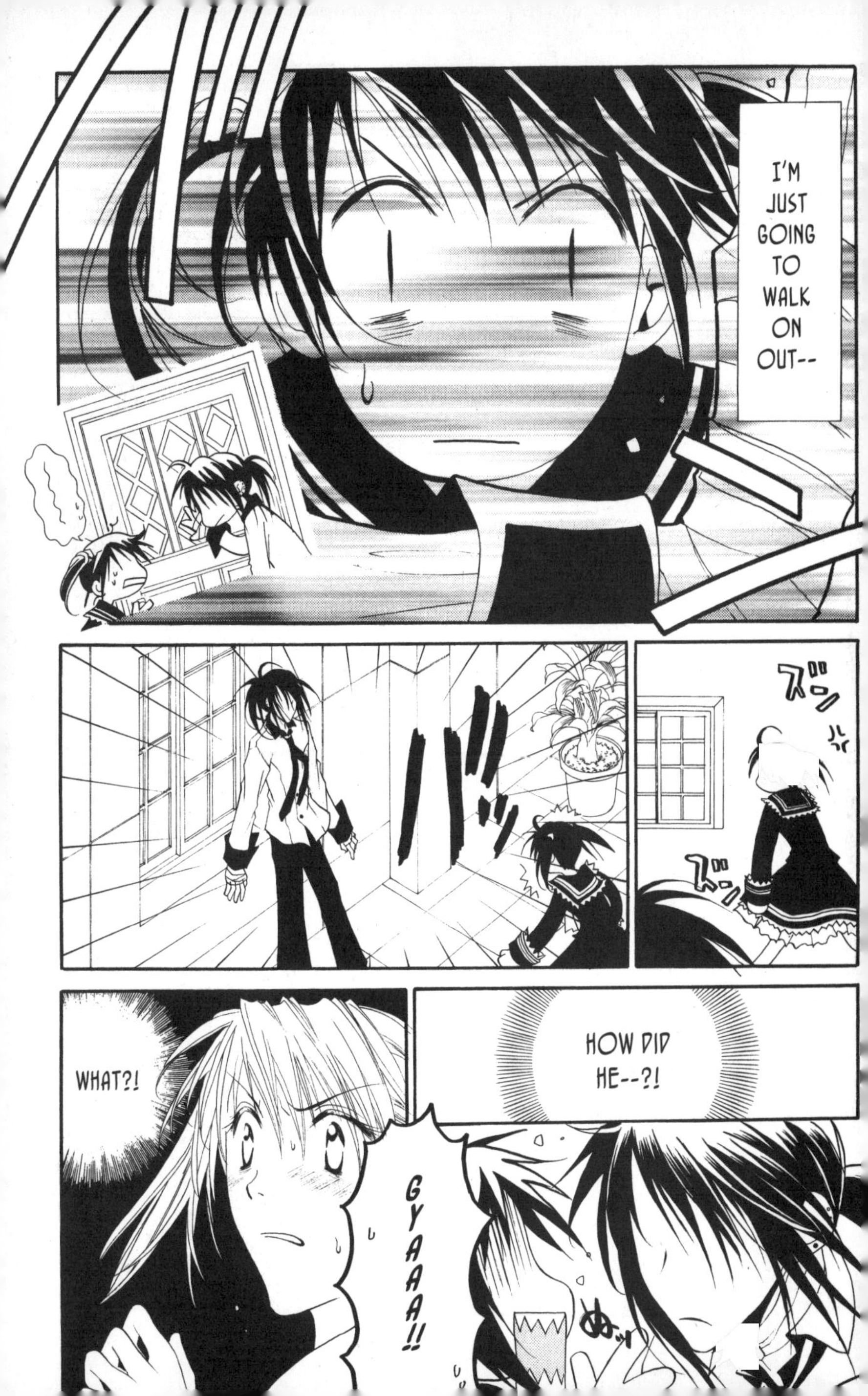
I'M JUST GOING TO WALK ON OUT--
バッ
HOW DID HE--?!
GYAAAA!!
WHAT?!

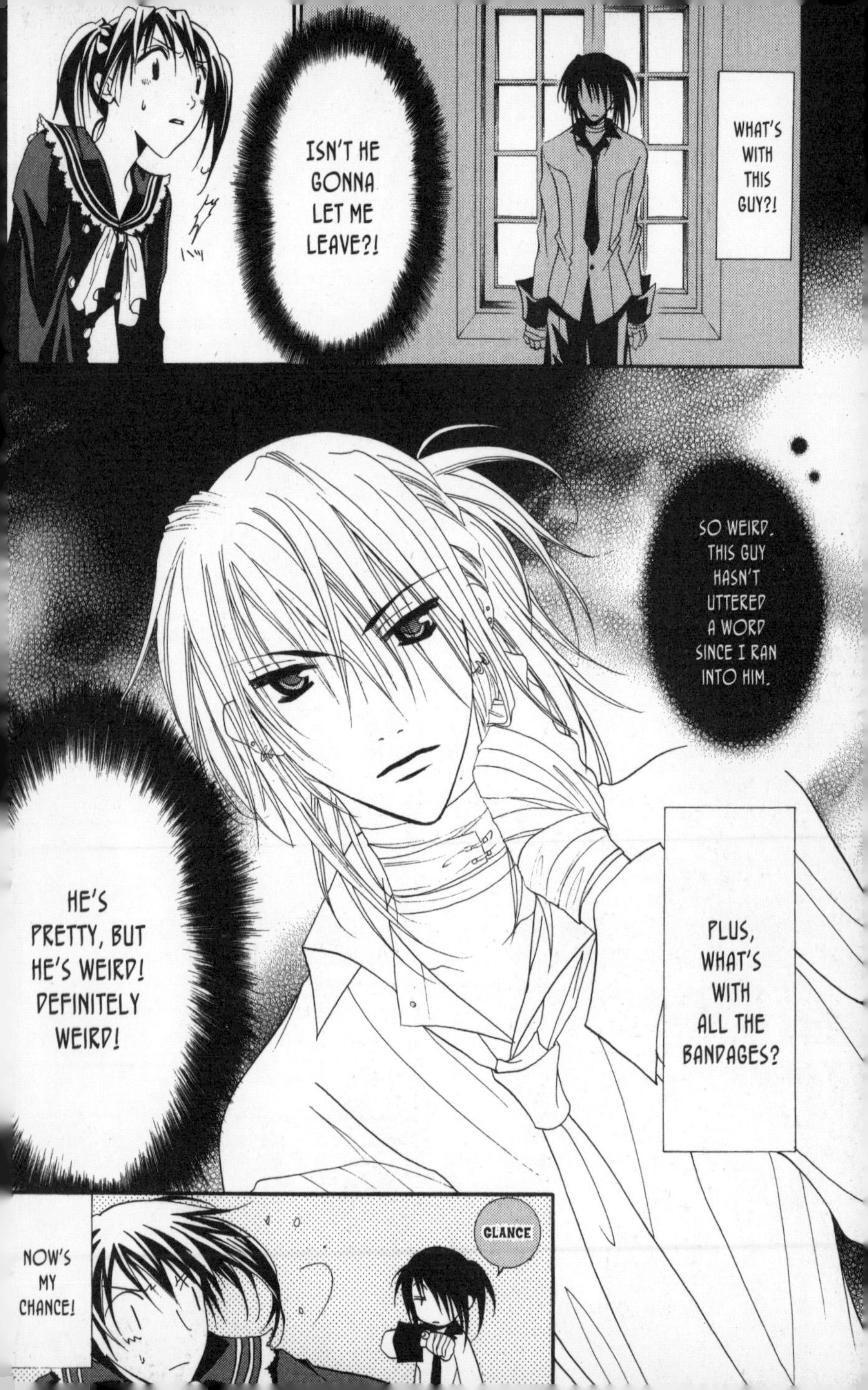
WHAT'S WITH THIS GUY?!
ISN'T HE GONNA LET ME LEAVE?!
SO WEIRD. THIS GUY HASN'T UTTERED A WORD SINCE I RAN INTO HIM.
PLUS, WHAT'S WITH ALL THE BANDAGES?
HE'S PRETTY, BUT HE'S WEIRD! DEFINITELY WEIRD!
GLANCE
NOW'S MY CHANCE!

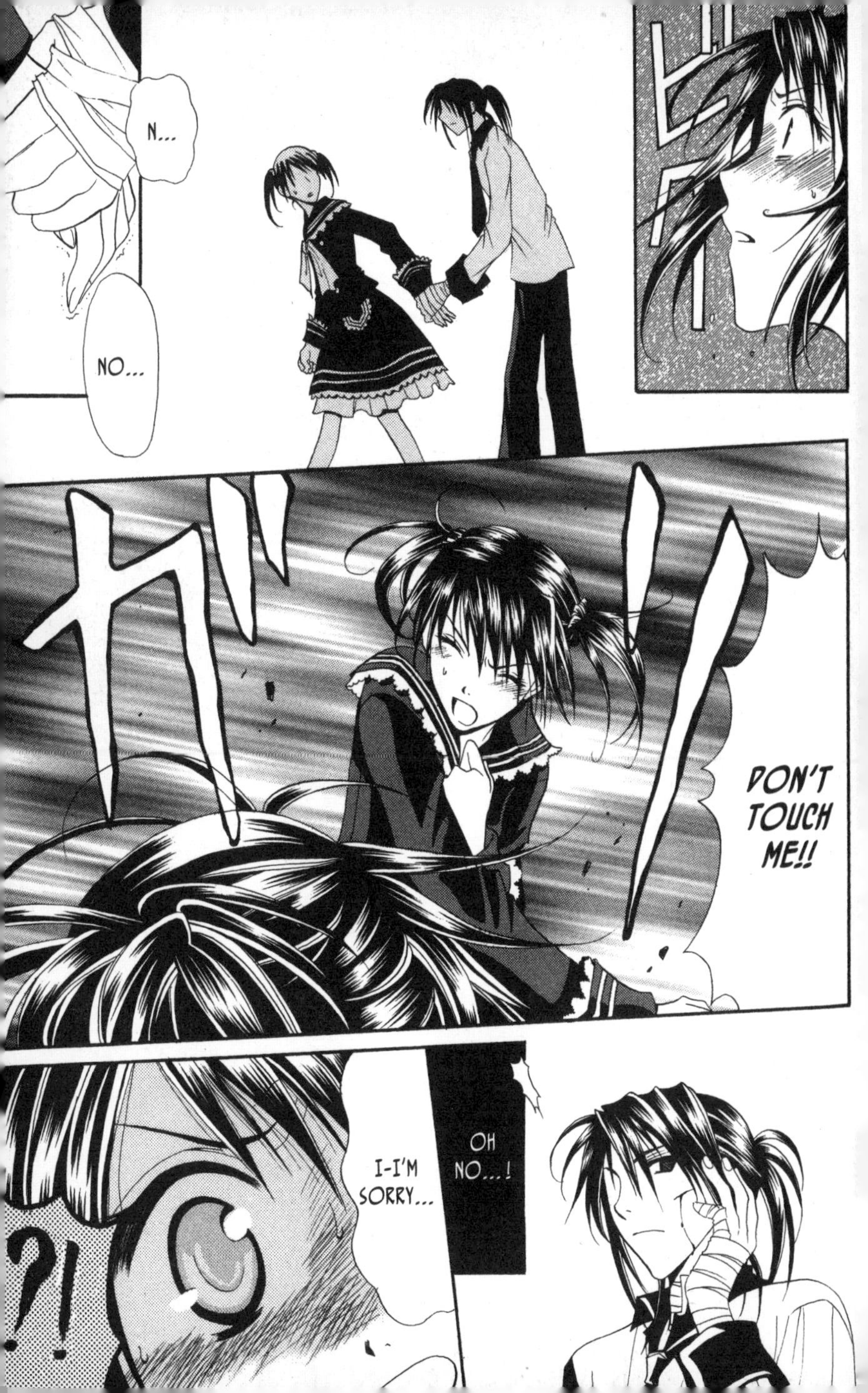

N...
NO...
DON'T TOUCH ME!!
OH NO...!
I-I'M SORRY...
?!

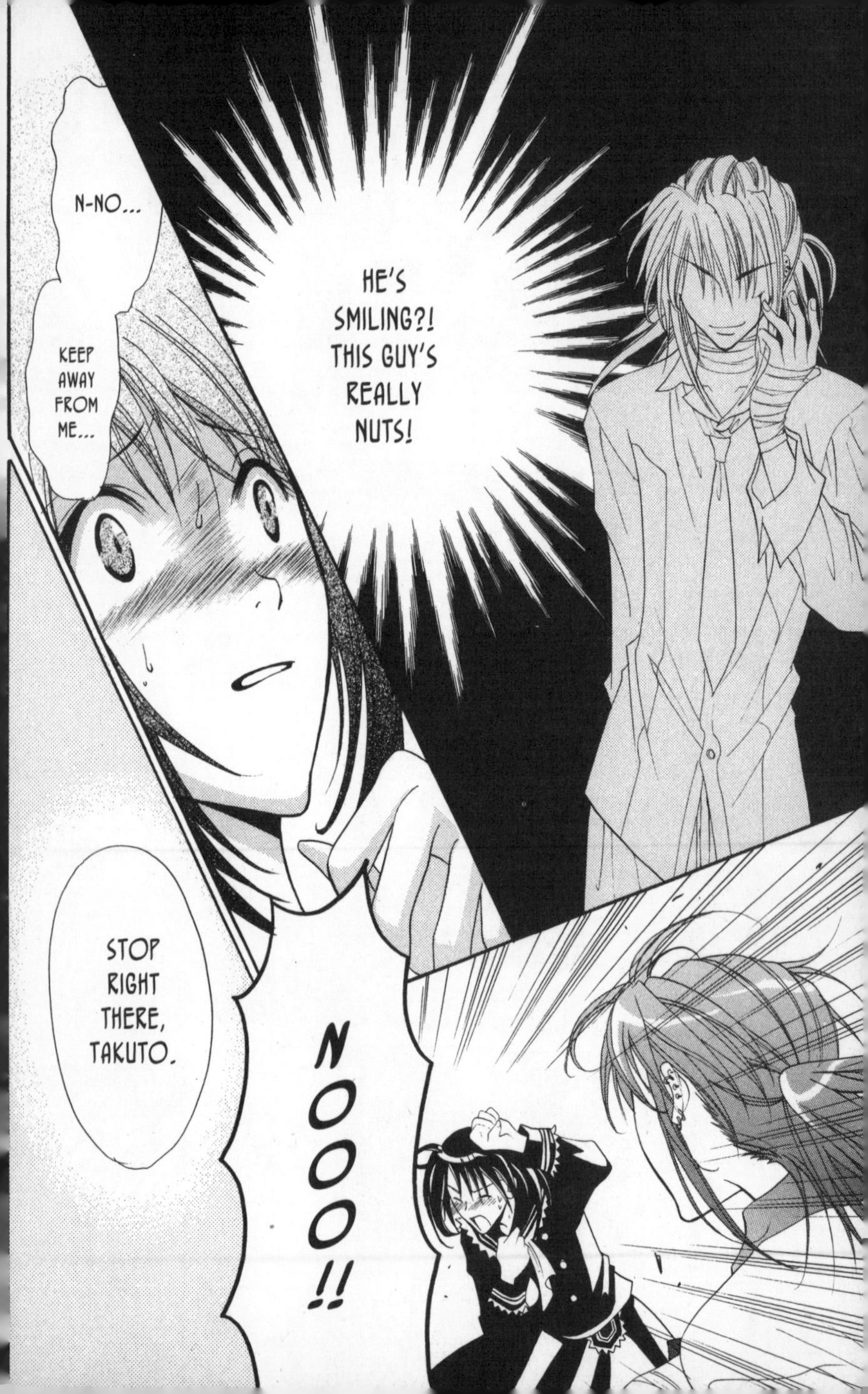
HE'S SMILING?! THIS GUY'S REALLY NUTS!
N-NO...
KEEP AWAY FROM ME...
NOOOO!!
STOP RIGHT THERE, TAKUTO.

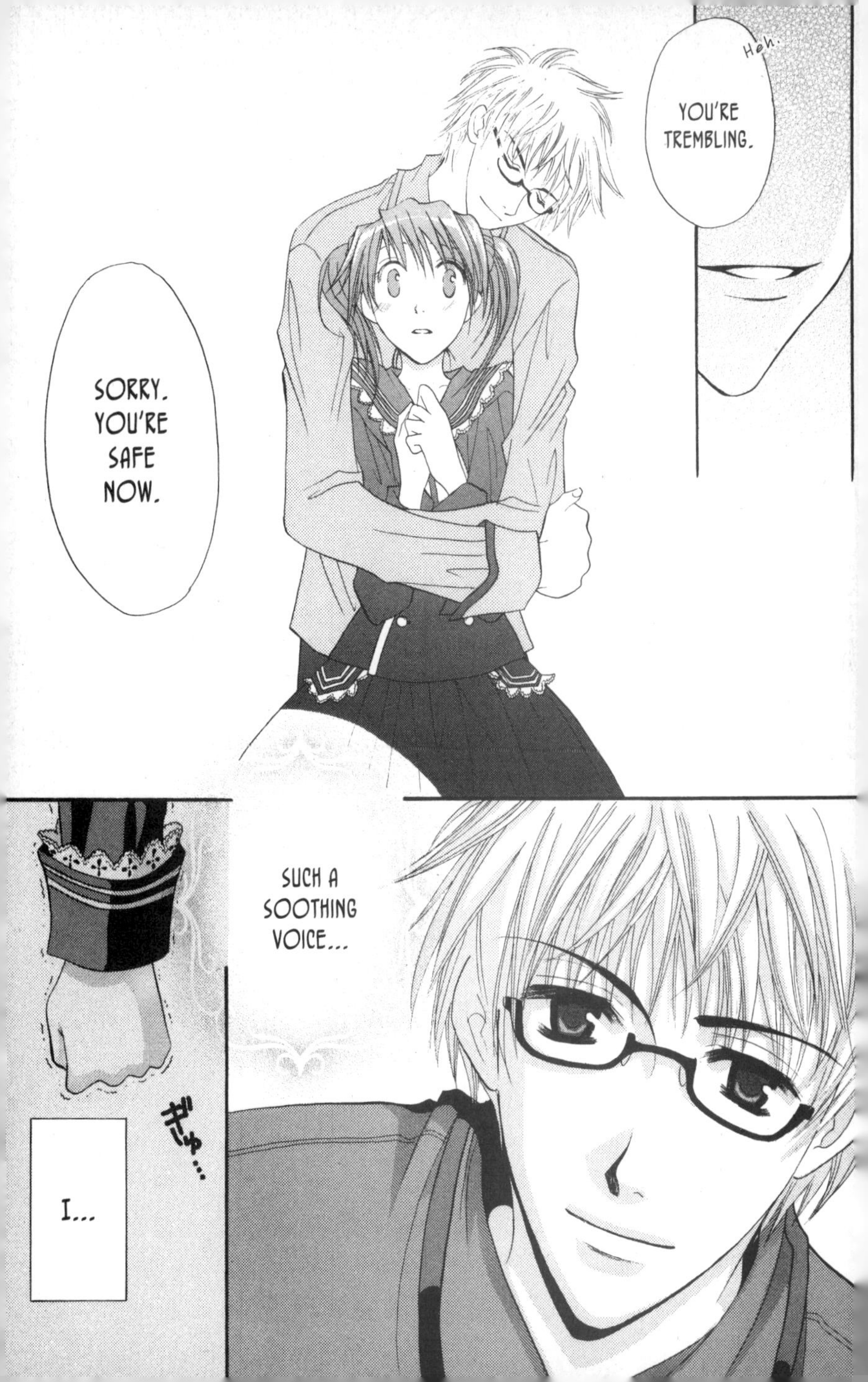
Heh.
YOU'RE TREMBLING.
SORRY. YOU'RE SAFE NOW.
SUCH A SOOTHING VOICE...
ギュ...
I...

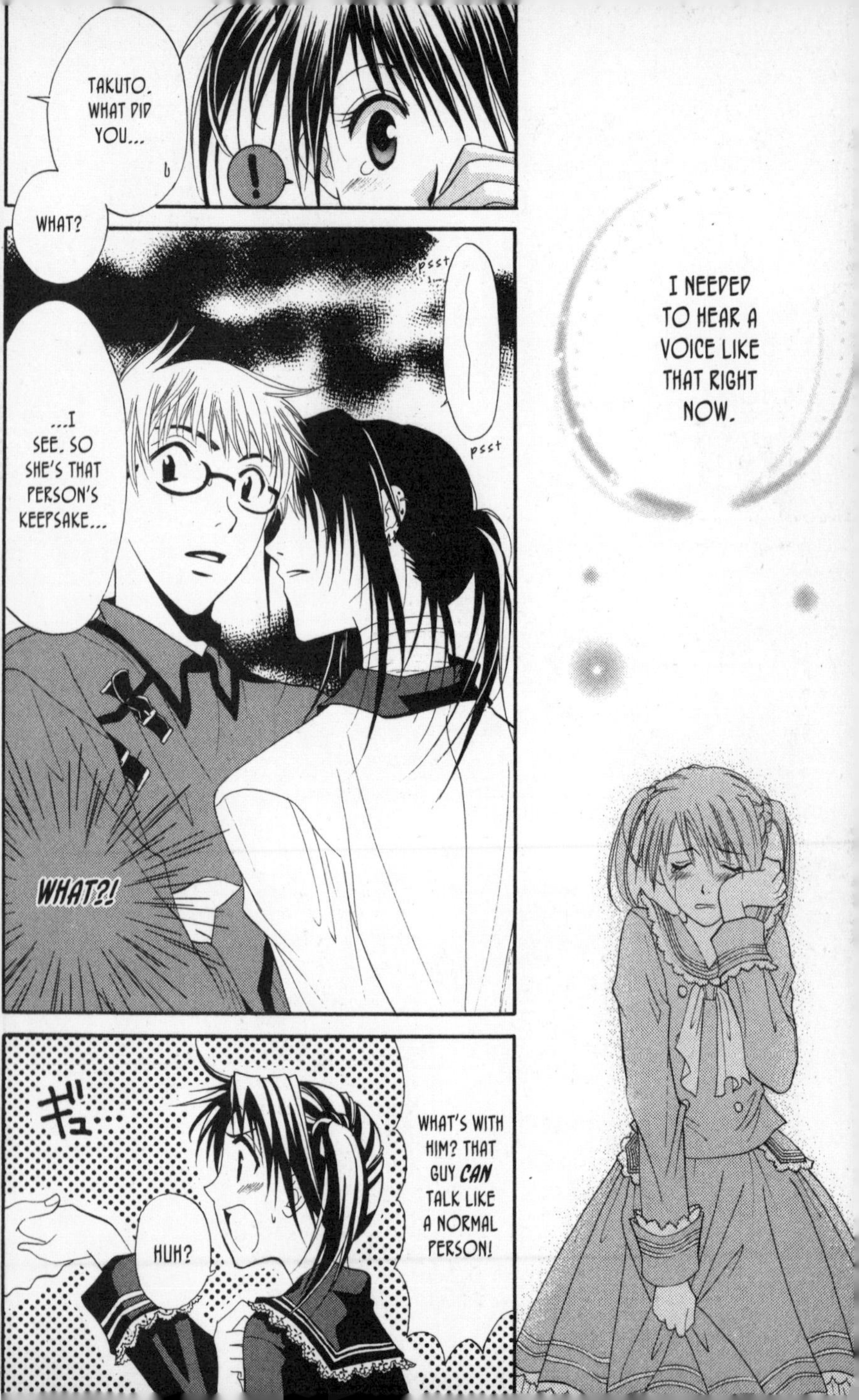
I NEEDED TO HEAR A VOICE LIKE THAT RIGHT NOW.
TAKUTO. WHAT DID YOU...
!
WHAT?
psst
psst
...I SEE. SO SHE'S THAT PERSON'S KEEPSAKE...
WHAT?!
ギュ…
WHAT'S WITH HIM? THAT GUY CAN TALK LIKE A NORMAL PERSON!
HUH?

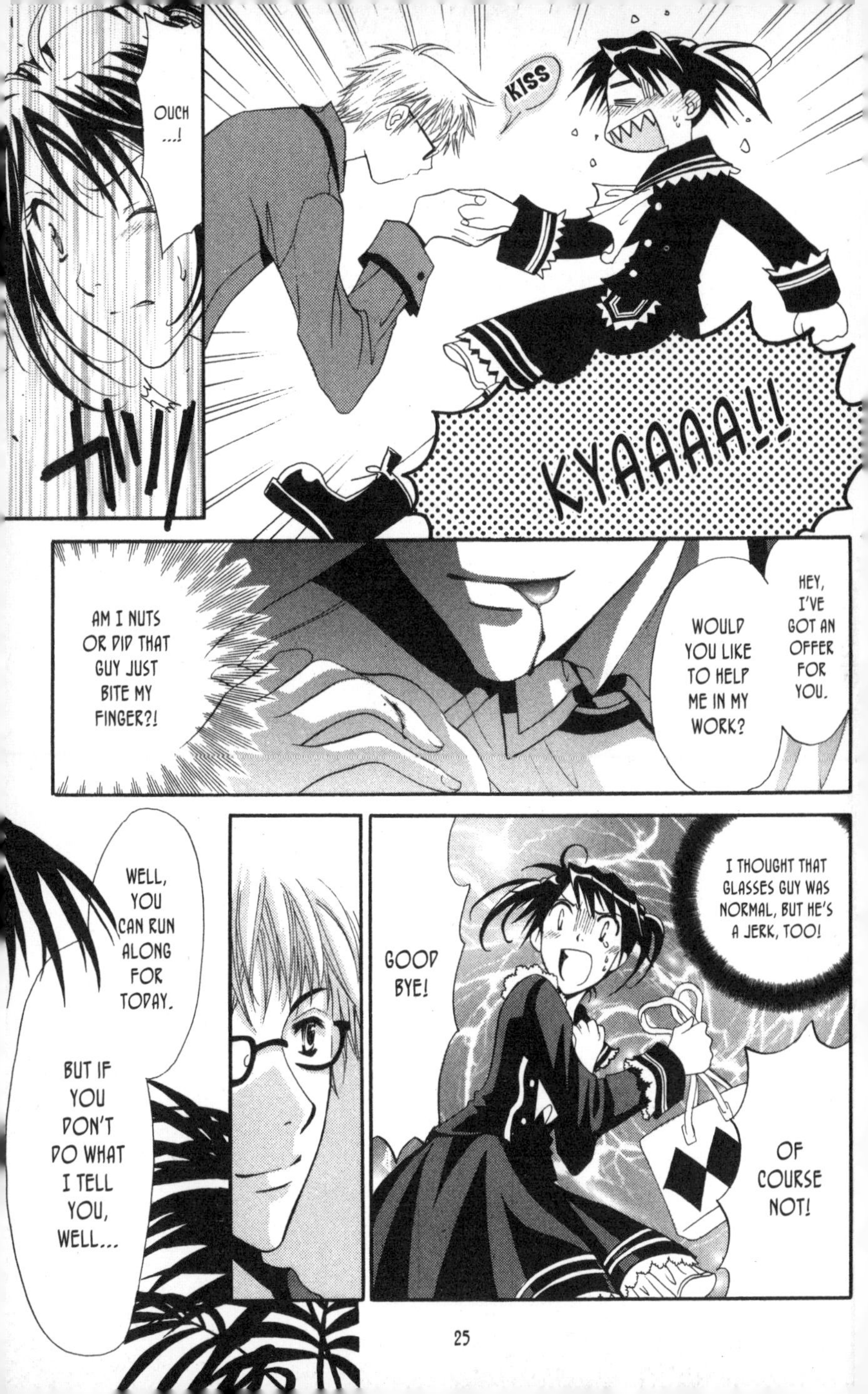
KISS
KYAAAA!!
OUCH ...!
HEY, I'VE GOT AN OFFER FOR YOU.
WOULD YOU LIKE TO HELP ME IN MY WORK?
AM I NUTS OR DID THAT GUY JUST BITE MY FINGER?!
I THOUGHT THAT GLASSES GUY WAS NORMAL, BUT HE'S A JERK, TOO!
OF COURSE NOT!
GOOD BYE!
WELL, YOU CAN RUN ALONG FOR TODAY.
BUT IF YOU DON'T DO WHAT I TELL YOU, WELL...

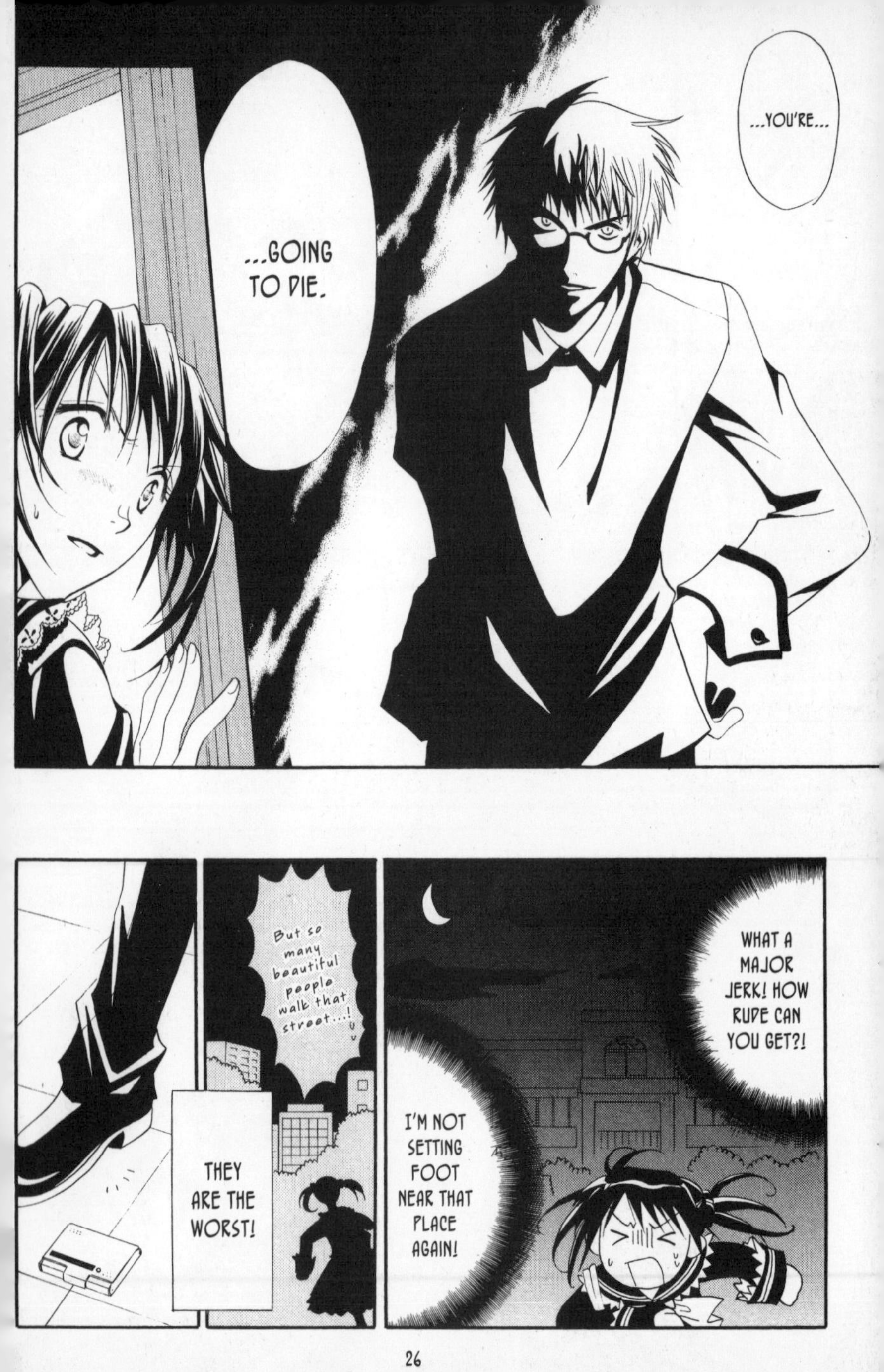
...YOU'RE...
...GOING TO DIE.
WHAT A MAJOR JERK! HOW RUDE CAN YOU GET?!
I'M NOT SETTING FOOT NEAR THAT PLACE AGAIN!
But so many beautiful people walk that street...!
THEY ARE THE WORST!

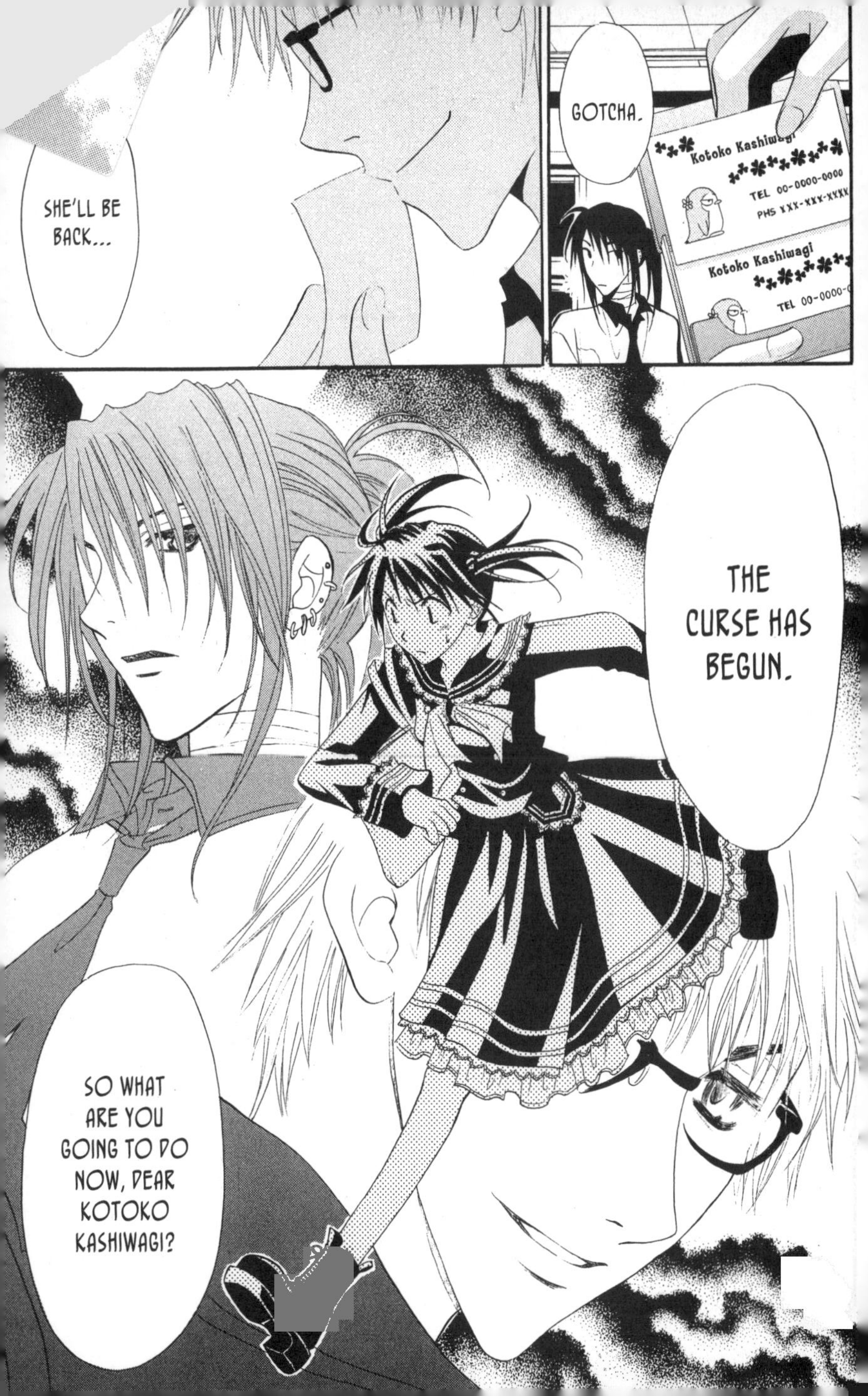
GOTCHA.
Kotoko Kashiwagi
TEL 00-0000-0000
PHS XXX-XXX-XXXX
Kotoko Kashiwagi
SHE'LL BE BACK...
THE CURSE HAS BEGUN.
SO WHAT ARE YOU GOING TO DO NOW, DEAR KOTOKO KASHIWAGI?

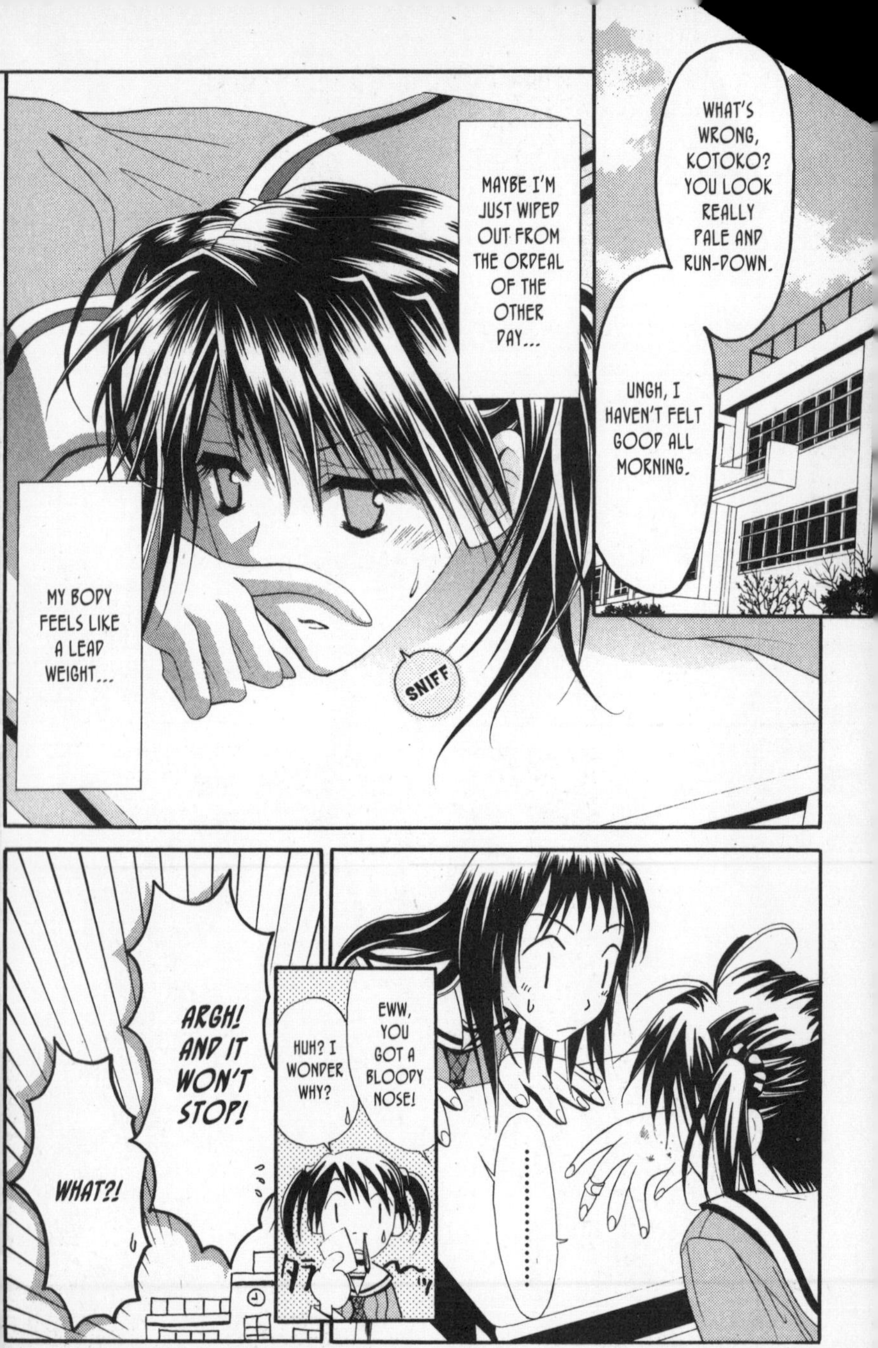
WHAT'S WRONG, KOTOKO? YOU LOOK REALLY PALE AND RUN-DOWN.
UNGH, I HAVEN'T FELT GOOD ALL MORNING.
MAYBE I'M JUST WIPED OUT FROM THE ORDEAL OF THE OTHER DAY...
MY BODY FEELS LIKE A LEAD WEIGHT...
SNIFF
......
EWW, YOU GOT A BLOODY NOSE!
HUH? I WONDER WHY?
ARGH! AND IT WON'T STOP!
WHAT?!

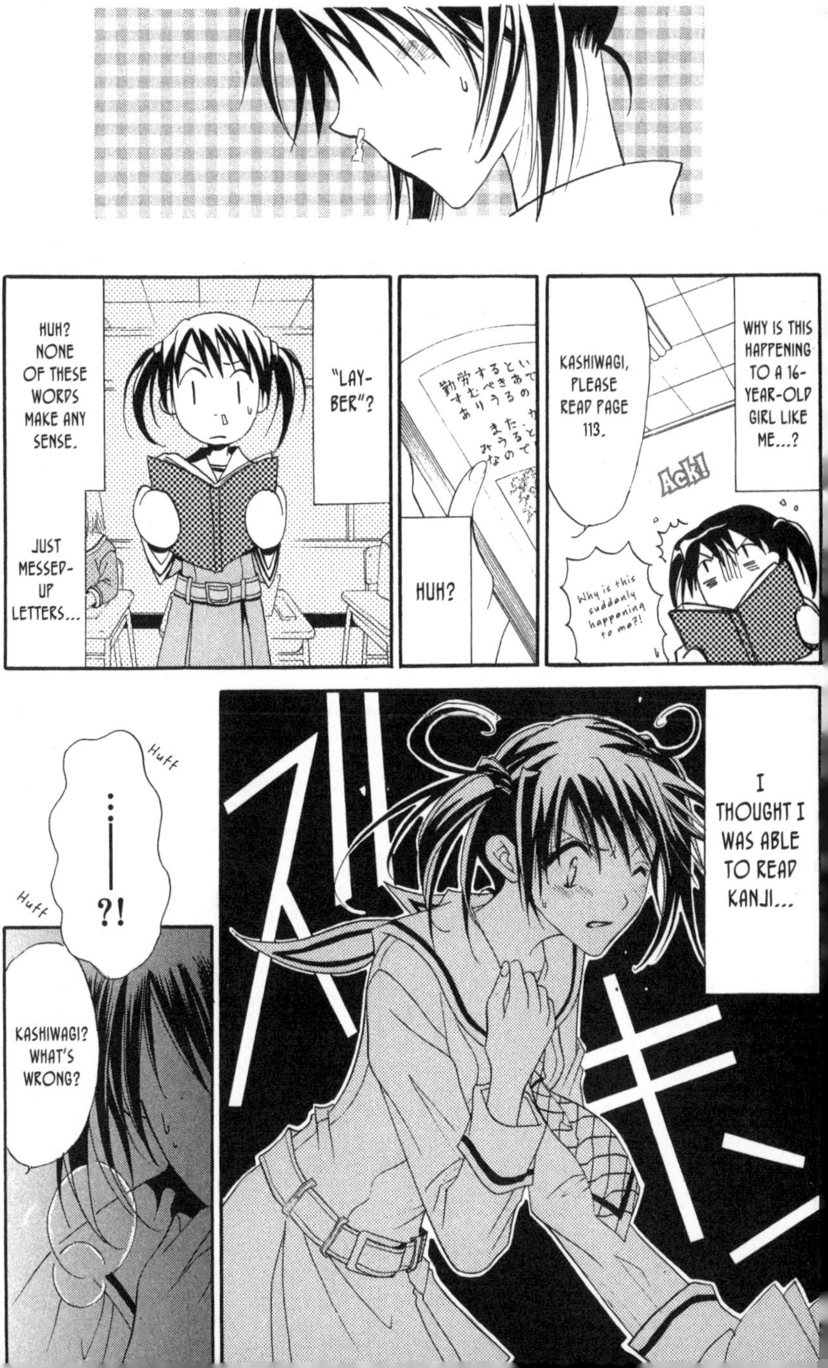
WHY IS THIS HAPPENING TO A 16-YEAR-OLD GIRL LIKE ME...?
KASHIWAGI, PLEASE READ PAGE 113.
Ack!
Why is this suddenly happening to me?!
HUH?
"LAY-BER"?
HUH? NONE OF THESE WORDS MAKE ANY SENSE.
JUST MESSED-UP LETTERS...
I THOUGHT I WAS ABLE TO READ KANJI...
Huff
...—?!
Huff
KASHIWAGI? WHAT'S WRONG?

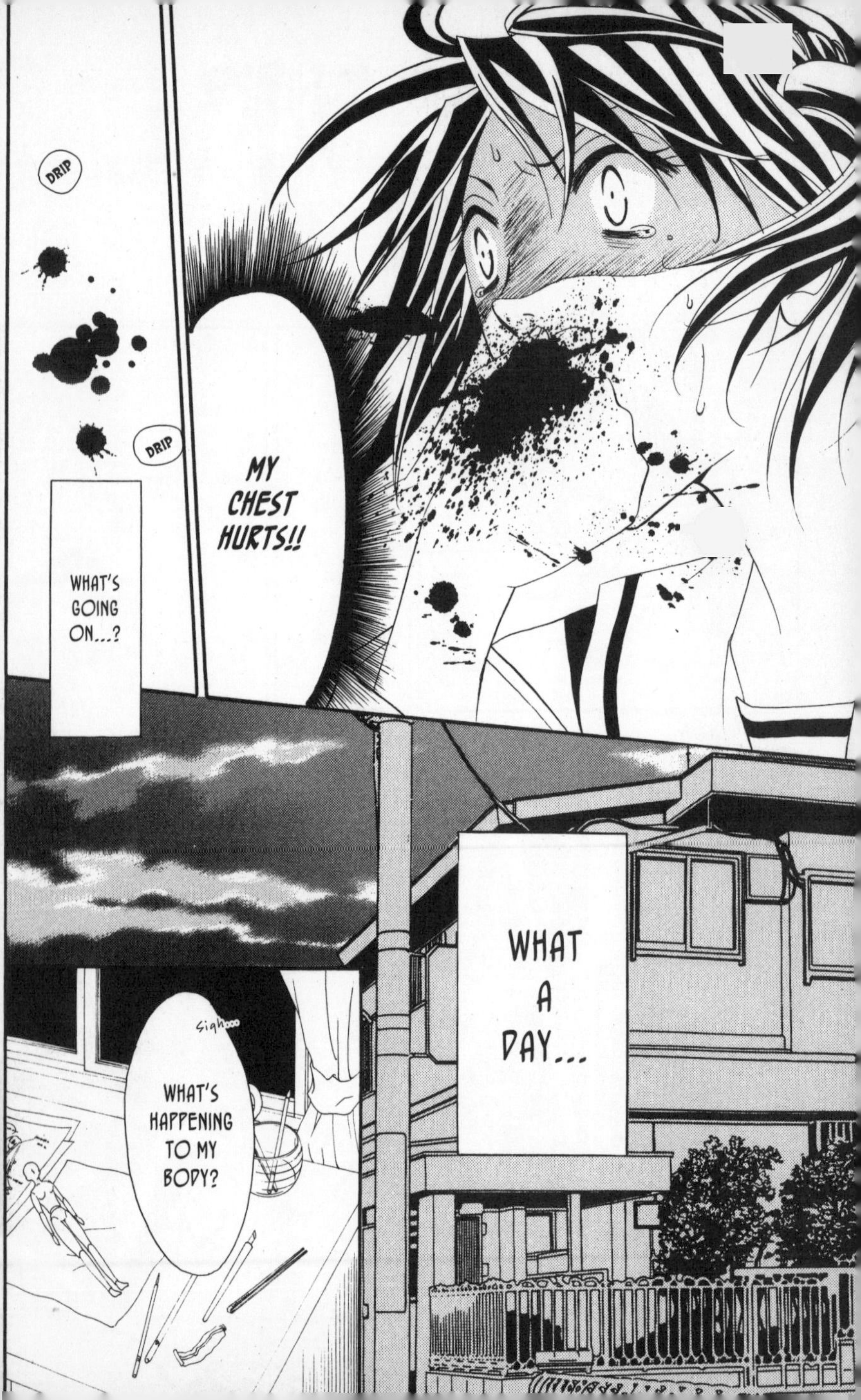
DRIP
MY CHEST HURTS!!
DRIP
WHAT'S GOING ON...?
WHAT A DAY...
Sigh...
WHAT'S HAPPENING TO MY BODY?

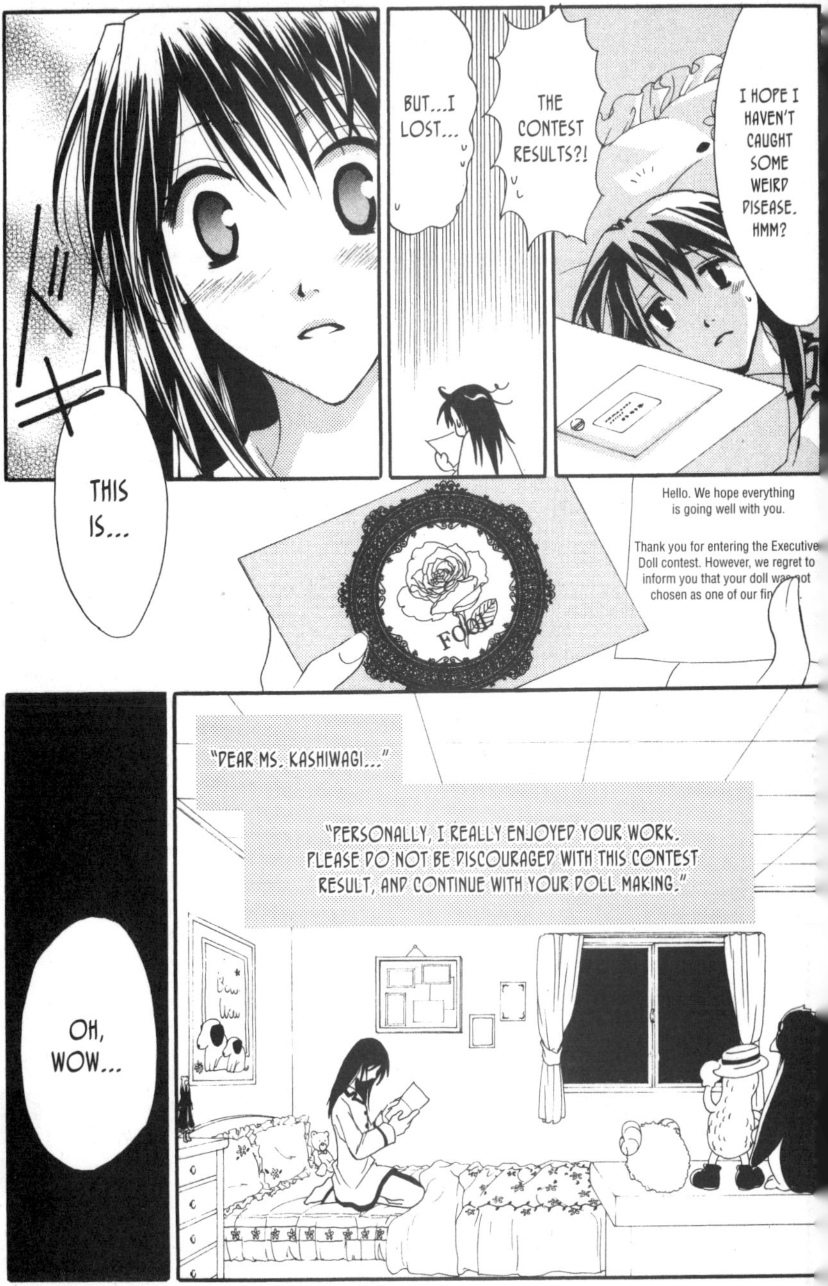
I HOPE I HAVEN'T CAUGHT SOME WEIRD DISEASE. HMM?
THE CONTEST RESULTS?!
BUT...I LOST...
THIS IS...
Hello. We hope everything is going well with you.
Thank you for entering the Executive Doll contest. However, we regret to inform you that your doll wa ot chosen as one of our fin
FOOL
"DEAR MS. KASHIWAGI..."
"PERSONALLY, I REALLY ENJOYED YOUR WORK. PLEASE DO NOT BE DISCOURAGED WITH THIS CONTEST RESULT, AND CONTINUE WITH YOUR DOLL MAKING."
OH, WOW...

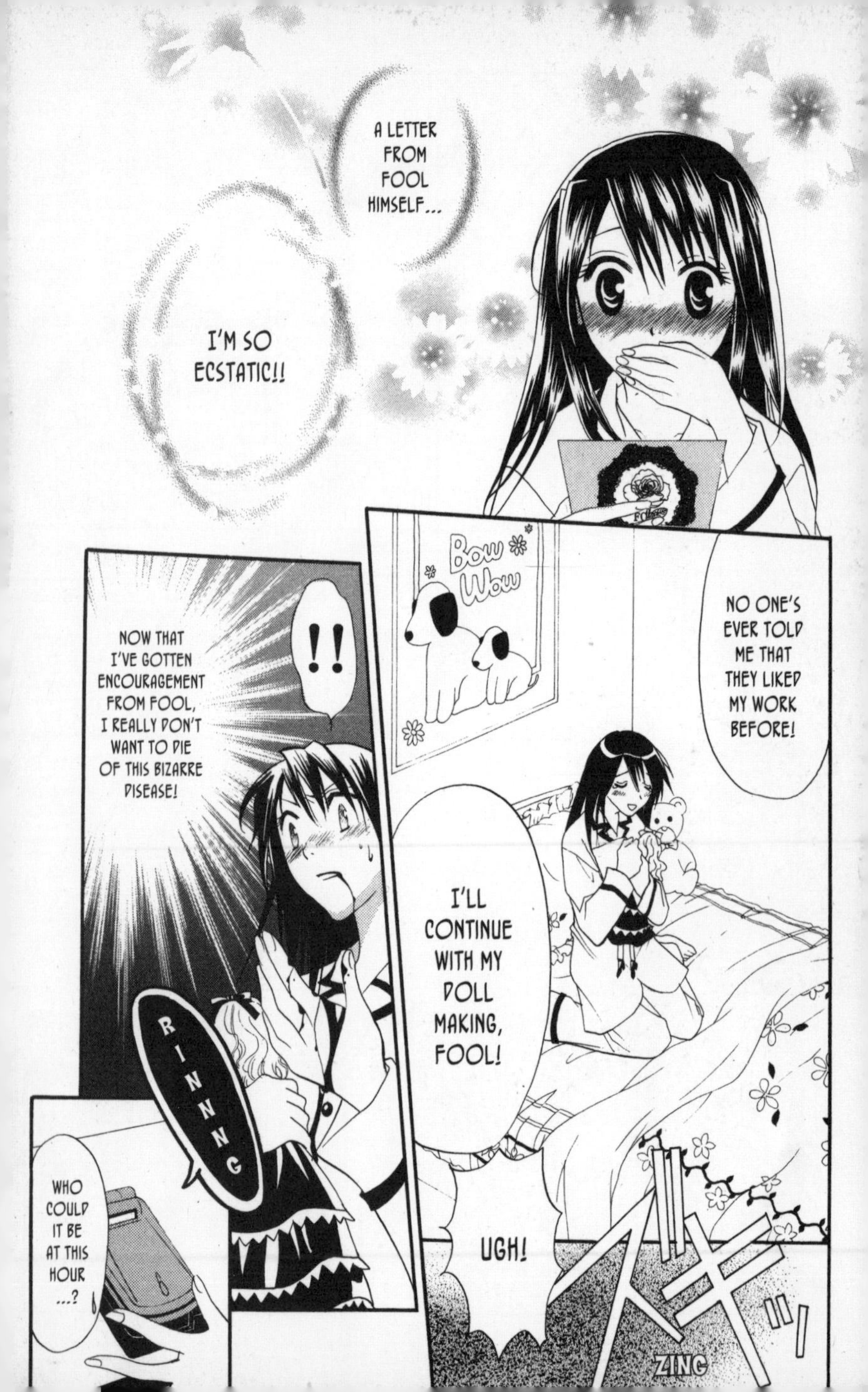

A LETTER FROM FOOL HIMSELF...
I'M SO ECSTATIC!!
NO ONE'S EVER TOLD ME THAT THEY LIKED MY WORK BEFORE!
I'LL CONTINUE WITH MY DOLL MAKING, FOOL!
UGH!
ZING
!!
NOW THAT I'VE GOTTEN ENCOURAGEMENT FROM FOOL, I REALLY DON'T WANT TO DIE OF THIS BIZARRE DISEASE!
RINNNG
WHO COULD IT BE AT THIS HOUR ...?

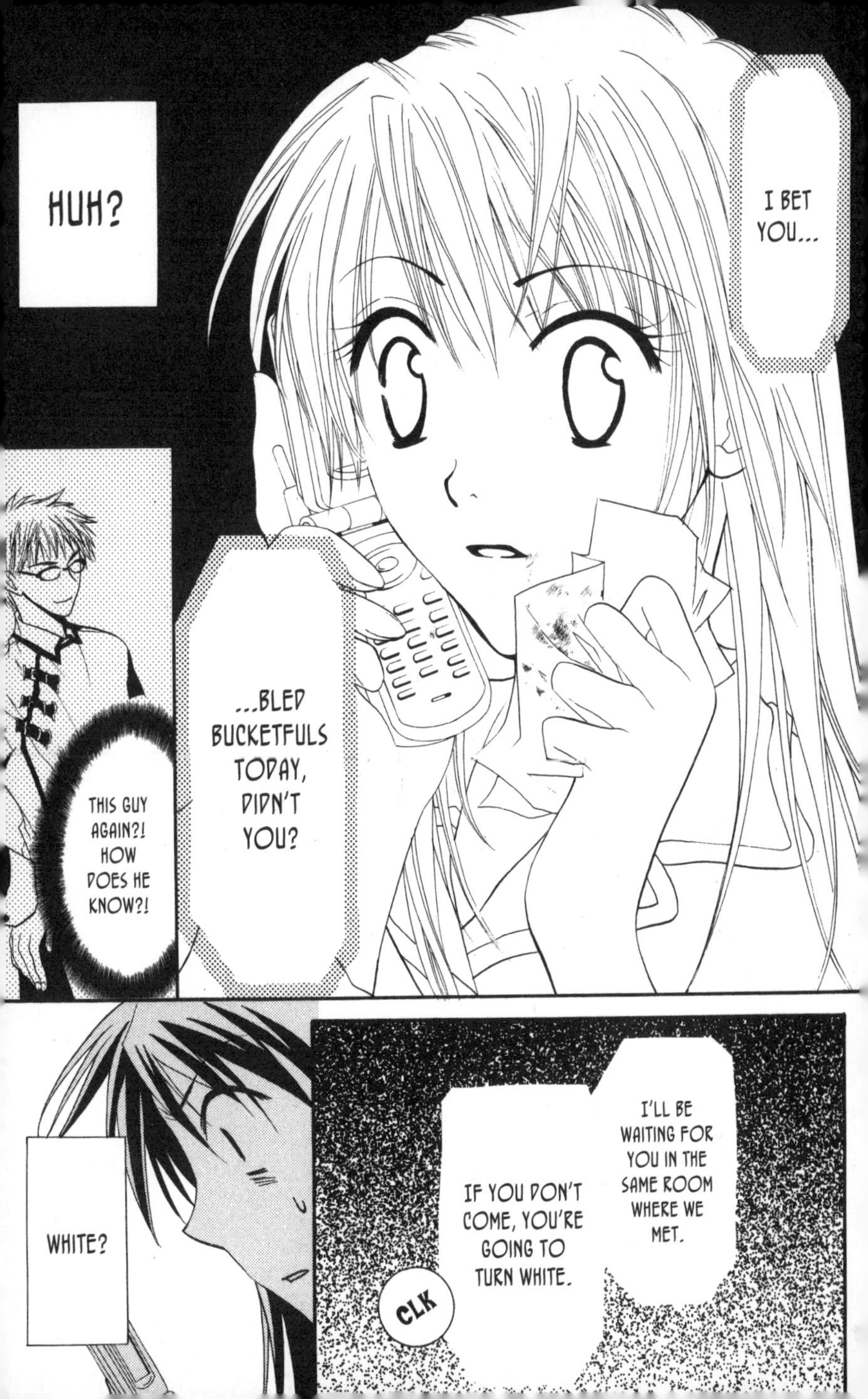
I BET YOU...
...BLED BUCKETFULS TODAY, DIDN'T YOU?
HUH?
THIS GUY AGAIN?! HOW DOES HE KNOW?!
I'LL BE WAITING FOR YOU IN THE SAME ROOM WHERE WE MET.
IF YOU DON'T COME, YOU'RE GOING TO TURN WHITE.
CLK
WHITE?

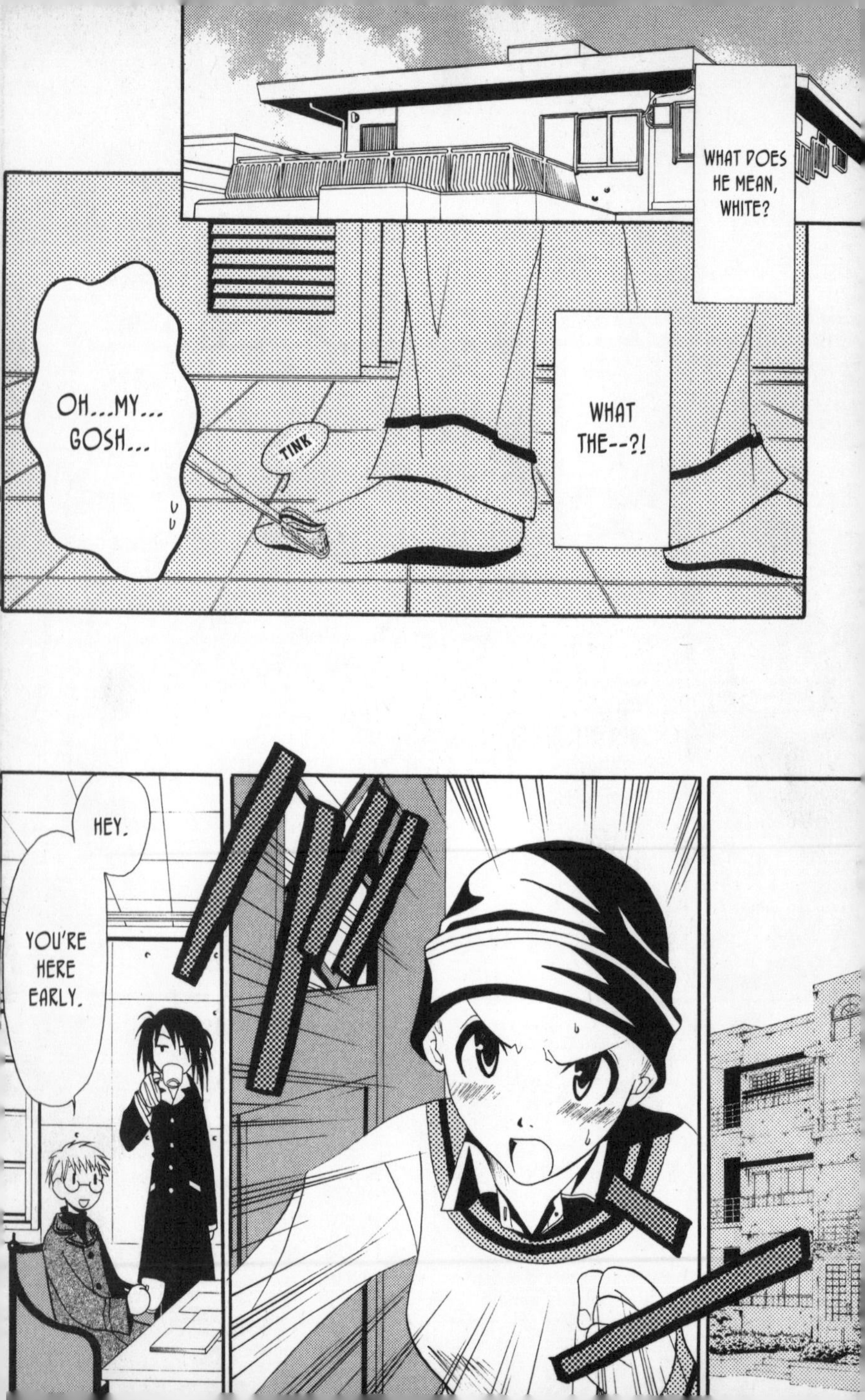
WHAT DOES HE MEAN, WHITE?
WHAT THE--?!
TINK
OH...MY... GOSH...
HEY.
YOU'RE HERE EARLY.

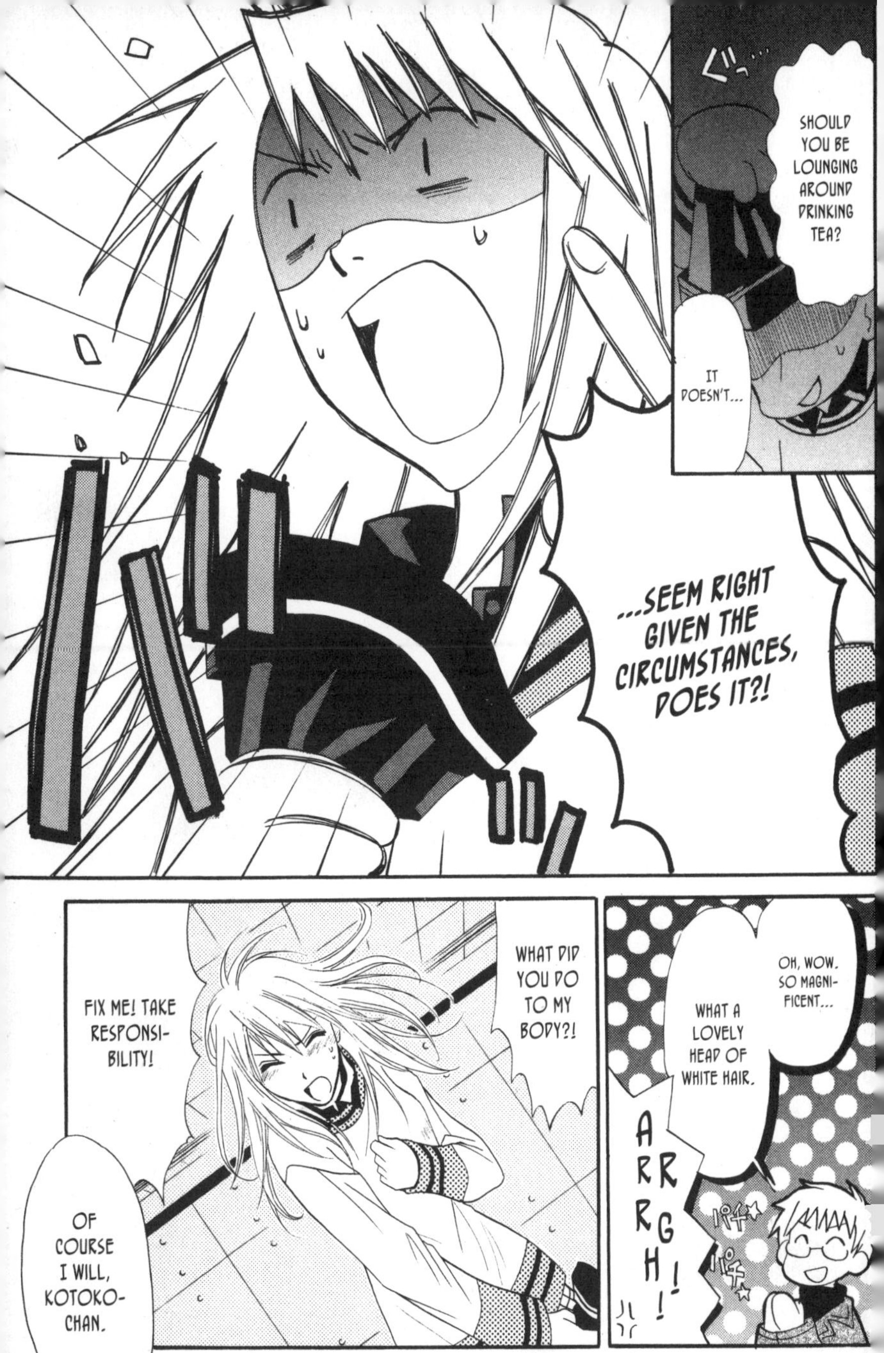
SHOULD YOU BE LOUNGING AROUND DRINKING TEA?
IT DOESN'T...
...SEEM RIGHT GIVEN THE CIRCUMSTANCES, DOES IT?!
OH, WOW. SO MAGNI-FICENT...
WHAT A LOVELY HEAD OF WHITE HAIR.
ARRRGH!!
パチ
パチ
WHAT DID YOU DO TO MY BODY?!
FIX ME! TAKE RESPONSI-BILITY!
OF COURSE I WILL, KOTOKO-CHAN.

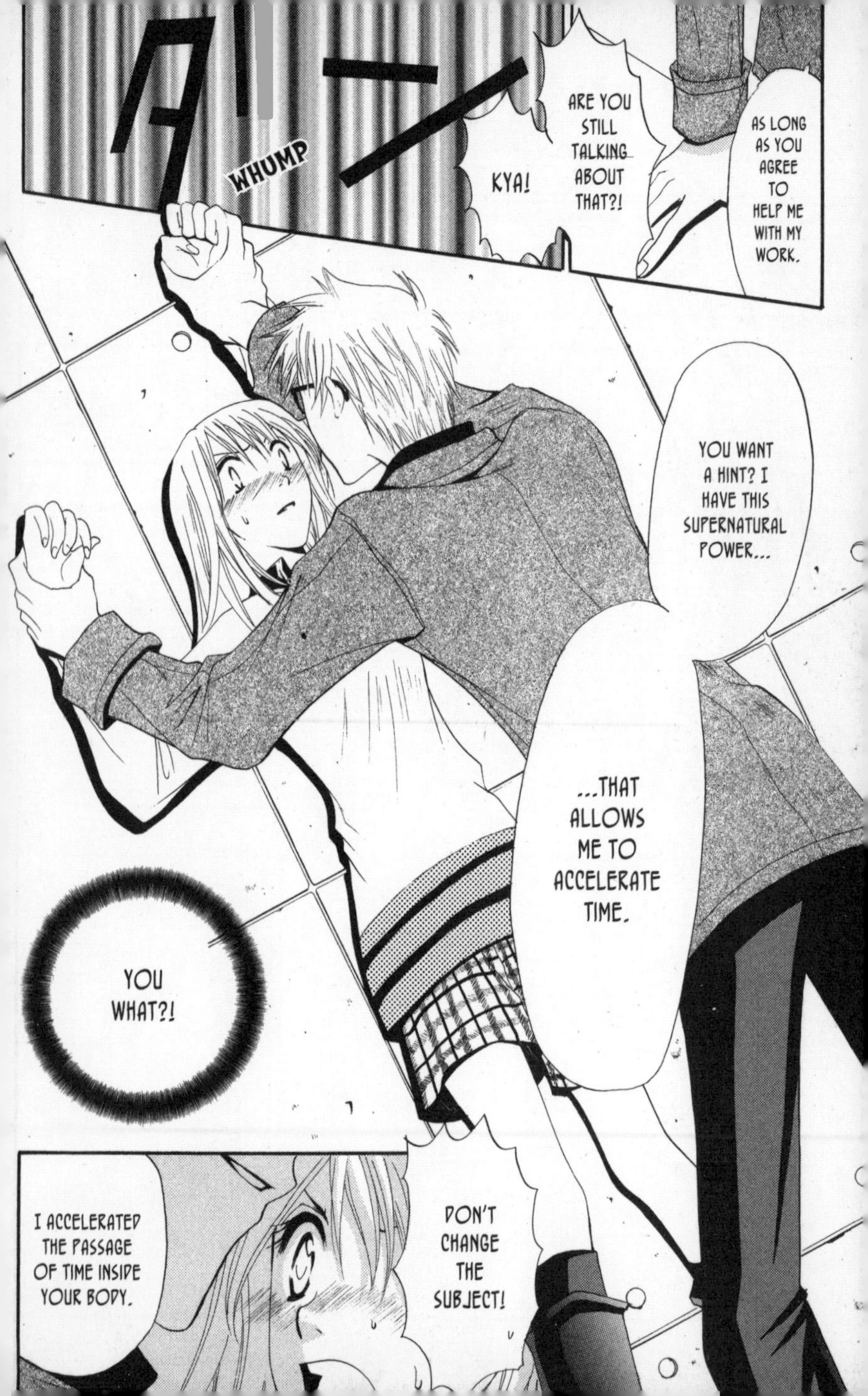
AS LONG AS YOU AGREE TO HELP ME WITH MY WORK.
ARE YOU STILL TALKING ABOUT THAT?!
KYA!
WHUMP
YOU WANT A HINT? I HAVE THIS SUPERNATURAL POWER...
...THAT ALLOWS ME TO ACCELERATE TIME.
YOU WHAT?!
DON'T CHANGE THE SUBJECT!
I ACCELERATED THE PASSAGE OF TIME INSIDE YOUR BODY.

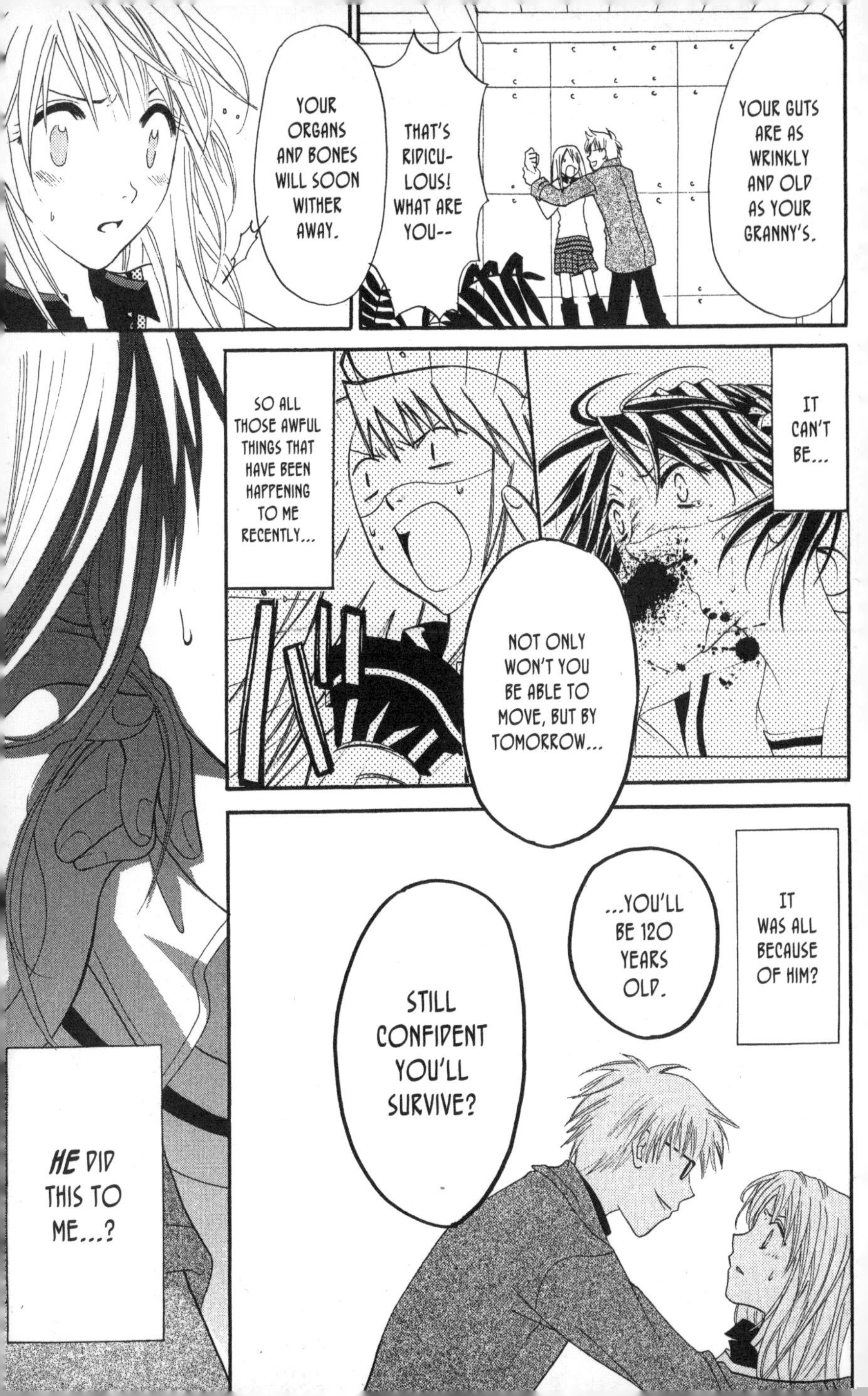
YOUR GUTS ARE AS WRINKLY AND OLD AS YOUR GRANNY'S.
THAT'S RIDICU-LOUS! WHAT ARE YOU--
YOUR ORGANS AND BONES WILL SOON WITHER AWAY.
IT CAN'T BE...
NOT ONLY WON'T YOU BE ABLE TO MOVE, BUT BY TOMORROW...
SO ALL THOSE AWFUL THINGS THAT HAVE BEEN HAPPENING TO ME RECENTLY...
IT WAS ALL BECAUSE OF HIM?
...YOU'LL BE 120 YEARS OLD.
STILL CONFIDENT YOU'LL SURVIVE?
HE DID THIS TO ME...?

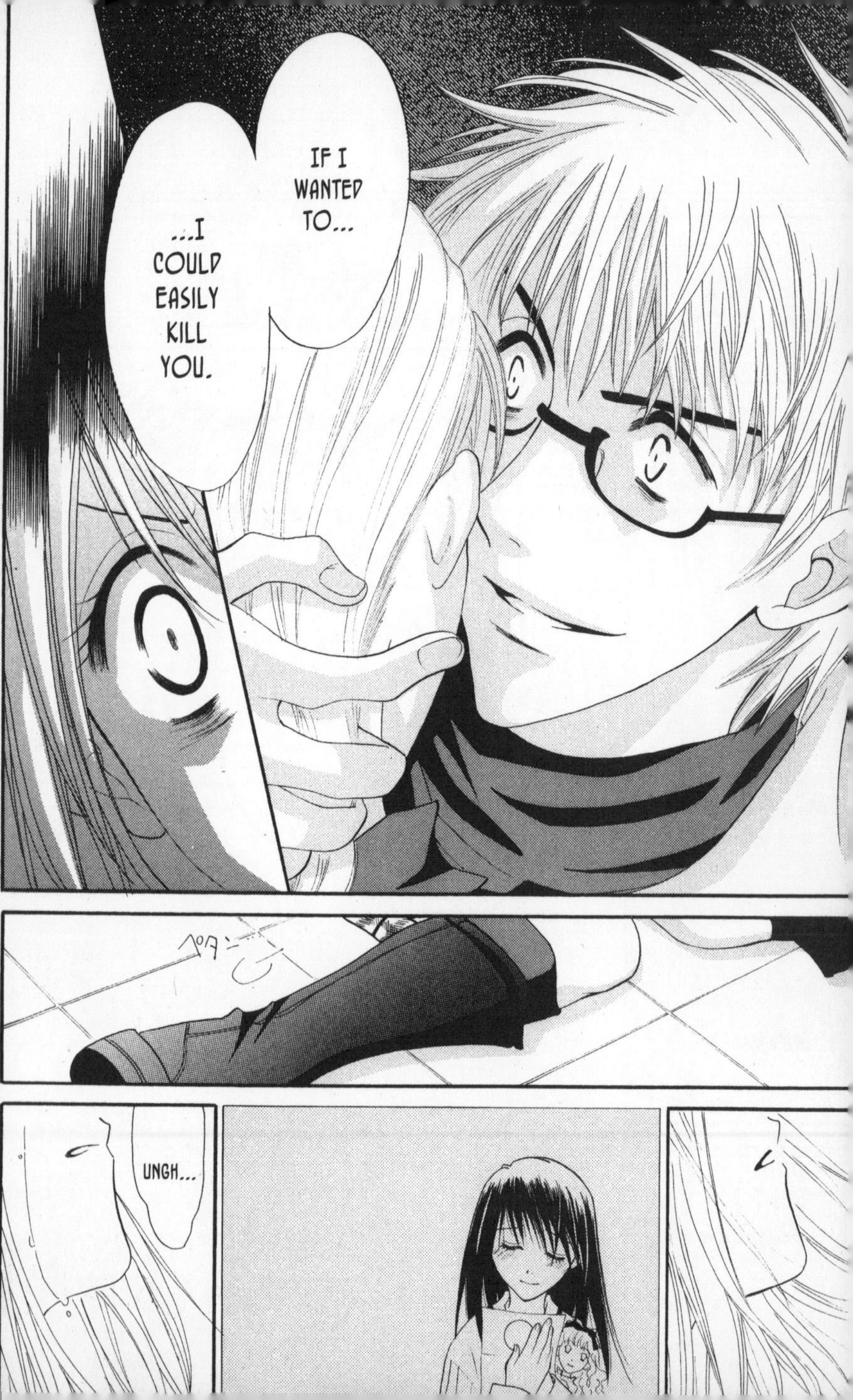
IF I WANTED TO...
...I COULD EASILY KILL YOU.
UNGH...

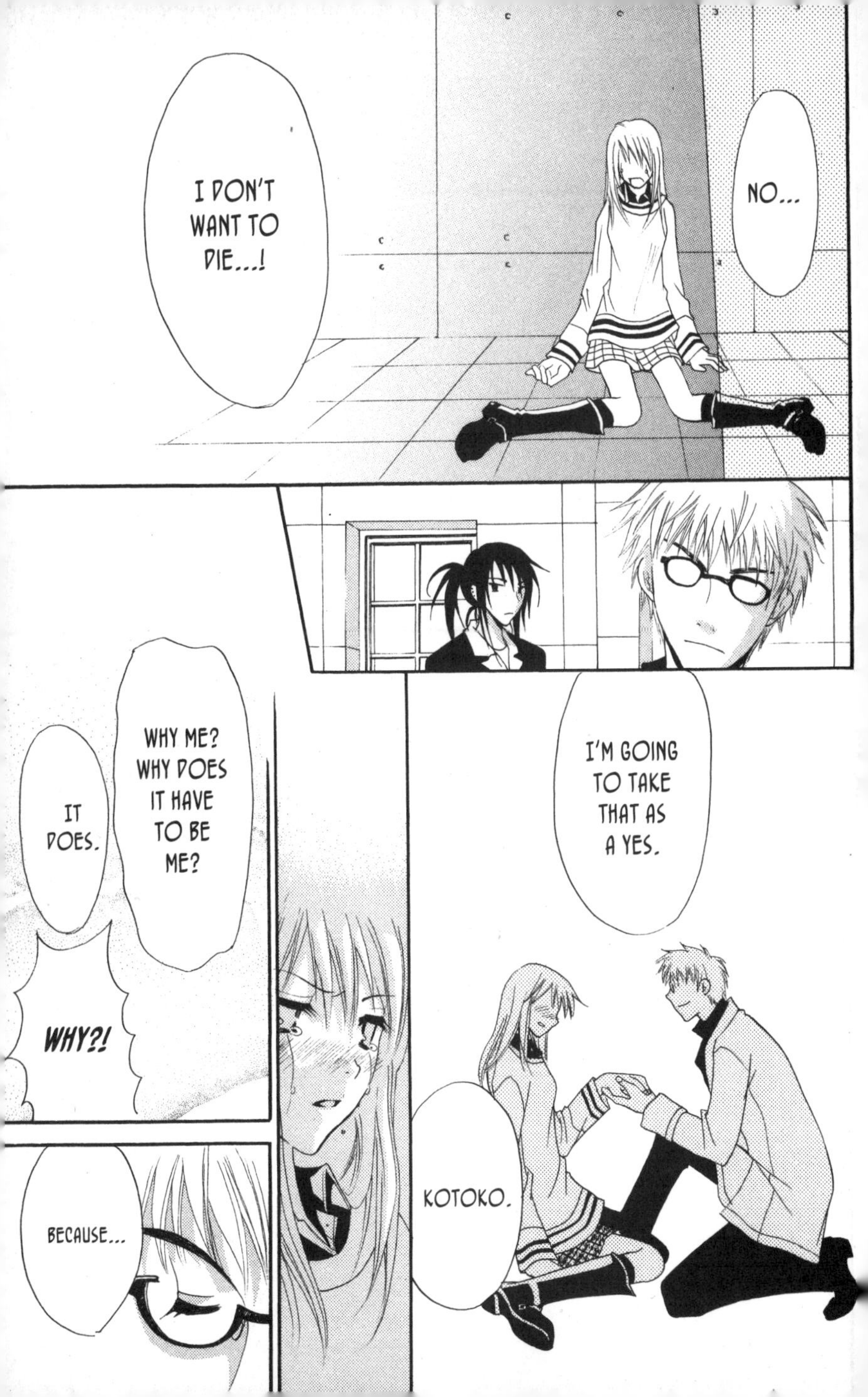
NO...
I DON'T WANT TO DIE...!
I'M GOING TO TAKE THAT AS A YES.
KOTOKO.
WHY ME? WHY DOES IT HAVE TO BE ME?
IT DOES.
WHY?!
BECAUSE...

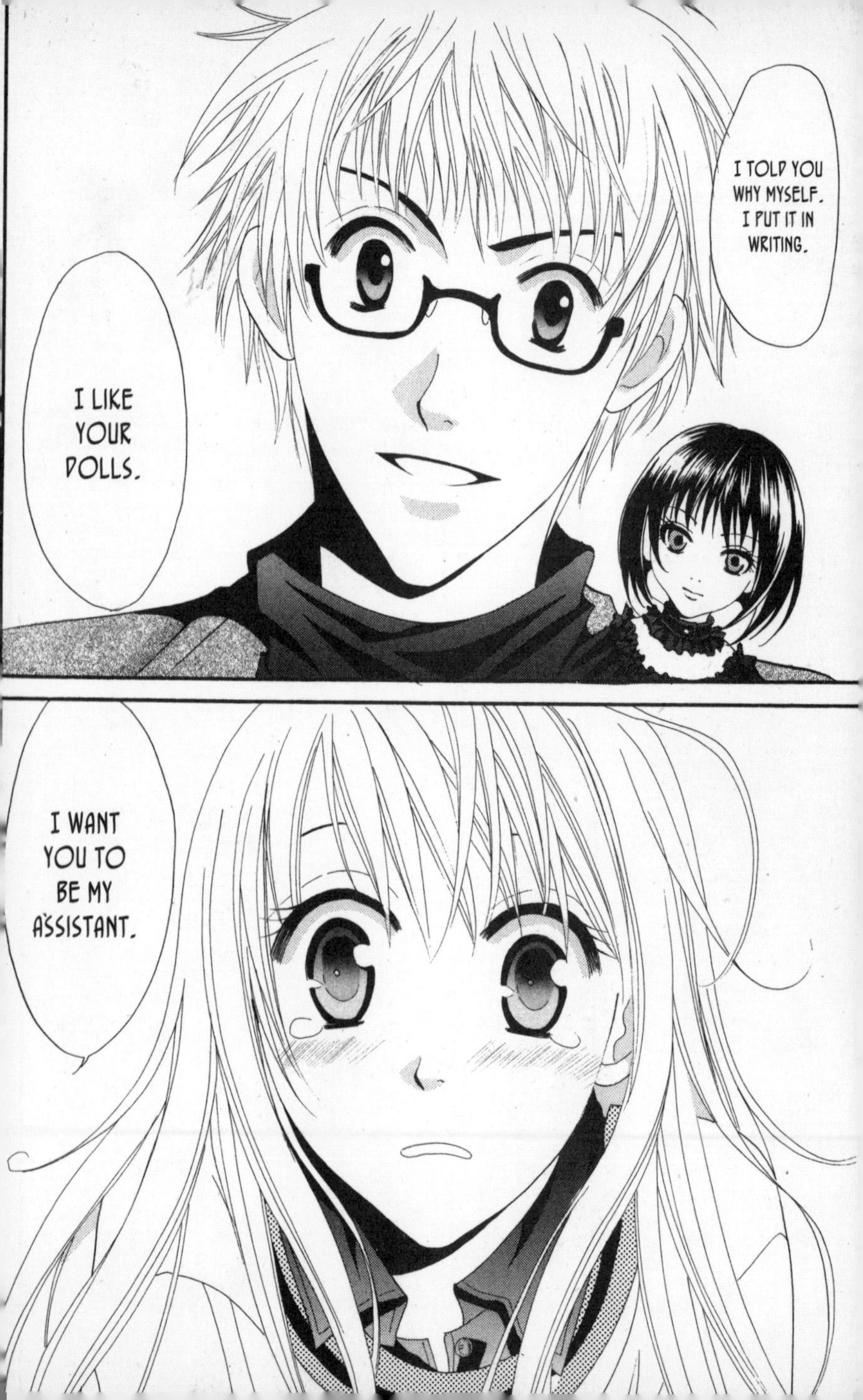
I TOLD YOU WHY MYSELF. I PUT IT IN WRITING.
I LIKE YOUR DOLLS.
I WANT YOU TO BE MY ASSISTANT.

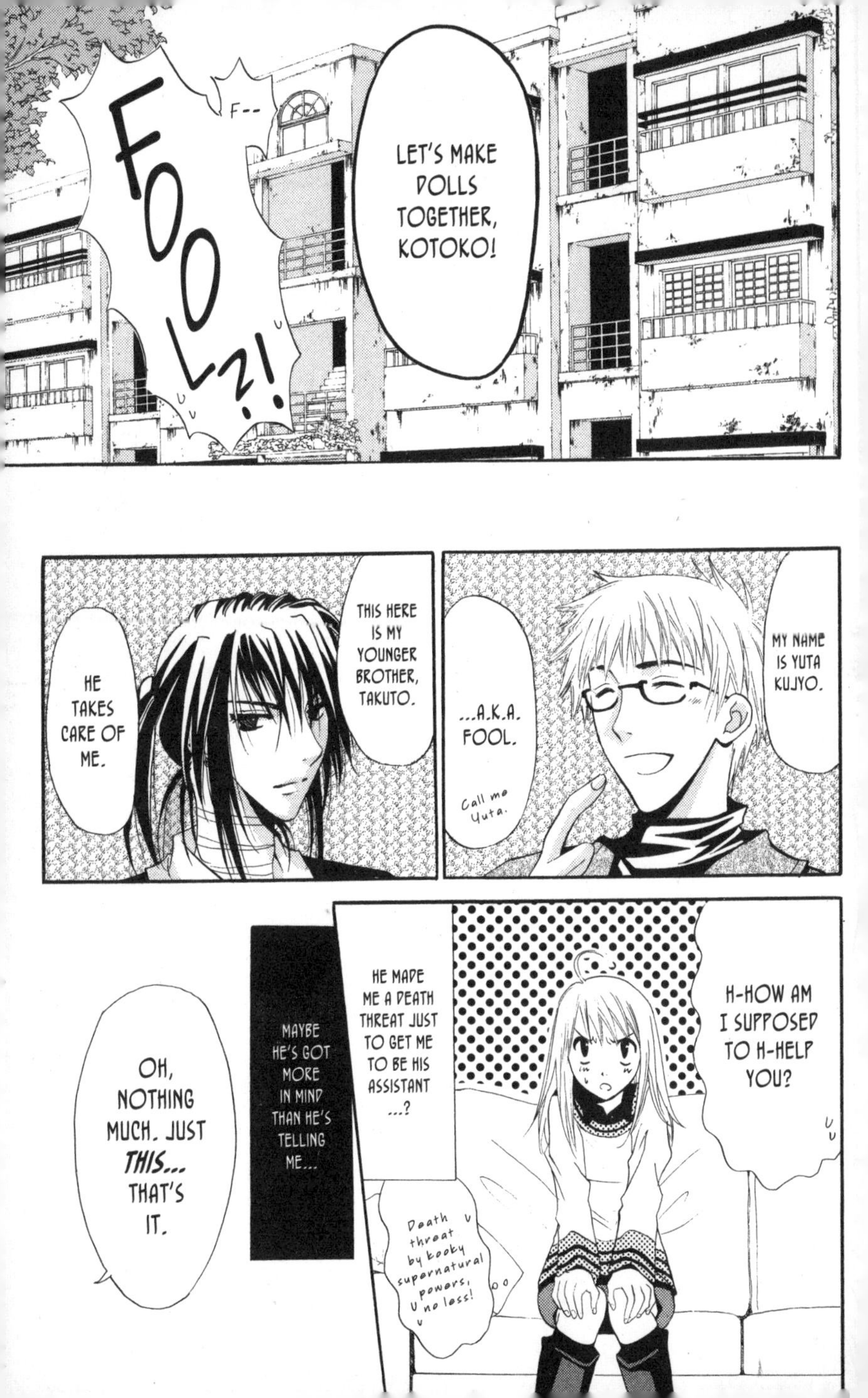
LET'S MAKE DOLLS TOGETHER, KOTOKO!
F--
FOOL?!
MY NAME IS YUTA KUJYO.
...A.K.A. FOOL.
Call me Yuta.
THIS HERE IS MY YOUNGER BROTHER, TAKUTO.
HE TAKES CARE OF ME.
H-HOW AM I SUPPOSED TO H-HELP YOU?
HE MADE ME A DEATH THREAT JUST TO GET ME TO BE HIS ASSISTANT ...?
Death threat by kooky supernatural powers, no less!
MAYBE HE'S GOT MORE IN MIND THAN HE'S TELLING ME...
OH, NOTHING MUCH. JUST *THIS...* THAT'S IT.

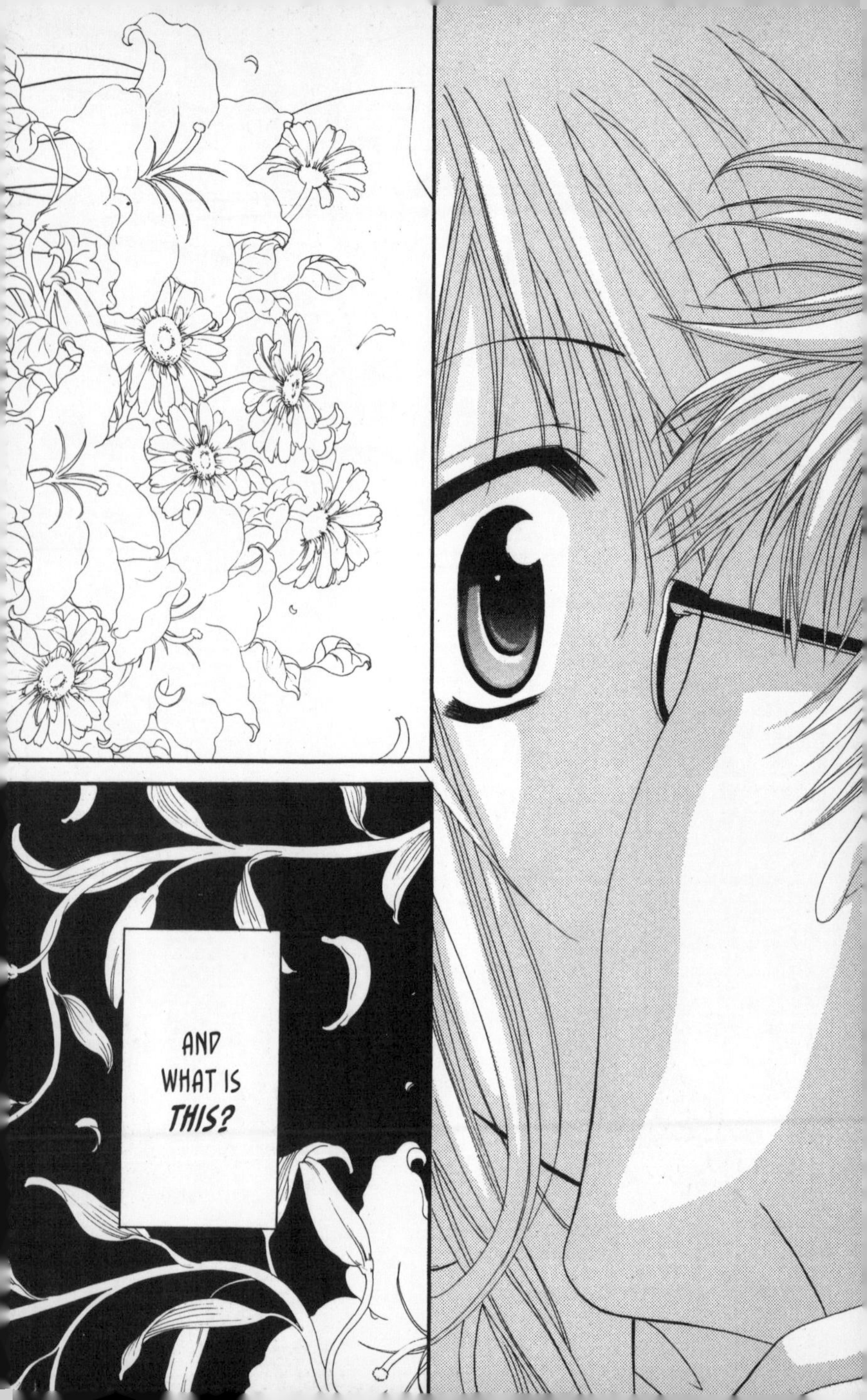
AND WHAT IS THIS?

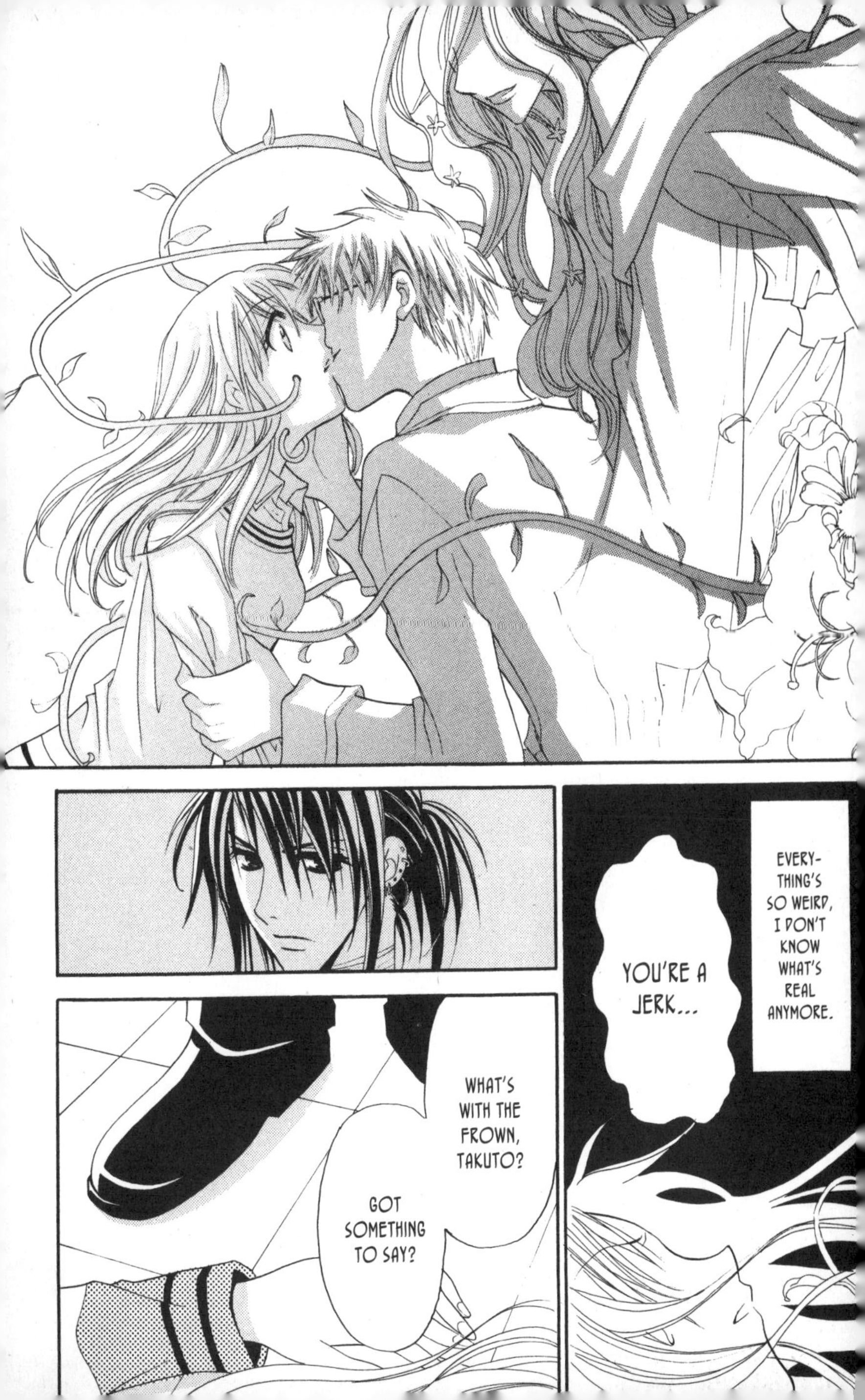
EVERY-THING'S SO WEIRD, I DON'T KNOW WHAT'S REAL ANYMORE.
YOU'RE A JERK...
WHAT'S WITH THE FROWN, TAKUTO?
GOT SOMETHING TO SAY?

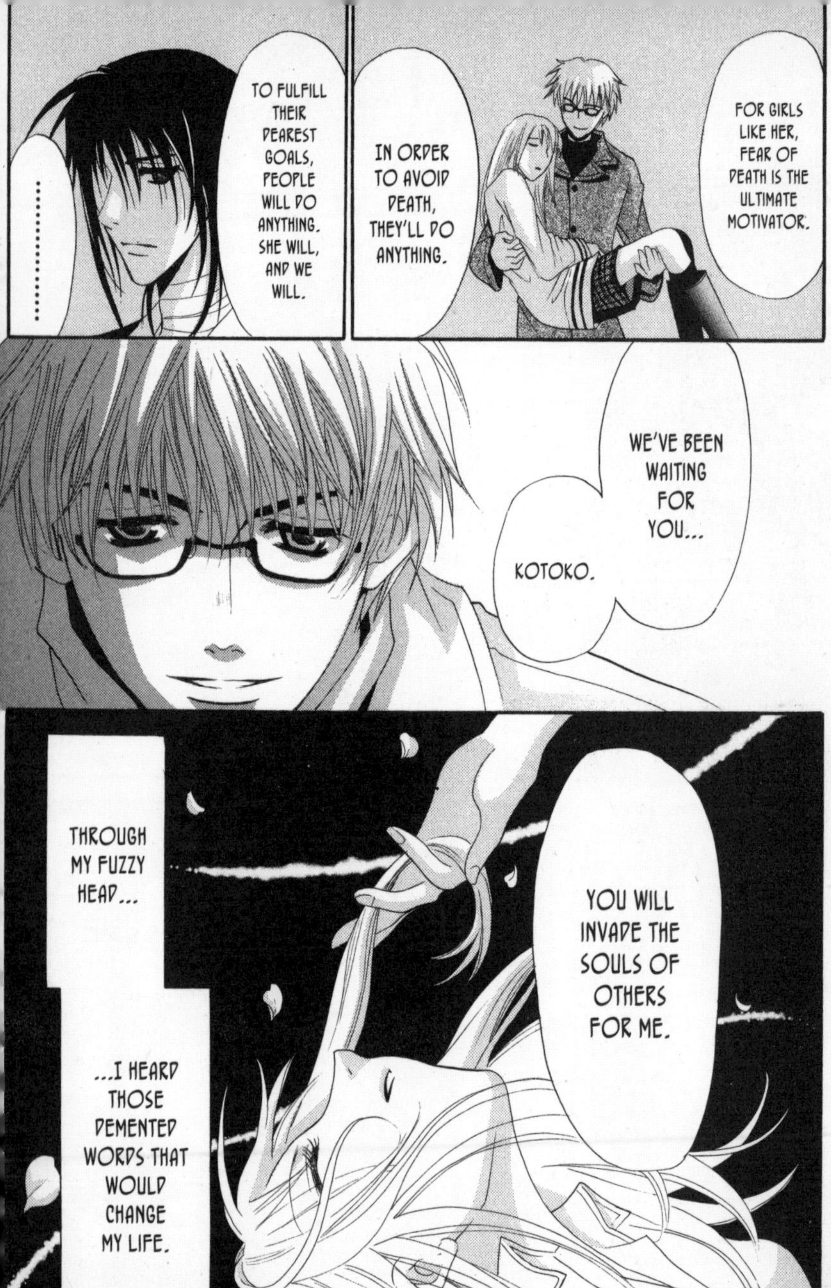
FOR GIRLS LIKE HER, FEAR OF DEATH IS THE ULTIMATE MOTIVATOR.
IN ORDER TO AVOID DEATH, THEY'LL DO ANYTHING.
TO FULFILL THEIR DEAREST GOALS, PEOPLE WILL DO ANYTHING. SHE WILL, AND WE WILL.
......
WE'VE BEEN WAITING FOR YOU...
KOTOKO.
YOU WILL INVADE THE SOULS OF OTHERS FOR ME.
THROUGH MY FUZZY HEAD...
...I HEARD THOSE DEMENTED WORDS THAT WOULD CHANGE MY LIFE.

1 End

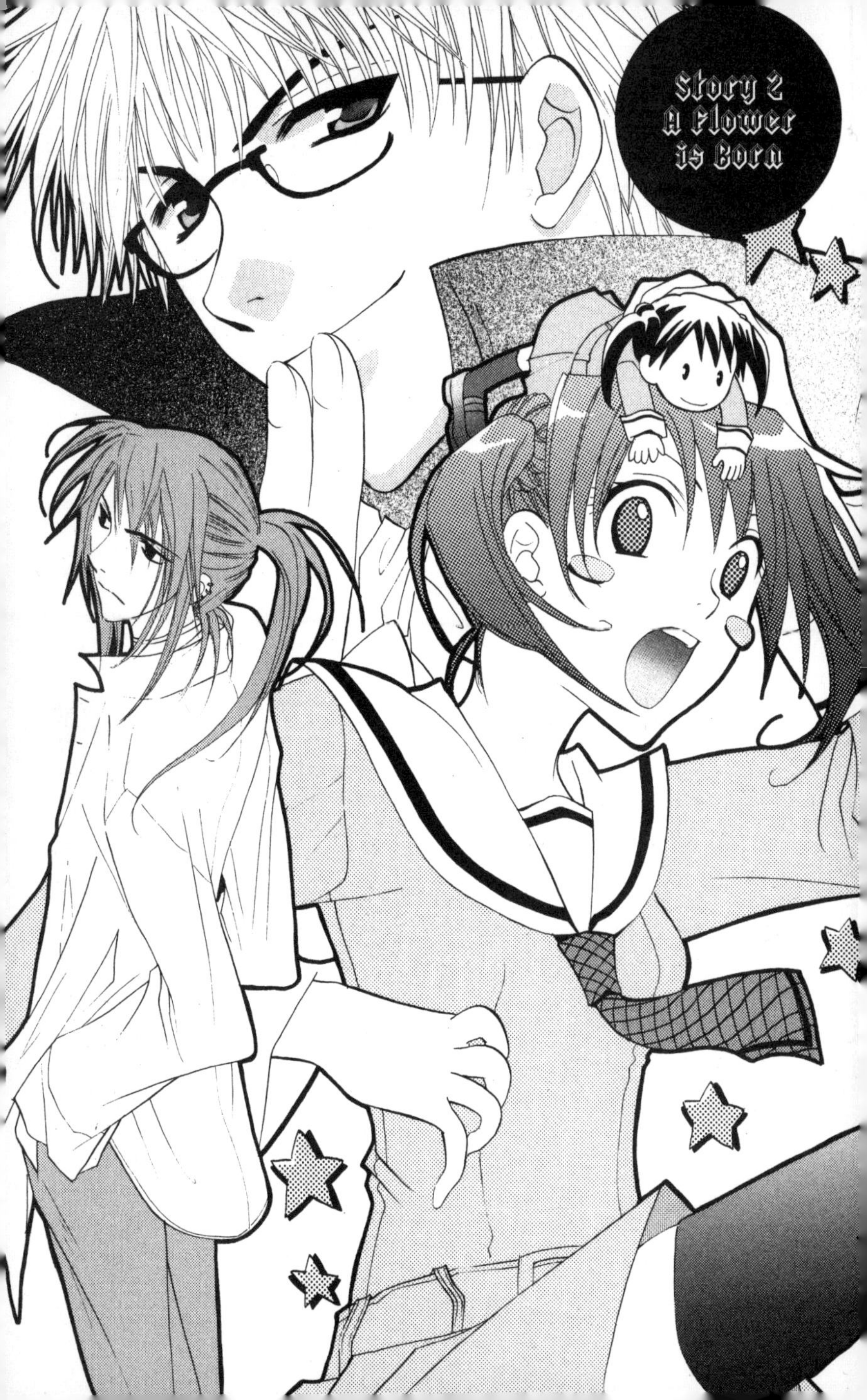
Story 2
A Flower
is Born

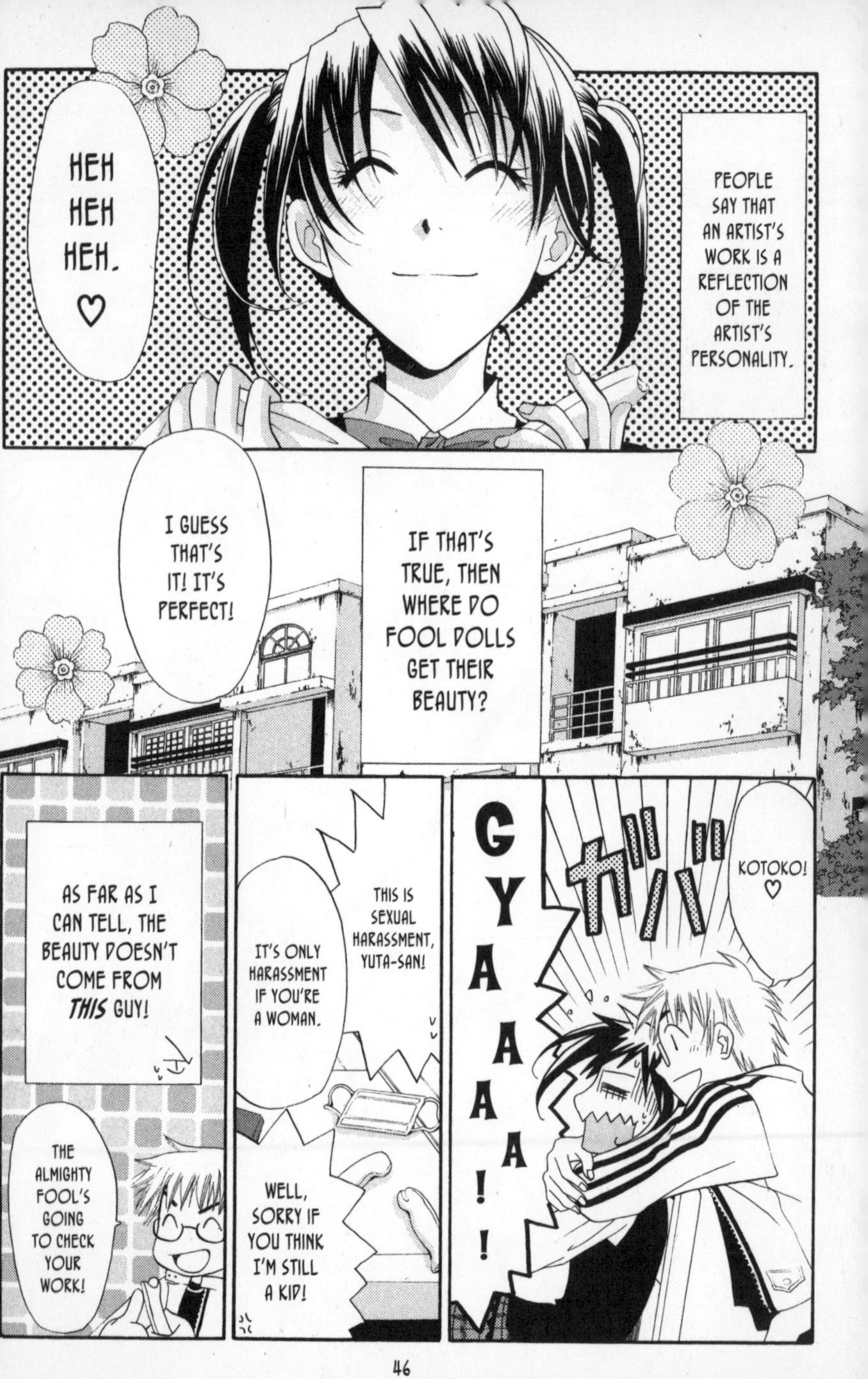
PEOPLE SAY THAT AN ARTIST'S WORK IS A REFLECTION OF THE ARTIST'S PERSONALITY.
HEH HEH HEH. ♡
IF THAT'S TRUE, THEN WHERE DO FOOL DOLLS GET THEIR BEAUTY?
I GUESS THAT'S IT! IT'S PERFECT!
KOTOKO! ♡
GYAAA!!
THIS IS SEXUAL HARASSMENT, YUTA-SAN!
IT'S ONLY HARASSMENT IF YOU'RE A WOMAN.
WELL, SORRY IF YOU THINK I'M STILL A KID!
AS FAR AS I CAN TELL, THE BEAUTY DOESN'T COME FROM *THIS* GUY!
THE ALMIGHTY FOOL'S GOING TO CHECK YOUR WORK!

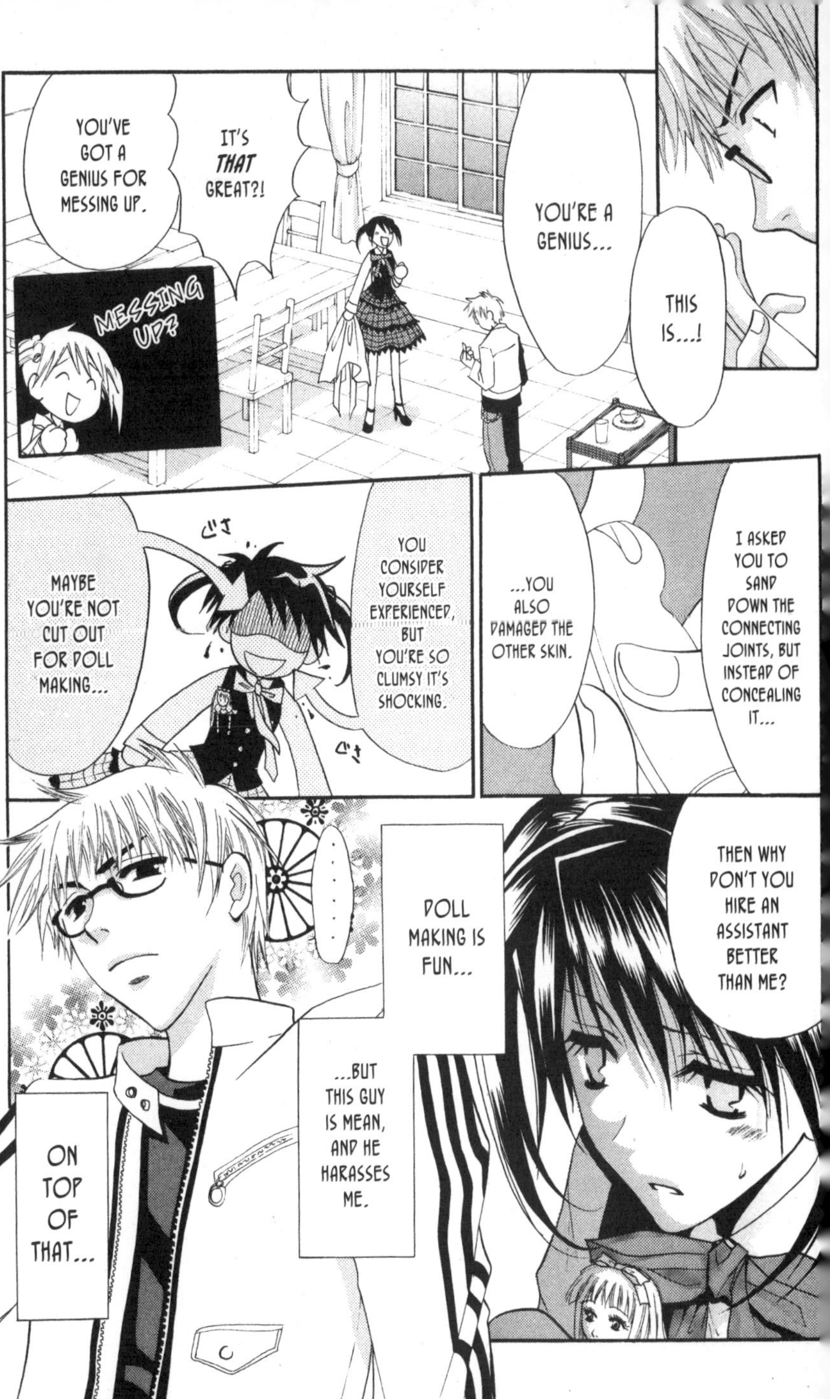
THIS IS...!
YOU'RE A GENIUS...
IT'S *THAT* GREAT?!
YOU'VE GOT A GENIUS FOR MESSING UP.
MESSING UP?
I ASKED YOU TO SAND DOWN THE CONNECTING JOINTS, BUT INSTEAD OF CONCEALING IT...
...YOU ALSO DAMAGED THE OTHER SKIN.
YOU CONSIDER YOURSELF EXPERIENCED, BUT YOU'RE SO CLUMSY IT'S SHOCKING.
MAYBE YOU'RE NOT CUT OUT FOR DOLL MAKING...
THEN WHY DON'T YOU HIRE AN ASSISTANT BETTER THAN ME?
......
DOLL MAKING IS FUN...
...BUT THIS GUY IS MEAN, AND HE HARASSES ME.
ON TOP OF THAT...

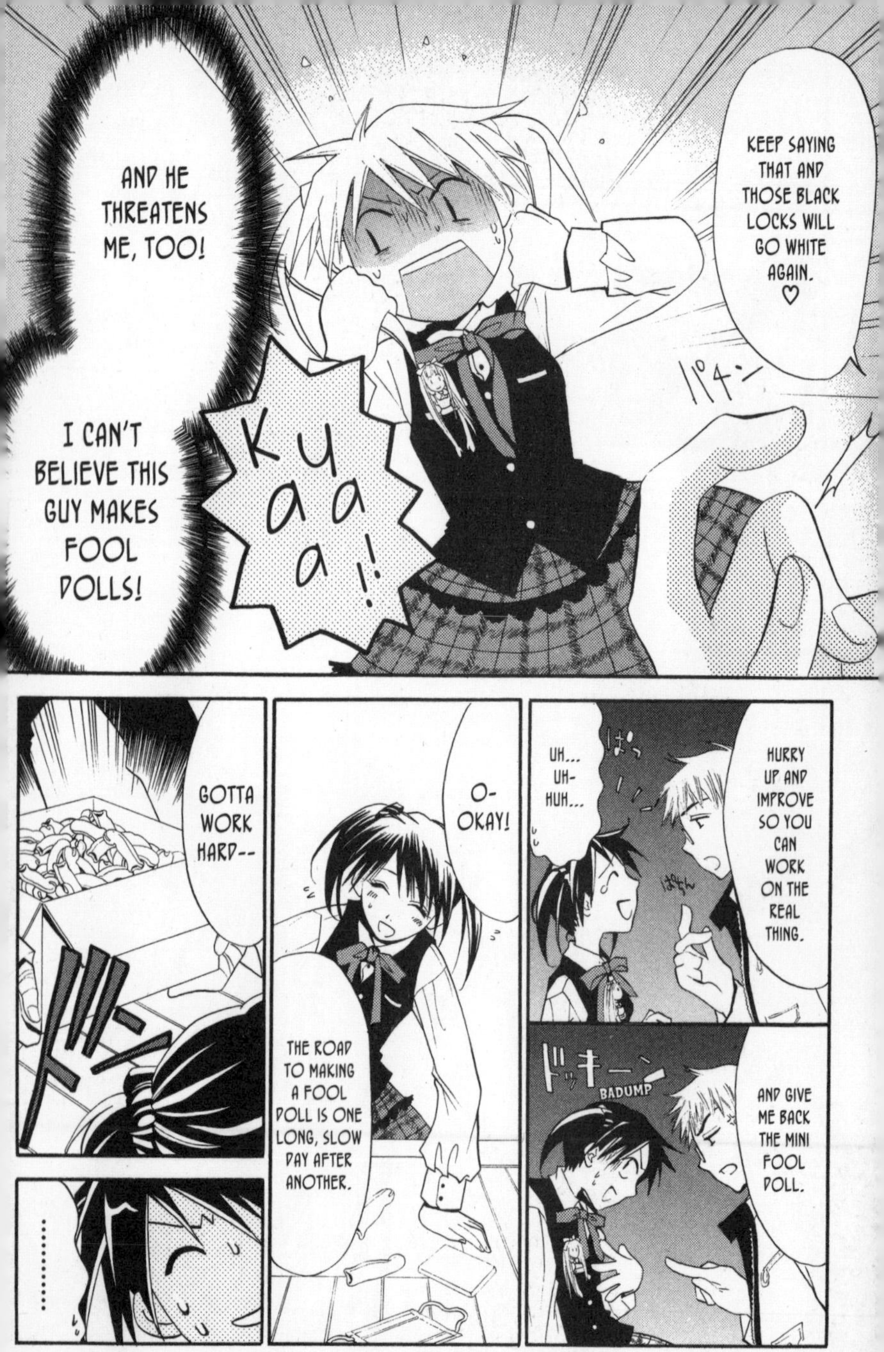
KEEP SAYING THAT AND THOSE BLACK LOCKS WILL GO WHITE AGAIN. ♡
KYAAA!!
AND HE THREATENS ME, TOO!
I CAN'T BELIEVE THIS GUY MAKES FOOL DOLLS!
HURRY UP AND IMPROVE SO YOU CAN WORK ON THE REAL THING.
UH... UH-HUH...
AND GIVE ME BACK THE MINI FOOL DOLL.
BADUMP
O-OKAY!
THE ROAD TO MAKING A FOOL DOLL IS ONE LONG, SLOW DAY AFTER ANOTHER.
GOTTA WORK HARD--
....

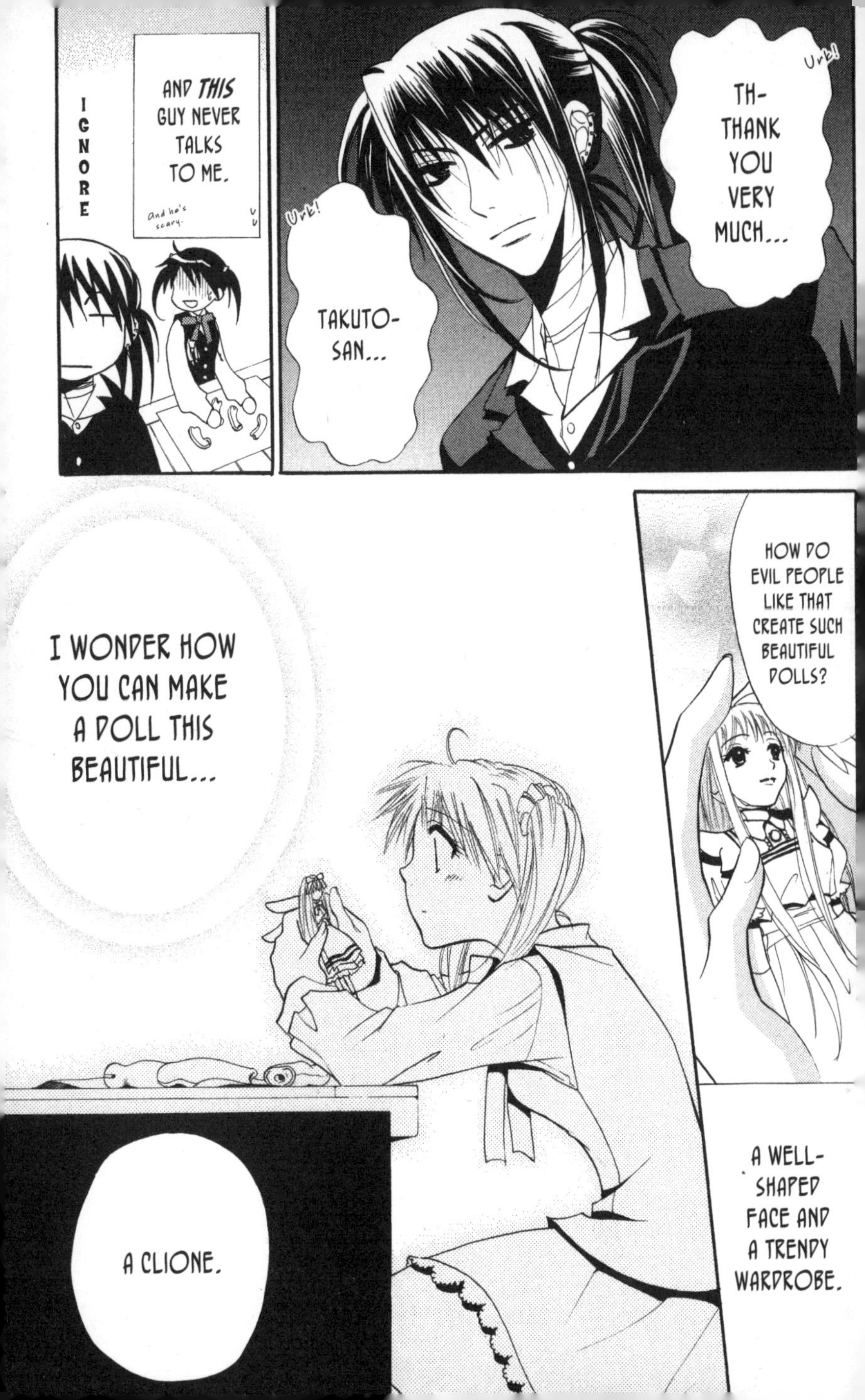
Urk!
TH- THANK YOU VERY MUCH...
Urk!
TAKUTO- SAN...
AND THIS GUY NEVER TALKS TO ME.
And he's scary.
IGNORE
HOW DO EVIL PEOPLE LIKE THAT CREATE SUCH BEAUTIFUL DOLLS?
I WONDER HOW YOU CAN MAKE A DOLL THIS BEAUTIFUL...
A WELL- SHAPED FACE AND A TRENDY WARDROBE.
A CLIONE.

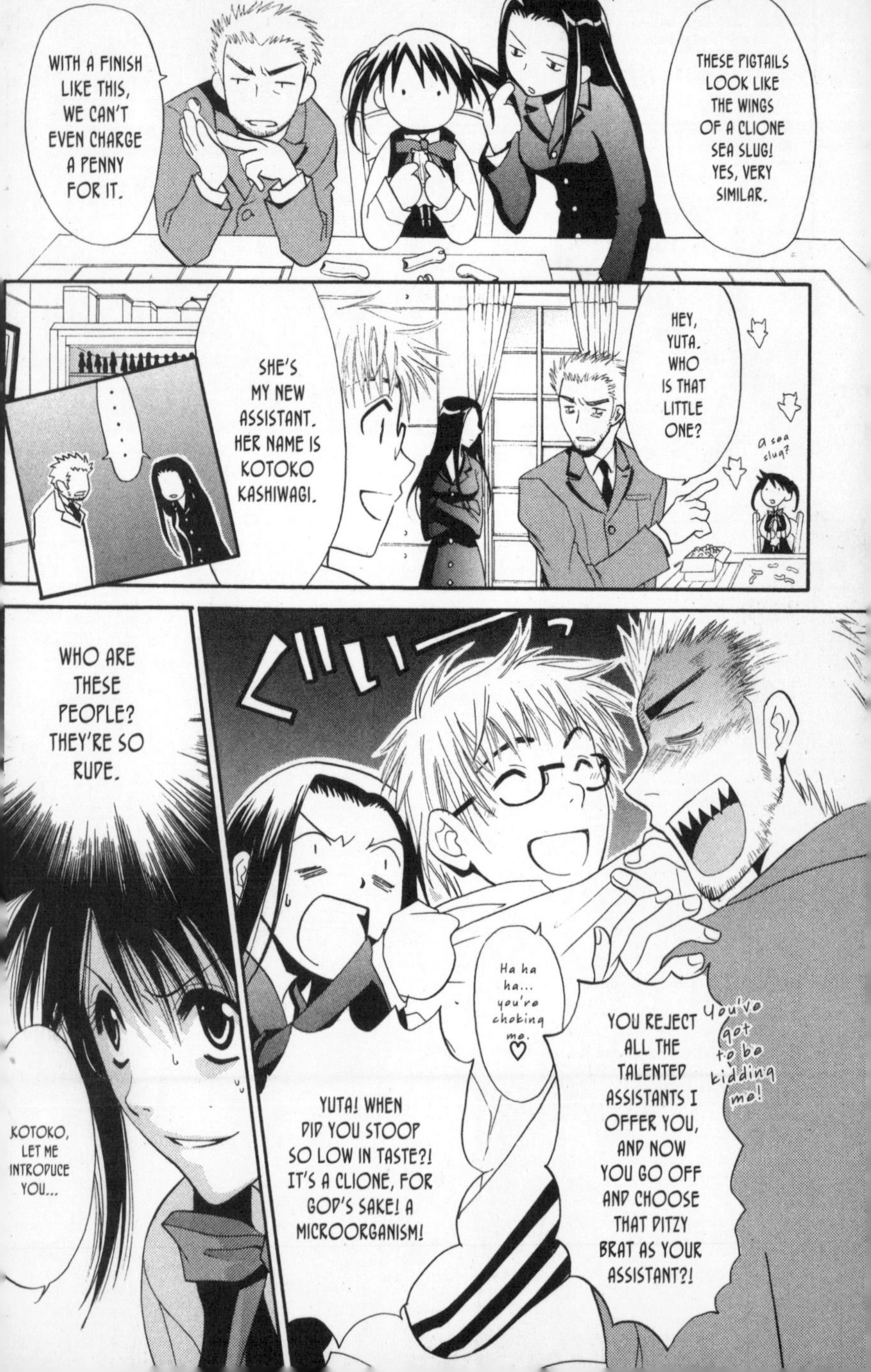
THESE PIGTAILS LOOK LIKE THE WINGS OF A CLIONE SEA SLUG! YES, VERY SIMILAR.
WITH A FINISH LIKE THIS, WE CAN'T EVEN CHARGE A PENNY FOR IT.
HEY, YUTA. WHO IS THAT LITTLE ONE?
a sea slug?
SHE'S MY NEW ASSISTANT. HER NAME IS KOTOKO KASHIWAGI.
......
You've got to be kidding me!
YOU REJECT ALL THE TALENTED ASSISTANTS I OFFER YOU, AND NOW YOU GO OFF AND CHOOSE THAT DITZY BRAT AS YOUR ASSISTANT?!
Ha ha ha... you're choking me. ♡
YUTA! WHEN DID YOU STOOP SO LOW IN TASTE?! IT'S A CLIONE, FOR GOD'S SAKE! A MICROORGANISM!
WHO ARE THESE PEOPLE? THEY'RE SO RUDE.
KOTOKO, LET ME INTRODUCE YOU...

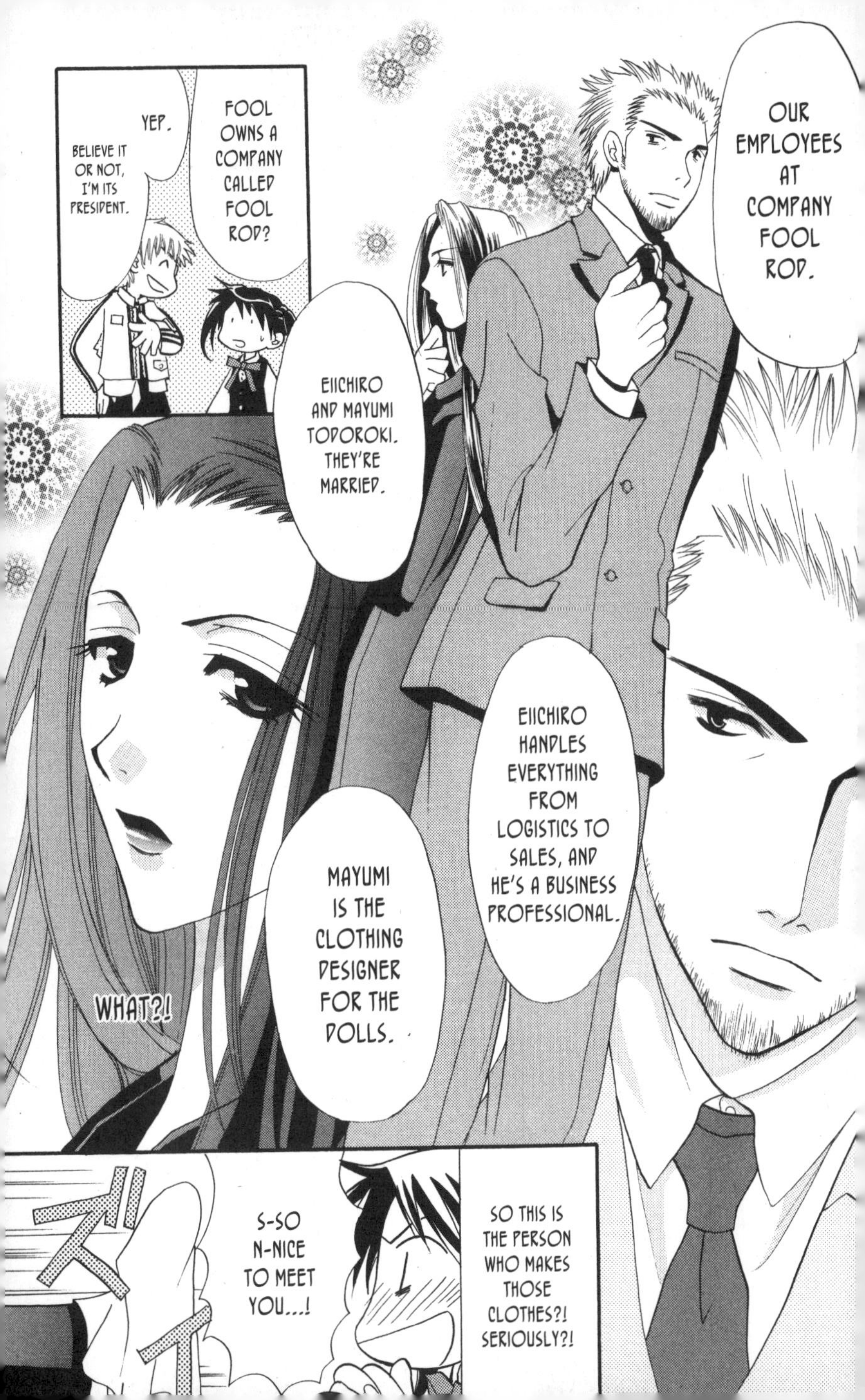
OUR EMPLOYEES AT COMPANY FOOL ROD.
FOOL OWNS A COMPANY CALLED FOOL ROD?
YEP.
BELIEVE IT OR NOT, I'M ITS PRESIDENT.
EIICHIRO AND MAYUMI TODOROKI. THEY'RE MARRIED.
EIICHIRO HANDLES EVERYTHING FROM LOGISTICS TO SALES, AND HE'S A BUSINESS PROFESSIONAL.
MAYUMI IS THE CLOTHING DESIGNER FOR THE DOLLS.
WHAT?!
SO THIS IS THE PERSON WHO MAKES THOSE CLOTHES?! SERIOUSLY?!
S-SO N-NICE TO MEET YOU...!

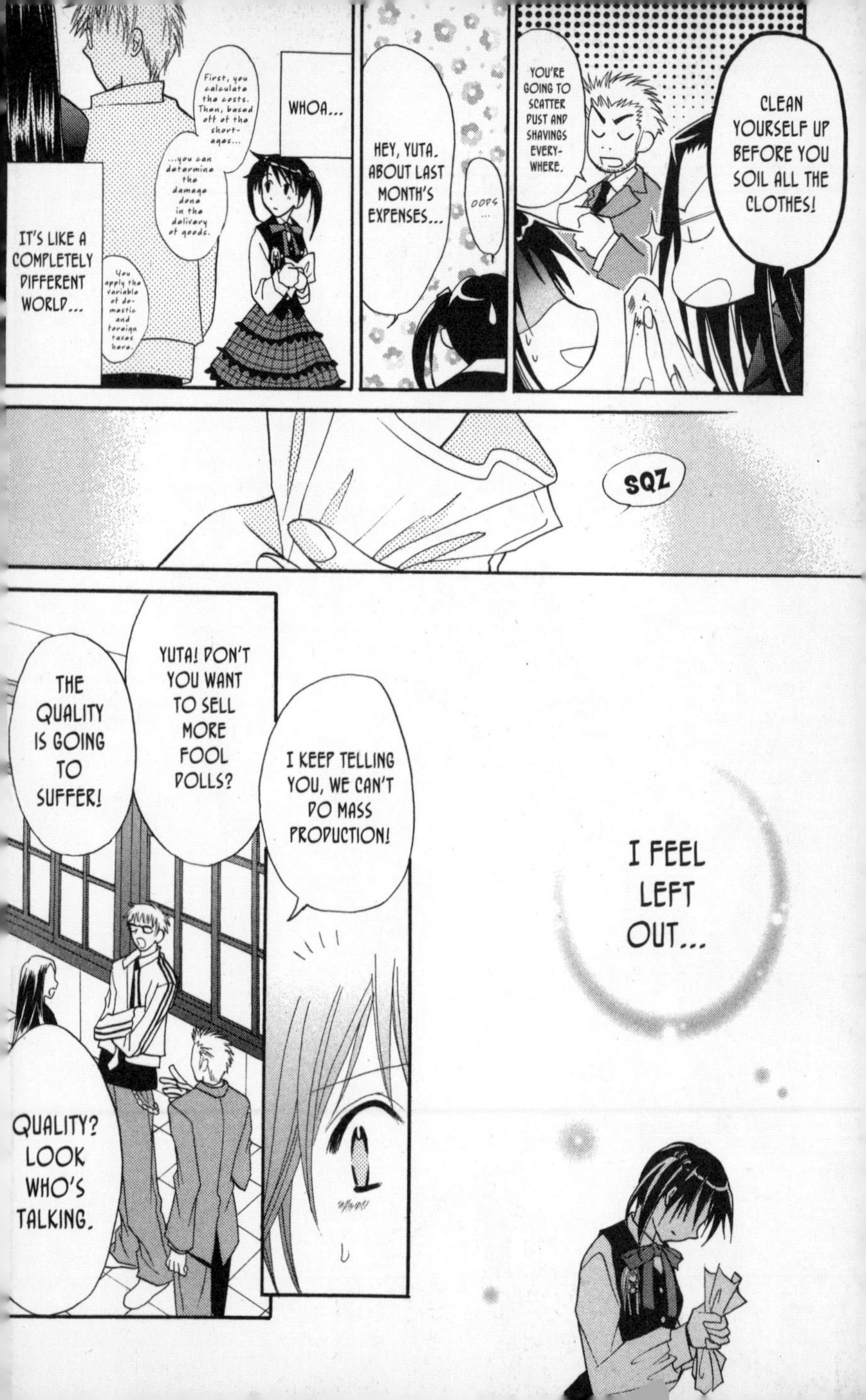
CLEAN YOURSELF UP BEFORE YOU SOIL ALL THE CLOTHES!
YOU'RE GOING TO SCATTER DUST AND SHAVINGS EVERY-WHERE.
HEY, YUTA. ABOUT LAST MONTH'S EXPENSES...
OOPS...
WHOA...
First, you calculate the costs. Then, based off of the short-ages...
...you can determine the damage done in the delivery of goods.
You apply the variable of do-mestic and foreign taxes here.
IT'S LIKE A COMPLETELY DIFFERENT WORLD...
SQZ
I FEEL LEFT OUT...
I KEEP TELLING YOU, WE CAN'T DO MASS PRODUCTION!
YUTA! DON'T YOU WANT TO SELL MORE FOOL DOLLS?
THE QUALITY IS GOING TO SUFFER!
QUALITY? LOOK WHO'S TALKING.

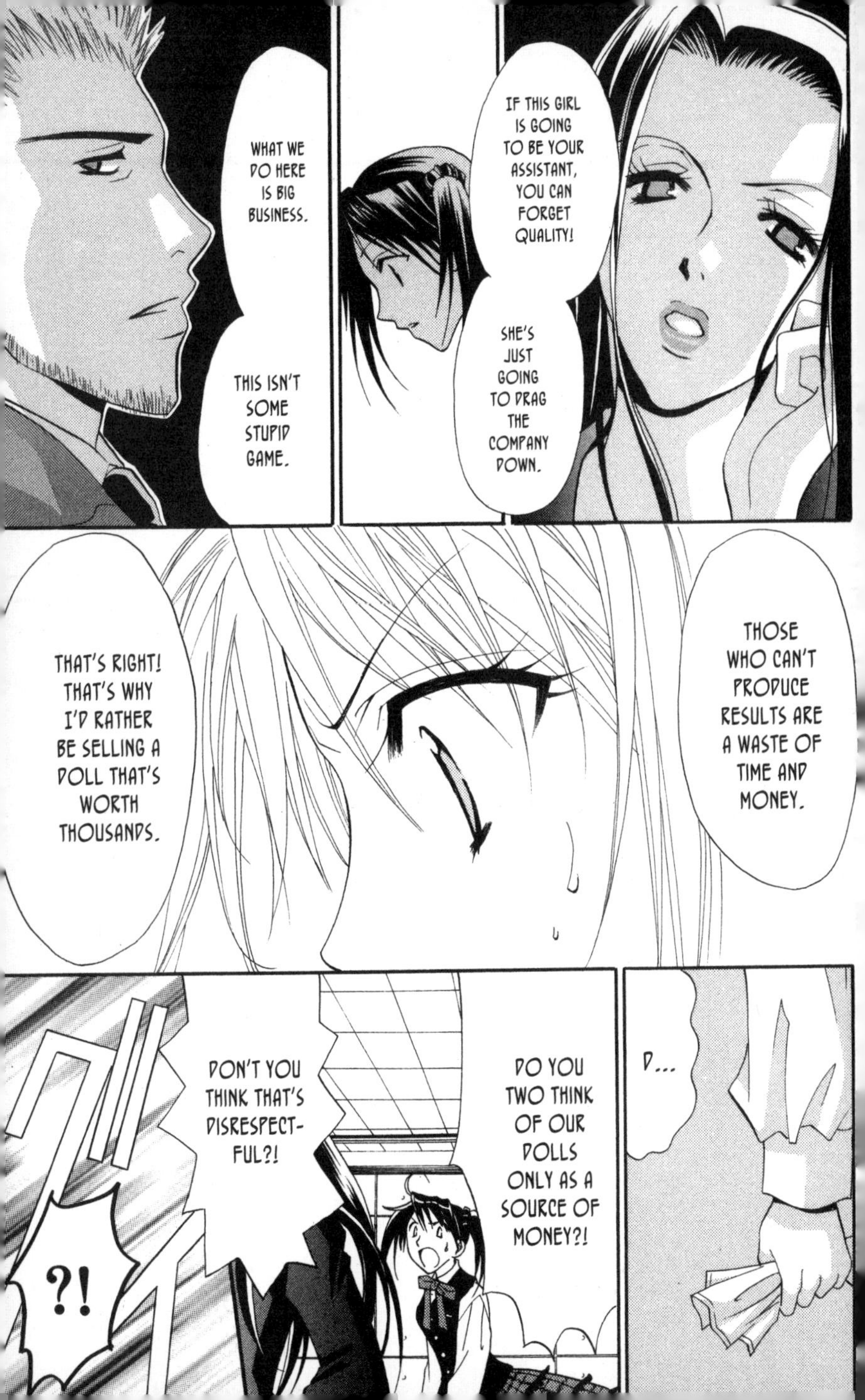
IF THIS GIRL IS GOING TO BE YOUR ASSISTANT, YOU CAN FORGET QUALITY!
SHE'S JUST GOING TO DRAG THE COMPANY DOWN.
WHAT WE DO HERE IS BIG BUSINESS.
THIS ISN'T SOME STUPID GAME.
THOSE WHO CAN'T PRODUCE RESULTS ARE A WASTE OF TIME AND MONEY.
THAT'S RIGHT! THAT'S WHY I'D RATHER BE SELLING A DOLL THAT'S WORTH THOUSANDS.
D...
DO YOU TWO THINK OF OUR DOLLS ONLY AS A SOURCE OF MONEY?!
DON'T YOU THINK THAT'S DISRESPECT-FUL?!
?!

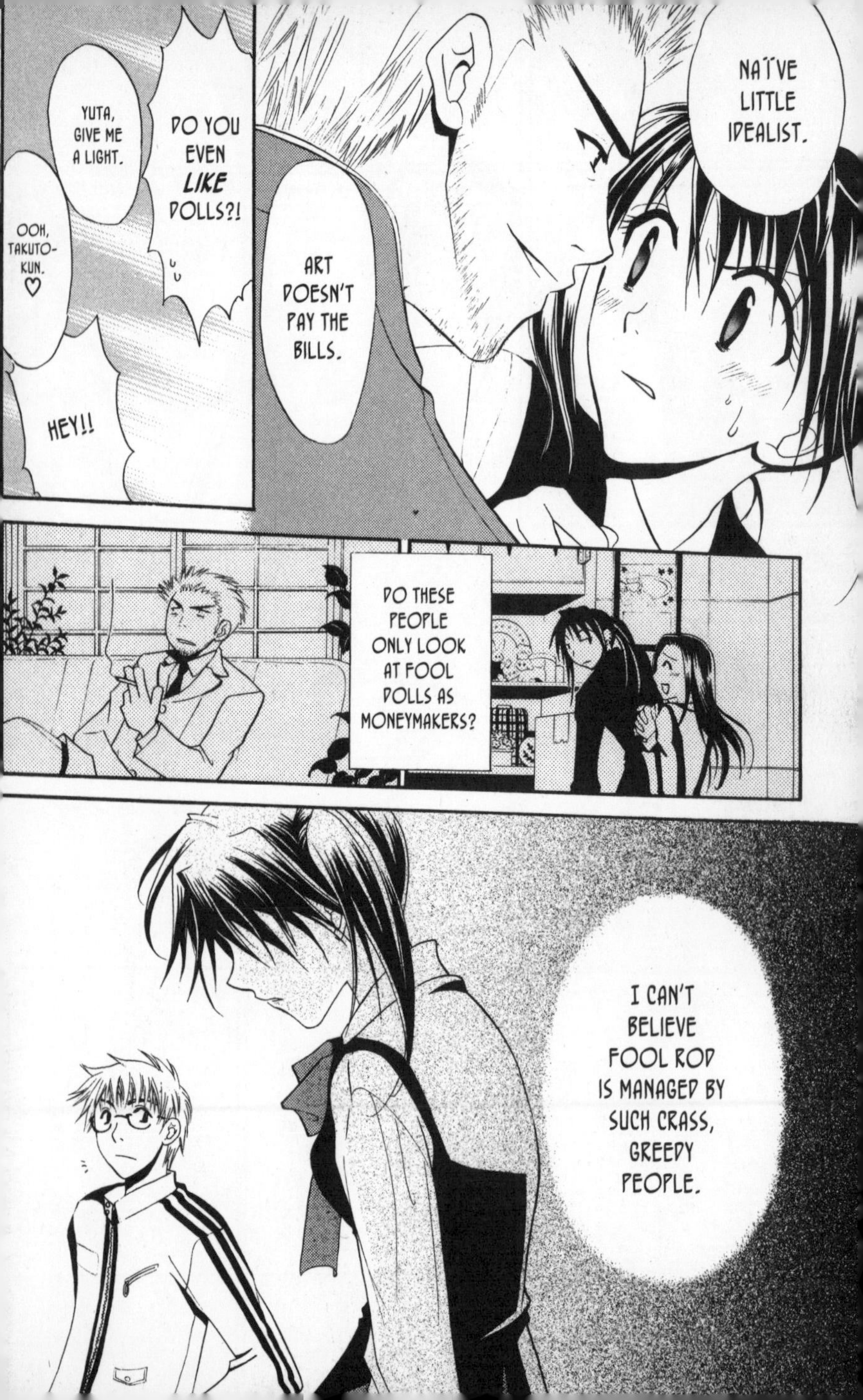
NAÏVE LITTLE IDEALIST.
ART DOESN'T PAY THE BILLS.
DO YOU EVEN *LIKE* DOLLS?!
YUTA, GIVE ME A LIGHT.
OOH, TAKUTO-KUN. ♡
HEY!!
DO THESE PEOPLE ONLY LOOK AT FOOL DOLLS AS MONEYMAKERS?
I CAN'T BELIEVE FOOL ROD IS MANAGED BY SUCH CRASS, GREEDY PEOPLE.

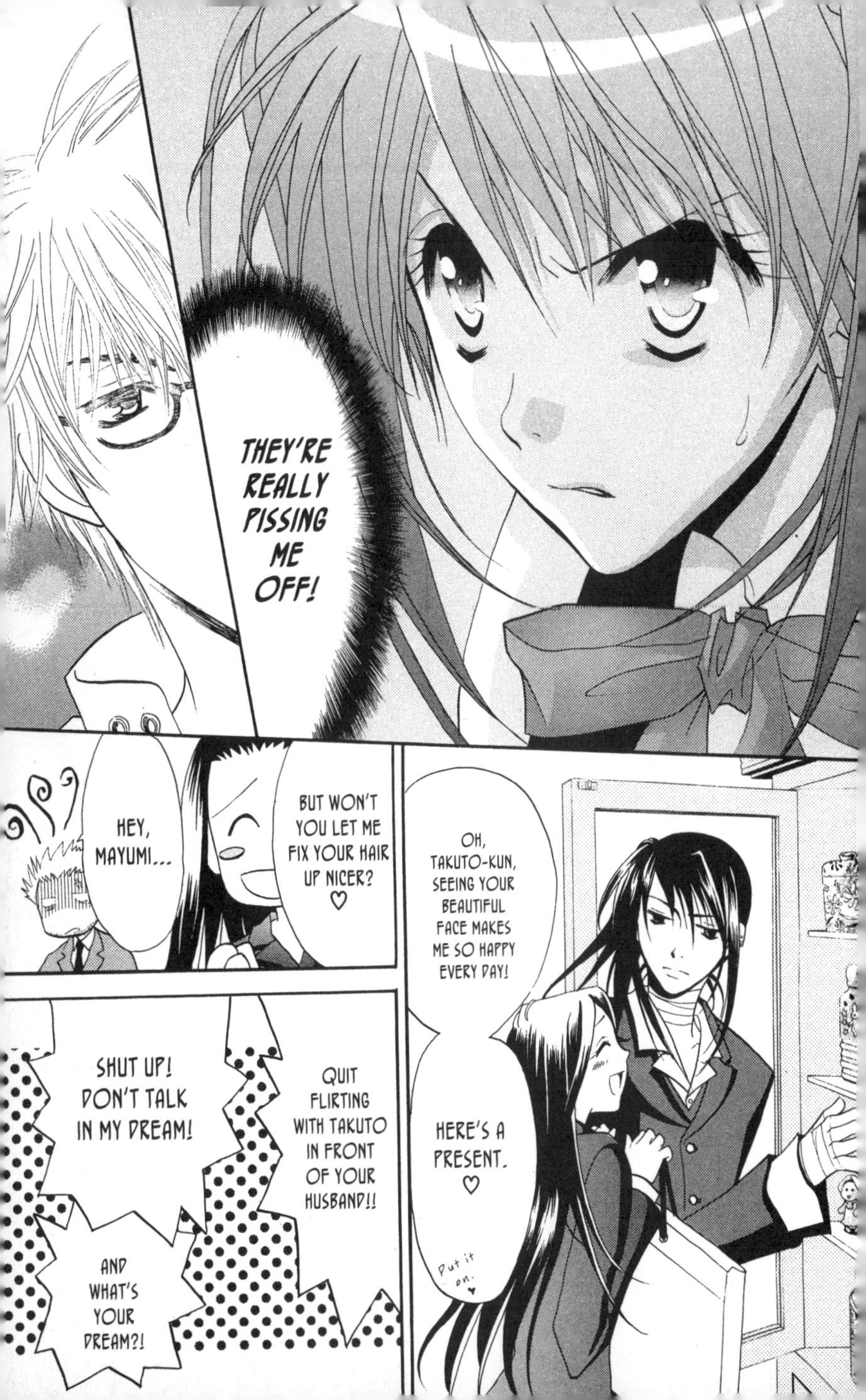
THEY'RE REALLY PISSING ME OFF!
OH, TAKUTO-KUN, SEEING YOUR BEAUTIFUL FACE MAKES ME SO HAPPY EVERY DAY!
HERE'S A PRESENT. ♡
Put it on. ♥
BUT WON'T YOU LET ME FIX YOUR HAIR UP NICER? ♡
HEY, MAYUMI...
QUIT FLIRTING WITH TAKUTO IN FRONT OF YOUR HUSBAND!!
SHUT UP! DON'T TALK IN MY DREAM!
AND WHAT'S YOUR DREAM?!

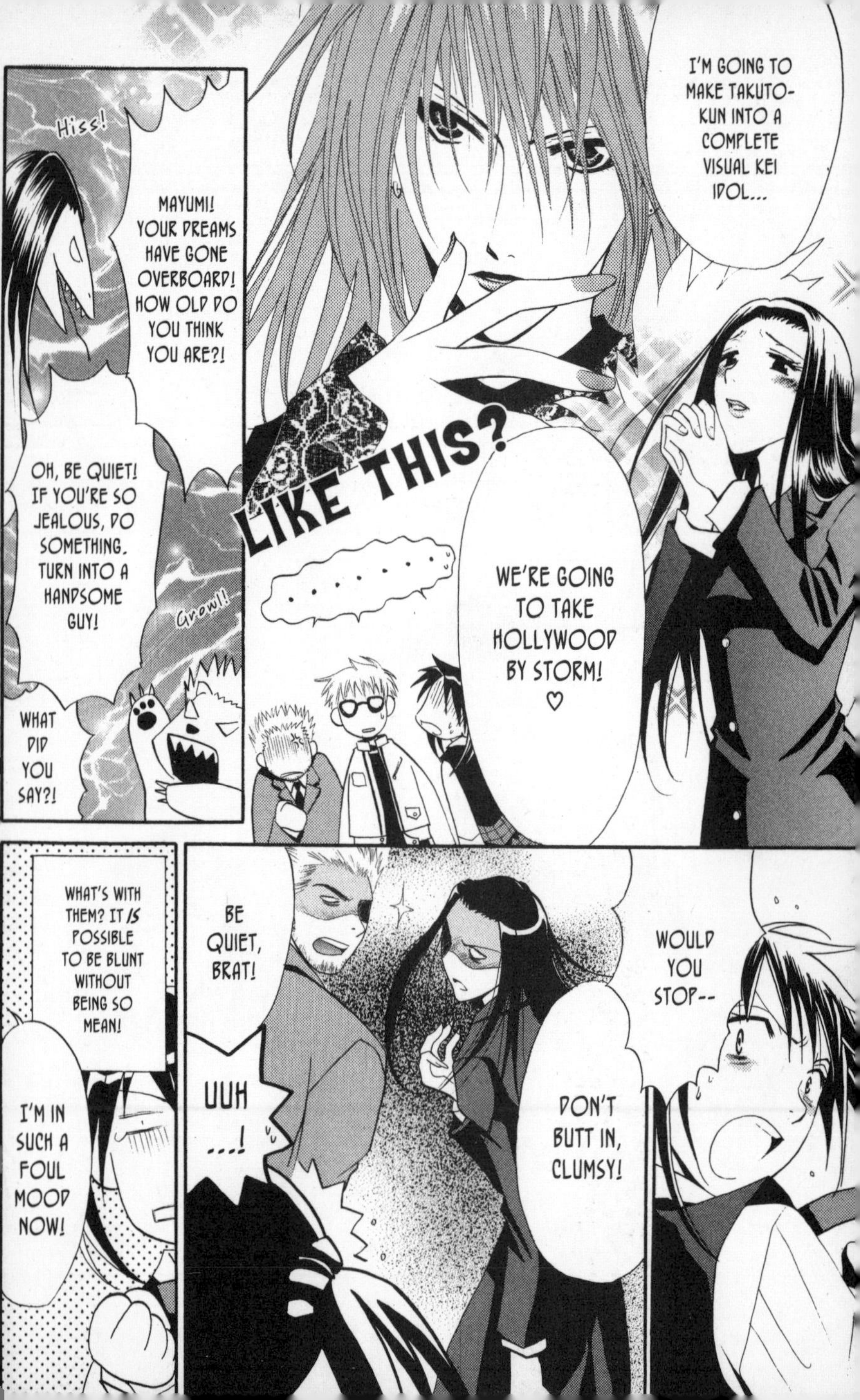
I'M GOING TO MAKE TAKUTO-KUN INTO A COMPLETE VISUAL KEI IDOL...
LIKE THIS?
WE'RE GOING TO TAKE HOLLYWOOD BY STORM! ♡
. . . .
Hiss!
MAYUMI! YOUR DREAMS HAVE GONE OVERBOARD! HOW OLD DO YOU THINK YOU ARE?!
OH, BE QUIET! IF YOU'RE SO JEALOUS, DO SOMETHING. TURN INTO A HANDSOME GUY!
Growl!
WHAT DID YOU SAY?!
WOULD YOU STOP--
DON'T BUTT IN, CLUMSY!
BE QUIET, BRAT!
UUH ...!
WHAT'S WITH THEM? IT *IS* POSSIBLE TO BE BLUNT WITHOUT BEING SO MEAN!
I'M IN SUCH A FOUL MOOD NOW!

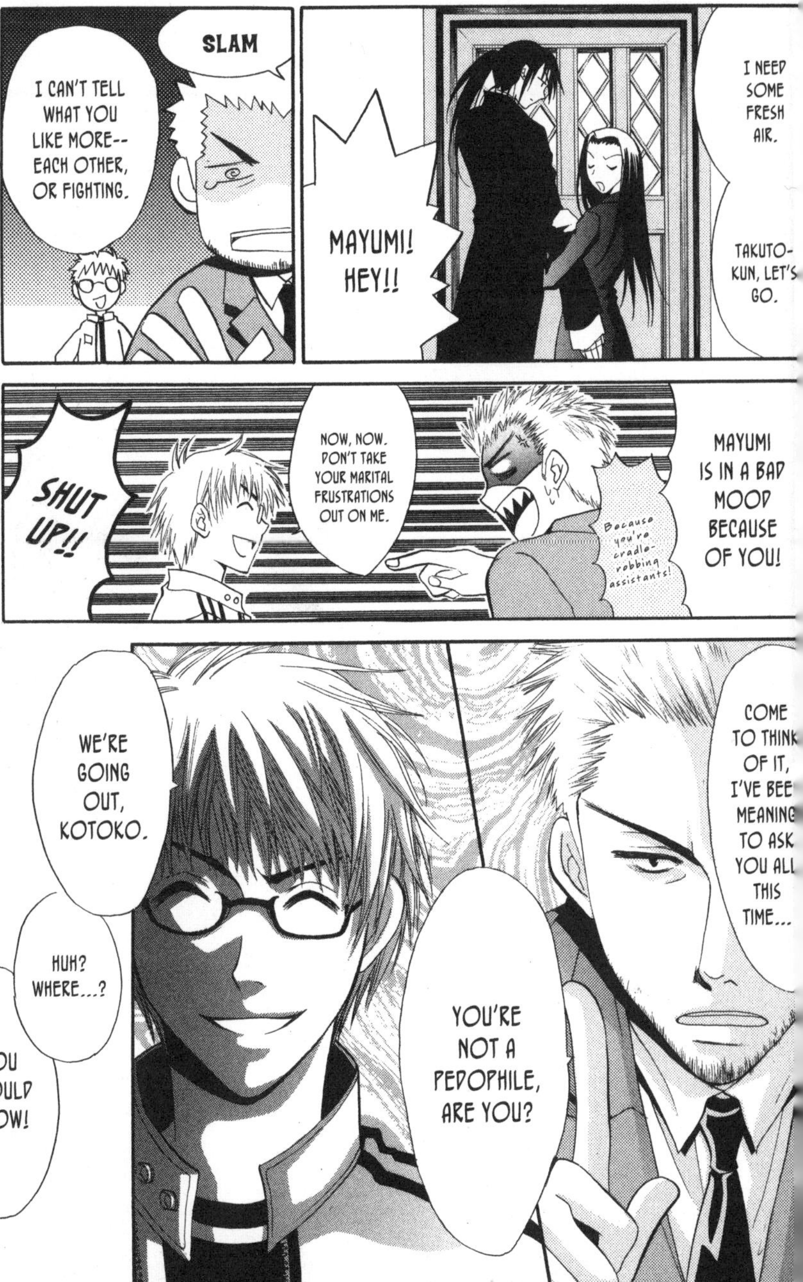
I NEED SOME FRESH AIR.
TAKUTO-KUN, LET'S GO.
MAYUMI! HEY!!
SLAM
I CAN'T TELL WHAT YOU LIKE MORE-- EACH OTHER, OR FIGHTING.
MAYUMI IS IN A BAD MOOD BECAUSE OF YOU!
Because you're cradle-robbing assistants!
NOW, NOW. DON'T TAKE YOUR MARITAL FRUSTRATIONS OUT ON ME.
SHUT UP!!
COME TO THINK OF IT, I'VE BEE MEANING TO ASK YOU ALL THIS TIME...
YOU'RE NOT A PEDOPHILE, ARE YOU?
WE'RE GOING OUT, KOTOKO.
HUH? WHERE...?
YOU SHOULD KNOW!

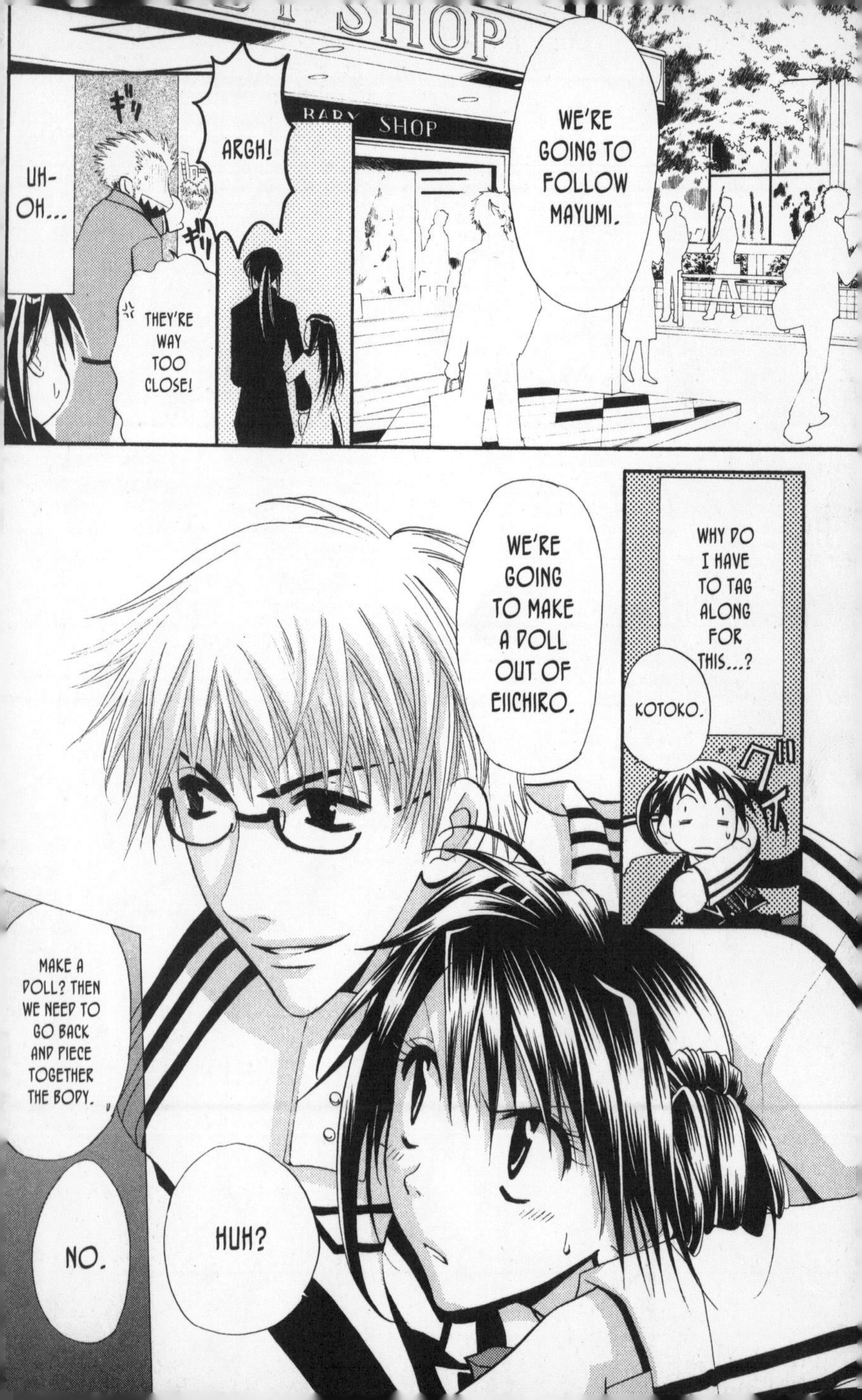
SHOP
BABY SHOP
WE'RE GOING TO FOLLOW MAYUMI.
ARGH!
ギッ
UH-OH...
THEY'RE WAY TOO CLOSE!
WHY DO I HAVE TO TAG ALONG FOR THIS...?
KOTOKO.
WE'RE GOING TO MAKE A DOLL OUT OF EIICHIRO.
MAKE A DOLL? THEN WE NEED TO GO BACK AND PIECE TOGETHER THE BODY.
HUH?
NO.

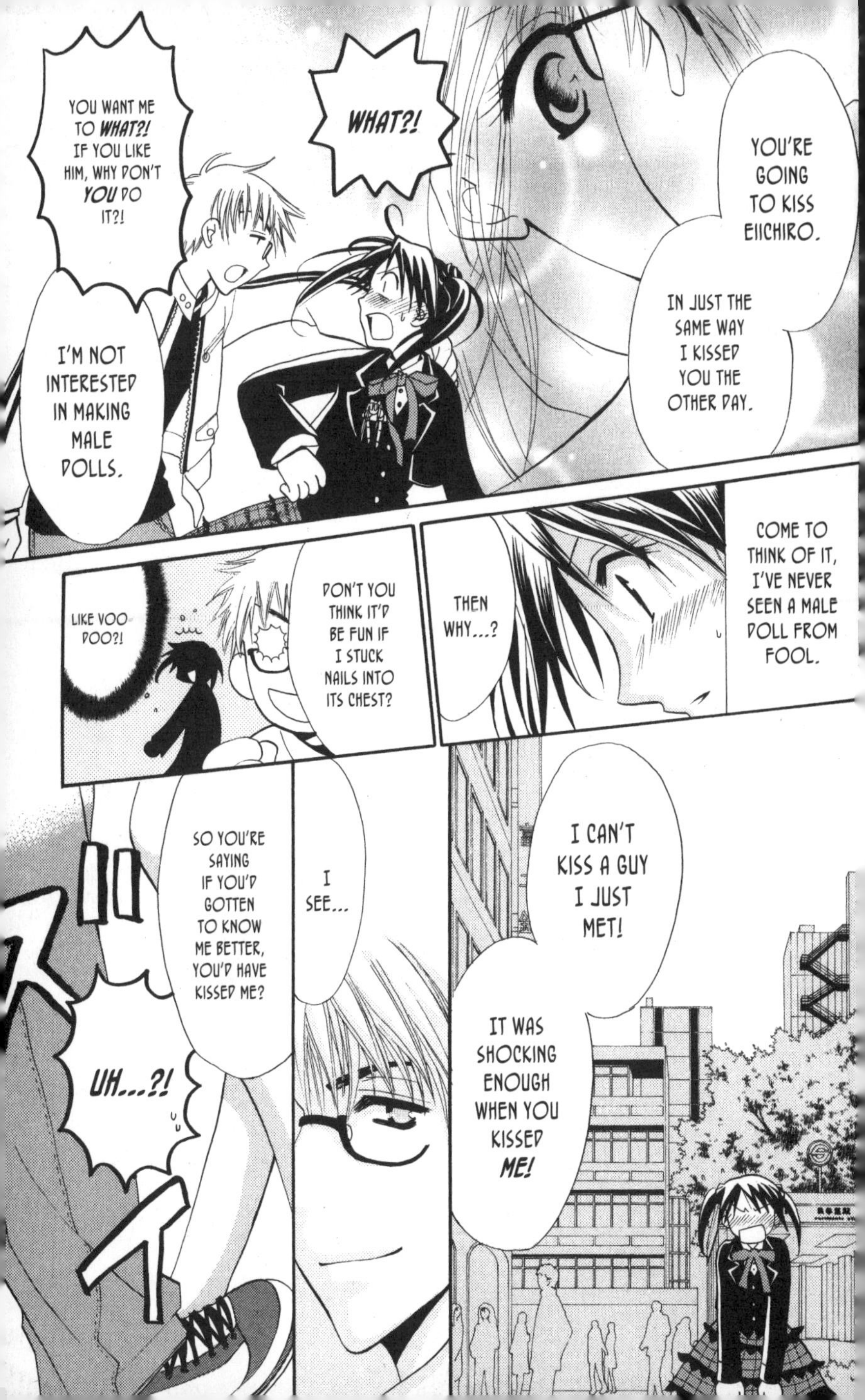
YOU'RE GOING TO KISS EIICHIRO.
IN JUST THE SAME WAY I KISSED YOU THE OTHER DAY.
WHAT?!
YOU WANT ME TO WHAT?! IF YOU LIKE HIM, WHY DON'T YOU DO IT?!
I'M NOT INTERESTED IN MAKING MALE DOLLS.
COME TO THINK OF IT, I'VE NEVER SEEN A MALE DOLL FROM FOOL.
THEN WHY...?
DON'T YOU THINK IT'D BE FUN IF I STUCK NAILS INTO ITS CHEST?
LIKE VOO-DOO?!
I CAN'T KISS A GUY I JUST MET!
IT WAS SHOCKING ENOUGH WHEN YOU KISSED ME!
I SEE...
SO YOU'RE SAYING IF YOU'D GOTTEN TO KNOW ME BETTER, YOU'D HAVE KISSED ME?
UH...?!

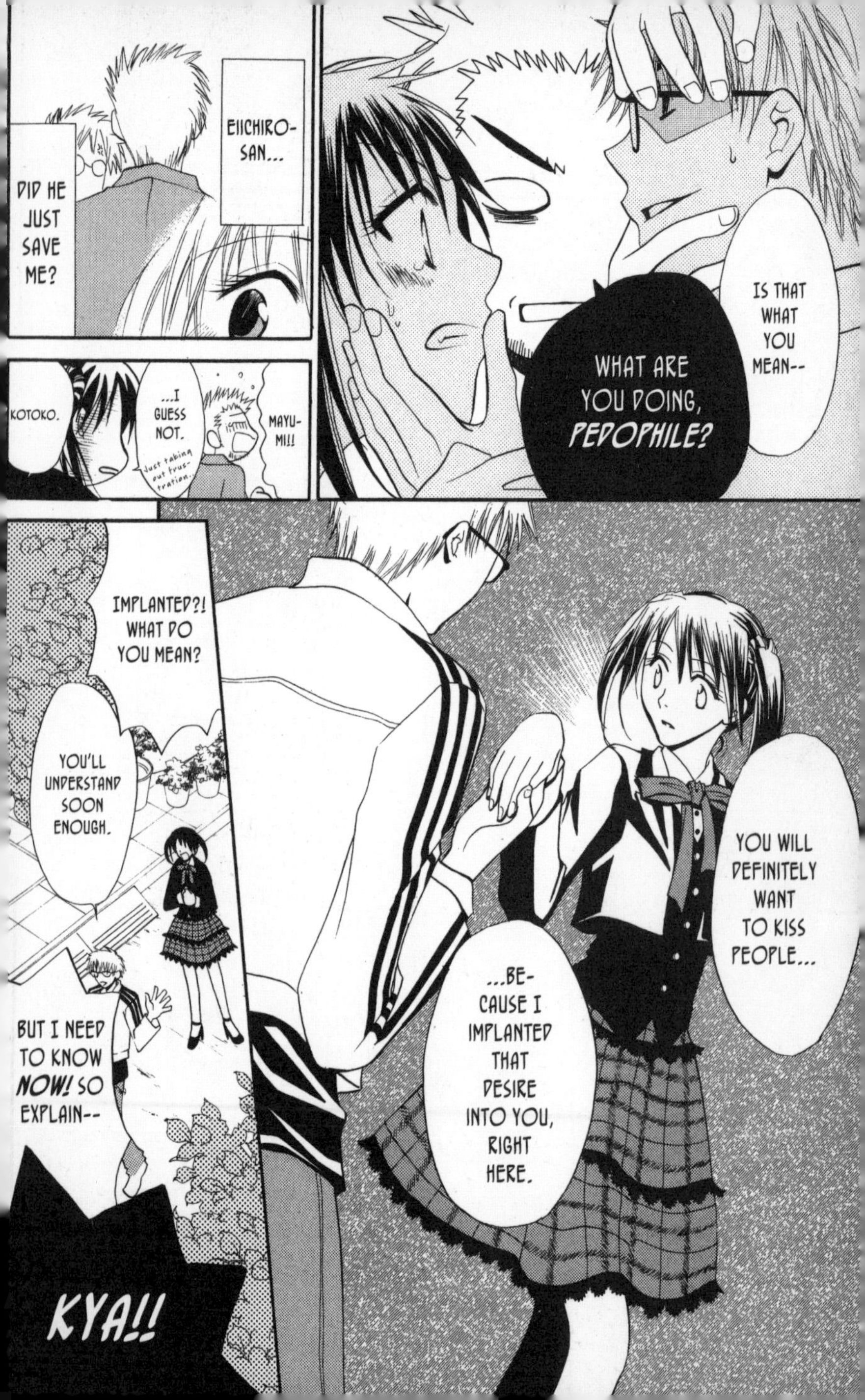
IS THAT WHAT YOU MEAN--
WHAT ARE YOU DOING, PEDOPHILE?
EIICHIRO-SAN...
DID HE JUST SAVE ME?
MAYU-MI!!
...I GUESS NOT.
Just taking out frus-tration.
KOTOKO.
YOU WILL DEFINITELY WANT TO KISS PEOPLE...
...BE-CAUSE I IMPLANTED THAT DESIRE INTO YOU, RIGHT HERE.
IMPLANTED?! WHAT DO YOU MEAN?
YOU'LL UNDERSTAND SOON ENOUGH.
BUT I NEED TO KNOW NOW! SO EXPLAIN--
KYA!!

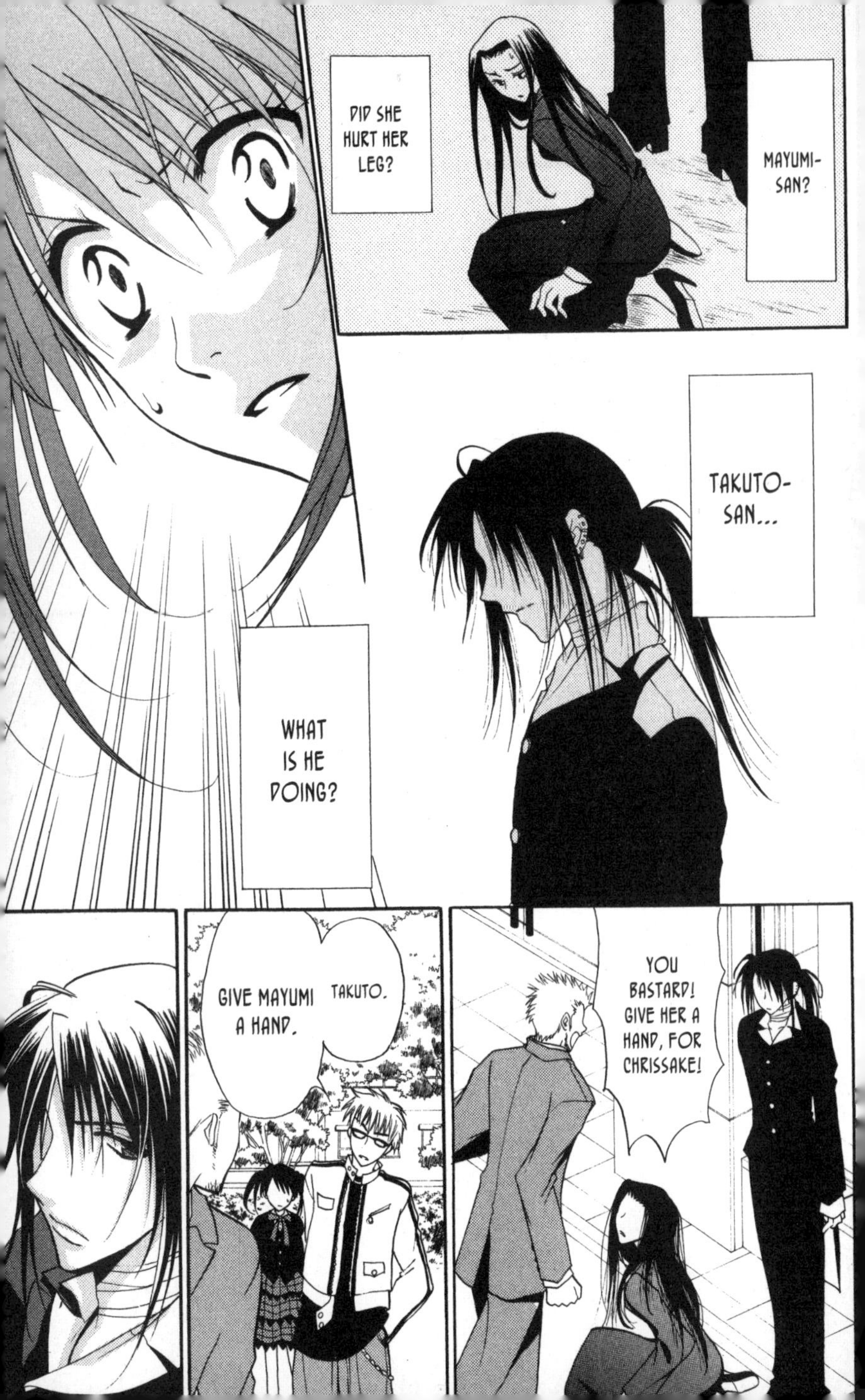
MAYUMI-SAN?
DID SHE HURT HER LEG?
TAKUTO-SAN...
WHAT IS HE DOING?
YOU BASTARD! GIVE HER A HAND, FOR CHRISSAKE!
TAKUTO.
GIVE MAYUMI A HAND.

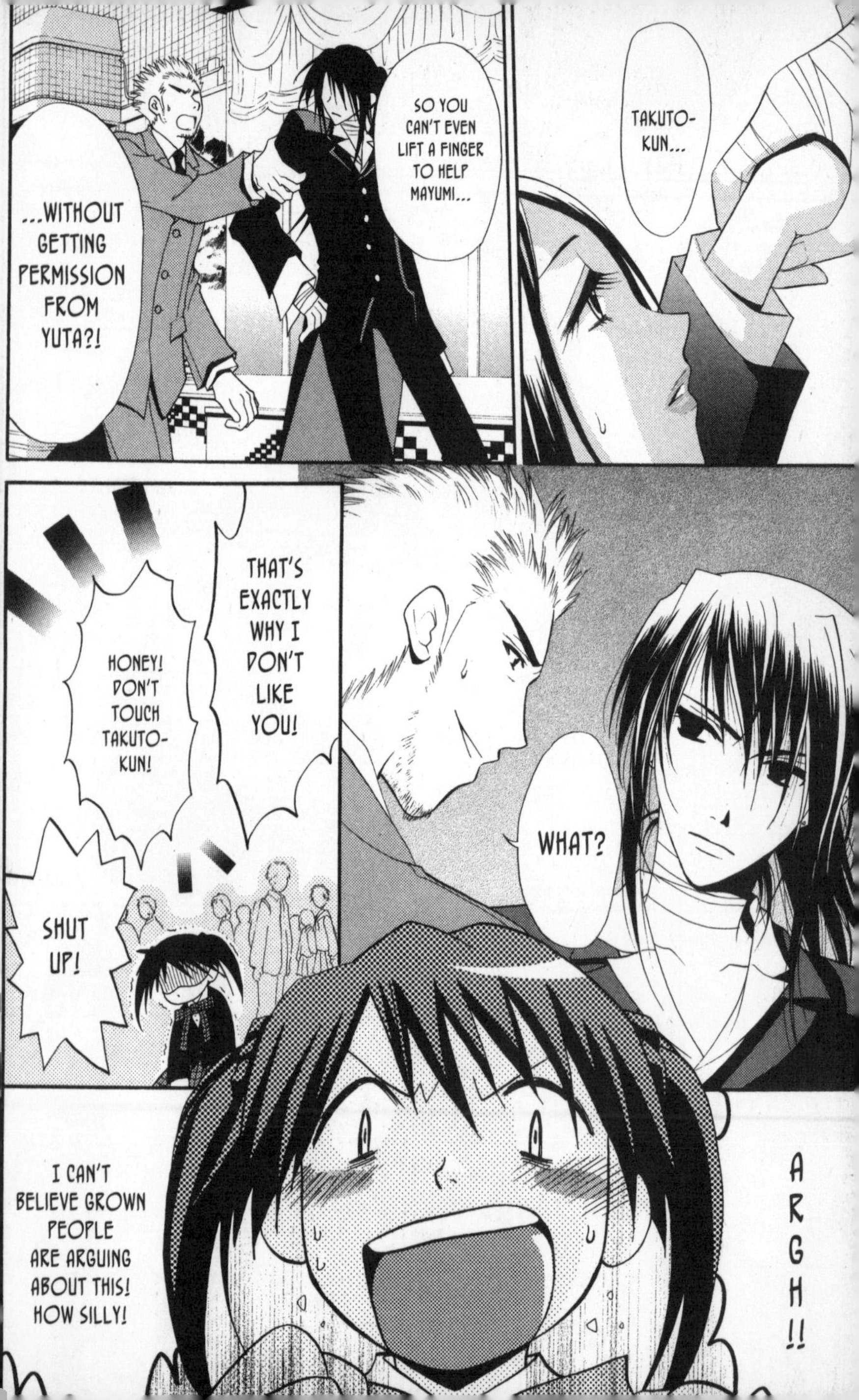
TAKUTO-KUN...
SO YOU CAN'T EVEN LIFT A FINGER TO HELP MAYUMI...
...WITHOUT GETTING PERMISSION FROM YUTA?!
WHAT?
THAT'S EXACTLY WHY I DON'T LIKE YOU!
HONEY! DON'T TOUCH TAKUTO-KUN!
SHUT UP!
ARGH!!
I CAN'T BELIEVE GROWN PEOPLE ARE ARGUING ABOUT THIS! HOW SILLY!

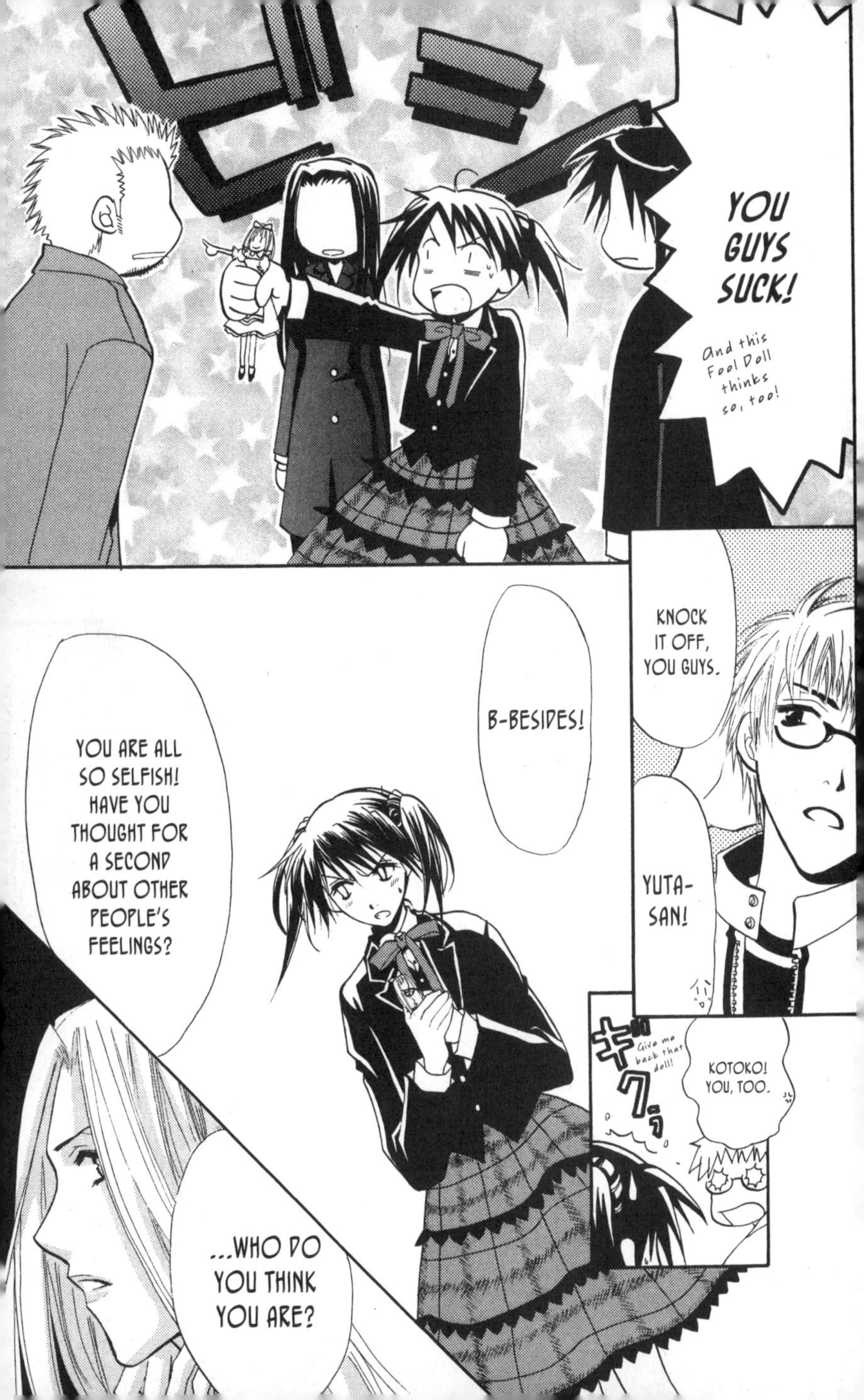
YOU GUYS SUCK!
And this Fool Doll thinks so, too!
KNOCK IT OFF, YOU GUYS.
YUTA-SAN!
Give me back that doll!
KOTOKO! YOU, TOO.
B-BESIDES!
YOU ARE ALL SO SELFISH! HAVE YOU THOUGHT FOR A SECOND ABOUT OTHER PEOPLE'S FEELINGS?
...WHO DO YOU THINK YOU ARE?

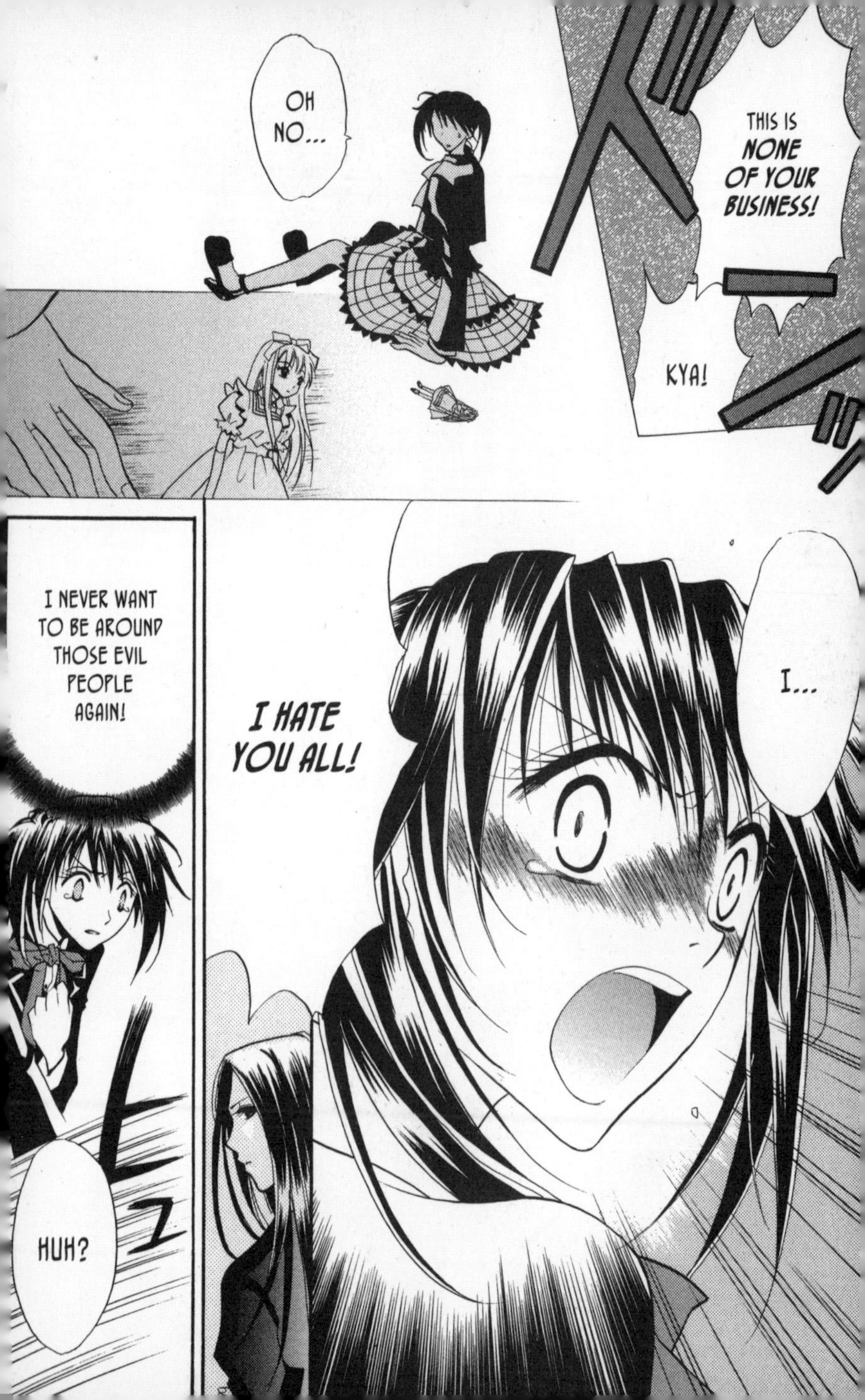
THIS IS NONE OF YOUR BUSINESS!
KYA!
OH NO...
I...
I HATE YOU ALL!
I NEVER WANT TO BE AROUND THOSE EVIL PEOPLE AGAIN!
HUH?

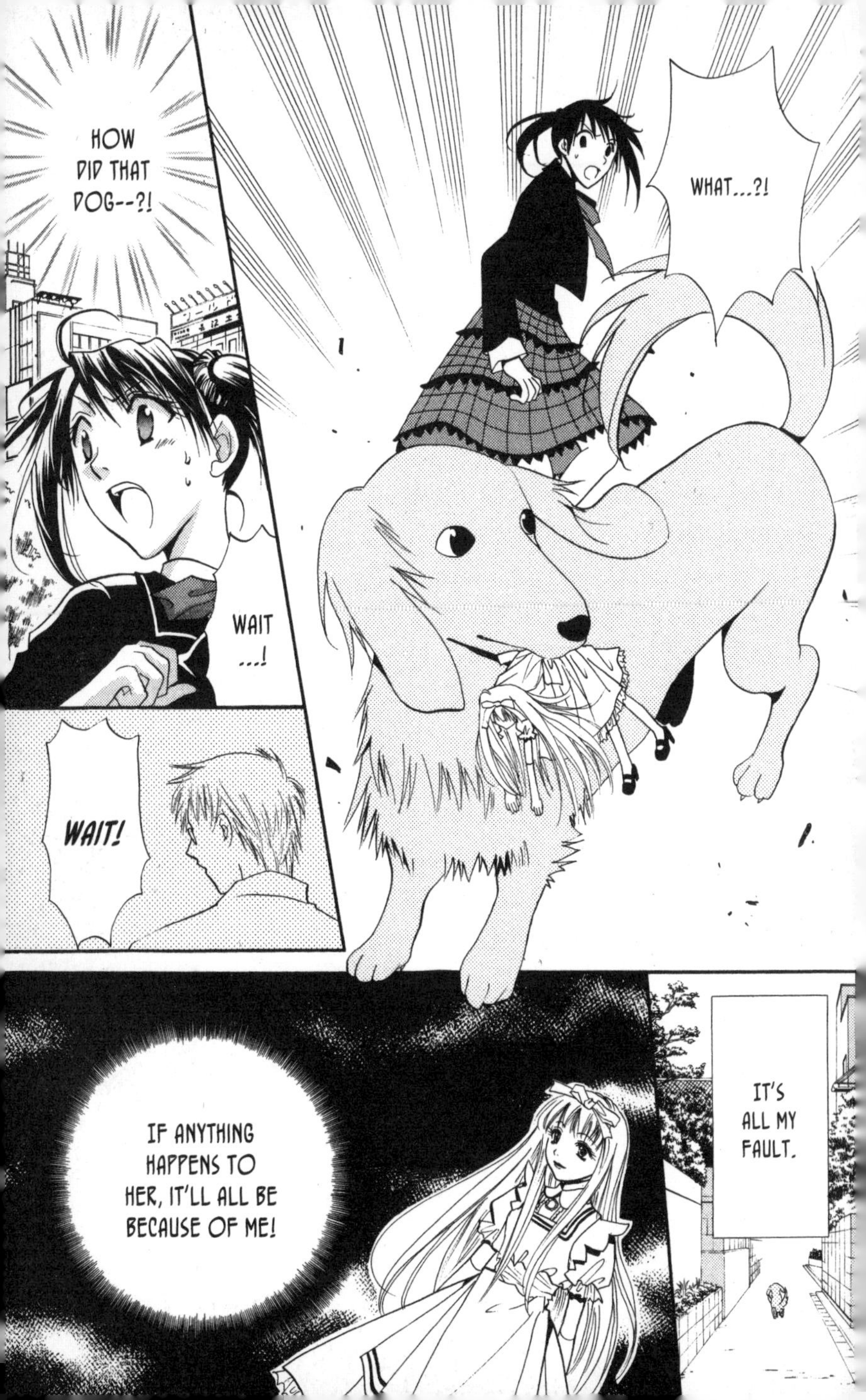
WHAT...?!
HOW DID THAT DOG--?!
WAIT ...!
WAIT!
IT'S ALL MY FAULT.
IF ANYTHING HAPPENS TO HER, IT'LL ALL BE BECAUSE OF ME!

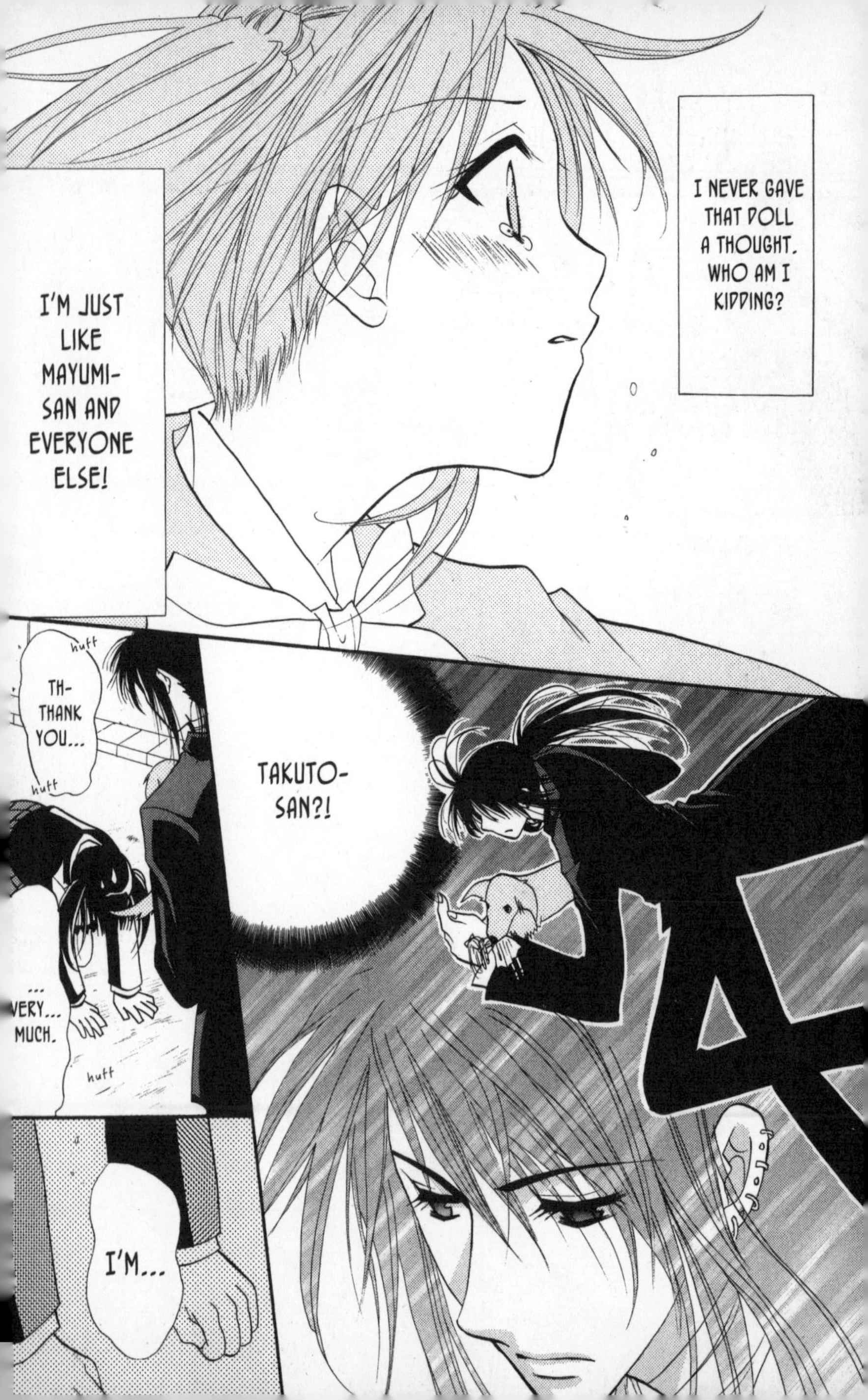
I NEVER GAVE THAT DOLL A THOUGHT. WHO AM I KIDDING?
I'M JUST LIKE MAYUMI-SAN AND EVERYONE ELSE!
TAKUTO-SAN?!
huff
TH-THANK YOU...
huff
...VERY... MUCH.
huff
I'M...

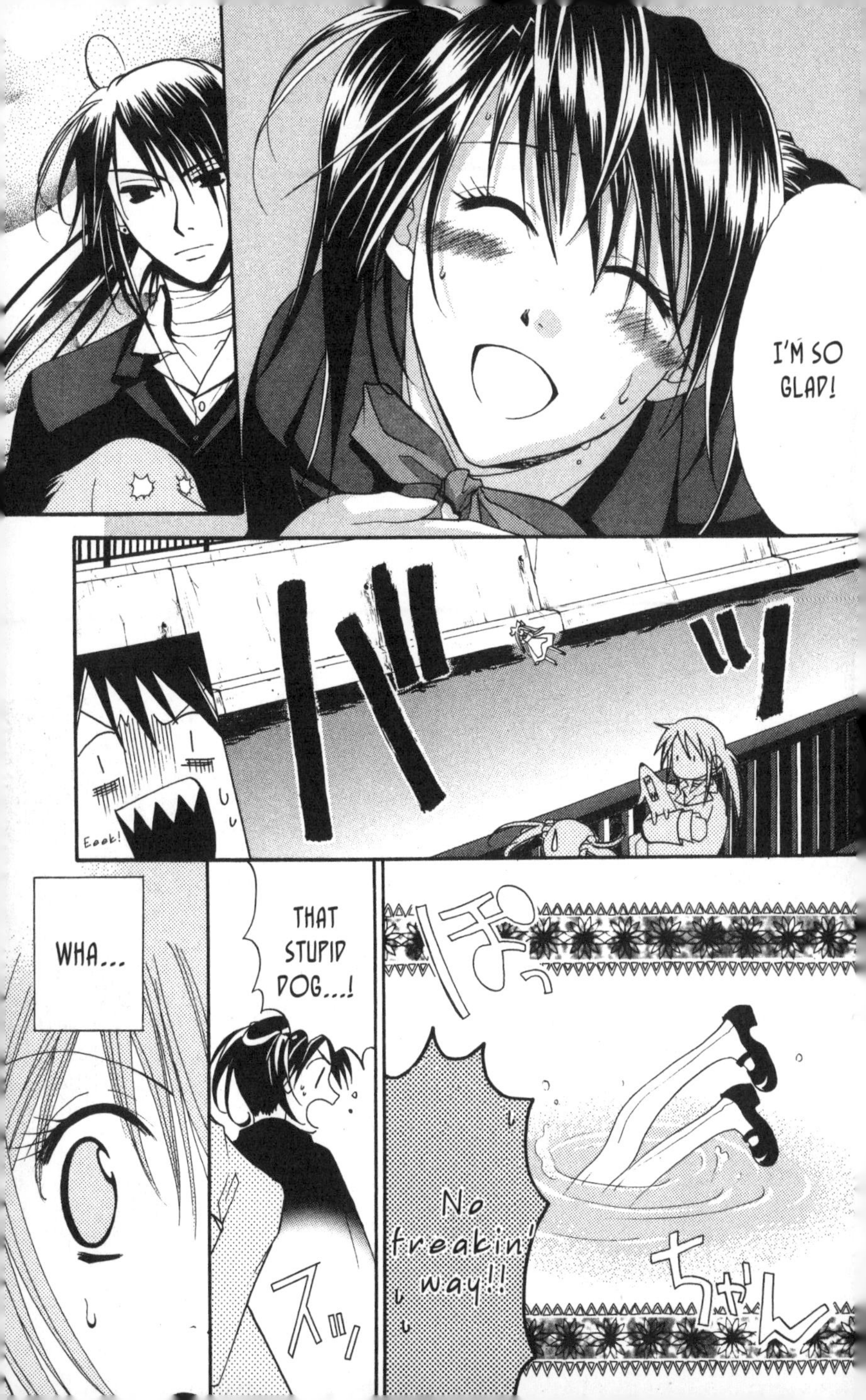
I'M SO GLAD!
ドッ
Eeek!
ぼっ
No freakin' way!!
ちゃん
THAT STUPID DOG...!
スッ
WHA...

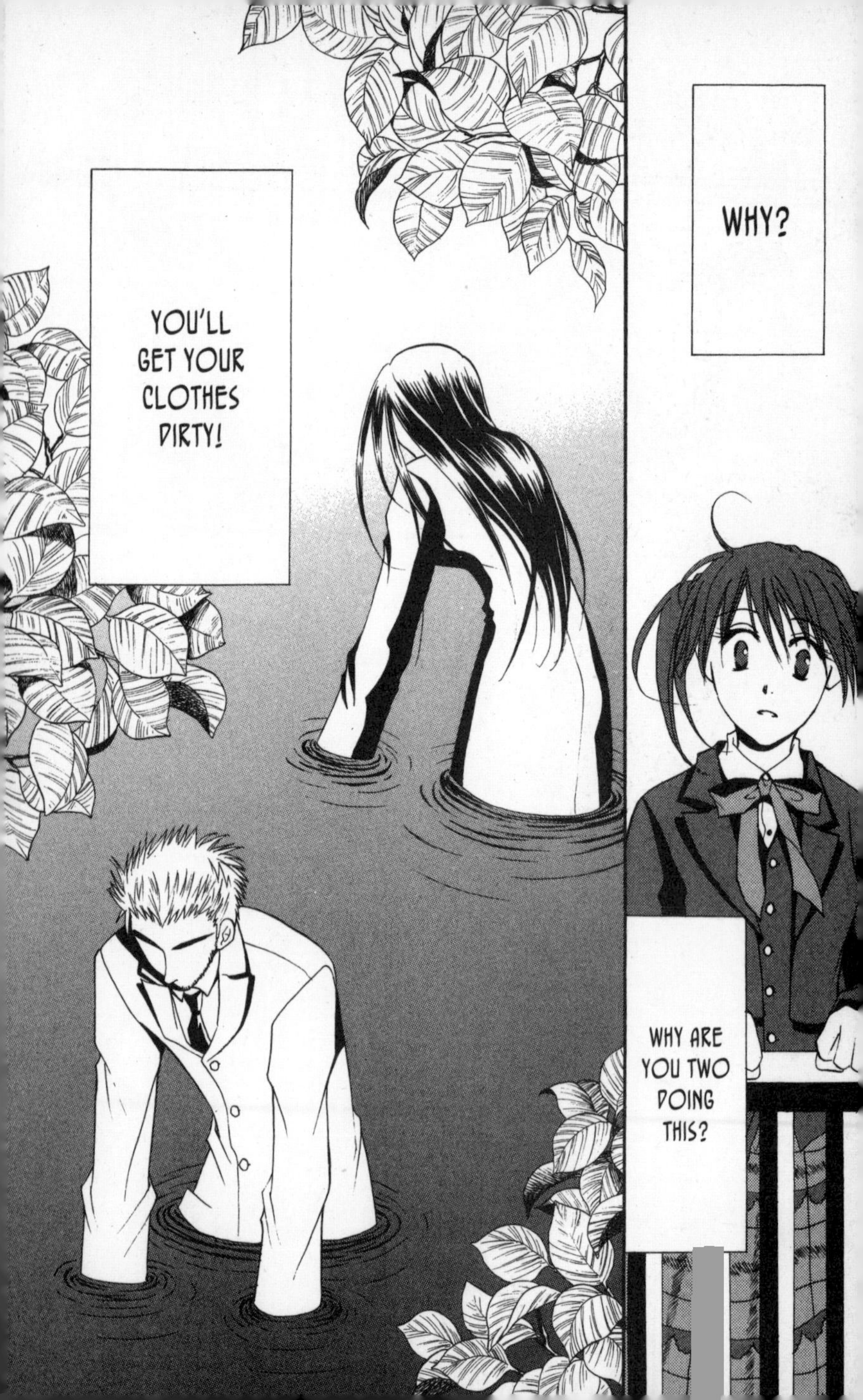
WHY?
WHY ARE YOU TWO DOING THIS?
YOU'LL GET YOUR CLOTHES DIRTY!

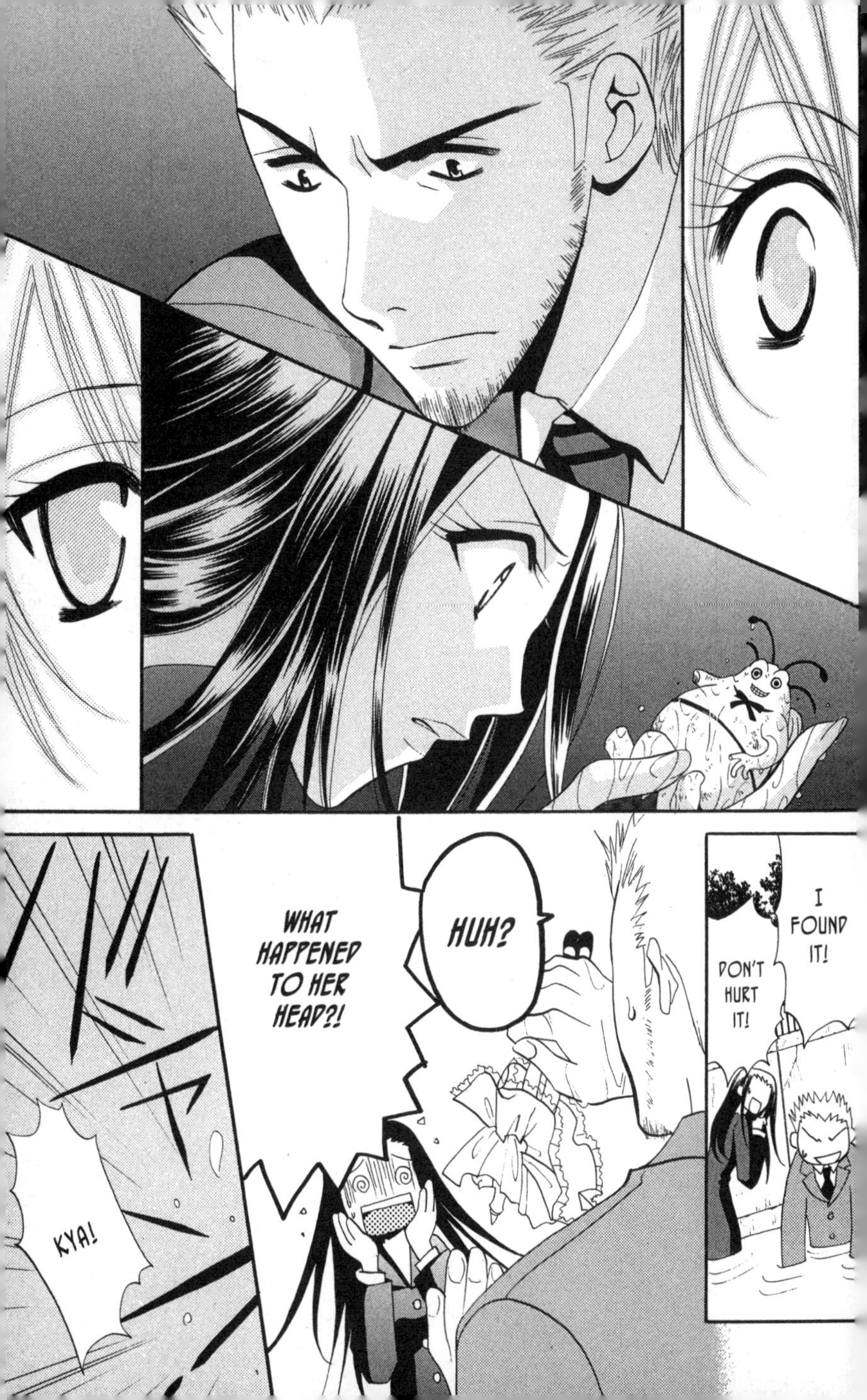
I FOUND IT!
DON'T HURT IT!
HUH?
WHAT HAPPENED TO HER HEAD?!
KYA!

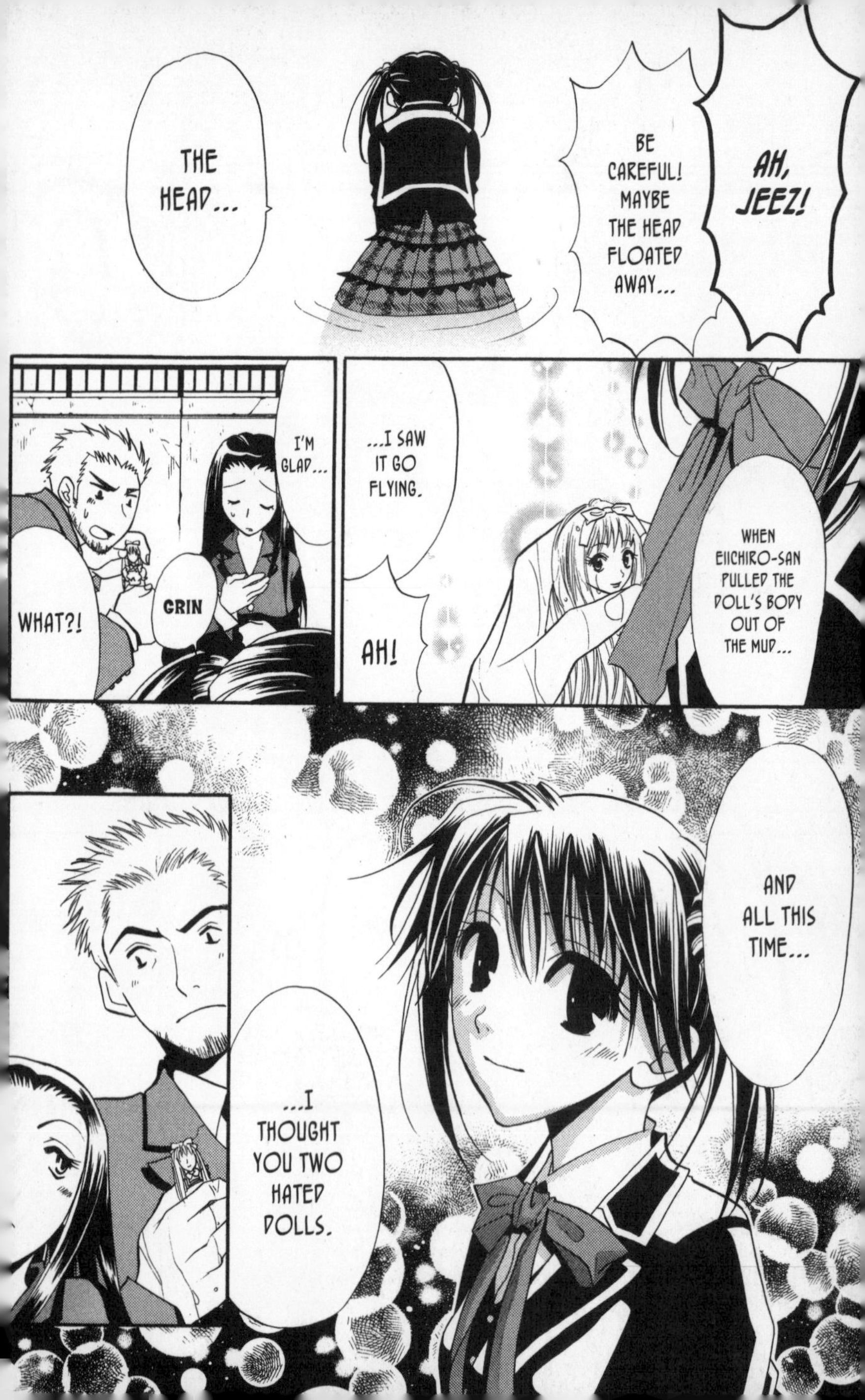
AH, JEEZ!
BE CAREFUL! MAYBE THE HEAD FLOATED AWAY...
THE HEAD...
WHEN EIICHIRO-SAN PULLED THE DOLL'S BODY OUT OF THE MUD...
...I SAW IT GO FLYING.
AH!
I'M GLAD...
GRIN
WHAT?!
AND ALL THIS TIME...
...I THOUGHT YOU TWO HATED DOLLS.

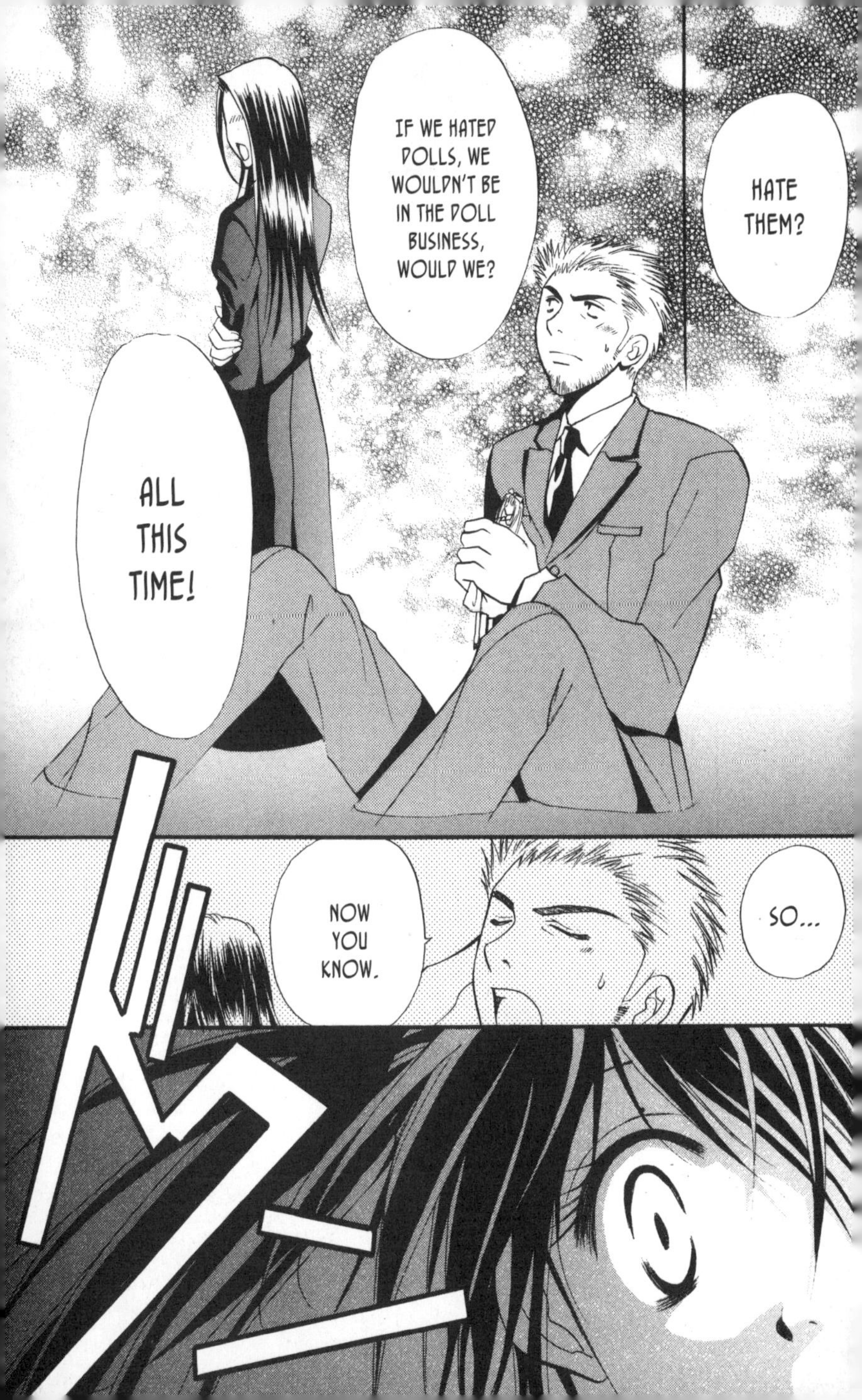
HATE THEM?
IF WE HATED DOLLS, WE WOULDN'T BE IN THE DOLL BUSINESS, WOULD WE?
ALL THIS TIME!
SO...
NOW YOU KNOW.

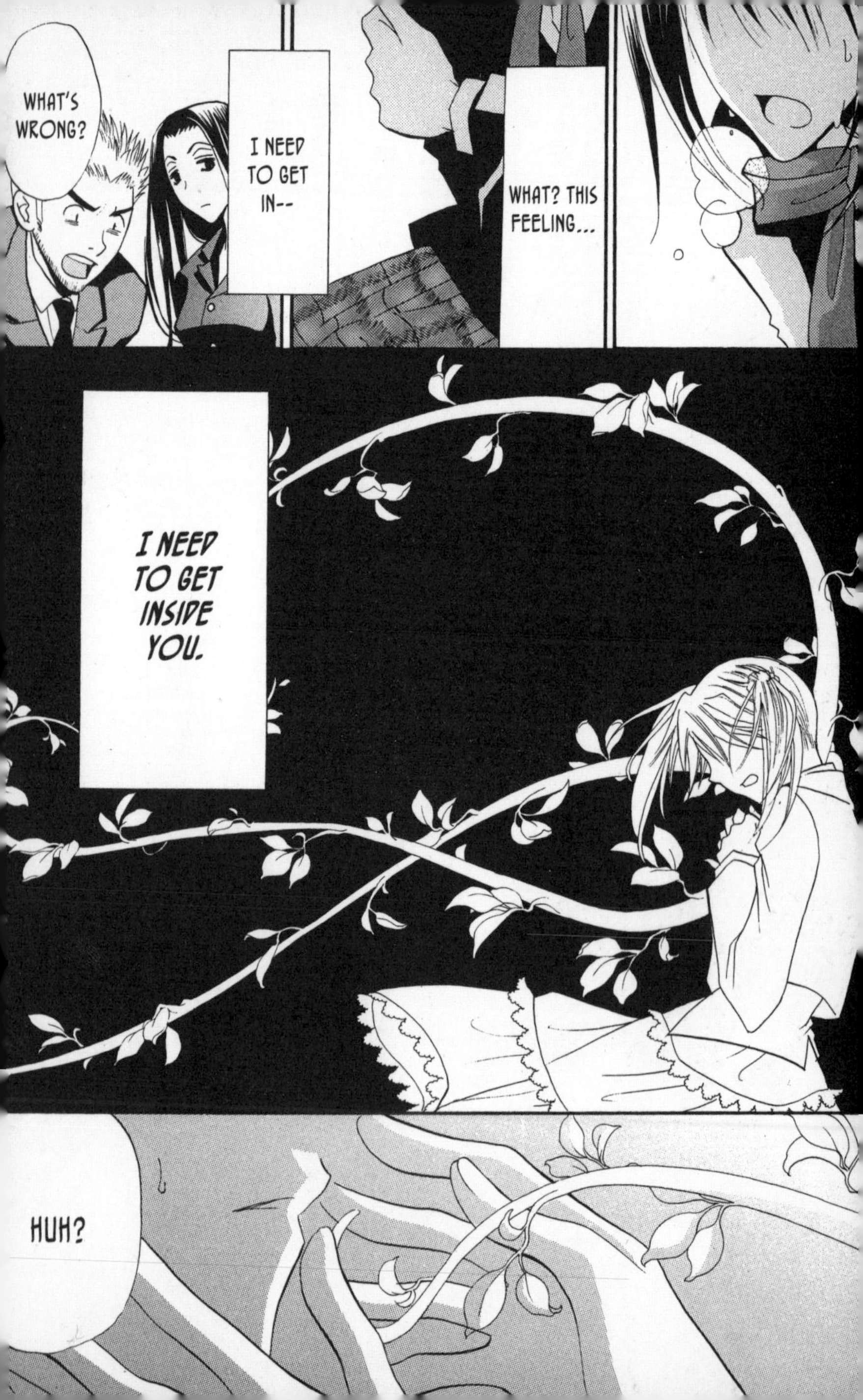
WHAT? THIS FEELING...
I NEED TO GET IN--
WHAT'S WRONG?
I NEED TO GET INSIDE YOU.
HUH?

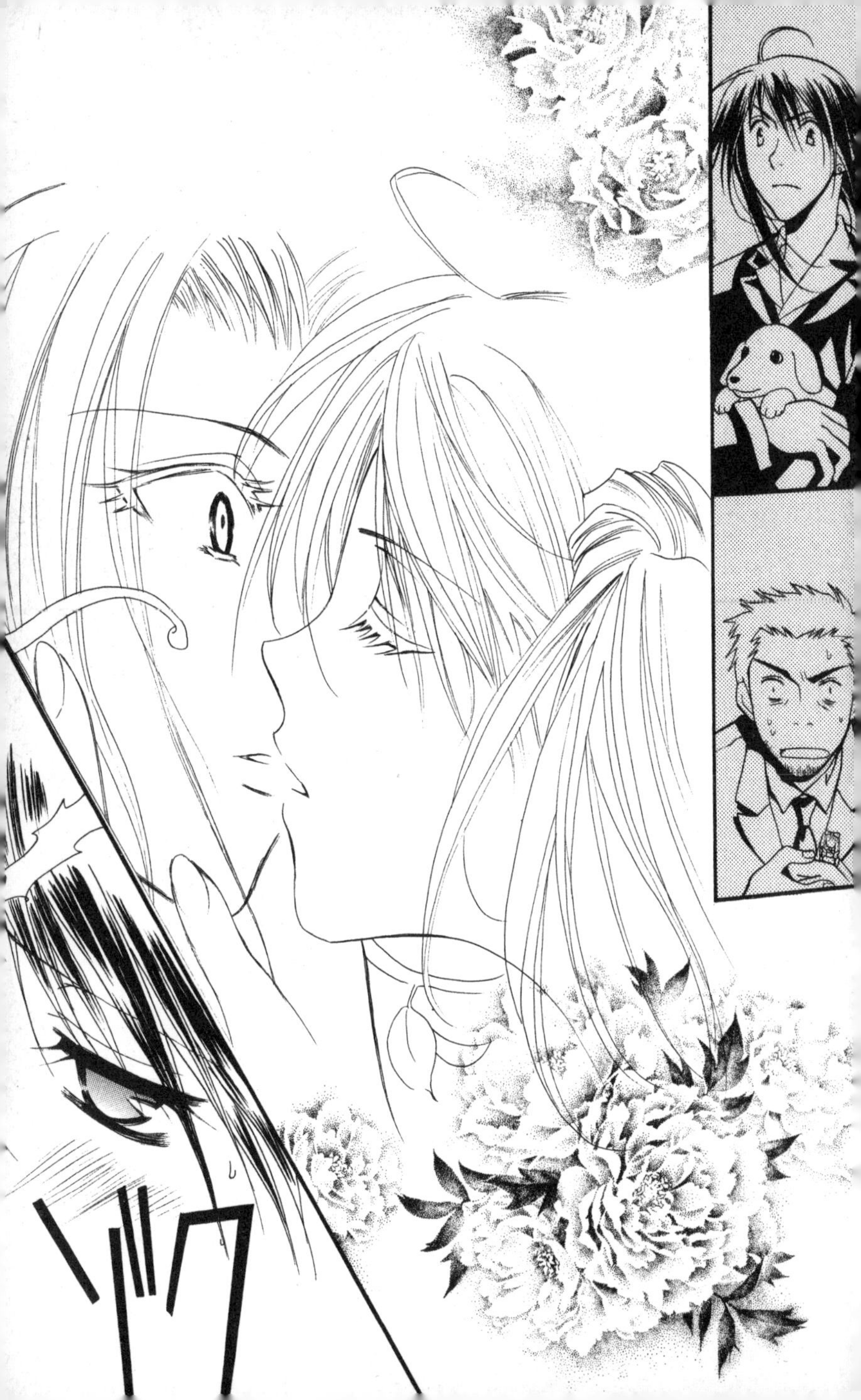

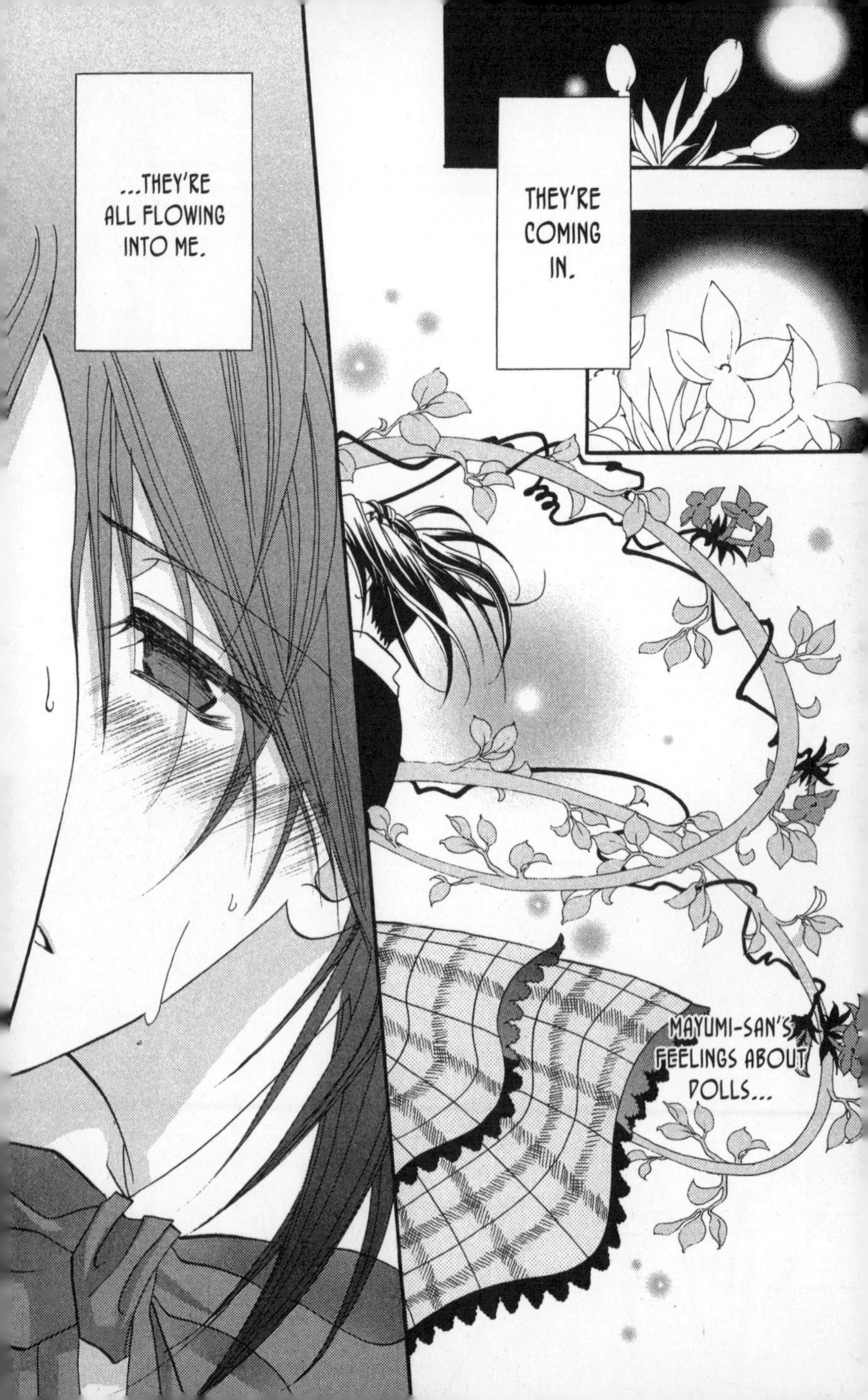
THEY'RE COMING IN.
...THEY'RE ALL FLOWING INTO ME.
MAYUMI-SAN'S FEELINGS ABOUT DOLLS...

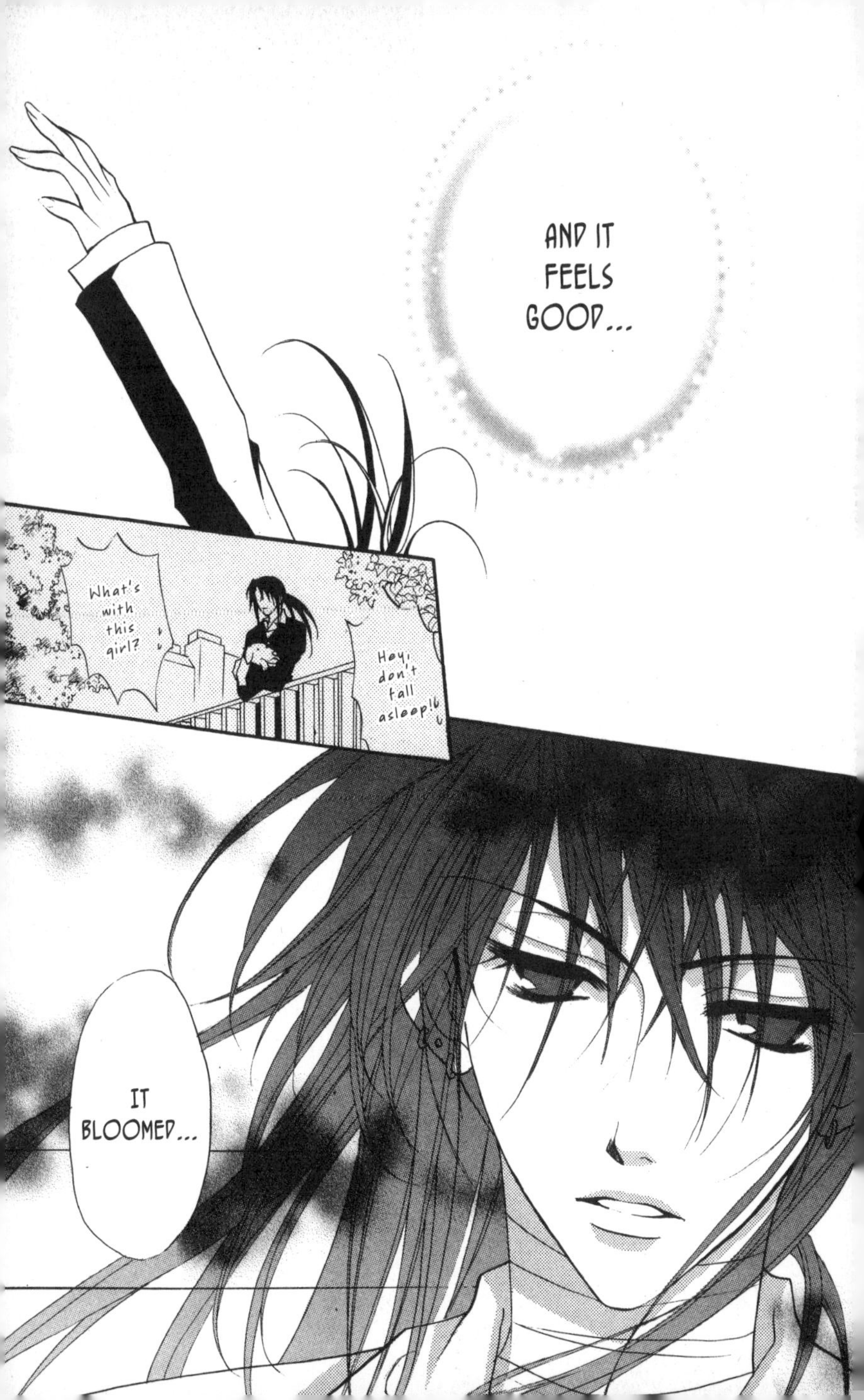
AND IT FEELS GOOD...
Hey, don't fall asleep!!
What's with this girl?
IT BLOOMED...

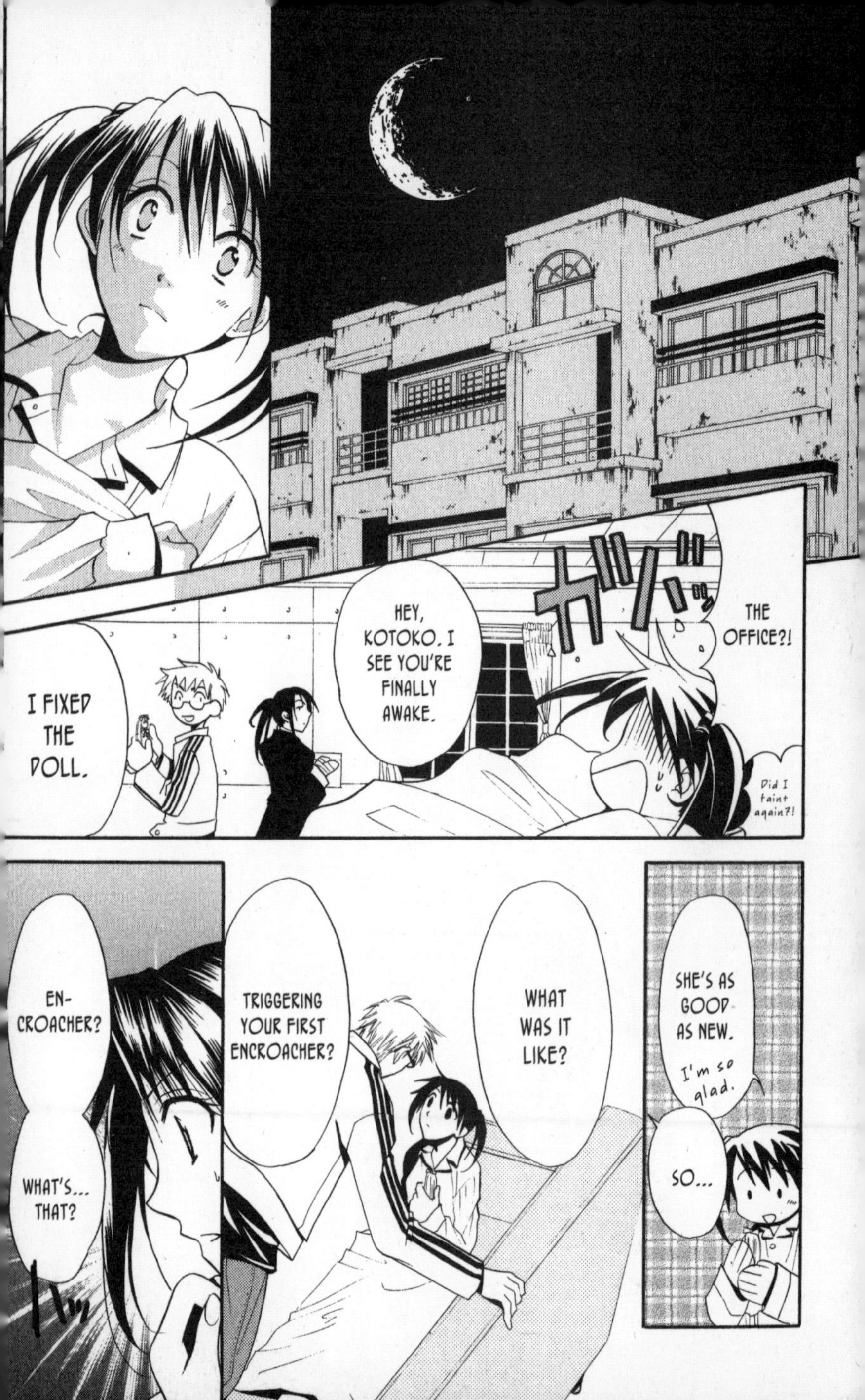
ガバッ
THE OFFICE?!
Did I faint again?!
HEY, KOTOKO. I SEE YOU'RE FINALLY AWAKE.
I FIXED THE DOLL.
SHE'S AS GOOD AS NEW.
I'm so glad.
SO...
WHAT WAS IT LIKE?
TRIGGERING YOUR FIRST ENCROACHER?
EN-CROACHER?
WHAT'S... THAT?

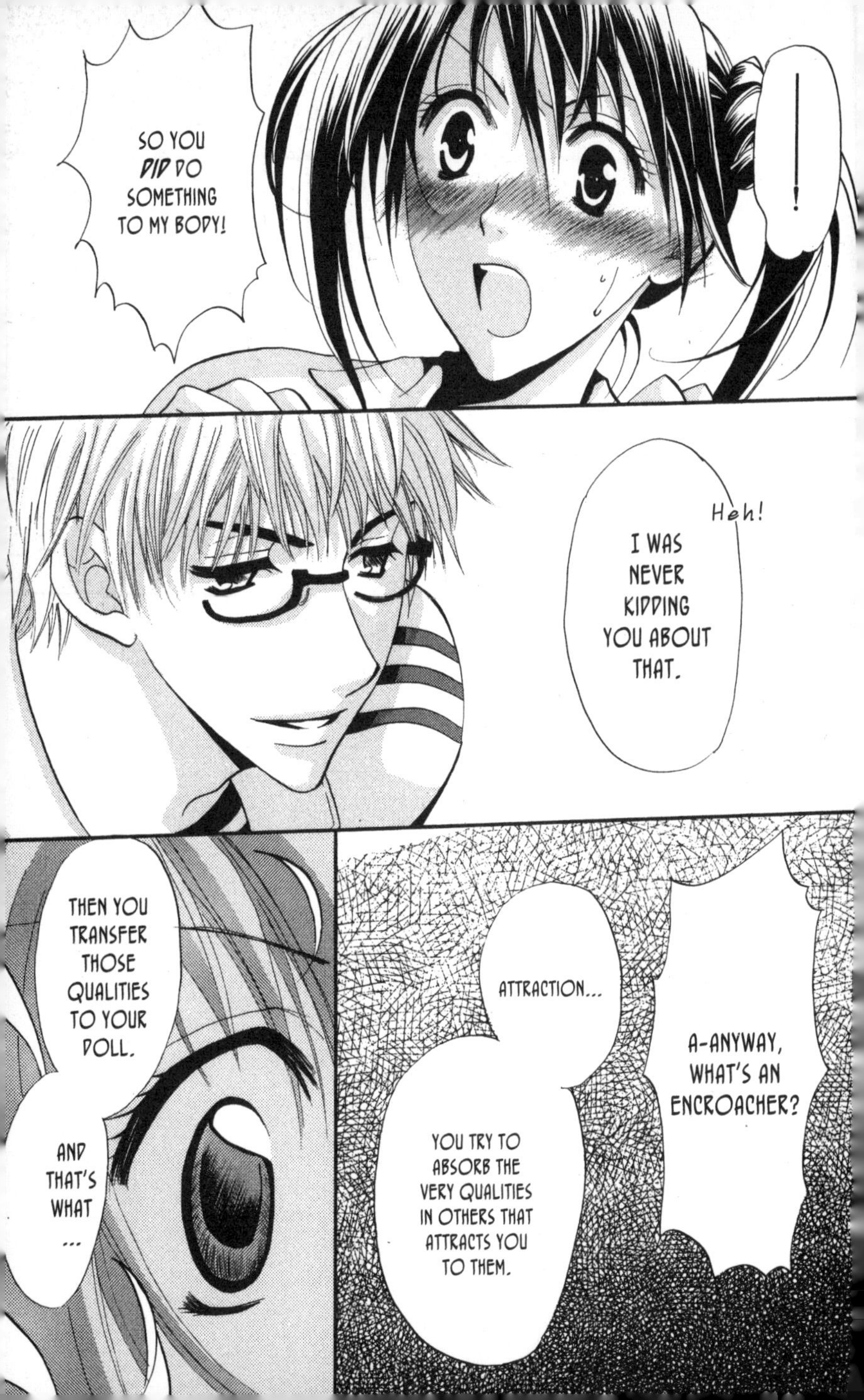
!
SO YOU DID DO SOMETHING TO MY BODY!
Heh!
I WAS NEVER KIDDING YOU ABOUT THAT.
A-ANYWAY, WHAT'S AN ENCROACHER?
ATTRACTION...
YOU TRY TO ABSORB THE VERY QUALITIES IN OTHERS THAT ATTRACTS YOU TO THEM.
THEN YOU TRANSFER THOSE QUALITIES TO YOUR DOLL.
AND THAT'S WHAT ...

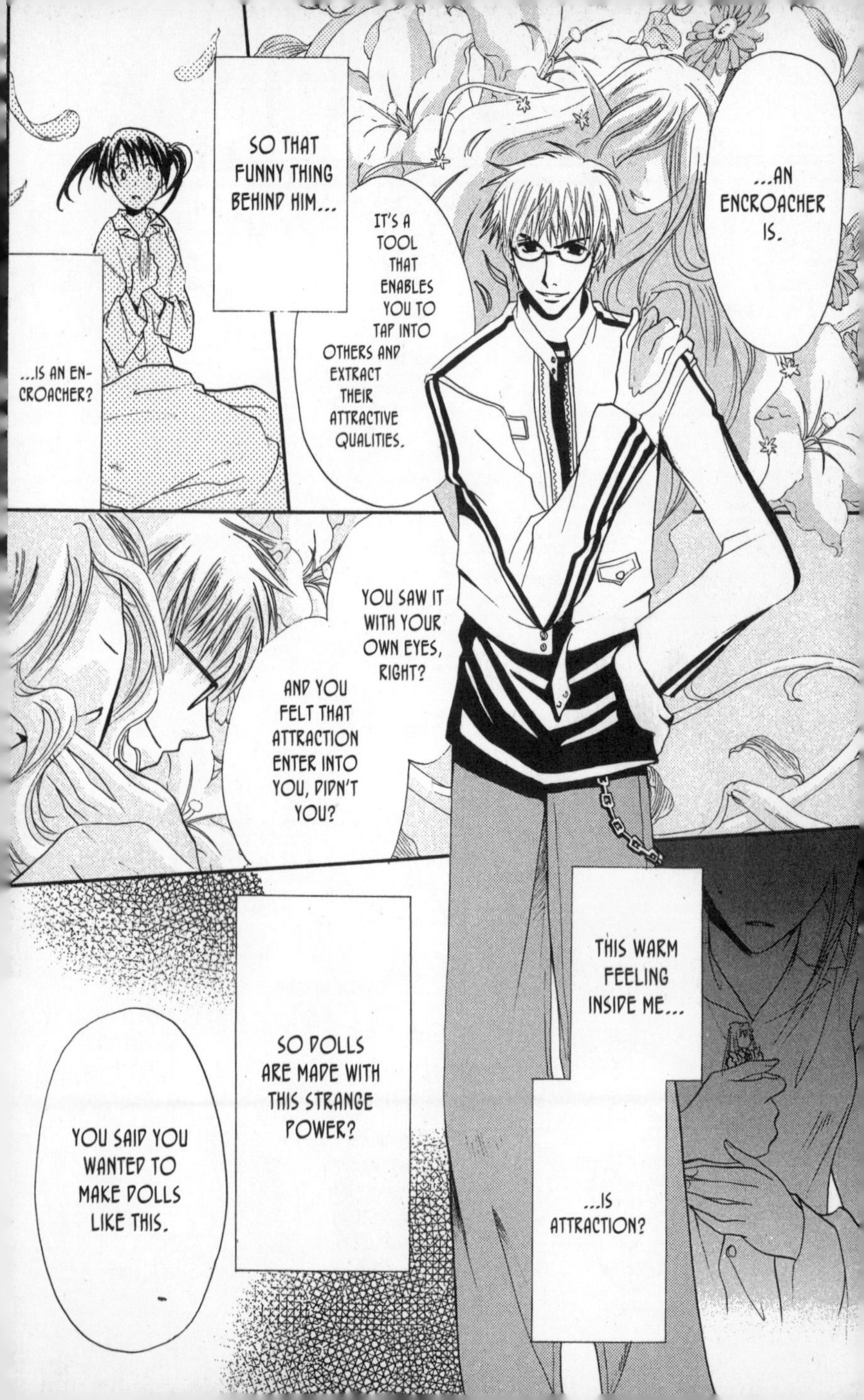
...AN ENCROACHER IS.
IT'S A TOOL THAT ENABLES YOU TO TAP INTO OTHERS AND EXTRACT THEIR ATTRACTIVE QUALITIES.
SO THAT FUNNY THING BEHIND HIM...
...IS AN EN-CROACHER?
YOU SAW IT WITH YOUR OWN EYES, RIGHT?
AND YOU FELT THAT ATTRACTION ENTER INTO YOU, DIDN'T YOU?
THIS WARM FEELING INSIDE ME...
...IS ATTRACTION?
SO DOLLS ARE MADE WITH THIS STRANGE POWER?
YOU SAID YOU WANTED TO MAKE DOLLS LIKE THIS.

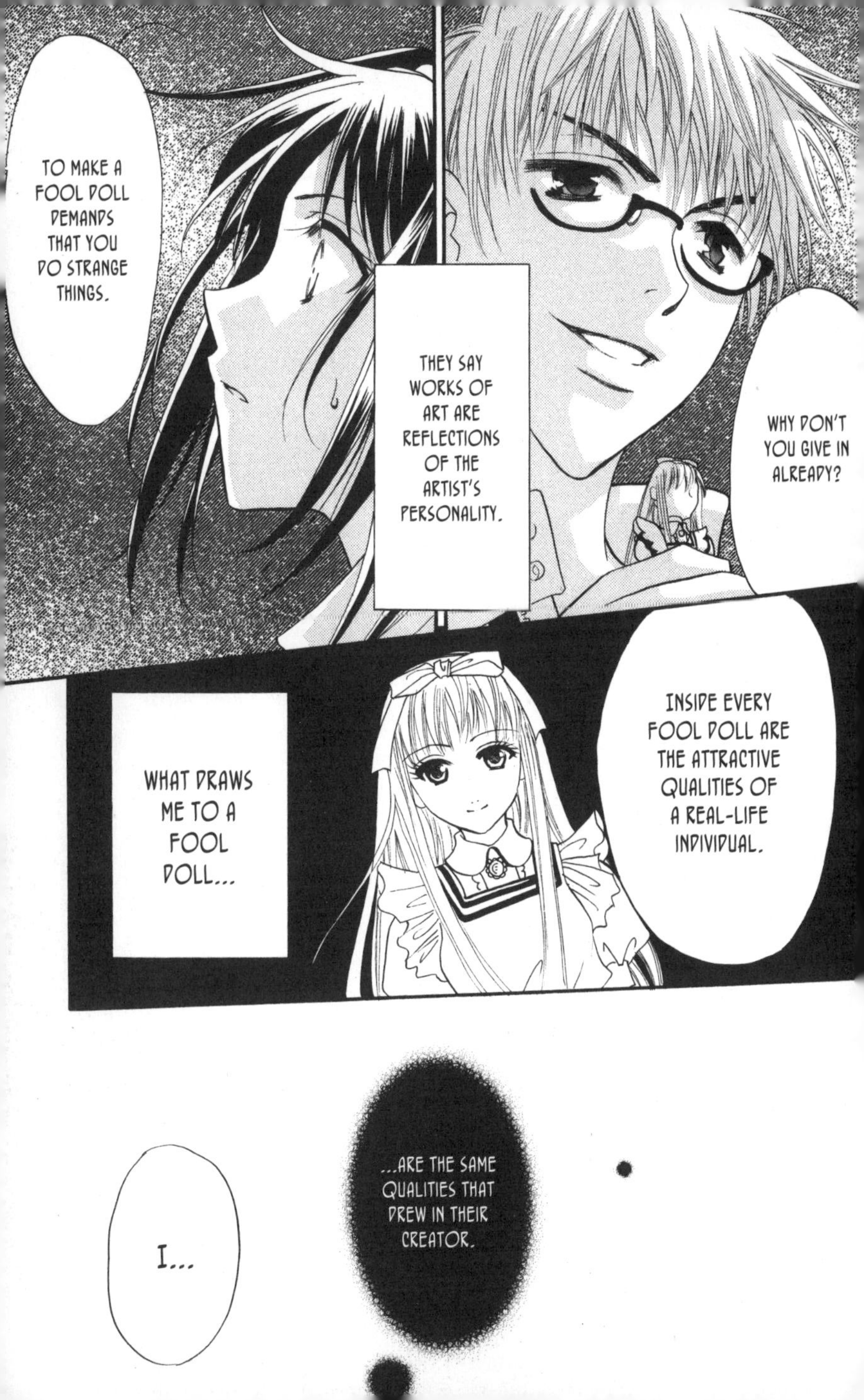
WHY DON'T YOU GIVE IN ALREADY?
THEY SAY WORKS OF ART ARE REFLECTIONS OF THE ARTIST'S PERSONALITY.
TO MAKE A FOOL DOLL DEMANDS THAT YOU DO STRANGE THINGS.
INSIDE EVERY FOOL DOLL ARE THE ATTRACTIVE QUALITIES OF A REAL-LIFE INDIVIDUAL.
WHAT DRAWS ME TO A FOOL DOLL...
...ARE THE SAME QUALITIES THAT DREW IN THEIR CREATOR.
I...

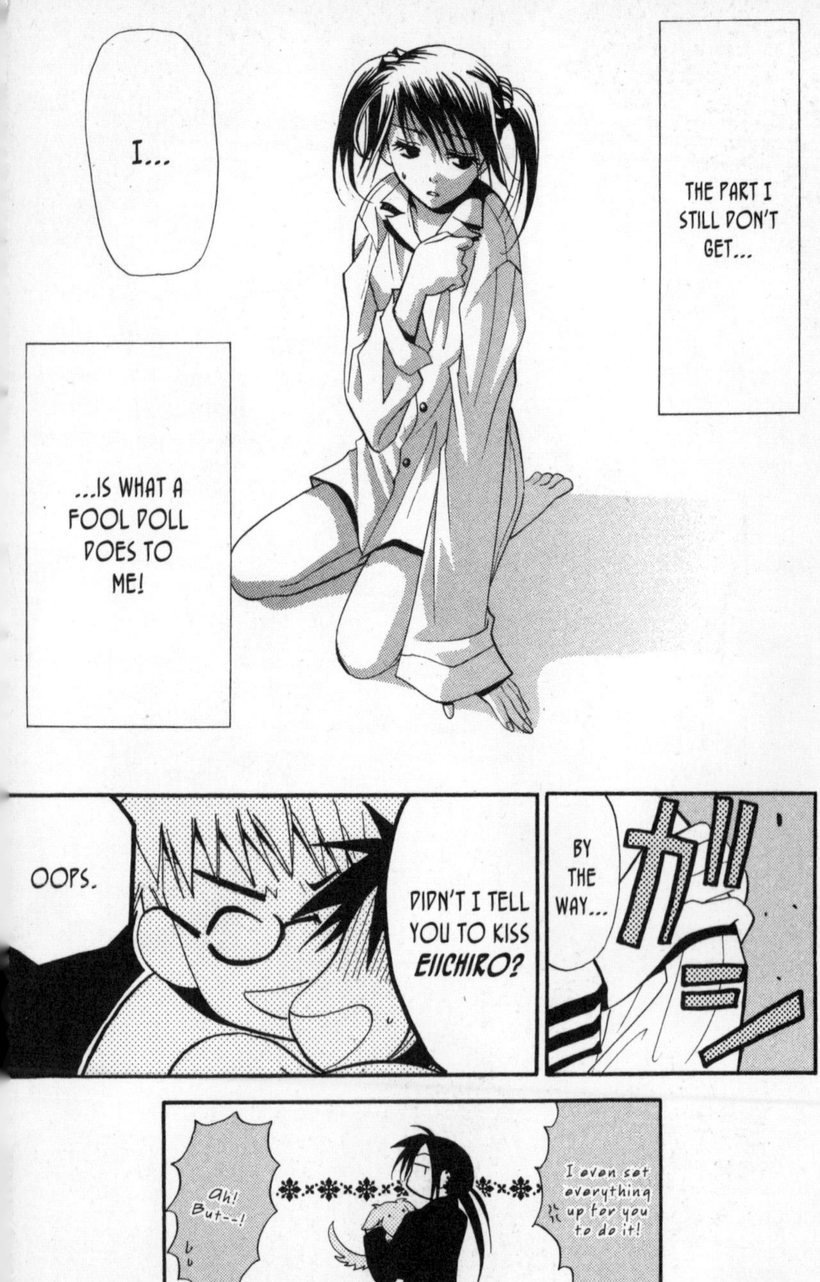
THE PART I STILL DON'T GET...
I...
...IS WHAT A FOOL DOLL DOES TO ME!
BY THE WAY...
カリ
DIDN'T I TELL YOU TO KISS EIICHIRO?
OOPS.
I even set everything up for you to do it!
Ah! But--!

2 End

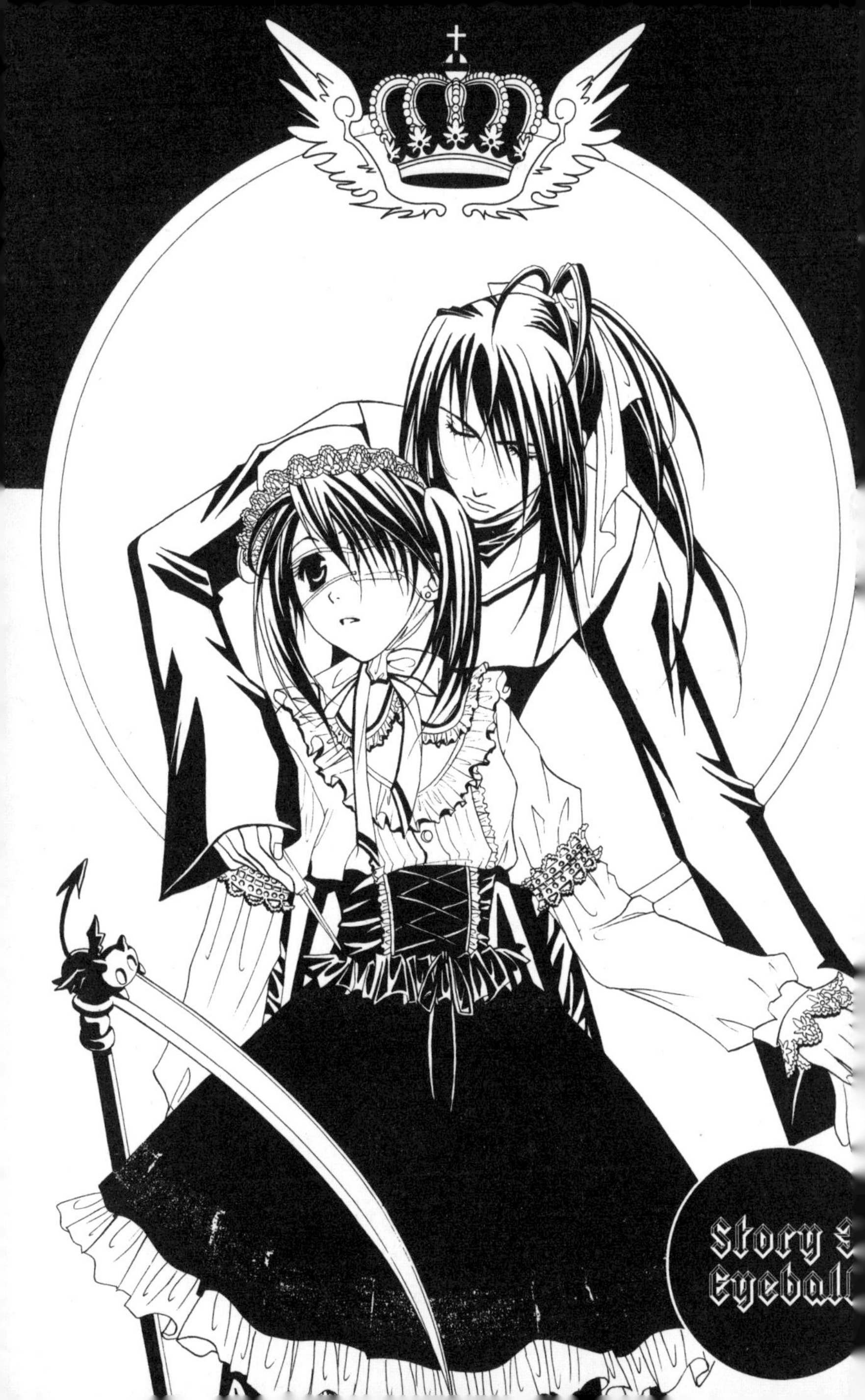
Story 3
Eyeball

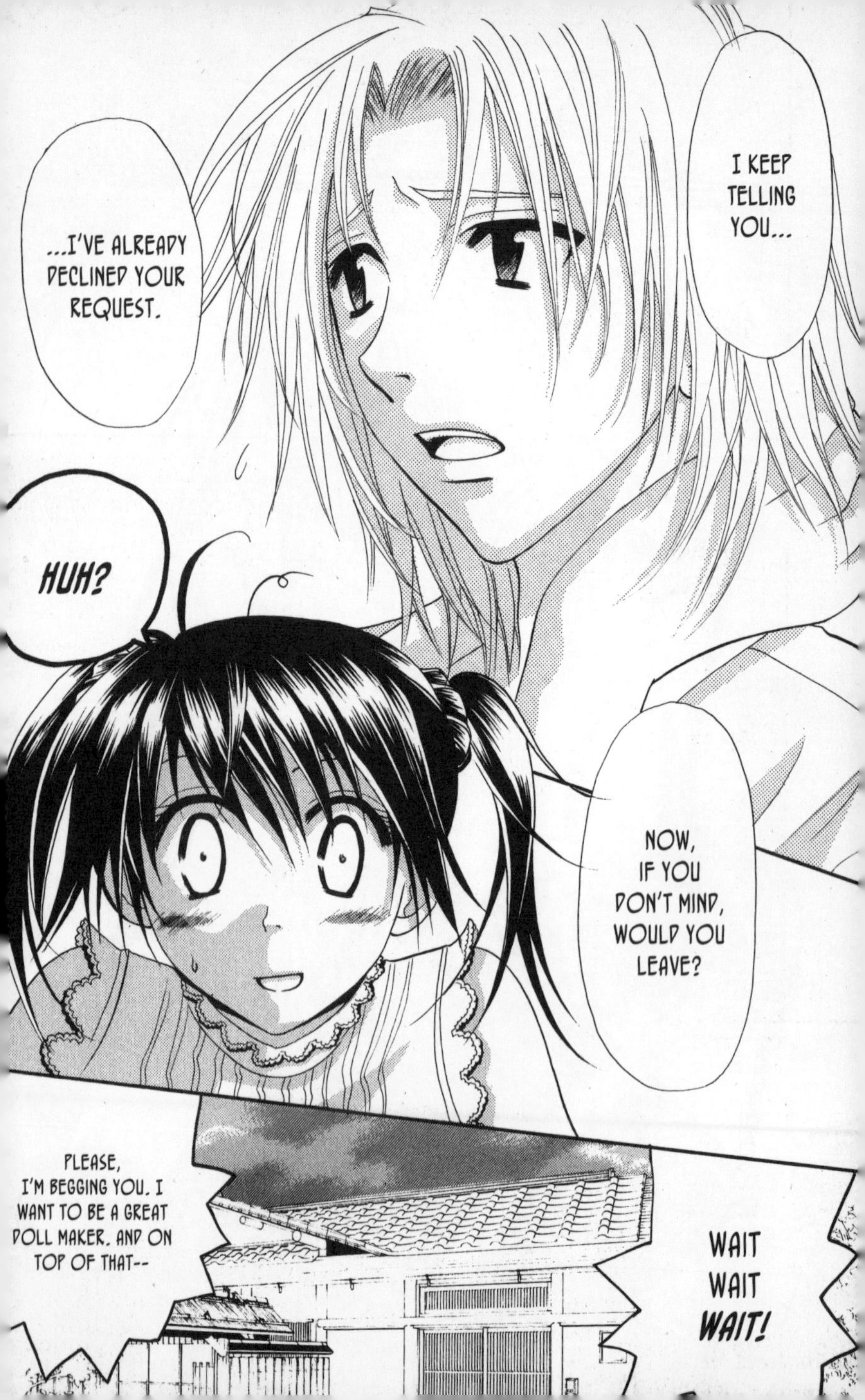
I KEEP TELLING YOU...
...I'VE ALREADY DECLINED YOUR REQUEST.
NOW, IF YOU DON'T MIND, WOULD YOU LEAVE?
HUH?
WAIT WAIT WAIT!
PLEASE, I'M BEGGING YOU. I WANT TO BE A GREAT DOLL MAKER. AND ON TOP OF THAT--

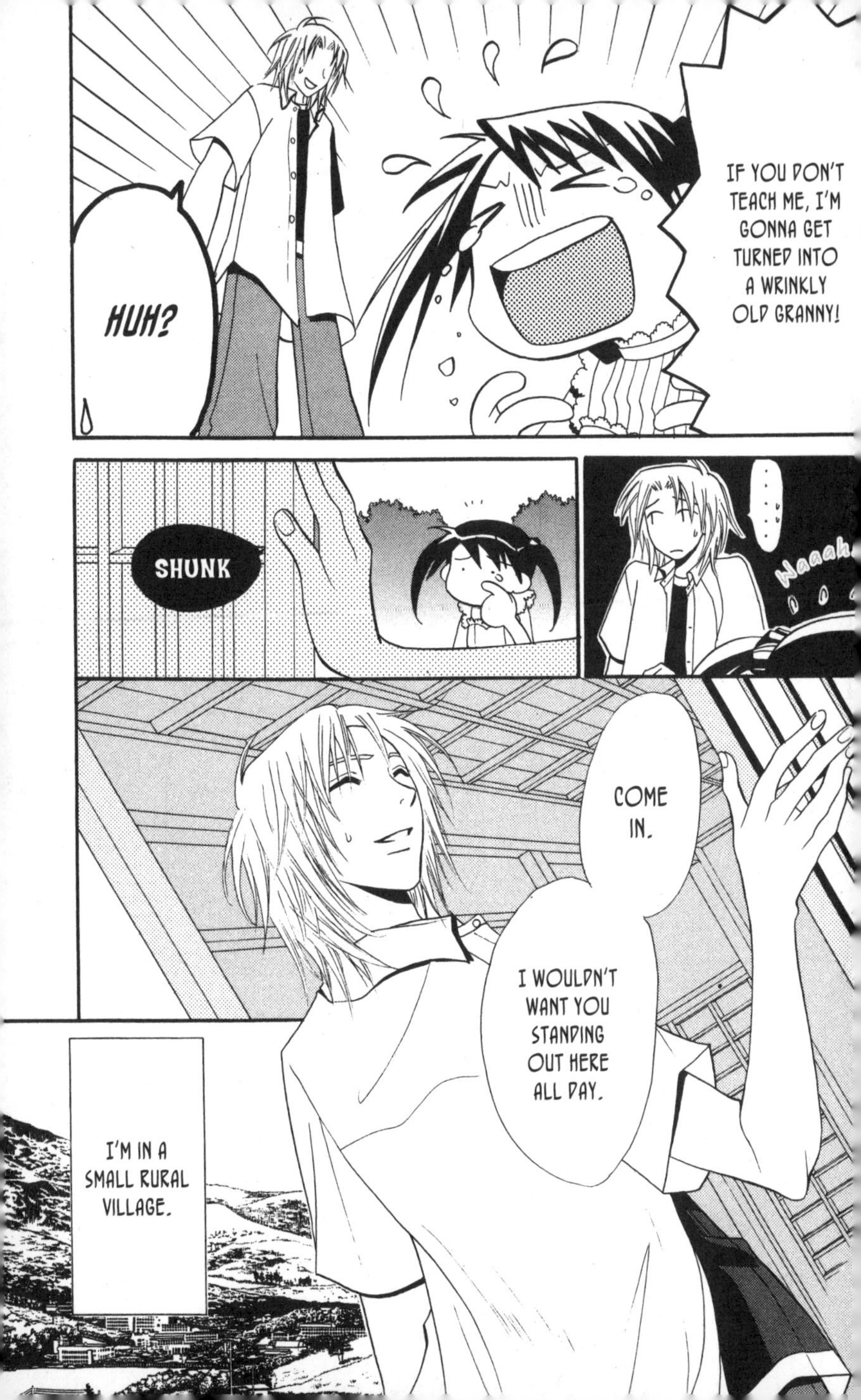

IF YOU DON'T TEACH ME, I'M GONNA GET TURNED INTO A WRINKLY OLD GRANNY!
HUH?
...
Waaah
SHUNK
COME IN.
I WOULDN'T WANT YOU STANDING OUT HERE ALL DAY.
I'M IN A SMALL RURAL VILLAGE.

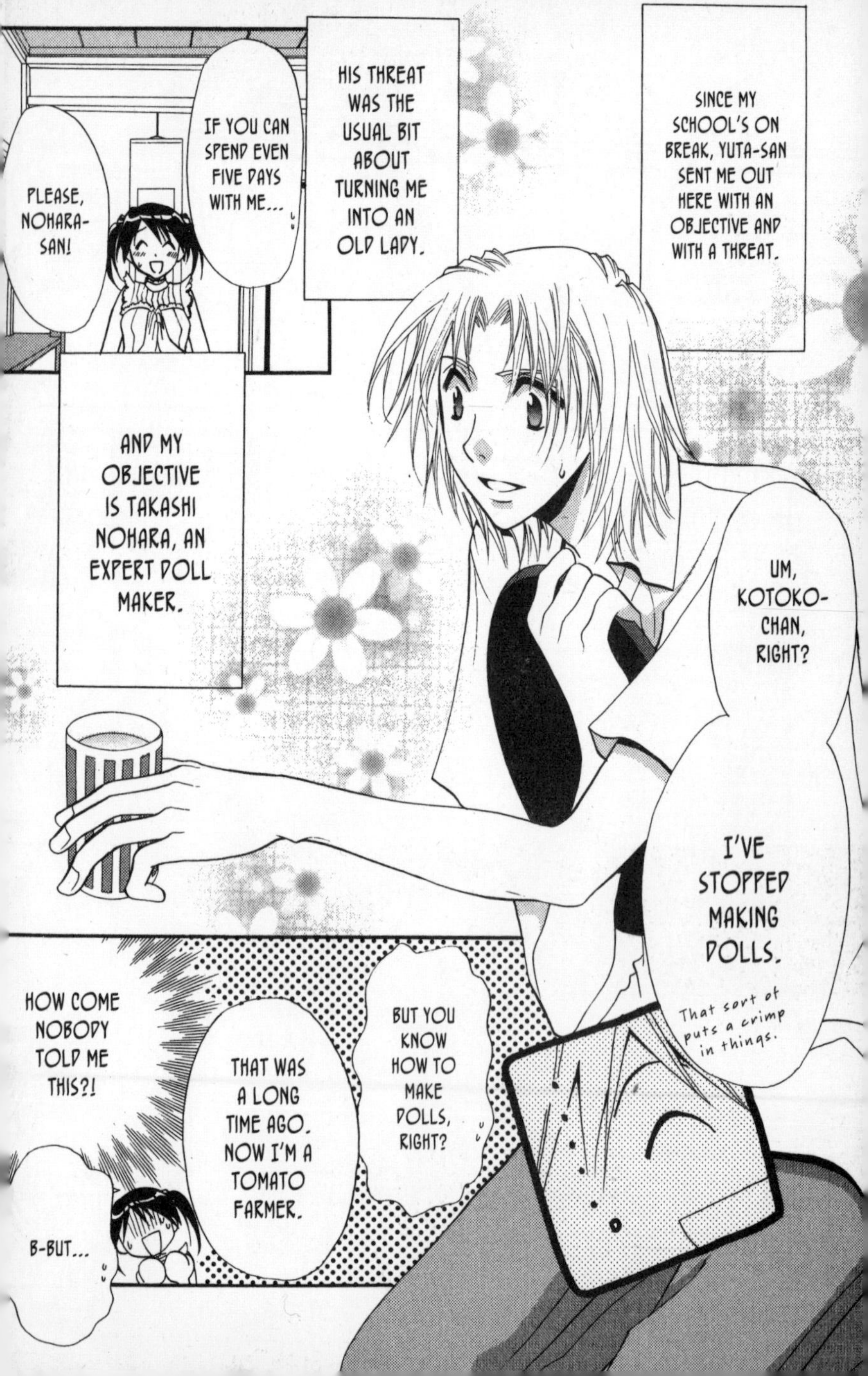

SINCE MY SCHOOL'S ON BREAK, YUTA-SAN SENT ME OUT HERE WITH AN OBJECTIVE AND WITH A THREAT.
HIS THREAT WAS THE USUAL BIT ABOUT TURNING ME INTO AN OLD LADY.
IF YOU CAN SPEND EVEN FIVE DAYS WITH ME...
PLEASE, NOHARA-SAN!
AND MY OBJECTIVE IS TAKASHI NOHARA, AN EXPERT DOLL MAKER.
UM, KOTOKO-CHAN, RIGHT?
I'VE STOPPED MAKING DOLLS.
That sort of puts a crimp in things.
BUT YOU KNOW HOW TO MAKE DOLLS, RIGHT?
THAT WAS A LONG TIME AGO. NOW I'M A TOMATO FARMER.
HOW COME NOBODY TOLD ME THIS?!
B-BUT...

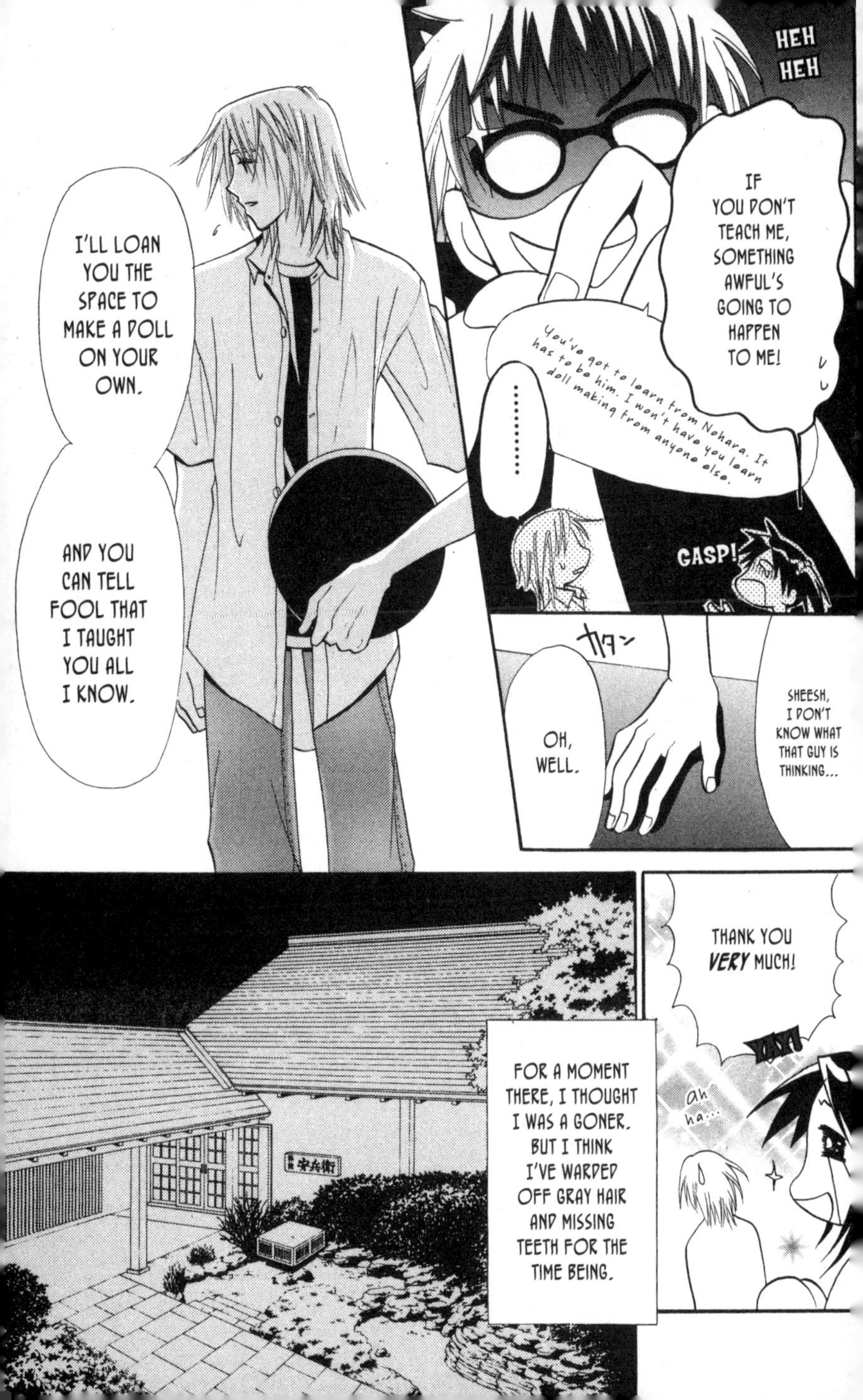
HEH HEH
IF YOU DON'T TEACH ME, SOMETHING AWFUL'S GOING TO HAPPEN TO ME!
You've got to learn from Nohara. It has to be him. I won't have you learn doll making from anyone else.
......
GASP!
カタン
SHEESH, I DON'T KNOW WHAT THAT GUY IS THINKING...
OH, WELL.
I'LL LOAN YOU THE SPACE TO MAKE A DOLL ON YOUR OWN.
AND YOU CAN TELL FOOL THAT I TAUGHT YOU ALL I KNOW.
THANK YOU **VERY** MUCH!
ah ha...
FOR A MOMENT THERE, I THOUGHT I WAS A GONER. BUT I THINK I'VE WARDED OFF GRAY HAIR AND MISSING TEETH FOR THE TIME BEING.

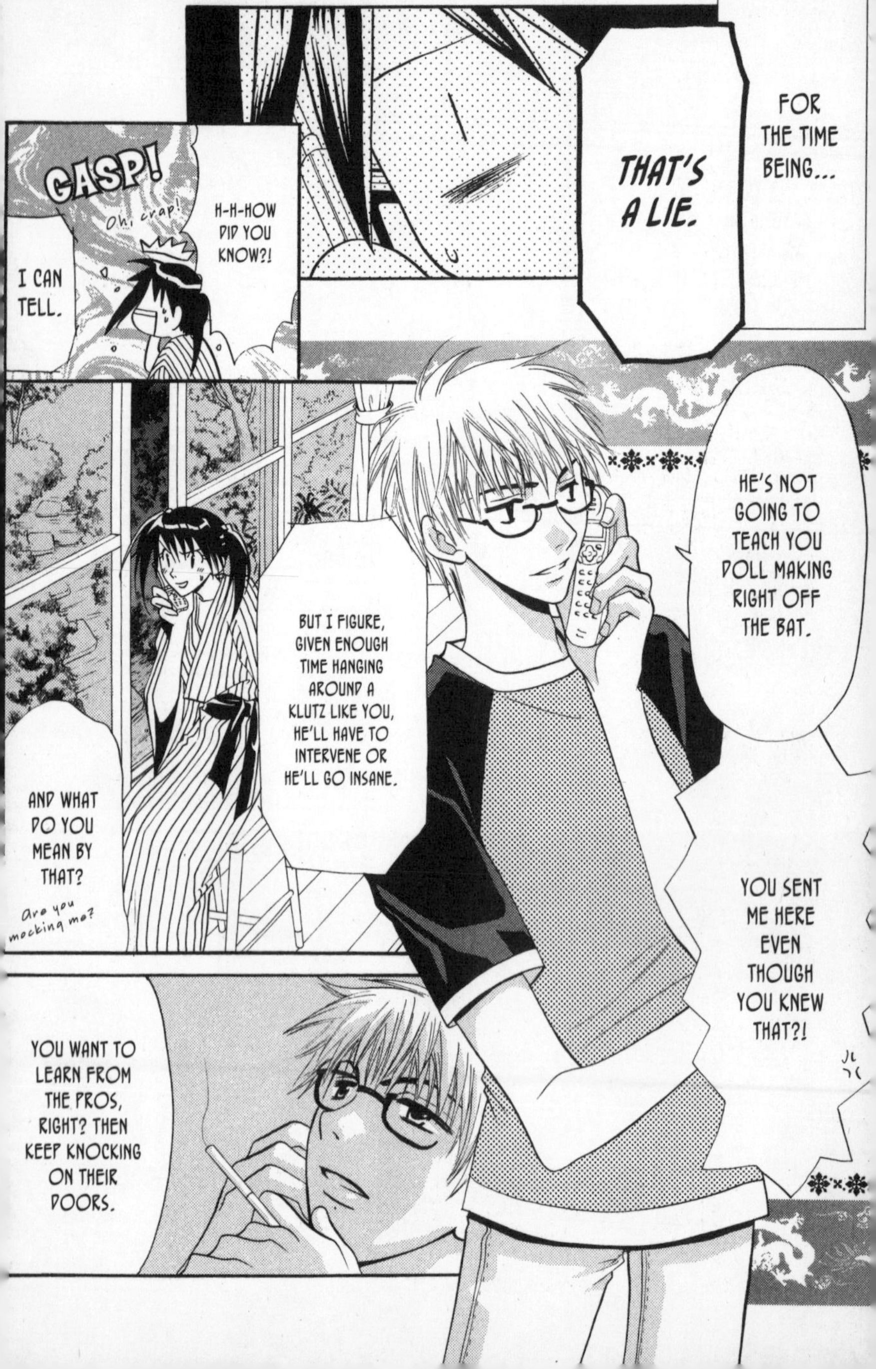
FOR THE TIME BEING...
THAT'S A LIE.
GASP!
Oh, crap!
H-H-HOW DID YOU KNOW?!
I CAN TELL.
HE'S NOT GOING TO TEACH YOU DOLL MAKING RIGHT OFF THE BAT.
YOU SENT ME HERE EVEN THOUGH YOU KNEW THAT?!
BUT I FIGURE, GIVEN ENOUGH TIME HANGING AROUND A KLUTZ LIKE YOU, HE'LL HAVE TO INTERVENE OR HE'LL GO INSANE.
AND WHAT DO YOU MEAN BY THAT?
Are you mocking me?
YOU WANT TO LEARN FROM THE PROS, RIGHT? THEN KEEP KNOCKING ON THEIR DOORS.

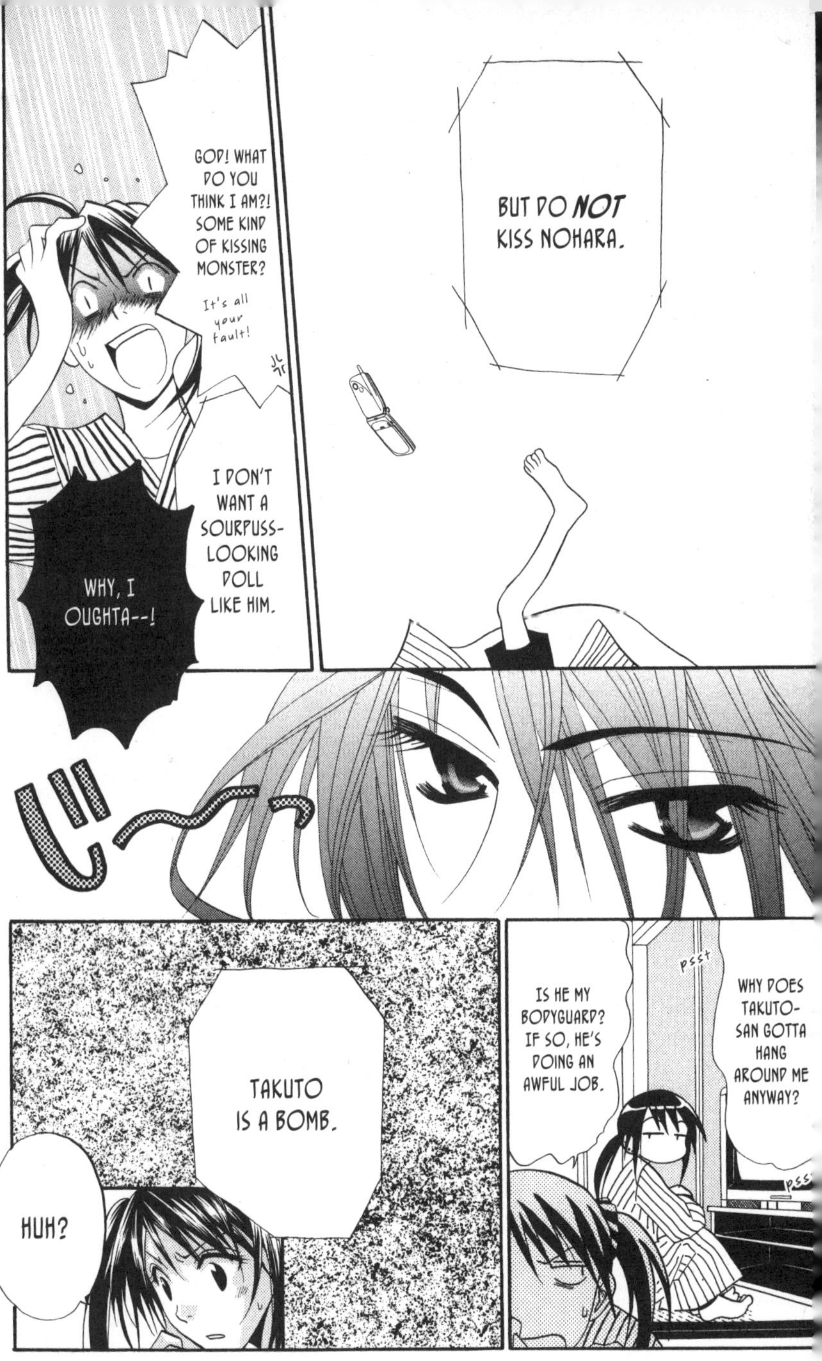
BUT DO **NOT** KISS NOHARA.
GOD! WHAT DO YOU THINK I AM?! SOME KIND OF KISSING MONSTER?
It's all your fault!
I DON'T WANT A SOURPUSS-LOOKING DOLL LIKE HIM.
WHY, I OUGHTA--!
じ〜〜
psst
WHY DOES TAKUTO-SAN GOTTA HANG AROUND ME ANYWAY?
IS HE MY BODYGUARD? IF SO, HE'S DOING AN AWFUL JOB.
psst
TAKUTO IS A BOMB.
HUH?

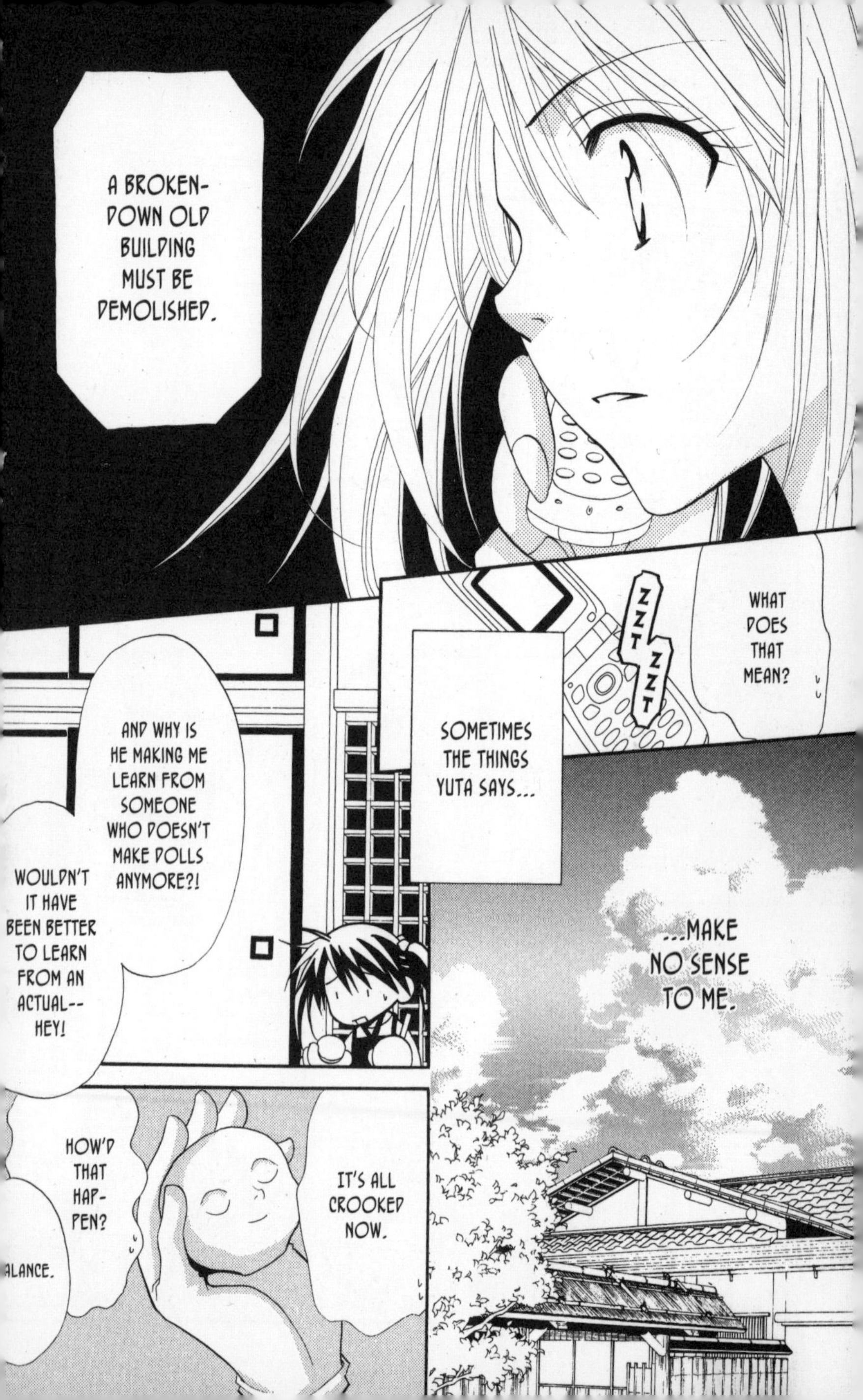
A BROKEN-DOWN OLD BUILDING MUST BE DEMOLISHED.
ZZT ZZT
WHAT DOES THAT MEAN?
SOMETIMES THE THINGS YUTA SAYS...
...MAKE NO SENSE TO ME.
AND WHY IS HE MAKING ME LEARN FROM SOMEONE WHO DOESN'T MAKE DOLLS ANYMORE?!
WOULDN'T IT HAVE BEEN BETTER TO LEARN FROM AN ACTUAL-- HEY!
IT'S ALL CROOKED NOW.
HOW'D THAT HAP-PEN?
ALANCE.

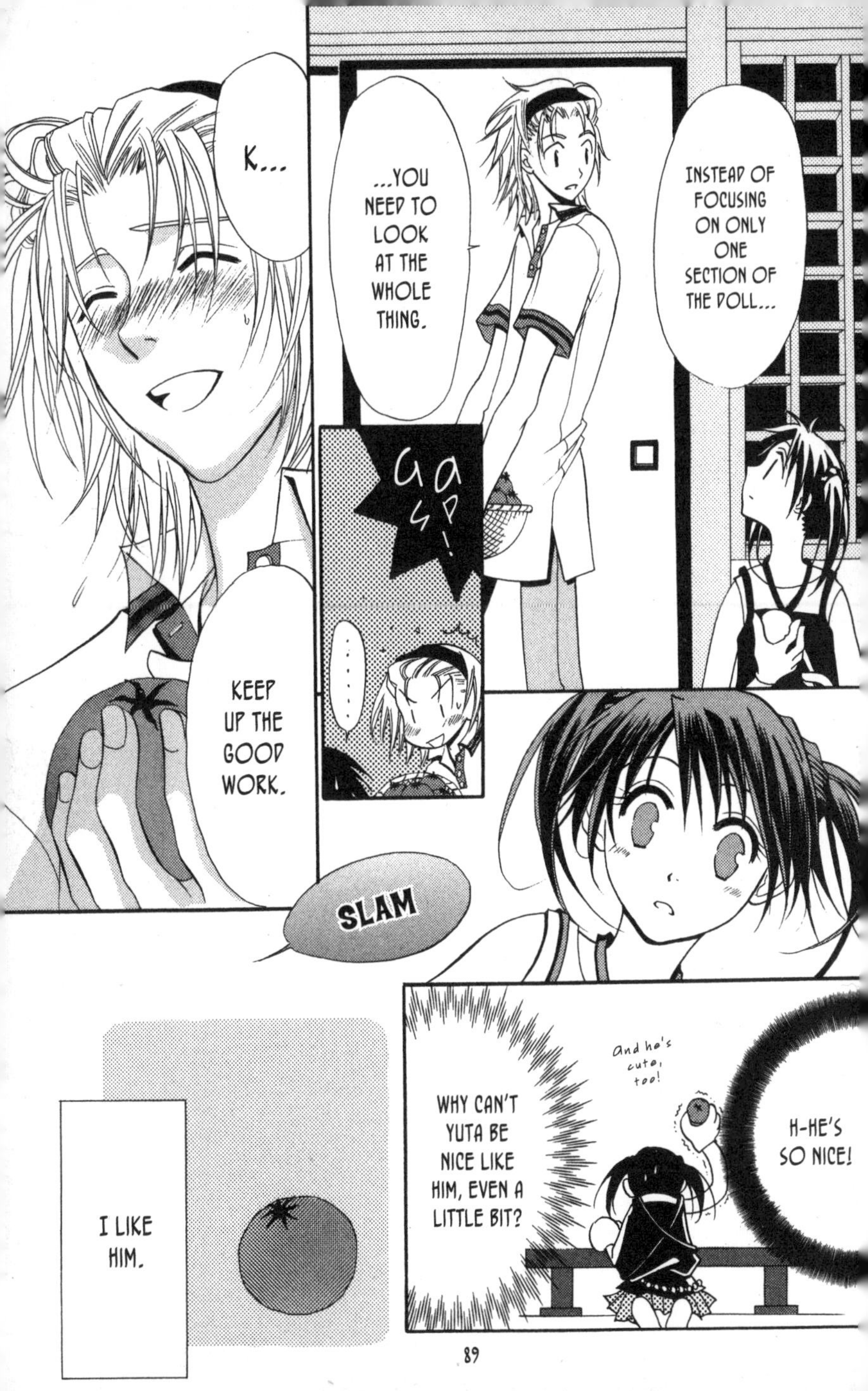
INSTEAD OF FOCUSING ON ONLY ONE SECTION OF THE DOLL...
...YOU NEED TO LOOK AT THE WHOLE THING.
GASP!
......
K...
KEEP UP THE GOOD WORK.
SLAM
H-HE'S SO NICE!
WHY CAN'T YUTA BE NICE LIKE HIM, EVEN A LITTLE BIT?
And he's cute, too!
I LIKE HIM.

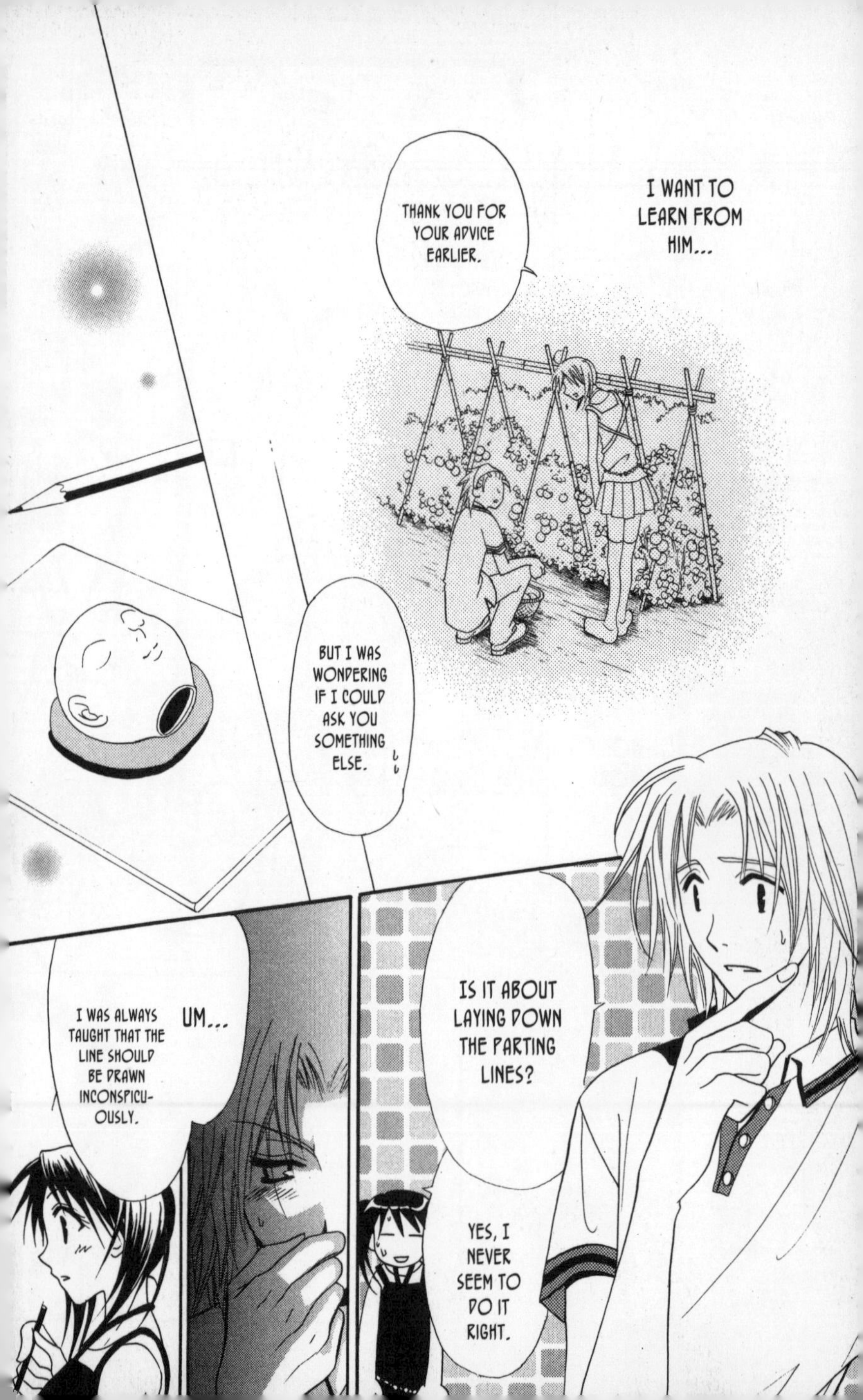
I WANT TO LEARN FROM HIM...
THANK YOU FOR YOUR ADVICE EARLIER.
BUT I WAS WONDERING IF I COULD ASK YOU SOMETHING ELSE.
IS IT ABOUT LAYING DOWN THE PARTING LINES?
YES, I NEVER SEEM TO DO IT RIGHT.
UM...
I WAS ALWAYS TAUGHT THAT THE LINE SHOULD BE DRAWN INCONSPICU-OUSLY.

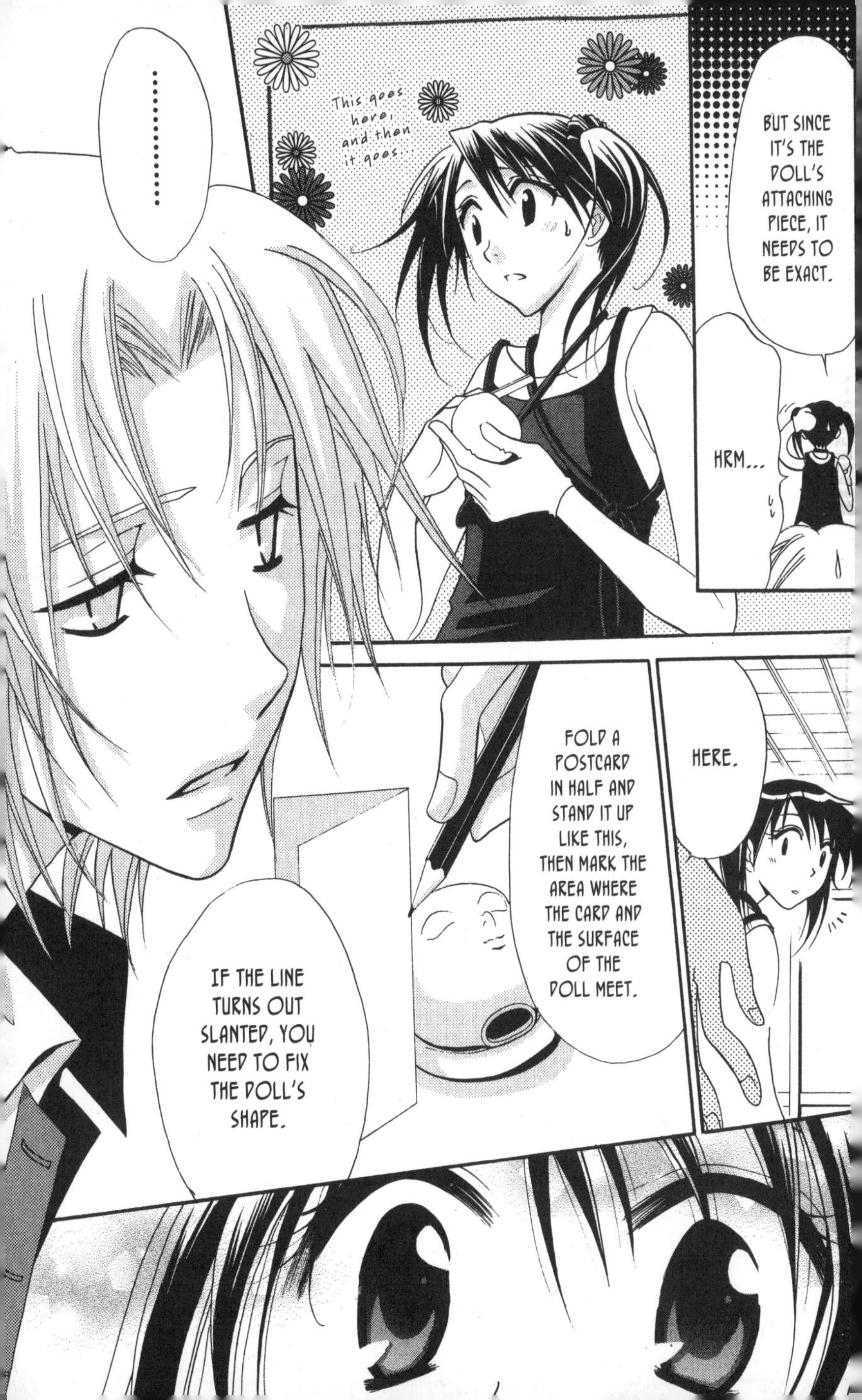

BUT SINCE IT'S THE DOLL'S ATTACHING PIECE, IT NEEDS TO BE EXACT.
HRM...
This goes here, and then it goes...
....
HERE.
FOLD A POSTCARD IN HALF AND STAND IT UP LIKE THIS, THEN MARK THE AREA WHERE THE CARD AND THE SURFACE OF THE DOLL MEET.
IF THE LINE TURNS OUT SLANTED, YOU NEED TO FIX THE DOLL'S SHAPE.

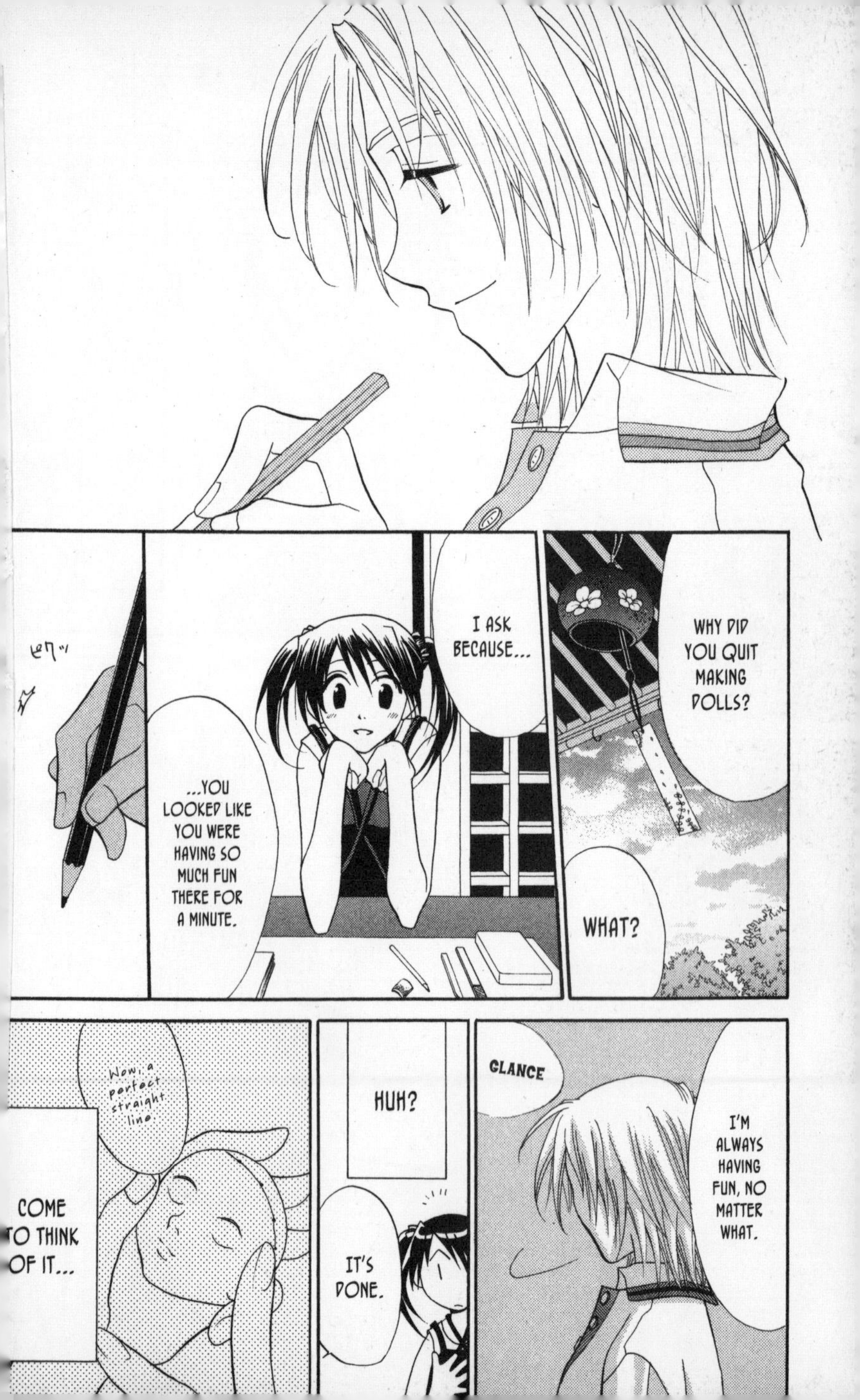
WHY DID YOU QUIT MAKING DOLLS?
WHAT?
I ASK BECAUSE...
...YOU LOOKED LIKE YOU WERE HAVING SO MUCH FUN THERE FOR A MINUTE.
ピクッ
I'M ALWAYS HAVING FUN, NO MATTER WHAT.
GLANCE
HUH?
IT'S DONE.
Wow, a perfect straight line
COME TO THINK OF IT...

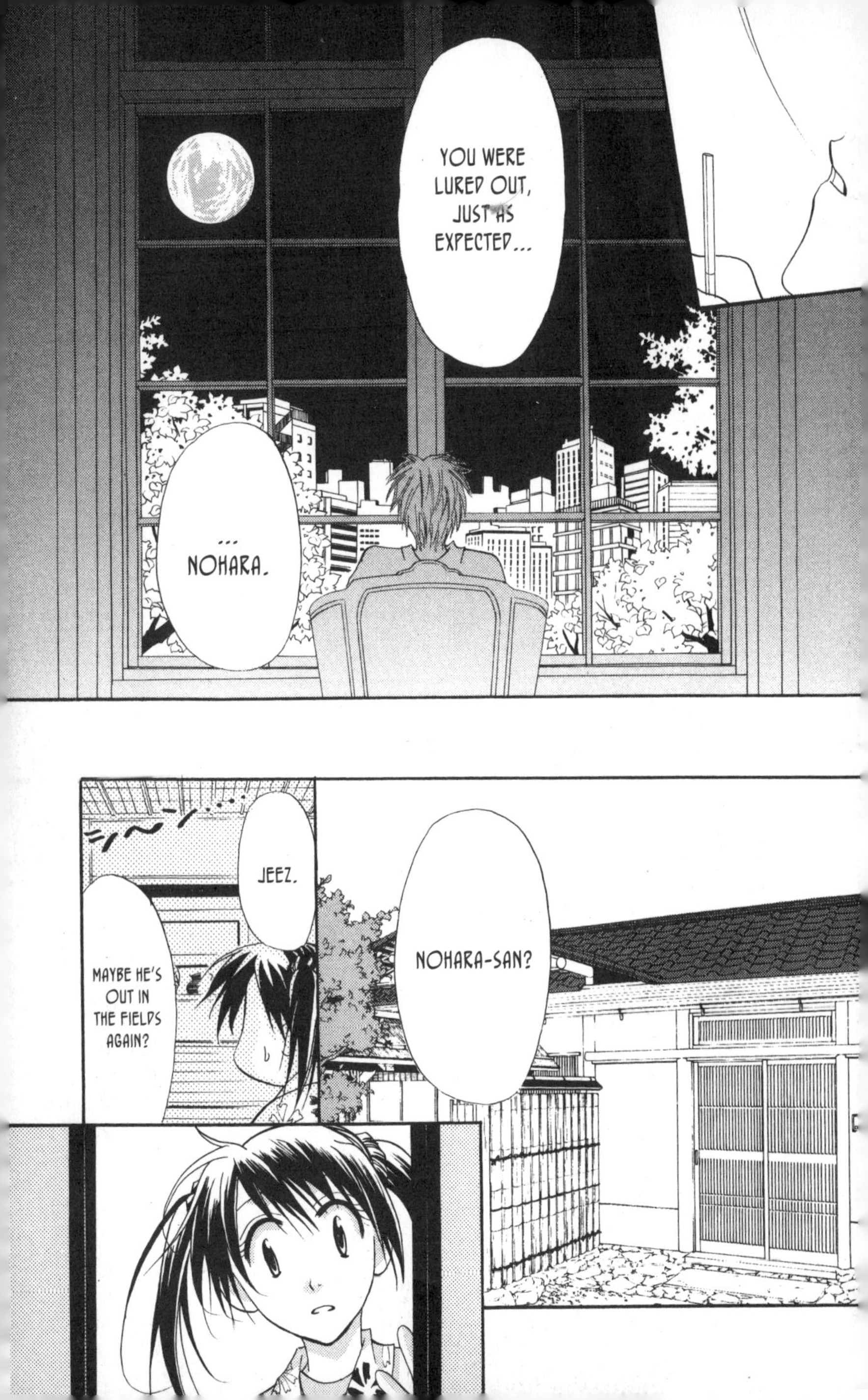
YOU WERE LURED OUT, JUST AS EXPECTED...
... NOHARA.
NOHARA-SAN?
JEEZ.
MAYBE HE'S OUT IN THE FIELDS AGAIN?

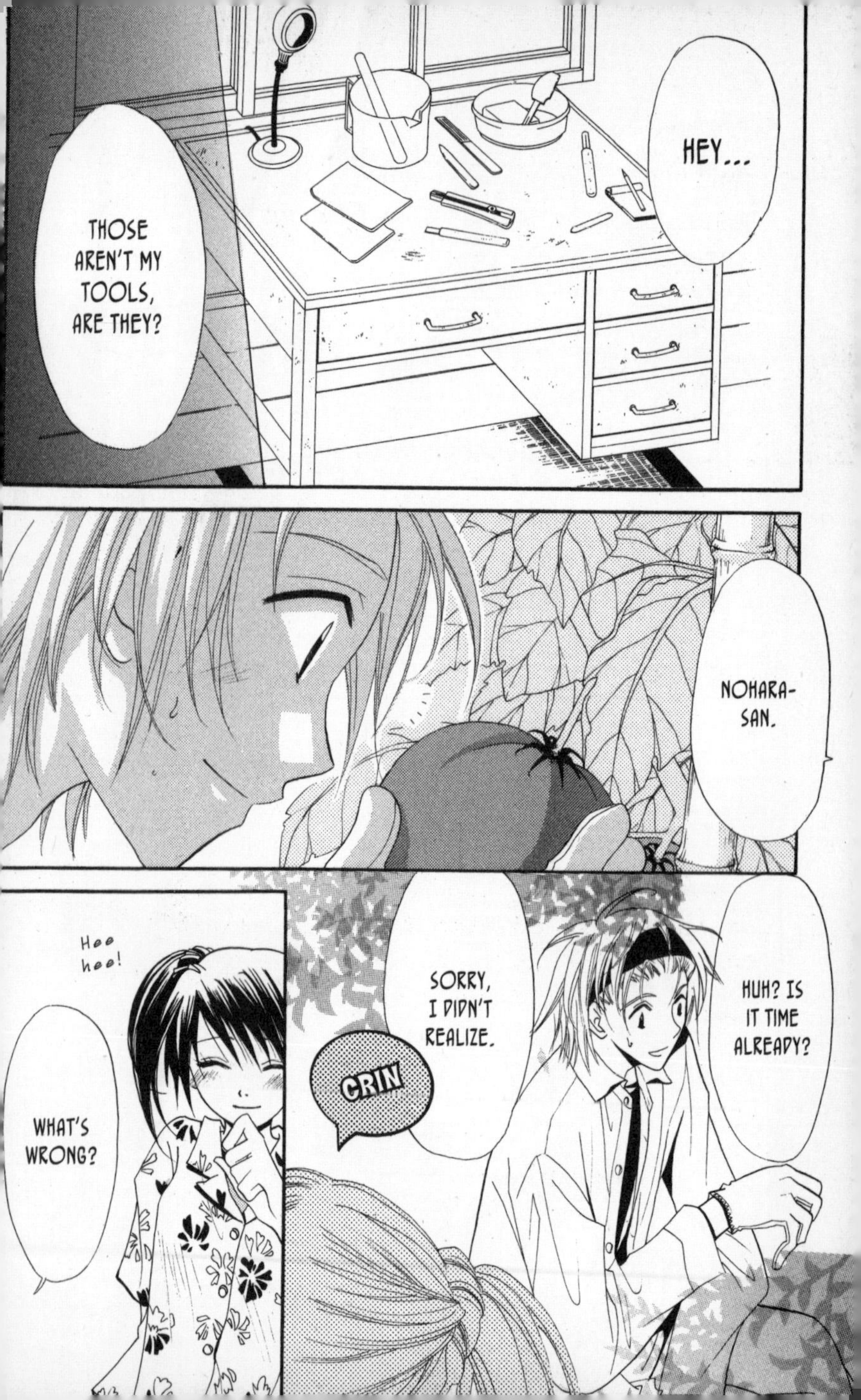
HEY...
THOSE AREN'T MY TOOLS, ARE THEY?
NOHARA-SAN.
HUH? IS IT TIME ALREADY?
SORRY, I DIDN'T REALIZE.
GRIN
Hee hee!
WHAT'S WRONG?

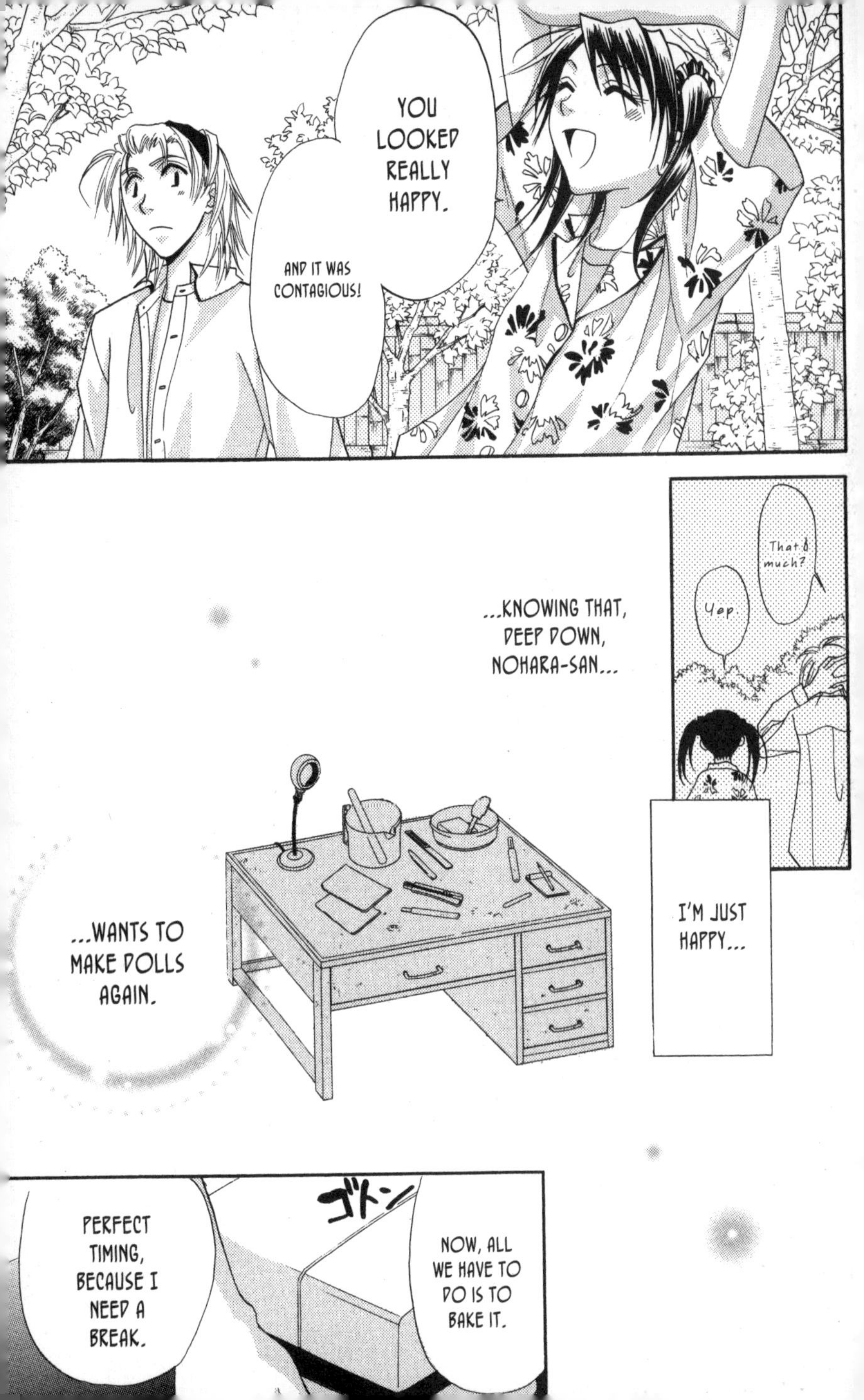
YOU LOOKED REALLY HAPPY.
AND IT WAS CONTAGIOUS!
That much?
Yep.
I'M JUST HAPPY...
...KNOWING THAT, DEEP DOWN, NOHARA-SAN...
...WANTS TO MAKE DOLLS AGAIN.
ゴトン
NOW, ALL WE HAVE TO DO IS TO BAKE IT.
PERFECT TIMING, BECAUSE I NEED A BREAK.

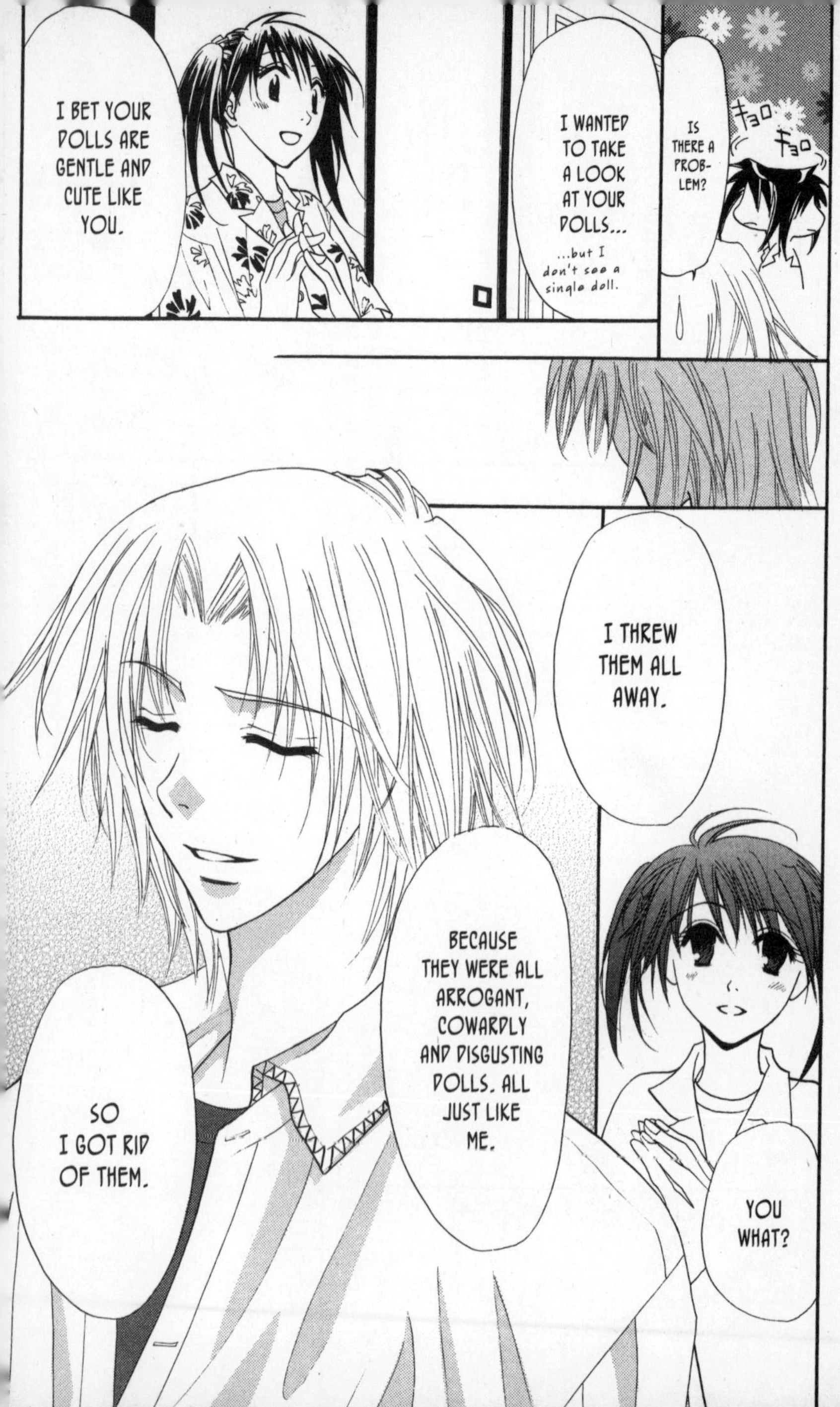
キョロ
キョロ
IS THERE A PROB-LEM?
I WANTED TO TAKE A LOOK AT YOUR DOLLS...
...but I don't see a single doll.
I BET YOUR DOLLS ARE GENTLE AND CUTE LIKE YOU.
I THREW THEM ALL AWAY.
YOU WHAT?
BECAUSE THEY WERE ALL ARROGANT, COWARDLY AND DISGUSTING DOLLS. ALL JUST LIKE ME.
SO I GOT RID OF THEM.

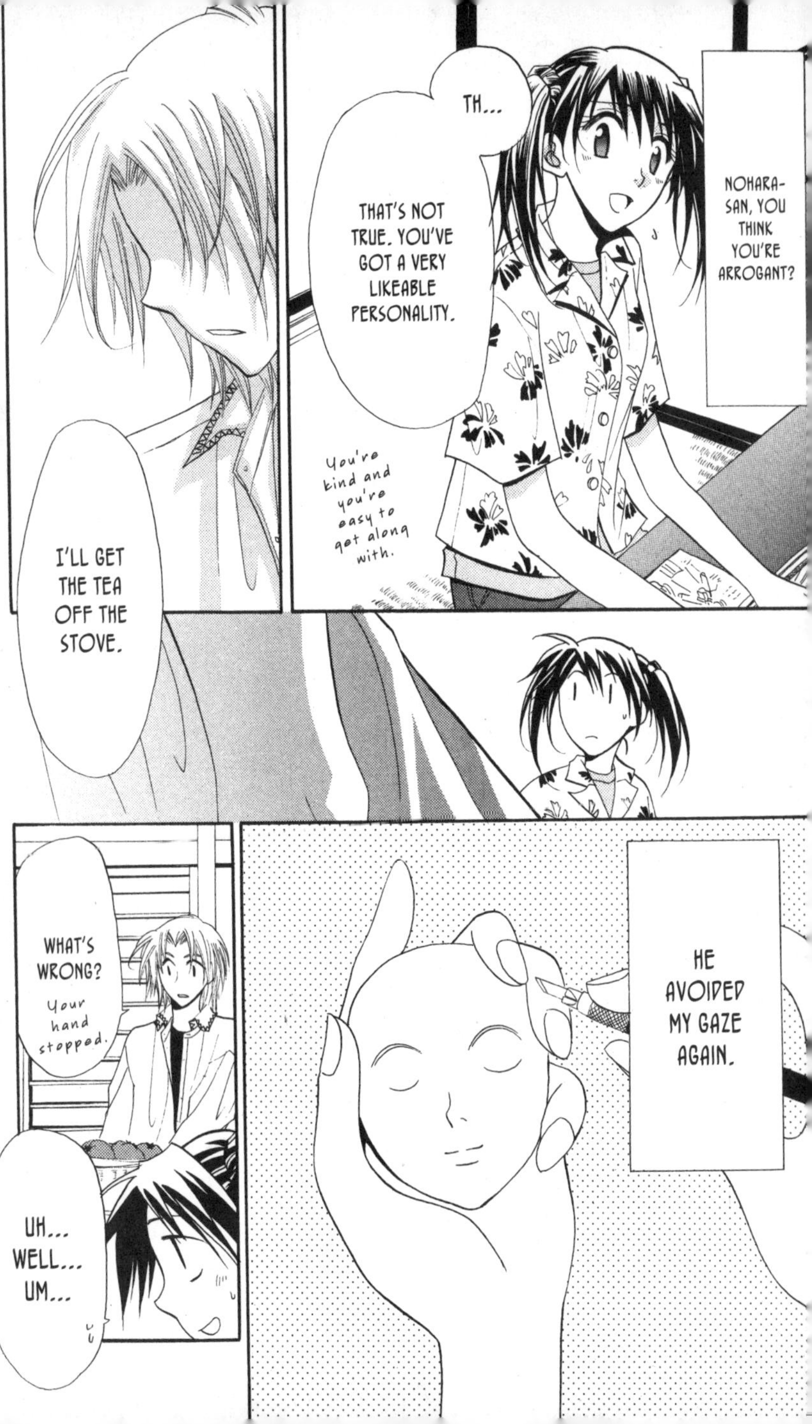
NOHARA-SAN, YOU THINK YOU'RE ARROGANT?
TH...
THAT'S NOT TRUE. YOU'VE GOT A VERY LIKEABLE PERSONALITY.
You're kind and you're easy to get along with.
I'LL GET THE TEA OFF THE STOVE.
HE AVOIDED MY GAZE AGAIN.
WHAT'S WRONG?
Your hand stopped.
UH... WELL... UM...

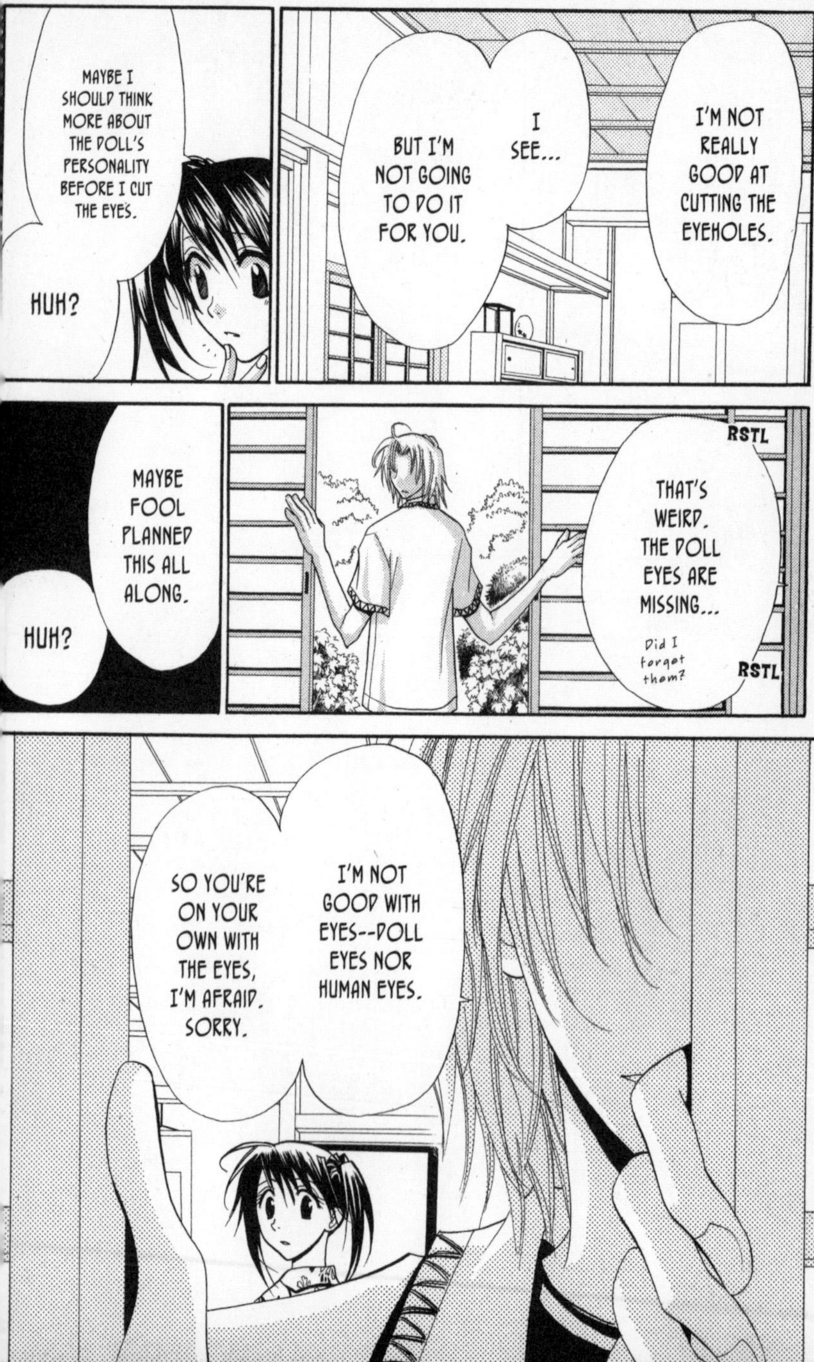
I'M NOT REALLY GOOD AT CUTTING THE EYEHOLES.
I SEE...
BUT I'M NOT GOING TO DO IT FOR YOU.
MAYBE I SHOULD THINK MORE ABOUT THE DOLL'S PERSONALITY BEFORE I CUT THE EYES.
HUH?
RSTL
THAT'S WEIRD. THE DOLL EYES ARE MISSING...
Did I forget them?
RSTL
MAYBE FOOL PLANNED THIS ALL ALONG.
HUH?
I'M NOT GOOD WITH EYES--DOLL EYES NOR HUMAN EYES.
SO YOU'RE ON YOUR OWN WITH THE EYES, I'M AFRAID. SORRY.

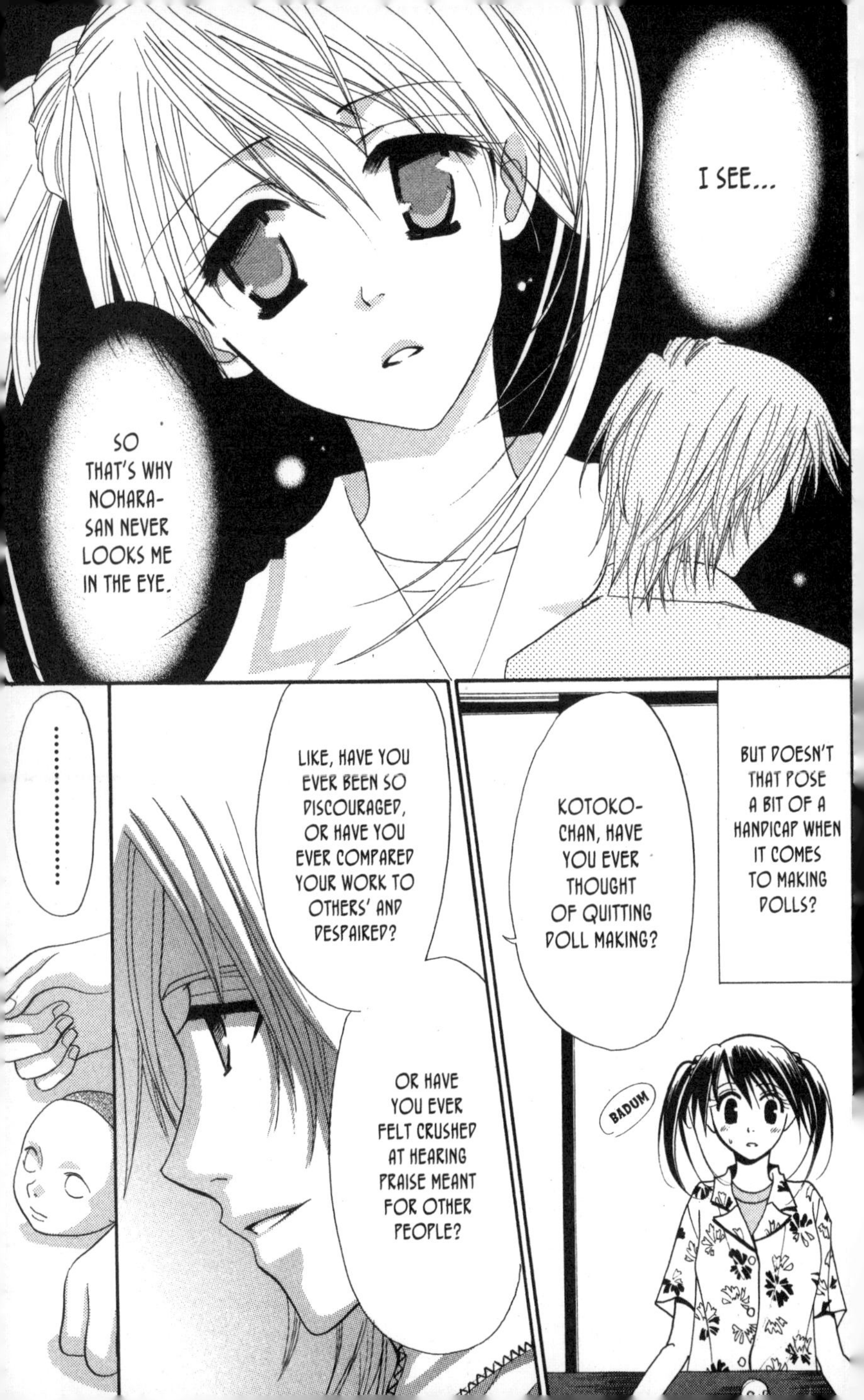
I SEE...
SO THAT'S WHY NOHARA-SAN NEVER LOOKS ME IN THE EYE.
BUT DOESN'T THAT POSE A BIT OF A HANDICAP WHEN IT COMES TO MAKING DOLLS?
KOTOKO-CHAN, HAVE YOU EVER THOUGHT OF QUITTING DOLL MAKING?
BADUM
LIKE, HAVE YOU EVER BEEN SO DISCOURAGED, OR HAVE YOU EVER COMPARED YOUR WORK TO OTHERS' AND DESPAIRED?
OR HAVE YOU EVER FELT CRUSHED AT HEARING PRAISE MEANT FOR OTHER PEOPLE?
....

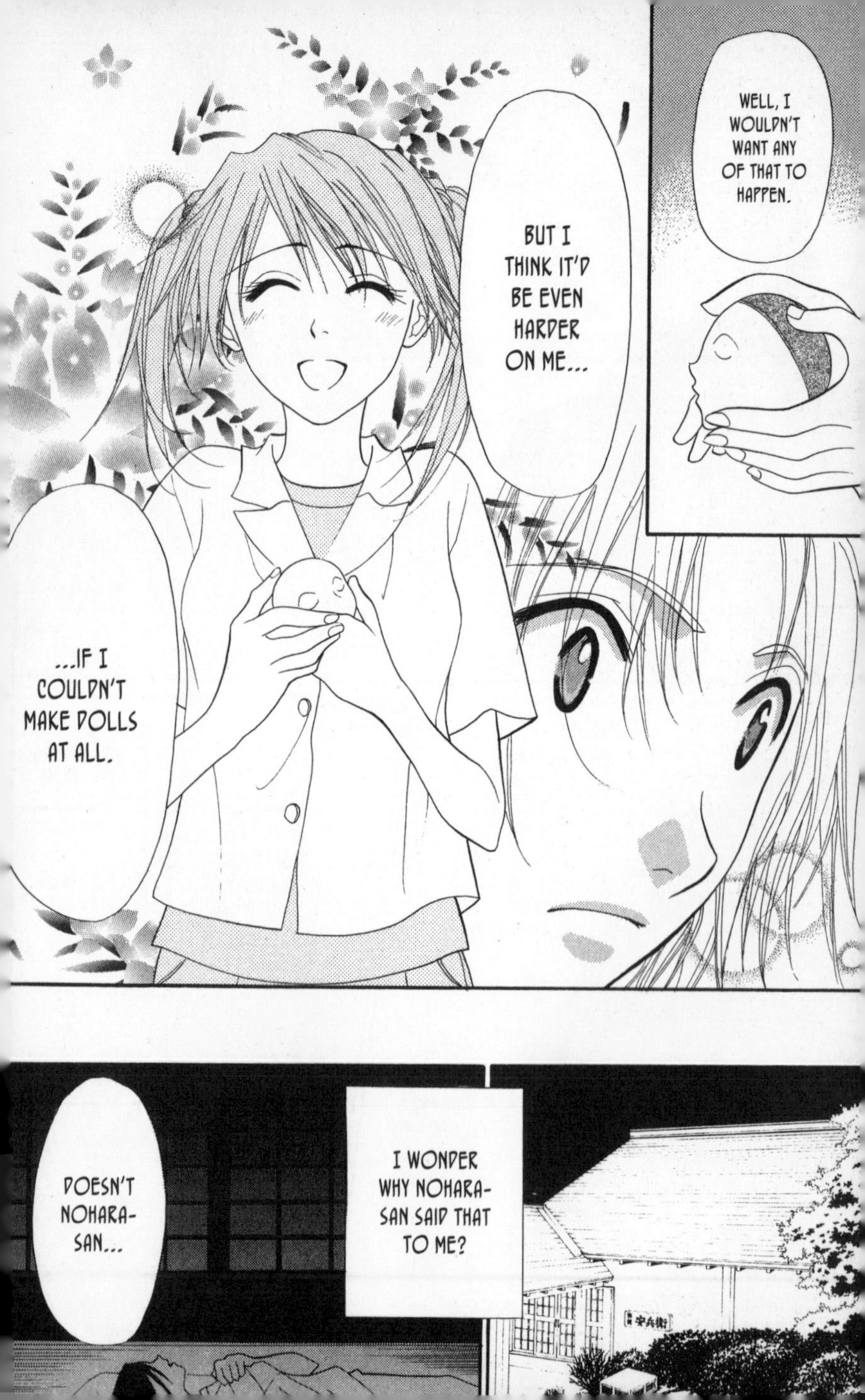
WELL, I WOULDN'T WANT ANY OF THAT TO HAPPEN.
BUT I THINK IT'D BE EVEN HARDER ON ME...
...IF I COULDN'T MAKE DOLLS AT ALL.
I WONDER WHY NOHARA-SAN SAID THAT TO ME?
DOESN'T NOHARA-SAN...

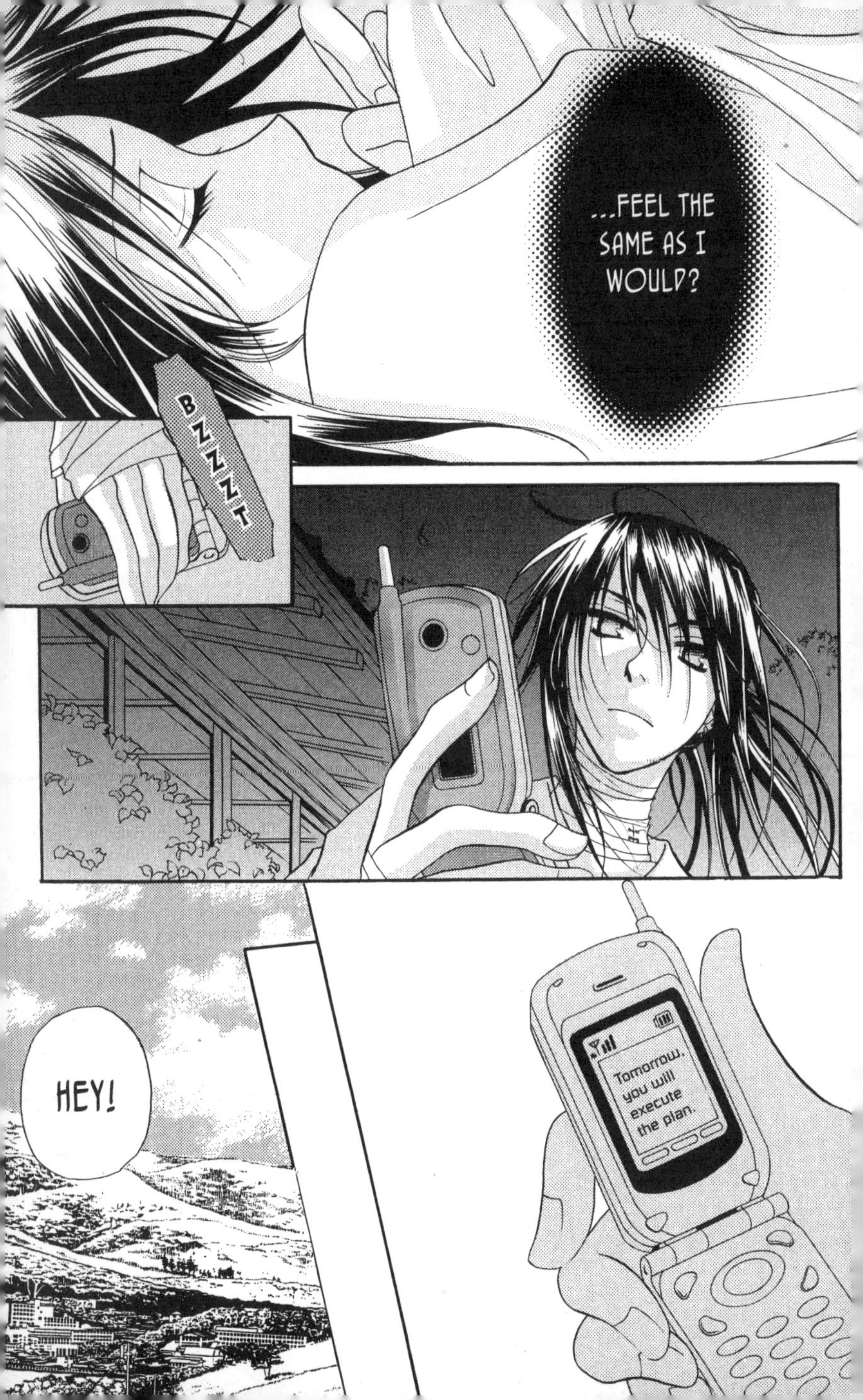
...FEEL THE SAME AS I WOULD?
BZZZT
Tomorrow, you will execute the plan.
HEY!

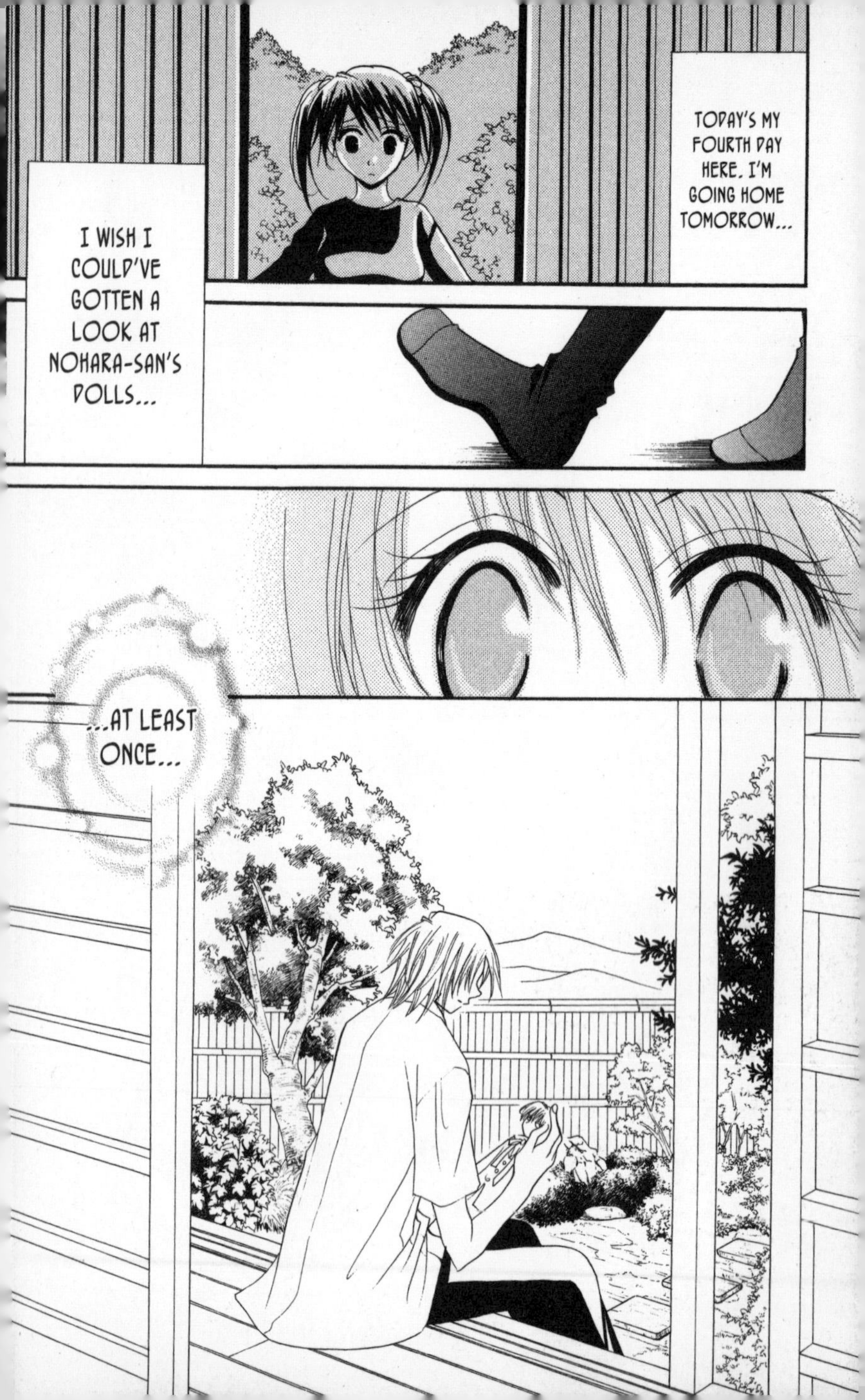
TODAY'S MY FOURTH DAY HERE. I'M GOING HOME TOMORROW...
I WISH I COULD'VE GOTTEN A LOOK AT NOHARA-SAN'S DOLLS...
...AT LEAST ONCE...

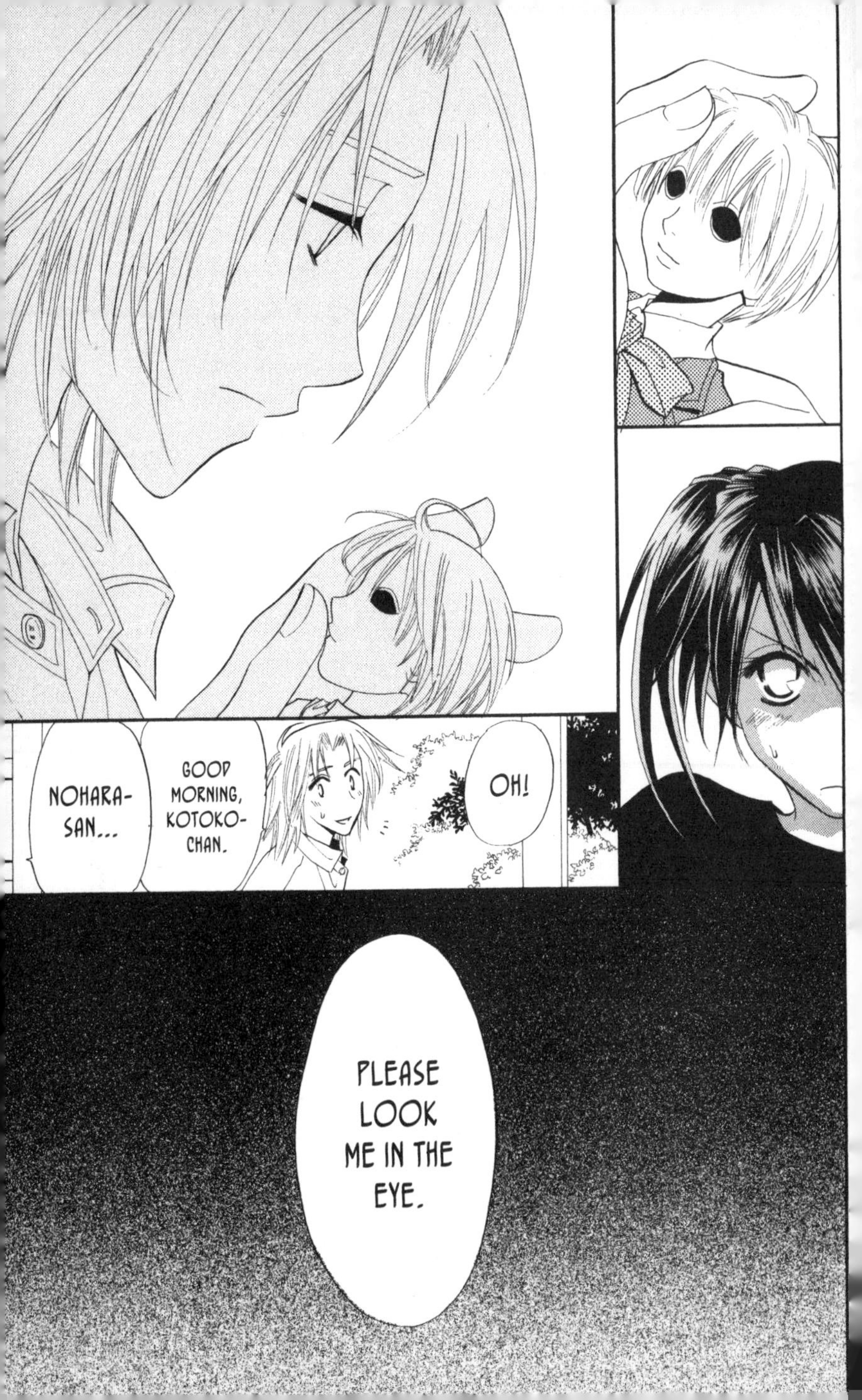
OH!
GOOD MORNING, KOTOKO-CHAN.
NOHARA-SAN...
PLEASE LOOK ME IN THE EYE.

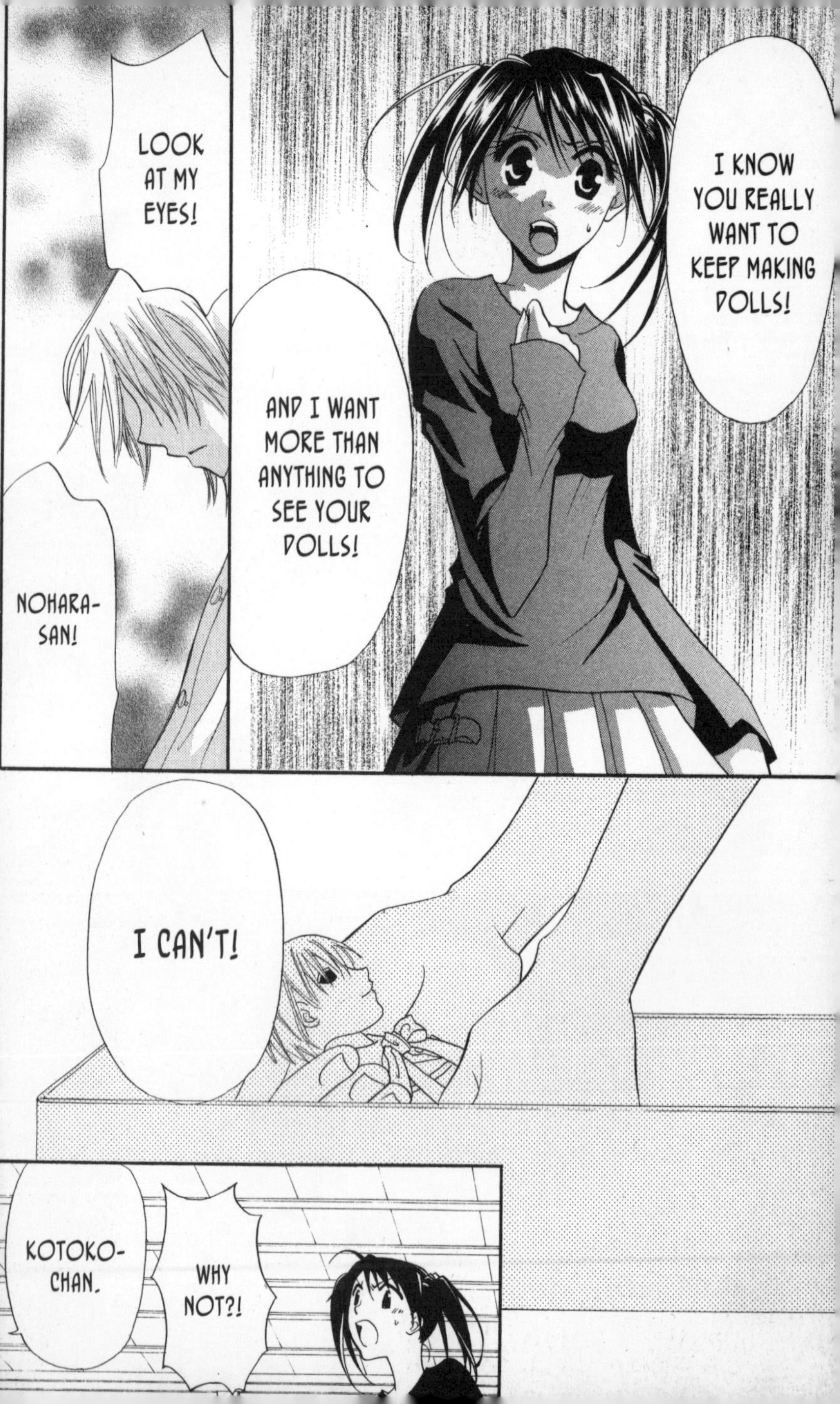
I KNOW YOU REALLY WANT TO KEEP MAKING DOLLS!
AND I WANT MORE THAN ANYTHING TO SEE YOUR DOLLS!
LOOK AT MY EYES!
NOHARA-SAN!
I CAN'T!
WHY NOT?!
KOTOKO-CHAN.

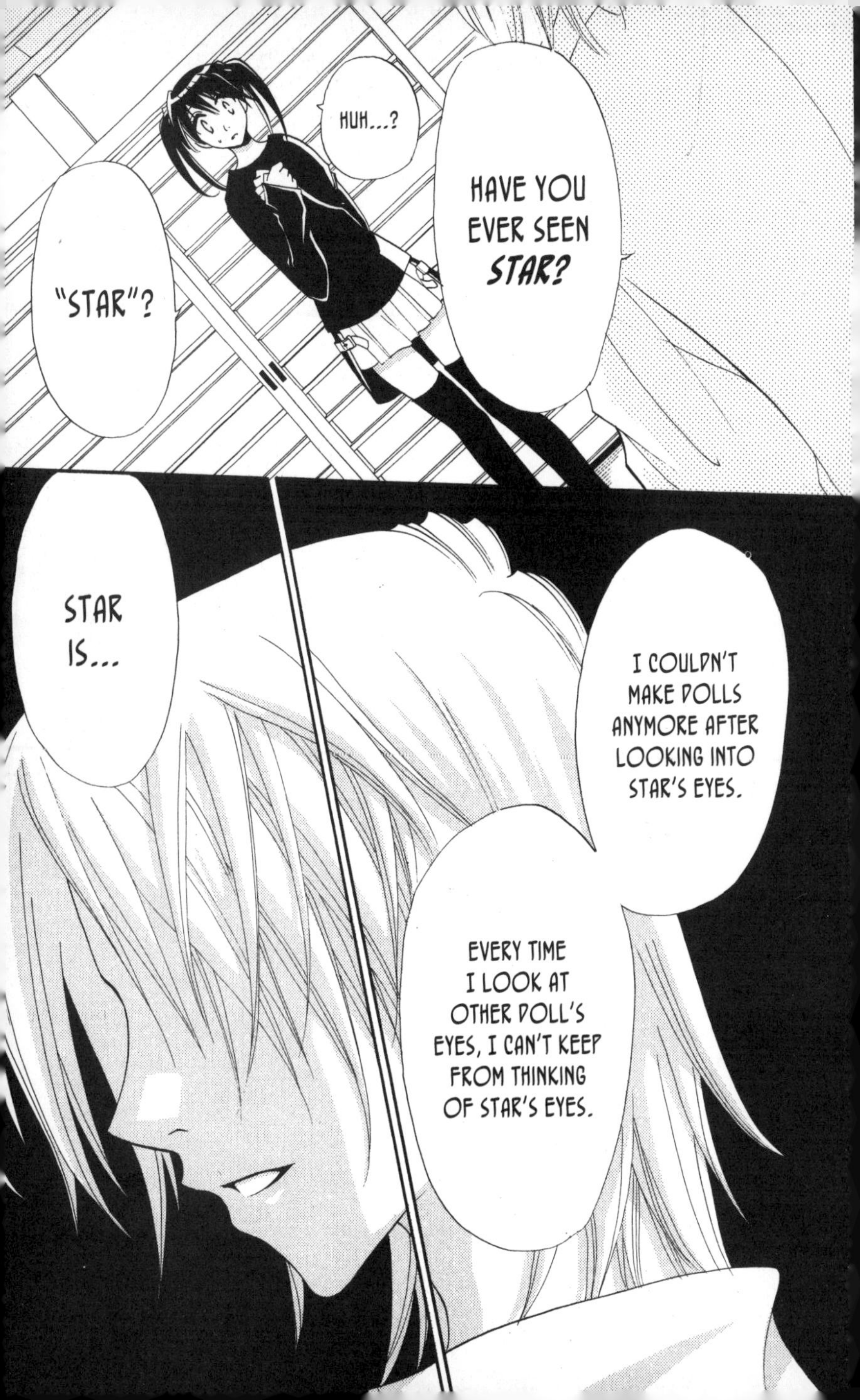
HAVE YOU EVER SEEN STAR?
HUH...?
"STAR"?
I COULDN'T MAKE DOLLS ANYMORE AFTER LOOKING INTO STAR'S EYES.
EVERY TIME I LOOK AT OTHER DOLL'S EYES, I CAN'T KEEP FROM THINKING OF STAR'S EYES.
STAR IS...

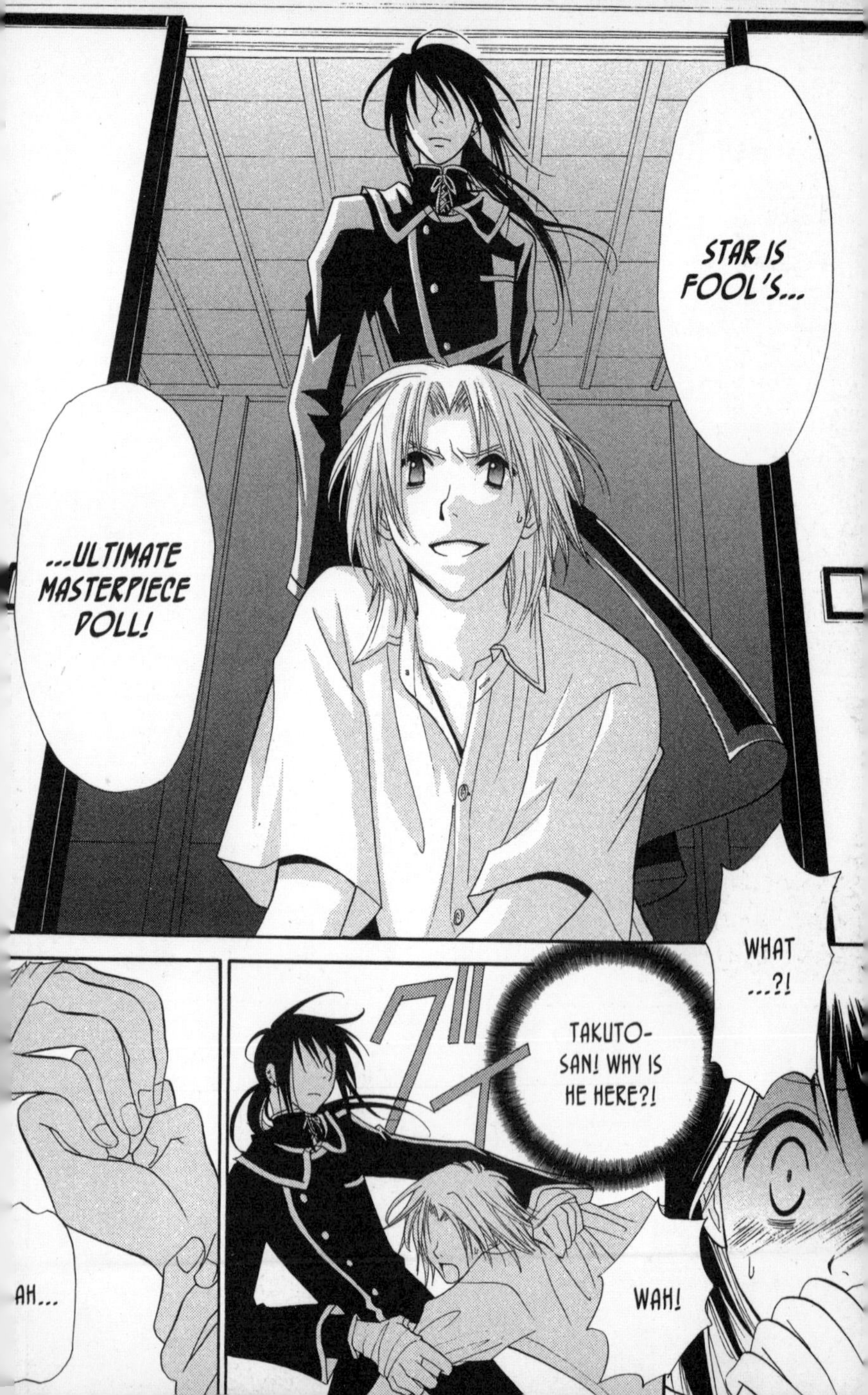
STAR IS FOOL'S...
...ULTIMATE MASTERPIECE DOLL!
WHAT ...?!
TAKUTO-SAN! WHY IS HE HERE?!
WAH!
AH...

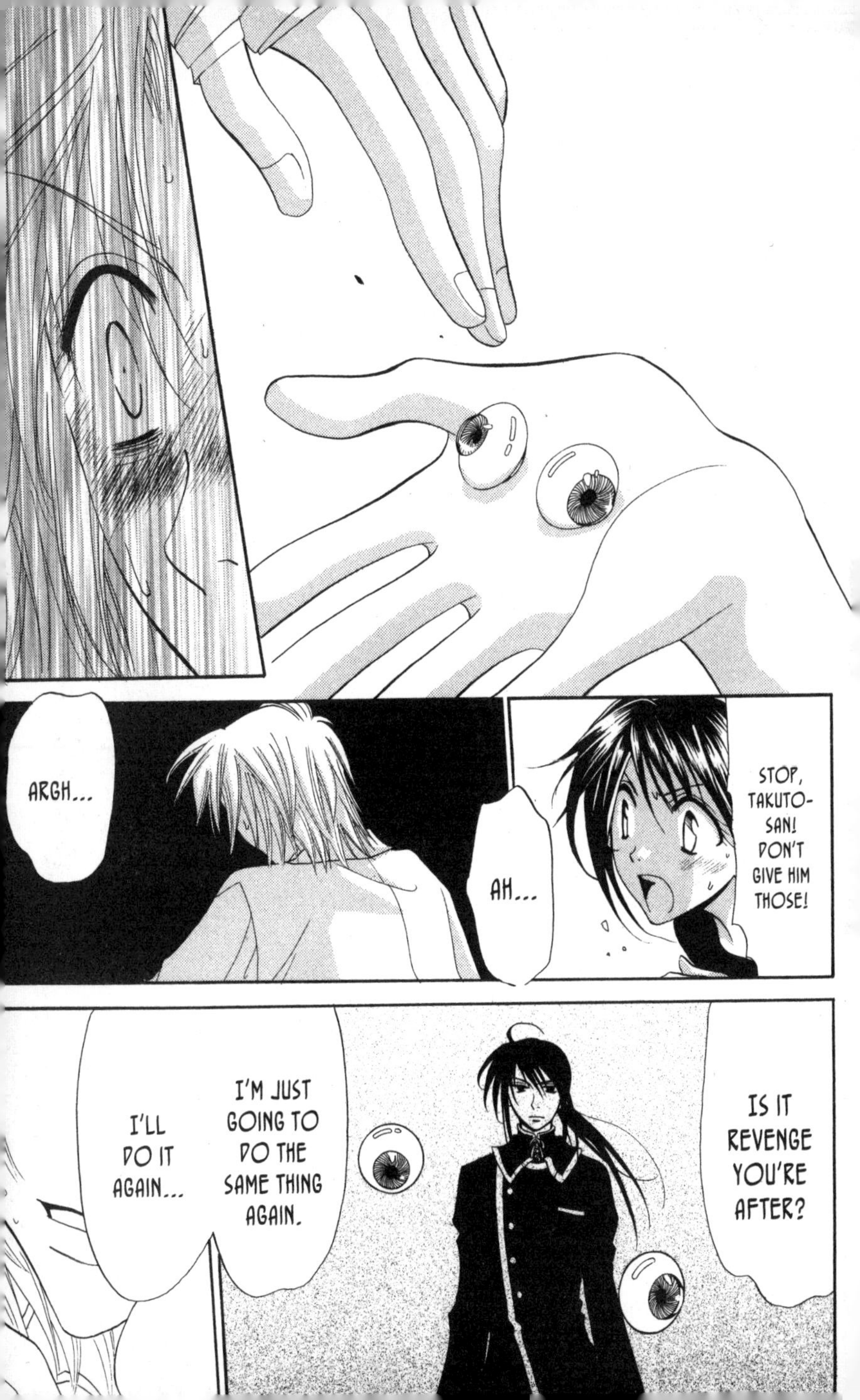
STOP, TAKUTO-SAN! DON'T GIVE HIM THOSE!
AH...
ARGH...
IS IT REVENGE YOU'RE AFTER?
I'M JUST GOING TO DO THE SAME THING AGAIN.
I'LL DO IT AGAIN...

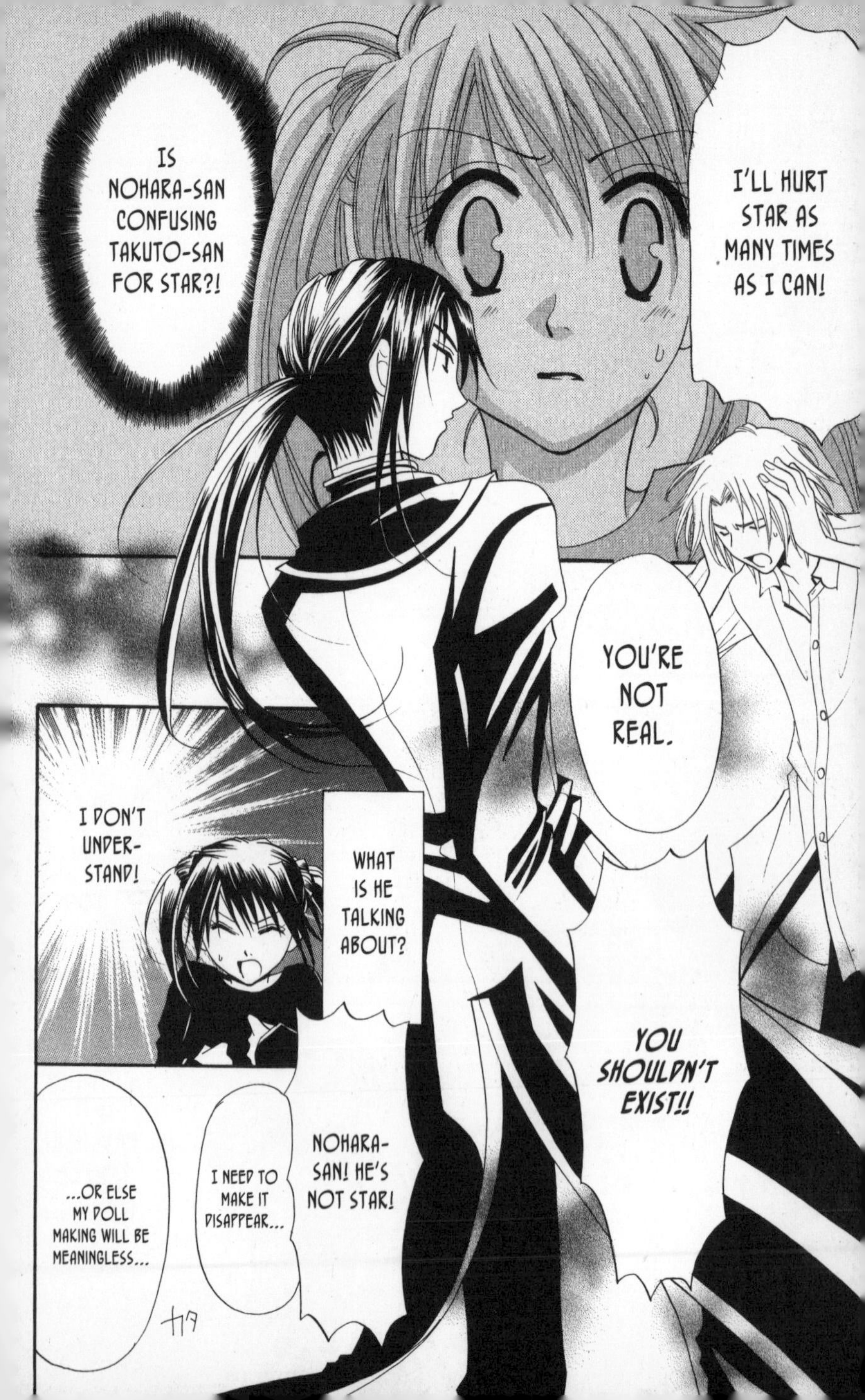
I'LL HURT STAR AS MANY TIMES AS I CAN!
IS NOHARA-SAN CONFUSING TAKUTO-SAN FOR STAR?!
YOU'RE NOT REAL.
YOU SHOULDN'T EXIST!!
WHAT IS HE TALKING ABOUT?
I DON'T UNDER-STAND!
NOHARA-SAN! HE'S NOT STAR!
I NEED TO MAKE IT DISAPPEAR...
...OR ELSE MY DOLL MAKING WILL BE MEANINGLESS...

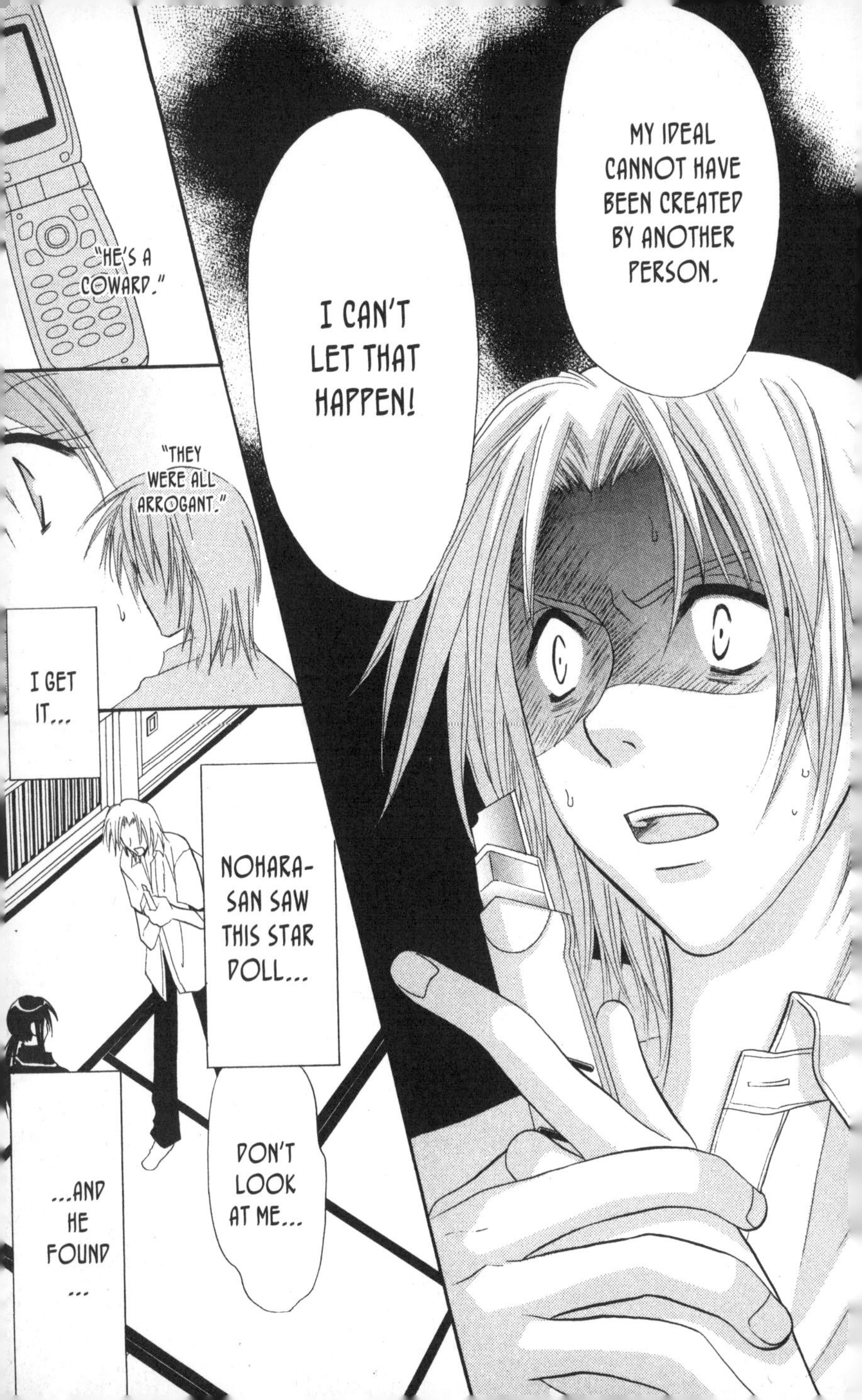
MY IDEAL CANNOT HAVE BEEN CREATED BY ANOTHER PERSON.
I CAN'T LET THAT HAPPEN!
"HE'S A COWARD."
"THEY WERE ALL ARROGANT."
I GET IT...
NOHARA-SAN SAW THIS STAR DOLL...
DON'T LOOK AT ME...
...AND HE FOUND ...

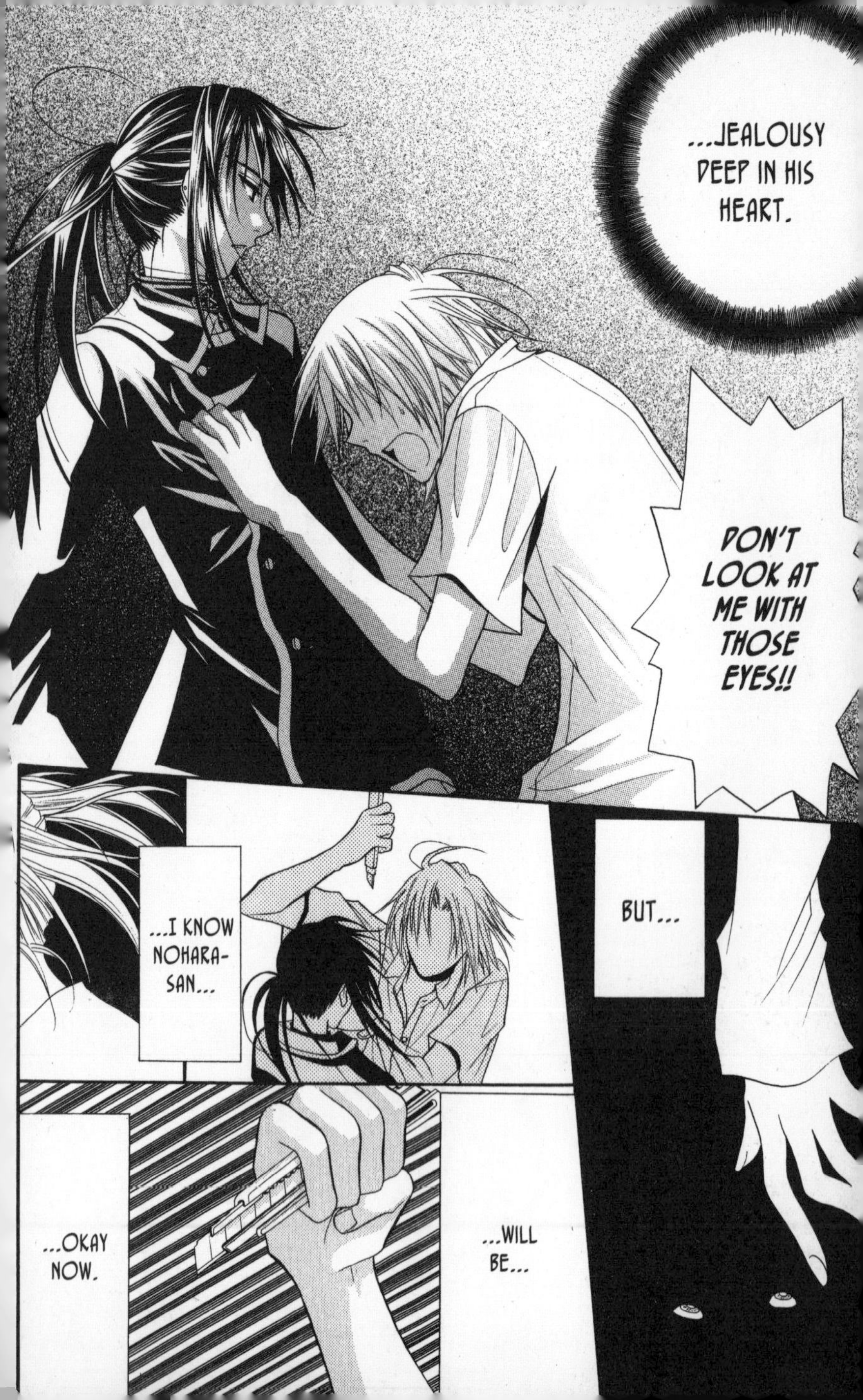
...JEALOUSY DEEP IN HIS HEART.
DON'T LOOK AT ME WITH THOSE EYES!!
BUT...
...I KNOW NOHARA-SAN...
...WILL BE...
...OKAY NOW.

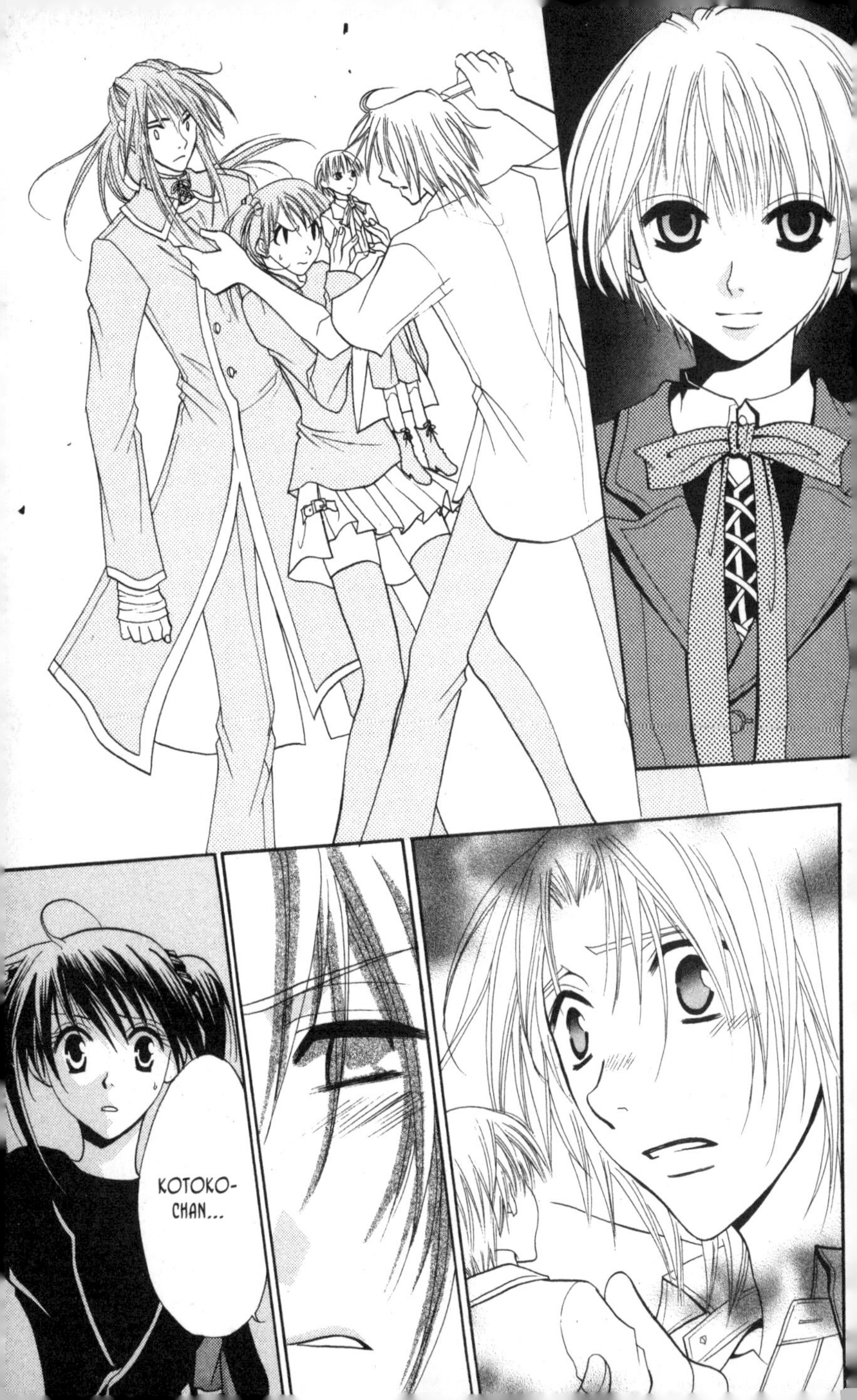
KOTOKO-CHAN...

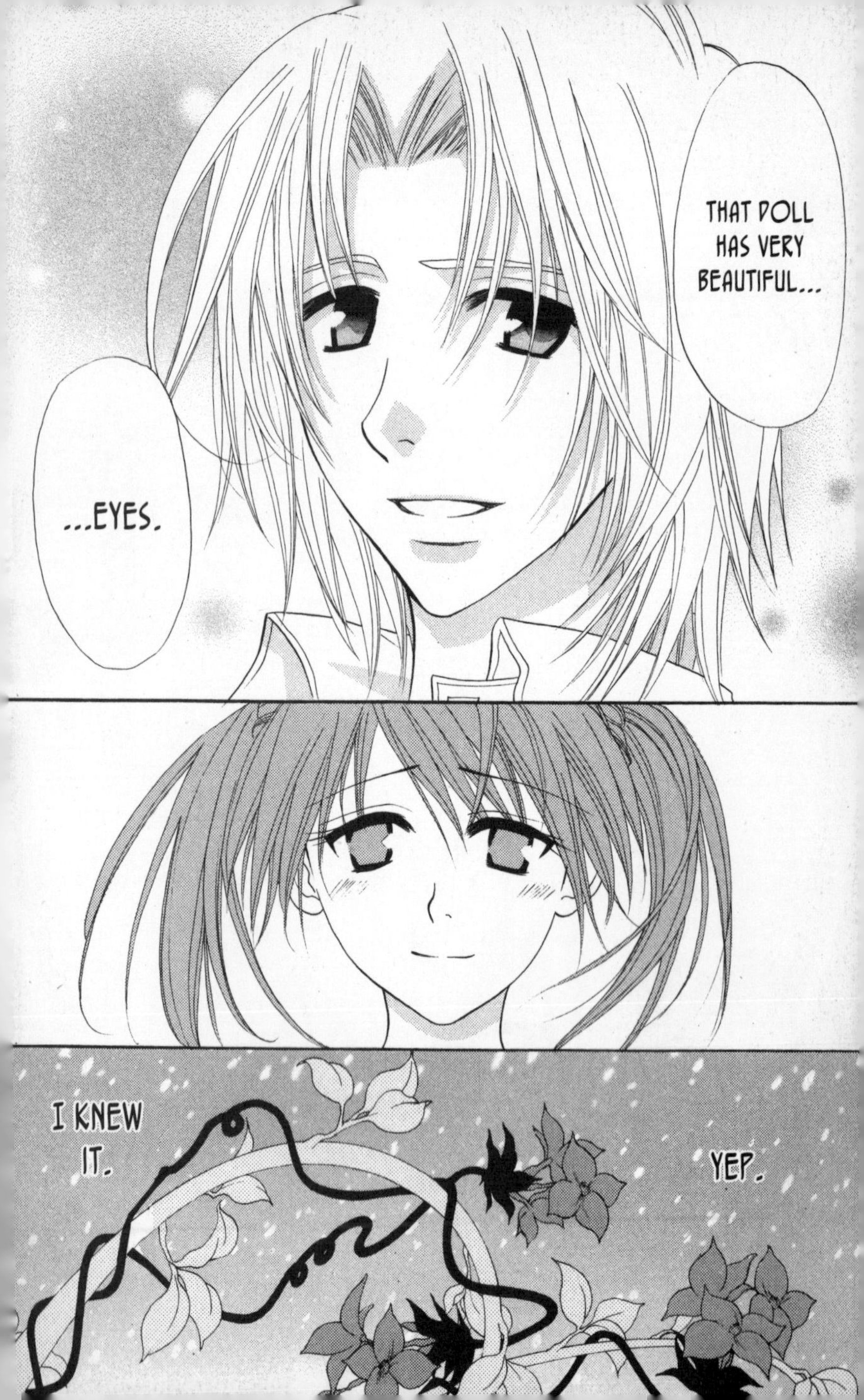
THAT DOLL HAS VERY BEAUTIFUL...
...EYES.
YEP.
I KNEW IT.

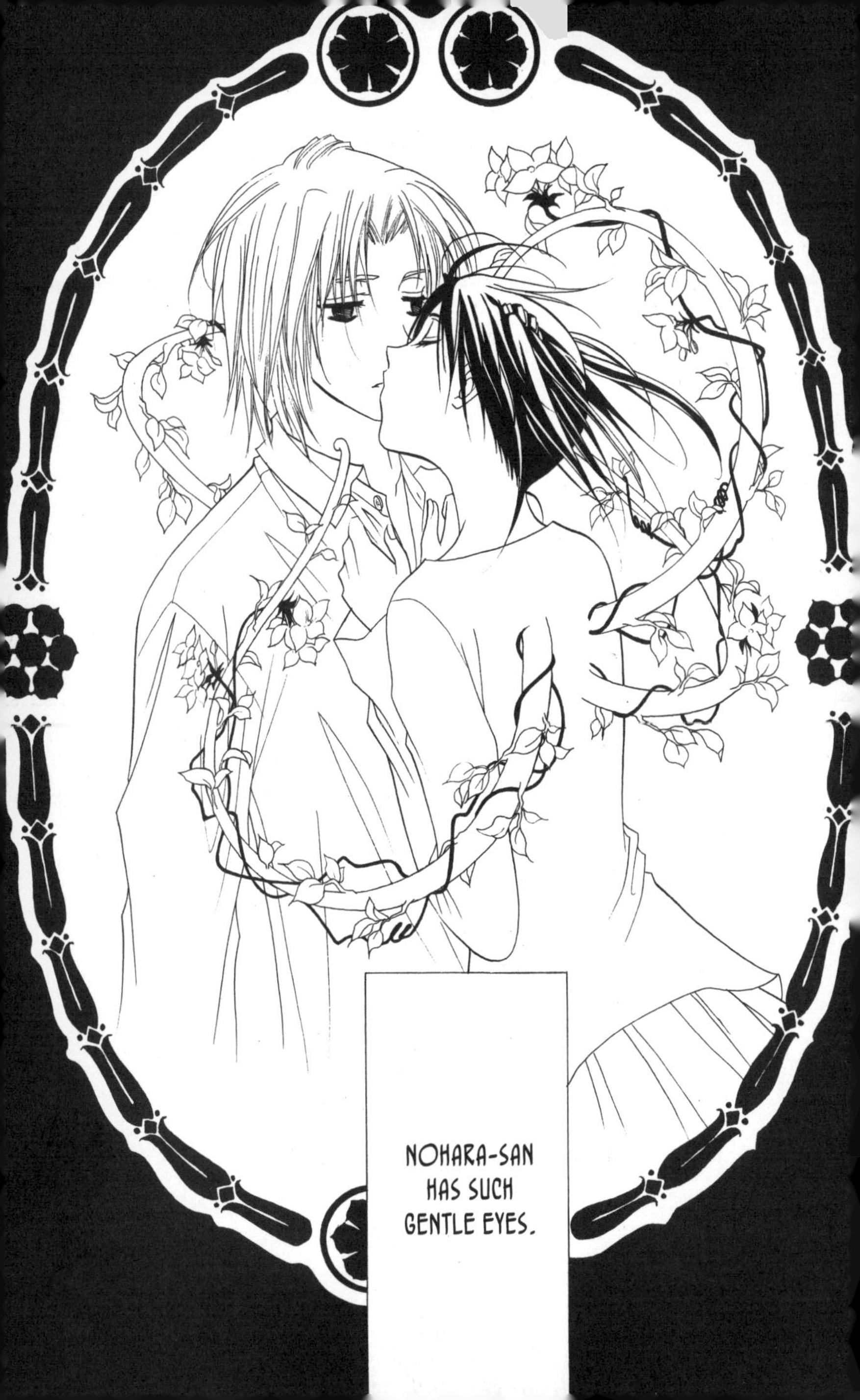
NOHARA-SAN HAS SUCH GENTLE EYES.

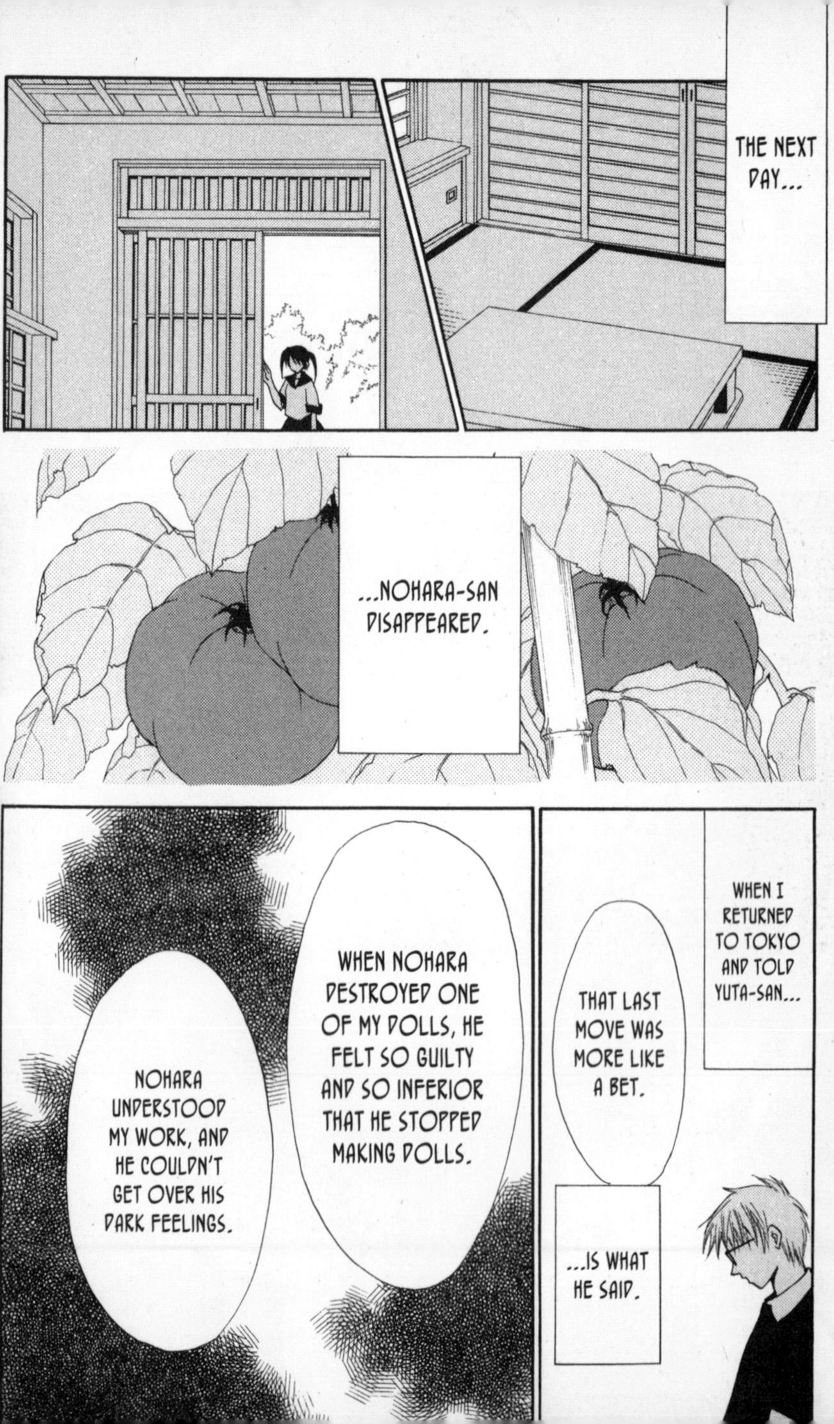
THE NEXT DAY...
...NOHARA-SAN DISAPPEARED.
WHEN I RETURNED TO TOKYO AND TOLD YUTA-SAN...
THAT LAST MOVE WAS MORE LIKE A BET.
...IS WHAT HE SAID.
WHEN NOHARA DESTROYED ONE OF MY DOLLS, HE FELT SO GUILTY AND SO INFERIOR THAT HE STOPPED MAKING DOLLS.
NOHARA UNDERSTOOD MY WORK, AND HE COULDN'T GET OVER HIS DARK FEELINGS.

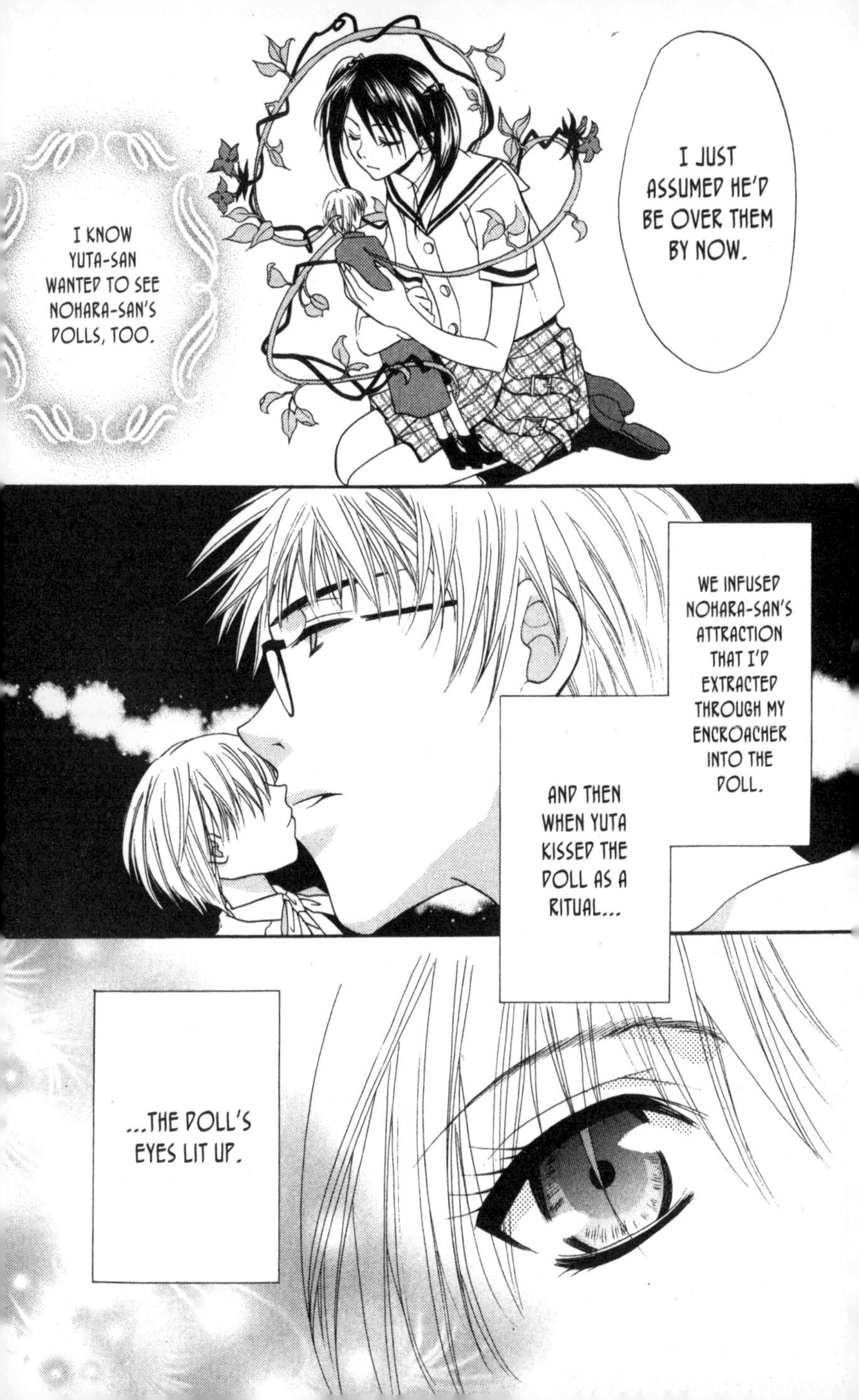
I JUST ASSUMED HE'D BE OVER THEM BY NOW.
I KNOW YUTA-SAN WANTED TO SEE NOHARA-SAN'S DOLLS, TOO.
WE INFUSED NOHARA-SAN'S ATTRACTION THAT I'D EXTRACTED THROUGH MY ENCROACHER INTO THE DOLL.
AND THEN WHEN YUTA KISSED THE DOLL AS A RITUAL...
...THE DOLL'S EYES LIT UP.

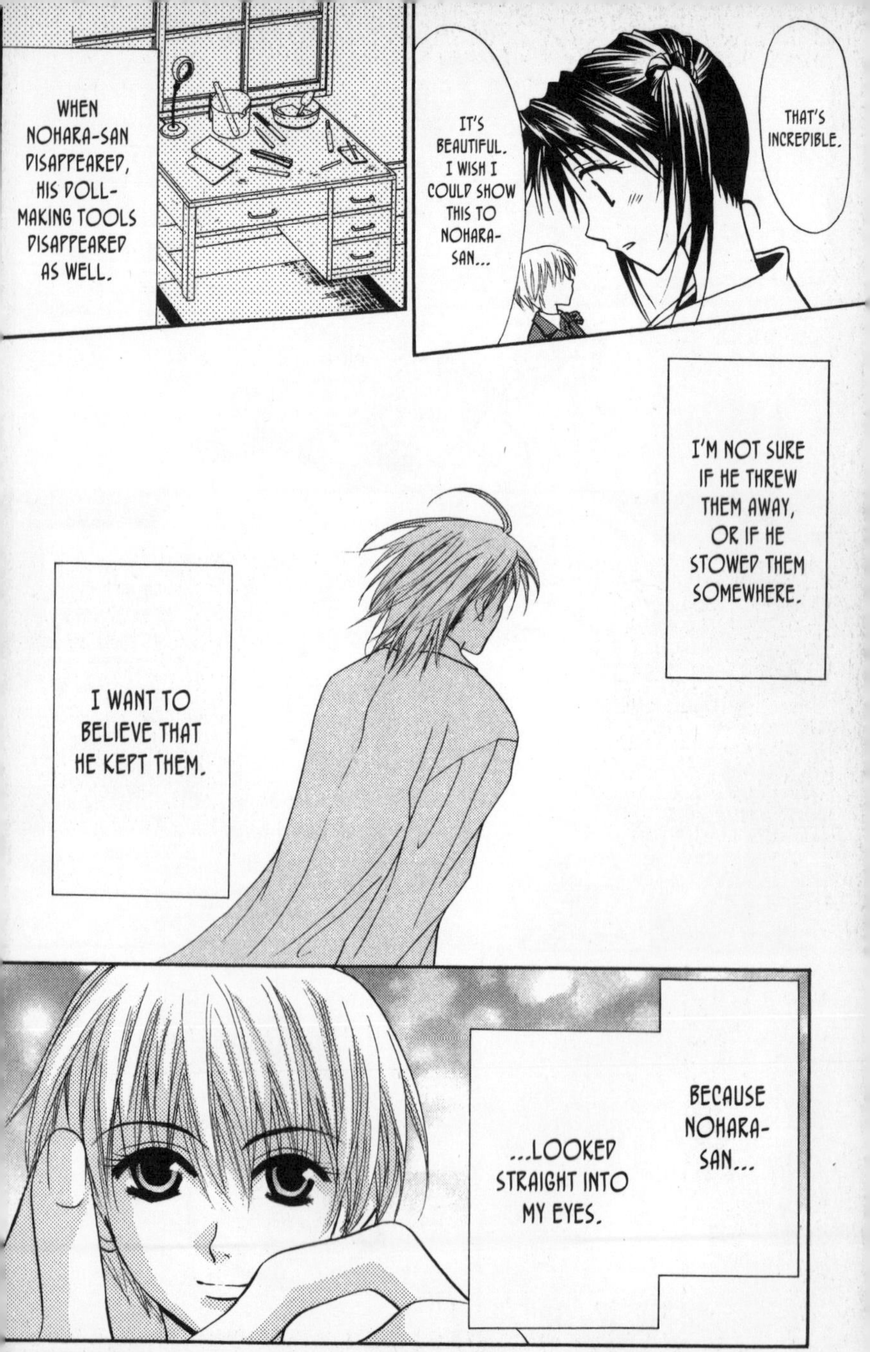
THAT'S INCREDIBLE.
IT'S BEAUTIFUL. I WISH I COULD SHOW THIS TO NOHARA-SAN...
WHEN NOHARA-SAN DISAPPEARED, HIS DOLL-MAKING TOOLS DISAPPEARED AS WELL.
I'M NOT SURE IF HE THREW THEM AWAY, OR IF HE STOWED THEM SOMEWHERE.
I WANT TO BELIEVE THAT HE KEPT THEM.
BECAUSE NOHARA-SAN...
...LOOKED STRAIGHT INTO MY EYES.

3 End

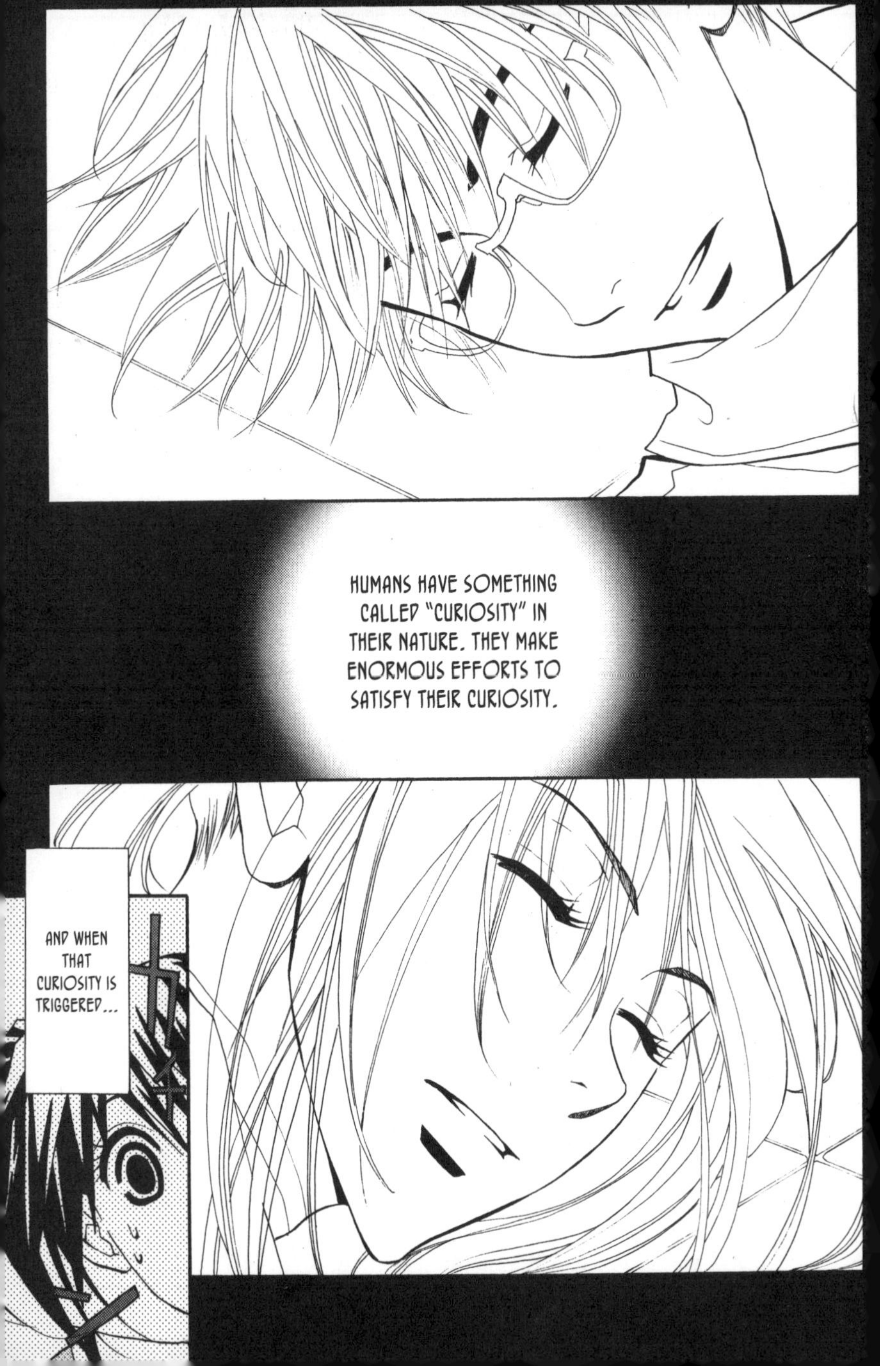
HUMANS HAVE SOMETHING CALLED "CURIOSITY" IN THEIR NATURE. THEY MAKE ENORMOUS EFFORTS TO SATISFY THEIR CURIOSITY.
AND WHEN THAT CURIOSITY IS TRIGGERED...

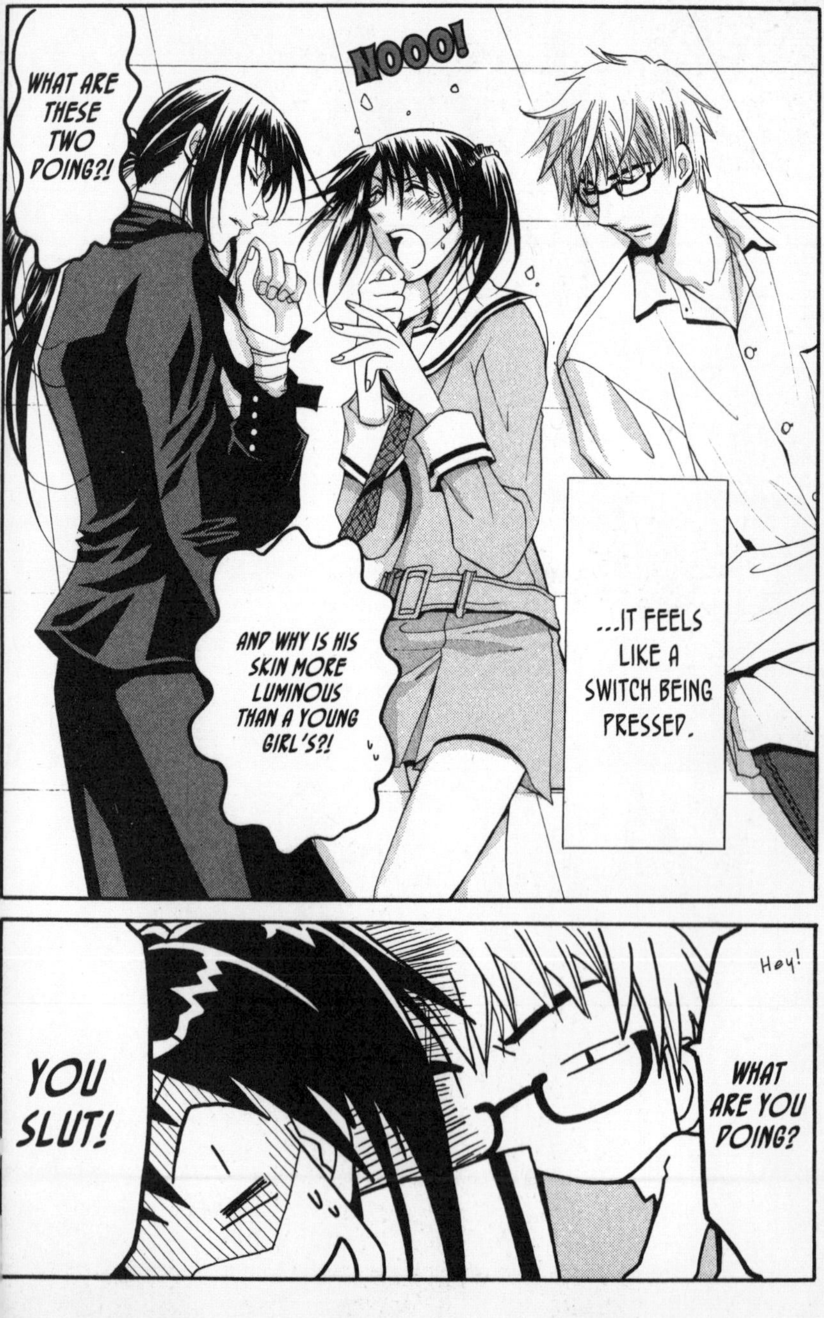
NOOO!
WHAT ARE THESE TWO DOING?!
...IT FEELS LIKE A SWITCH BEING PRESSED.
AND WHY IS HIS SKIN MORE LUMINOUS THAN A YOUNG GIRL'S?!
Hey!
WHAT ARE YOU DOING?
YOU SLUT!

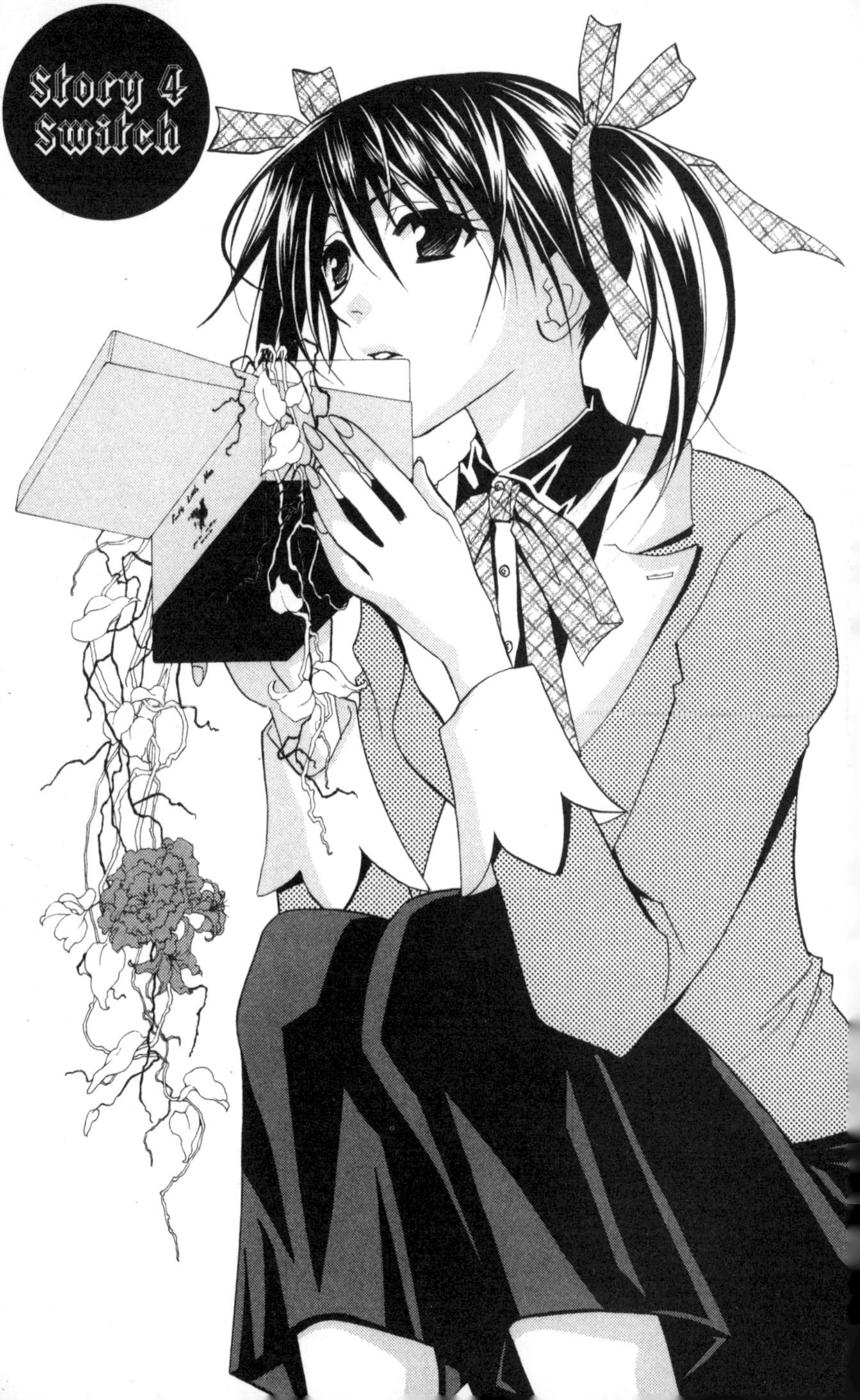
Story 4
switch

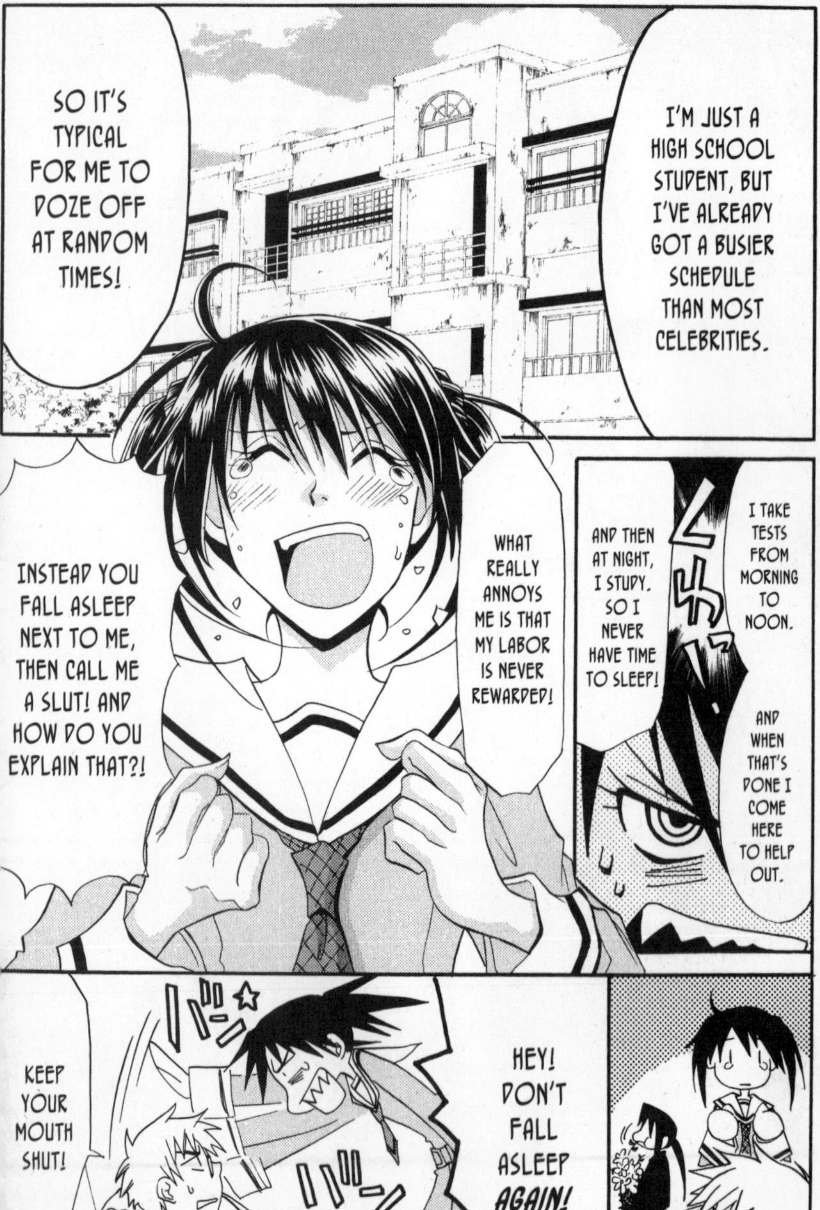
I'M JUST A HIGH SCHOOL STUDENT, BUT I'VE ALREADY GOT A BUSIER SCHEDULE THAN MOST CELEBRITIES.
SO IT'S TYPICAL FOR ME TO DOZE OFF AT RANDOM TIMES!
I TAKE TESTS FROM MORNING TO NOON.
AND THEN AT NIGHT, I STUDY. SO I NEVER HAVE TIME TO SLEEP!
AND WHEN THAT'S DONE I COME HERE TO HELP OUT.
WHAT REALLY ANNOYS ME IS THAT MY LABOR IS NEVER REWARDED!
INSTEAD YOU FALL ASLEEP NEXT TO ME, THEN CALL ME A SLUT! AND HOW DO YOU EXPLAIN THAT?!
HEY! DON'T FALL ASLEEP AGAIN!
KEEP YOUR MOUTH SHUT!

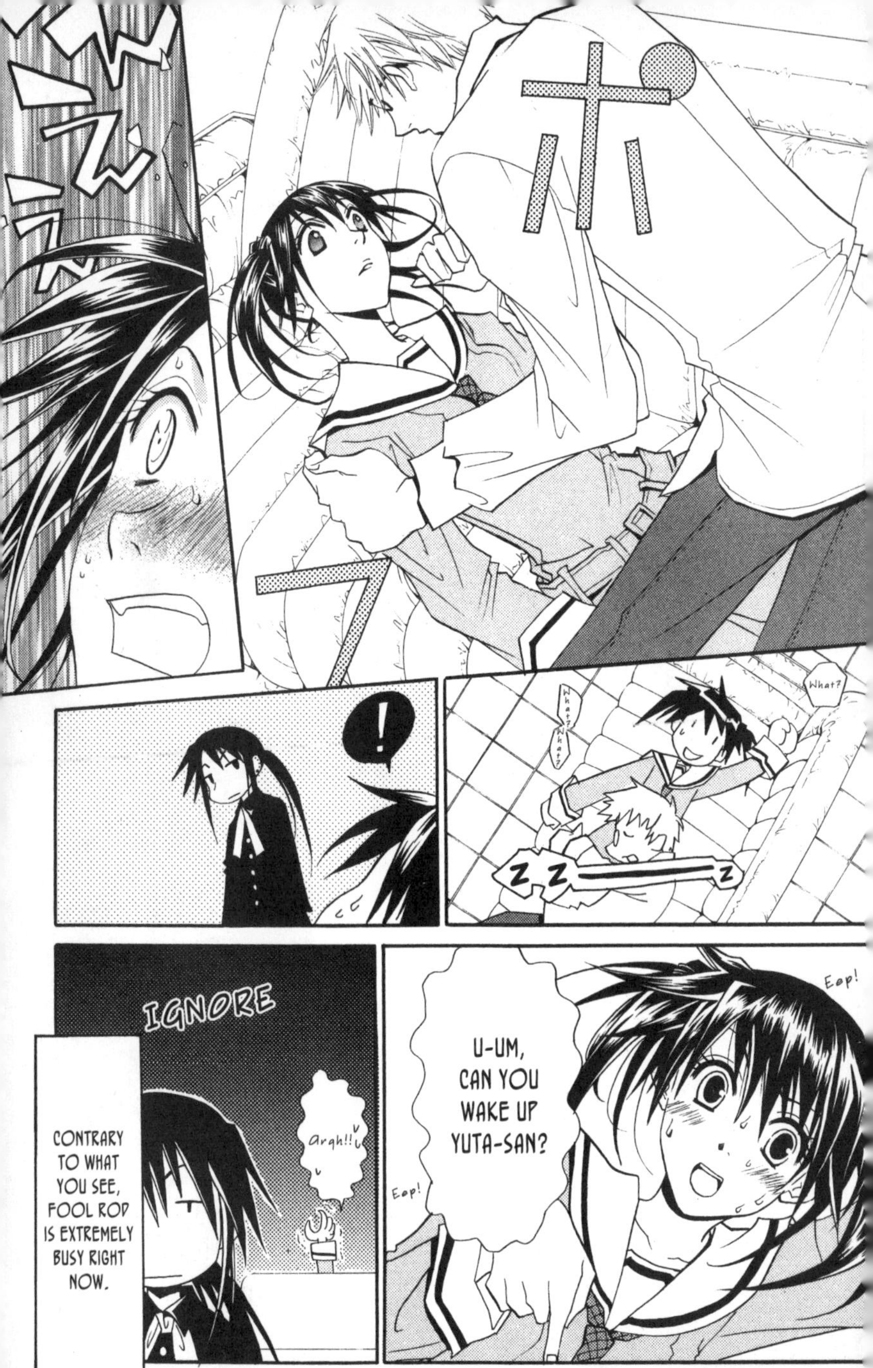

ポ
What?
What? What? What?
Z Z Z
!
Eep!
U-UM, CAN YOU WAKE UP YUTA-SAN?
Eep!
IGNORE
Argh!!
CONTRARY TO WHAT YOU SEE, FOOL ROD IS EXTREMELY BUSY RIGHT NOW.

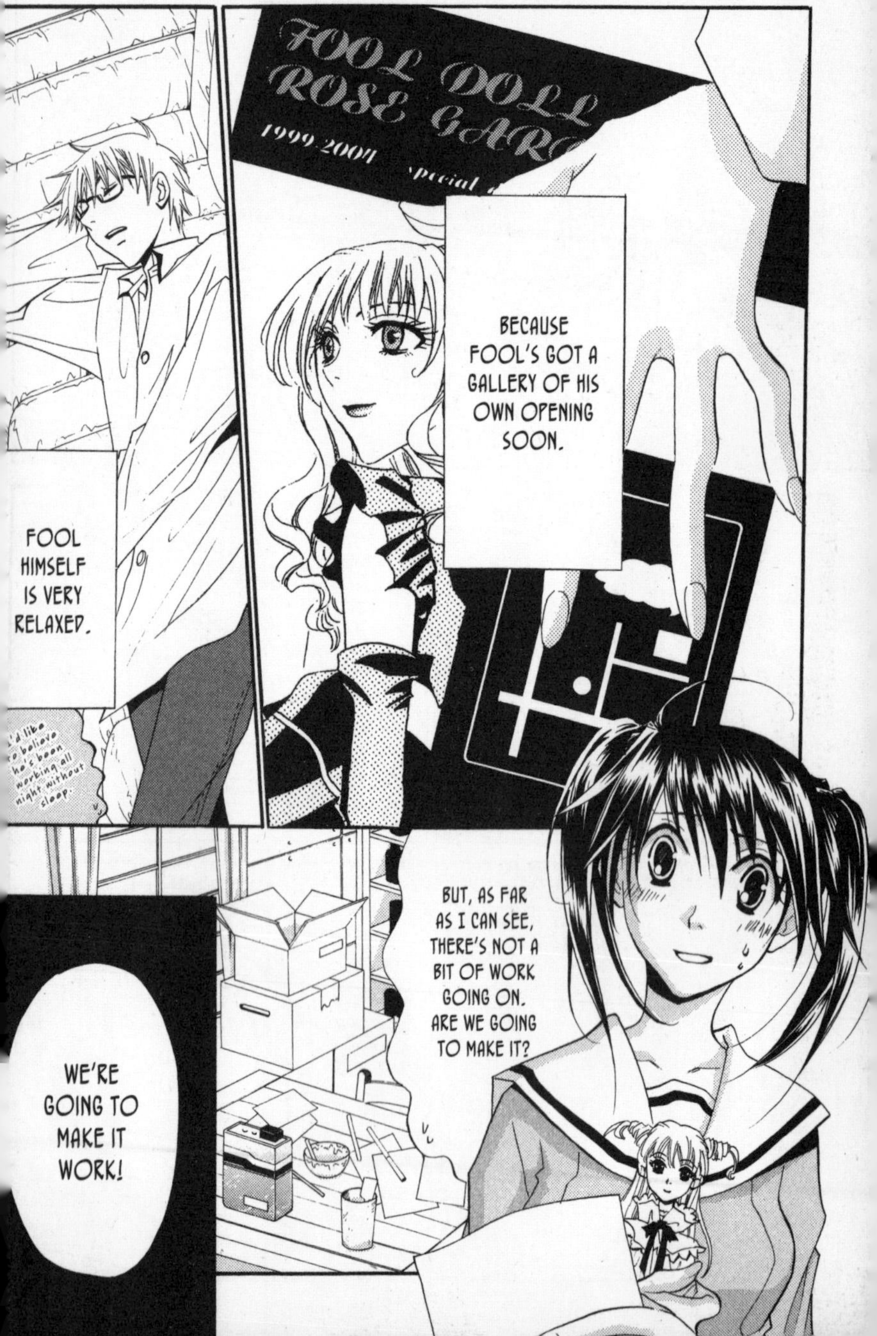
FOOL DOLL
ROSE GAR
1999-2004 special
BECAUSE FOOL'S GOT A GALLERY OF HIS OWN OPENING SOON.
FOOL HIMSELF IS VERY RELAXED.
'd like to believe he's been working all night without sleep.
BUT, AS FAR AS I CAN SEE, THERE'S NOT A BIT OF WORK GOING ON. ARE WE GOING TO MAKE IT?
WE'RE GOING TO MAKE IT WORK!

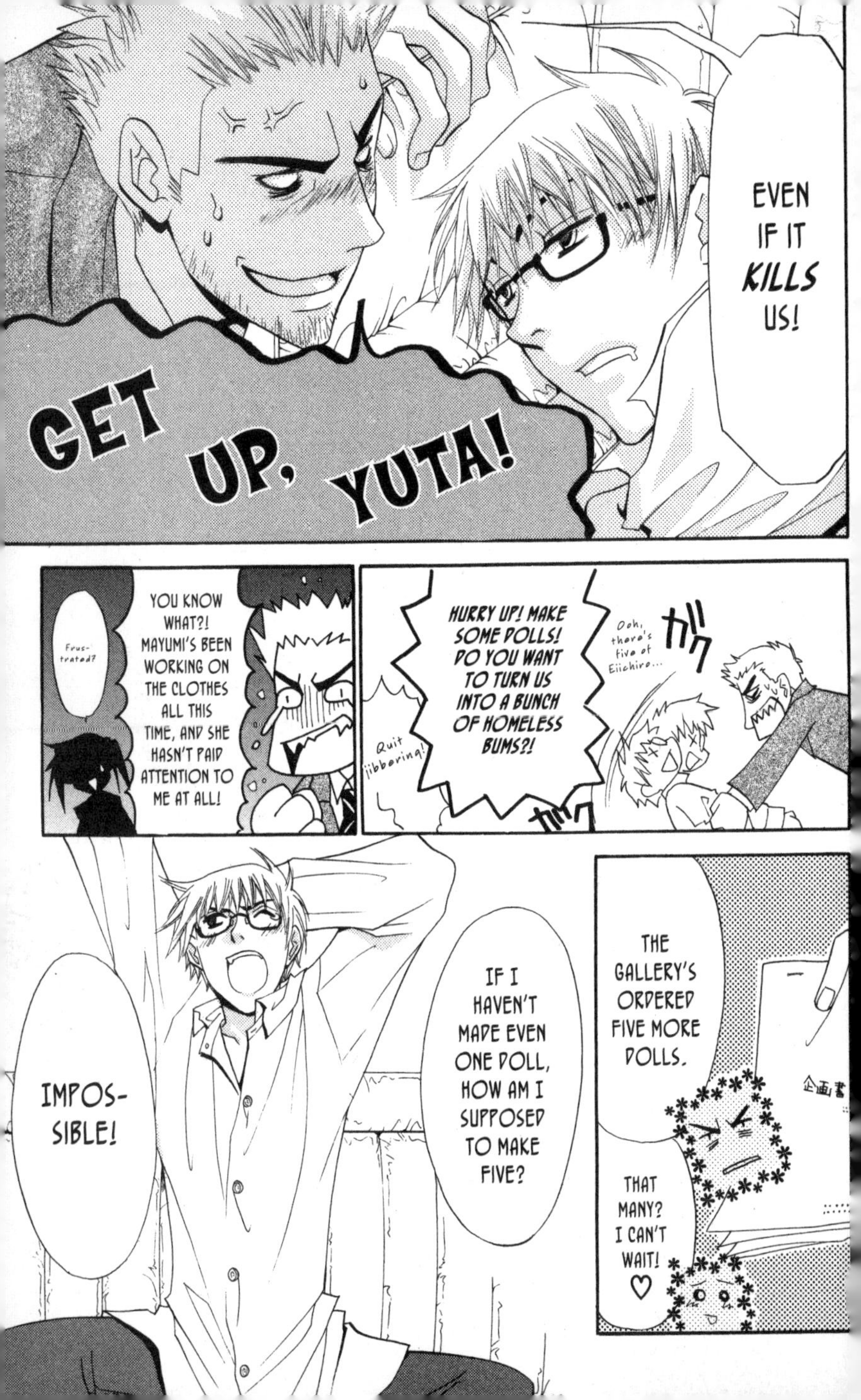
EVEN IF IT KILLS US!
GET UP, YUTA!
HURRY UP! MAKE SOME DOLLS! DO YOU WANT TO TURN US INTO A BUNCH OF HOMELESS BUMS?!
ガク
Ooh, there's five of Eiichiro...
Quit jibbering!
ガク
YOU KNOW WHAT?! MAYUMI'S BEEN WORKING ON THE CLOTHES ALL THIS TIME, AND SHE HASN'T PAID ATTENTION TO ME AT ALL!
Frus-trated?
THE GALLERY'S ORDERED FIVE MORE DOLLS.
企画書
THAT MANY? I CAN'T WAIT! ♡
IF I HAVEN'T MADE EVEN ONE DOLL, HOW AM I SUPPOSED TO MAKE FIVE?
IMPOS-SIBLE!

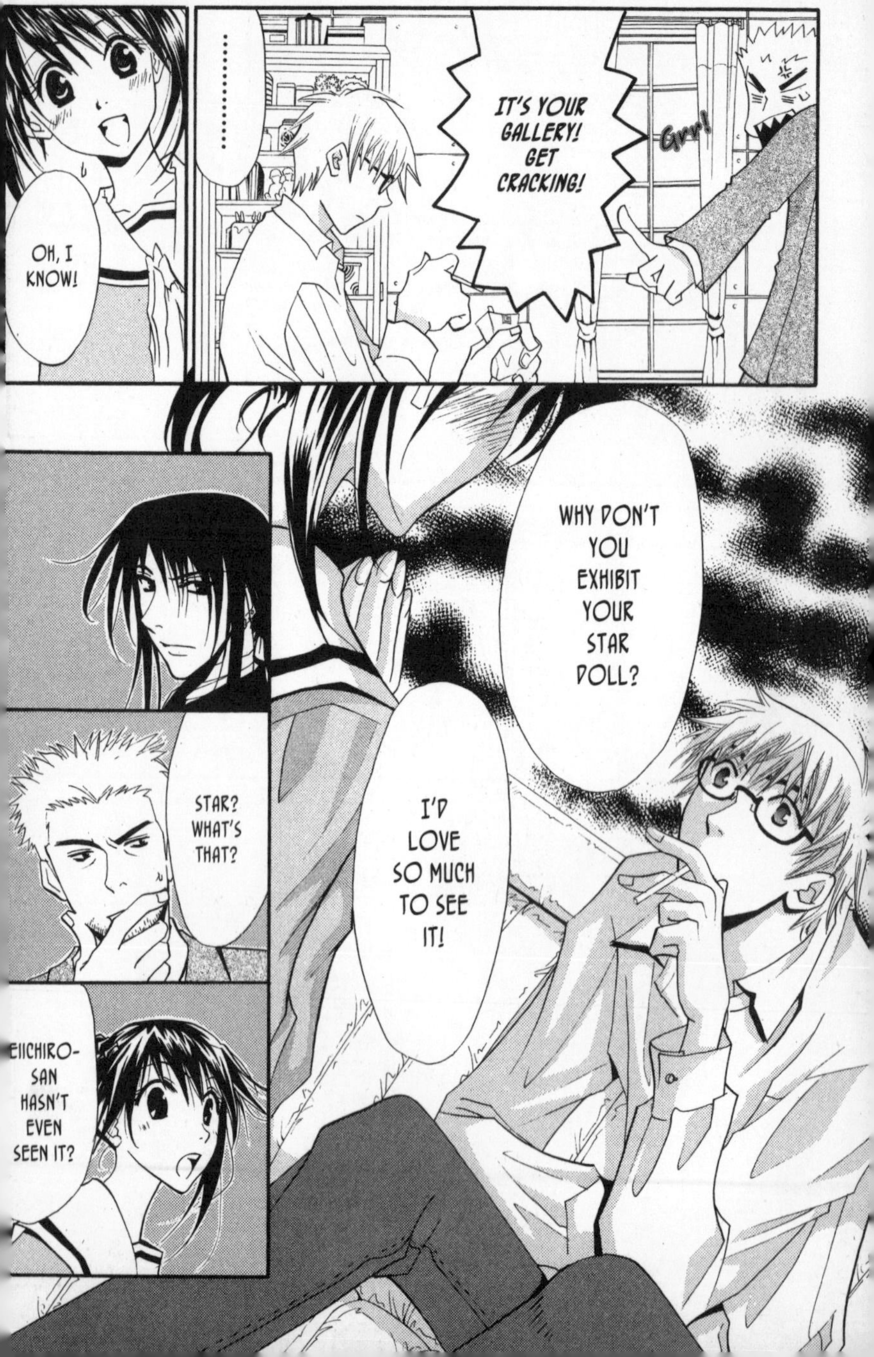
Grr!
IT'S YOUR GALLERY! GET CRACKING!
......
OH, I KNOW!
WHY DON'T YOU EXHIBIT YOUR STAR DOLL?
I'D LOVE SO MUCH TO SEE IT!
STAR? WHAT'S THAT?
EIICHIRO-SAN HASN'T EVEN SEEN IT?

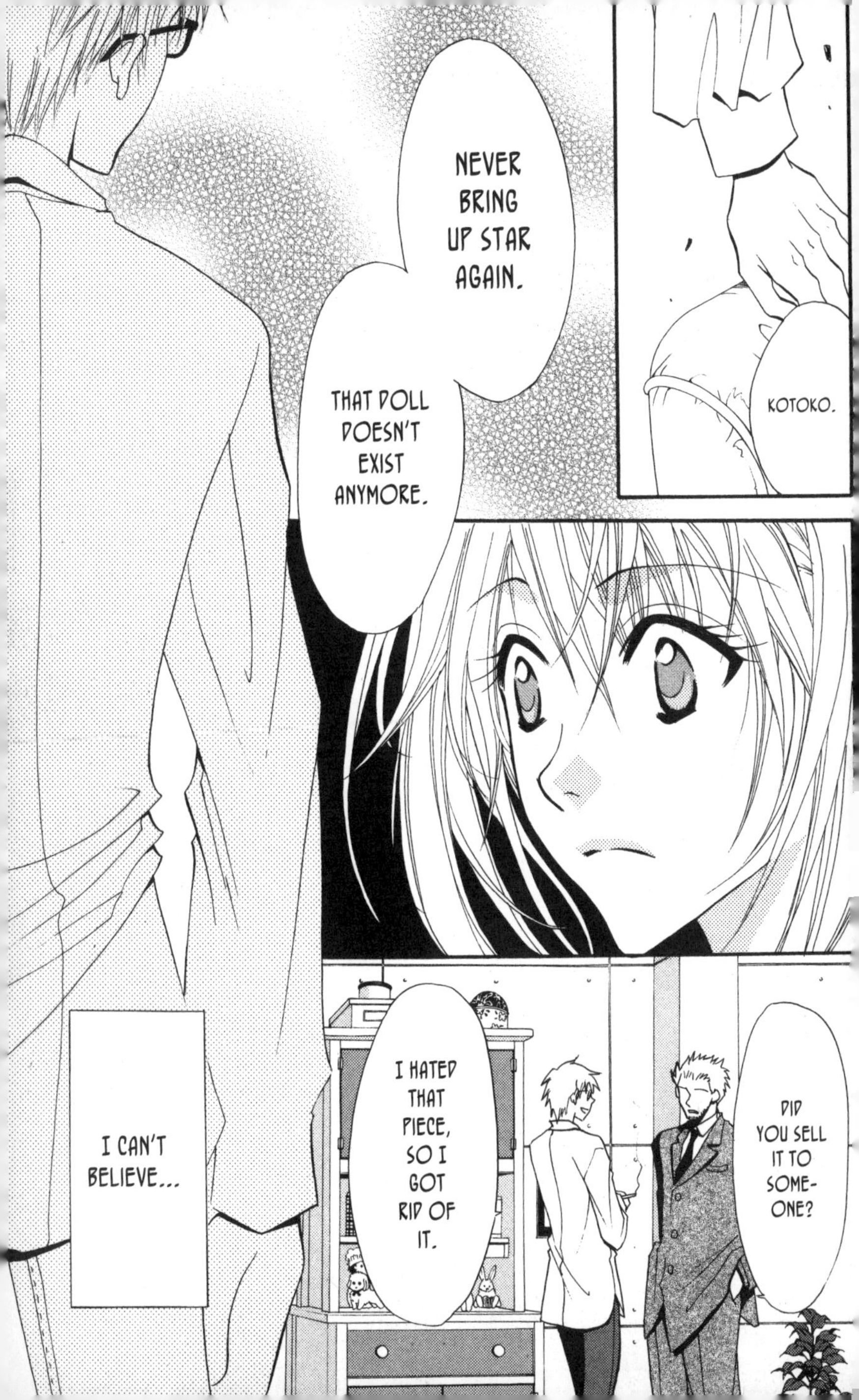
KOTOKO.
NEVER BRING UP STAR AGAIN.
THAT DOLL DOESN'T EXIST ANYMORE.
DID YOU SELL IT TO SOME-ONE?
I HATED THAT PIECE, SO I GOT RID OF IT.
I CAN'T BELIEVE...

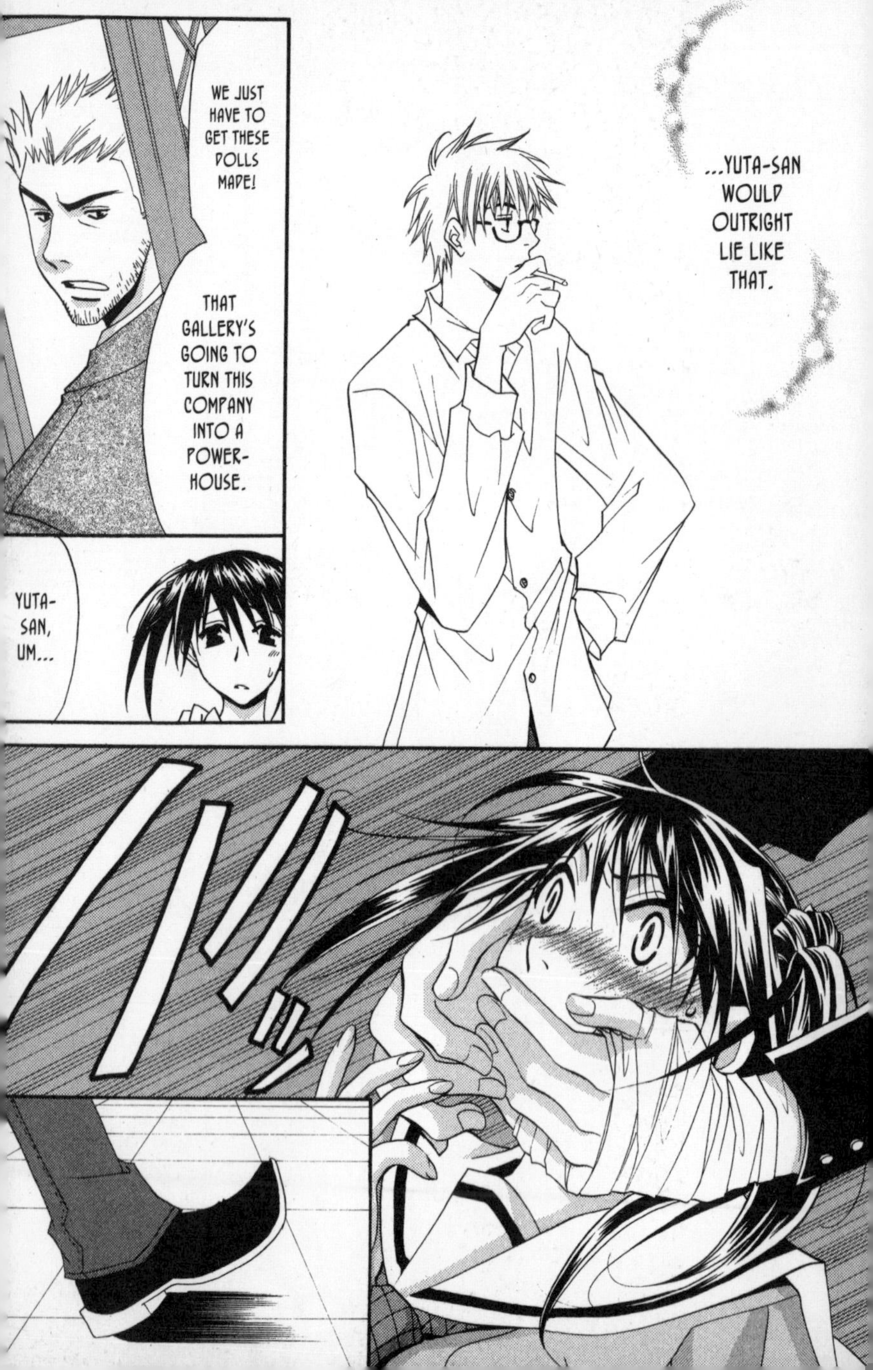
...YUTA-SAN WOULD OUTRIGHT LIE LIKE THAT.
WE JUST HAVE TO GET THESE DOLLS MADE!
THAT GALLERY'S GOING TO TURN THIS COMPANY INTO A POWER-HOUSE.
YUTA-SAN, UM...

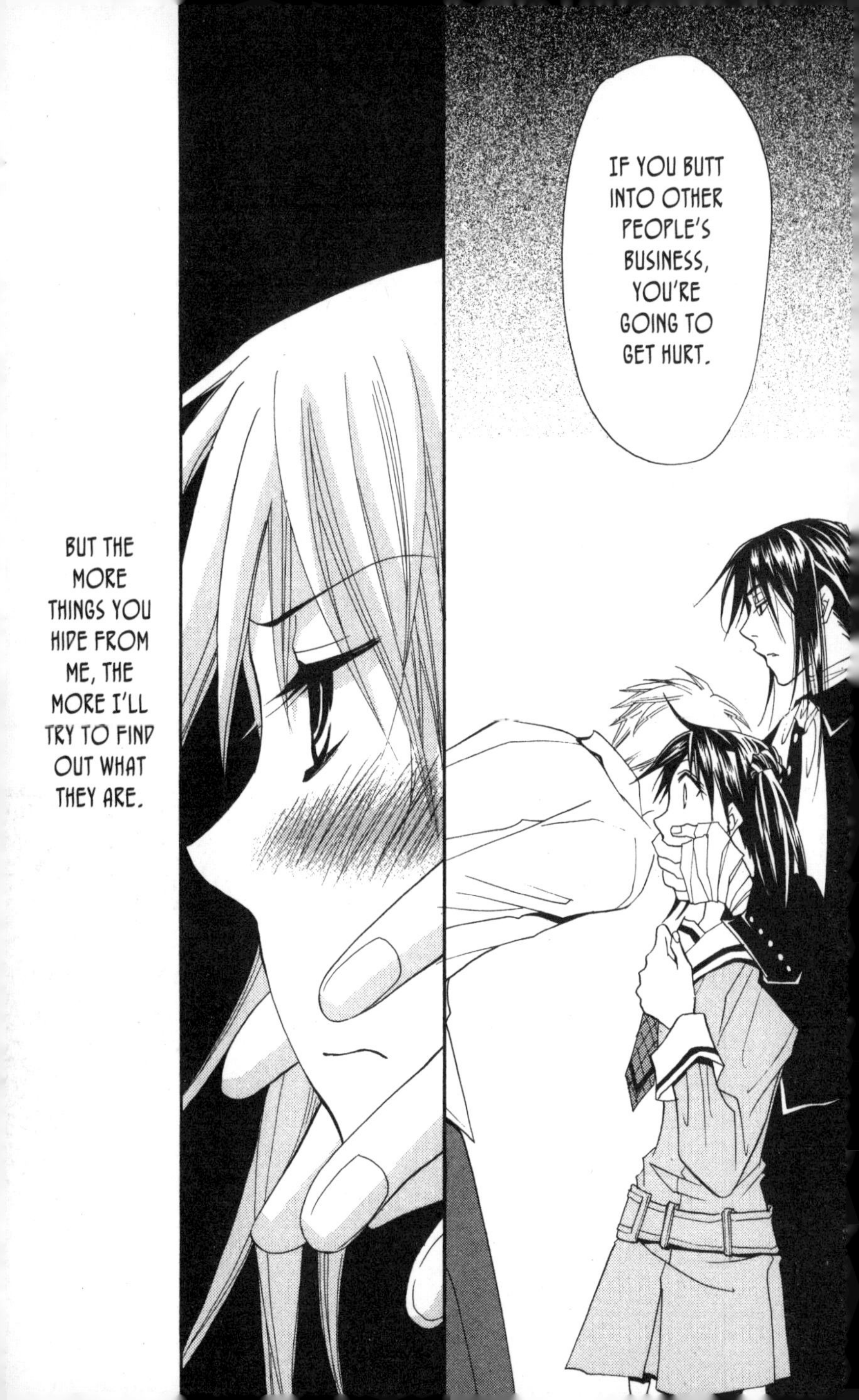
IF YOU BUTT INTO OTHER PEOPLE'S BUSINESS, YOU'RE GOING TO GET HURT.
BUT THE MORE THINGS YOU HIDE FROM ME, THE MORE I'LL TRY TO FIND OUT WHAT THEY ARE.

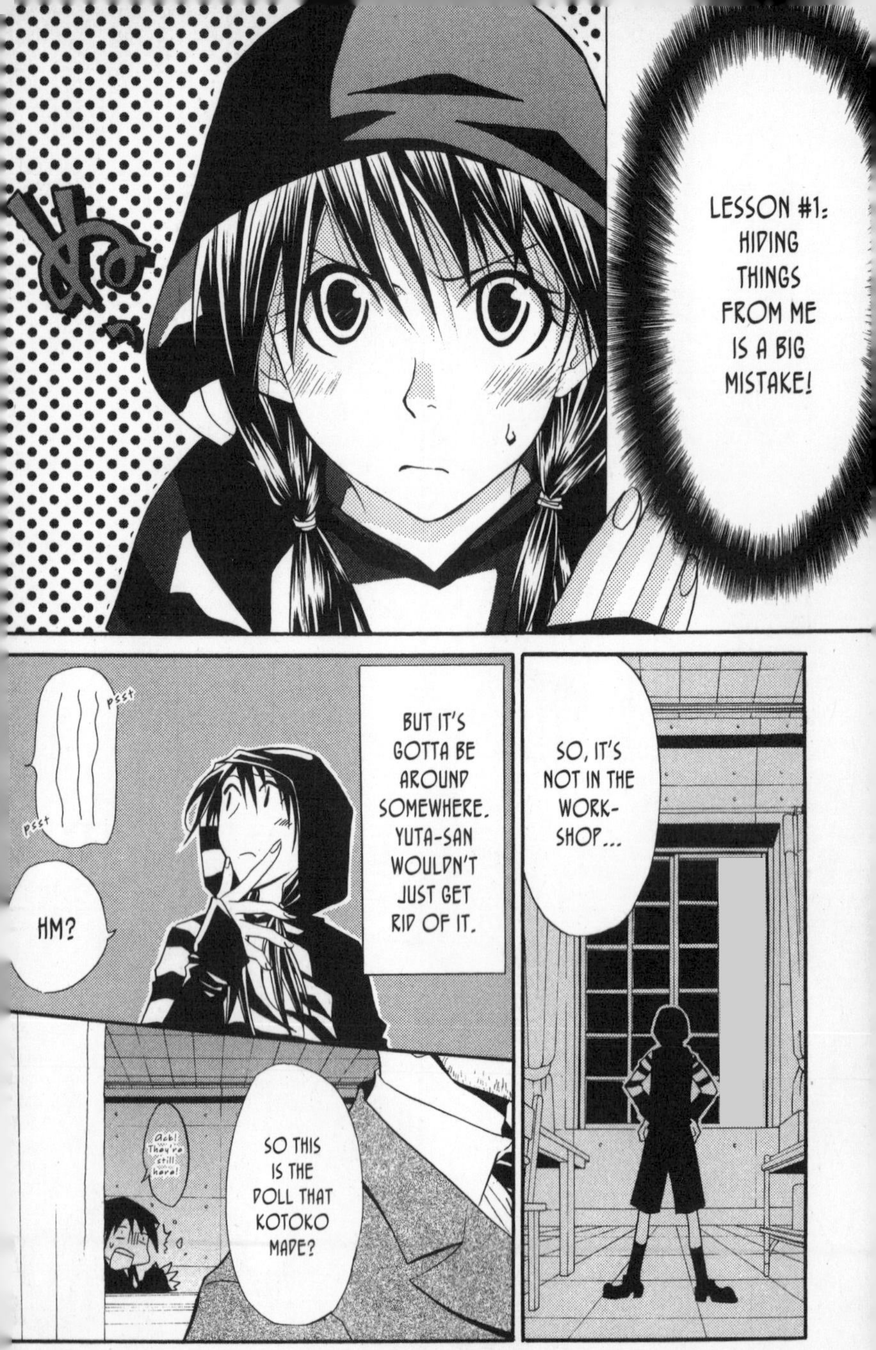
LESSON #1: HIDING THINGS FROM ME IS A BIG MISTAKE!
SO, IT'S NOT IN THE WORK-SHOP...
BUT IT'S GOTTA BE AROUND SOMEWHERE. YUTA-SAN WOULDN'T JUST GET RID OF IT.
psst
psst
HM?
SO THIS IS THE DOLL THAT KOTOKO MADE?
Ack! They're still here!

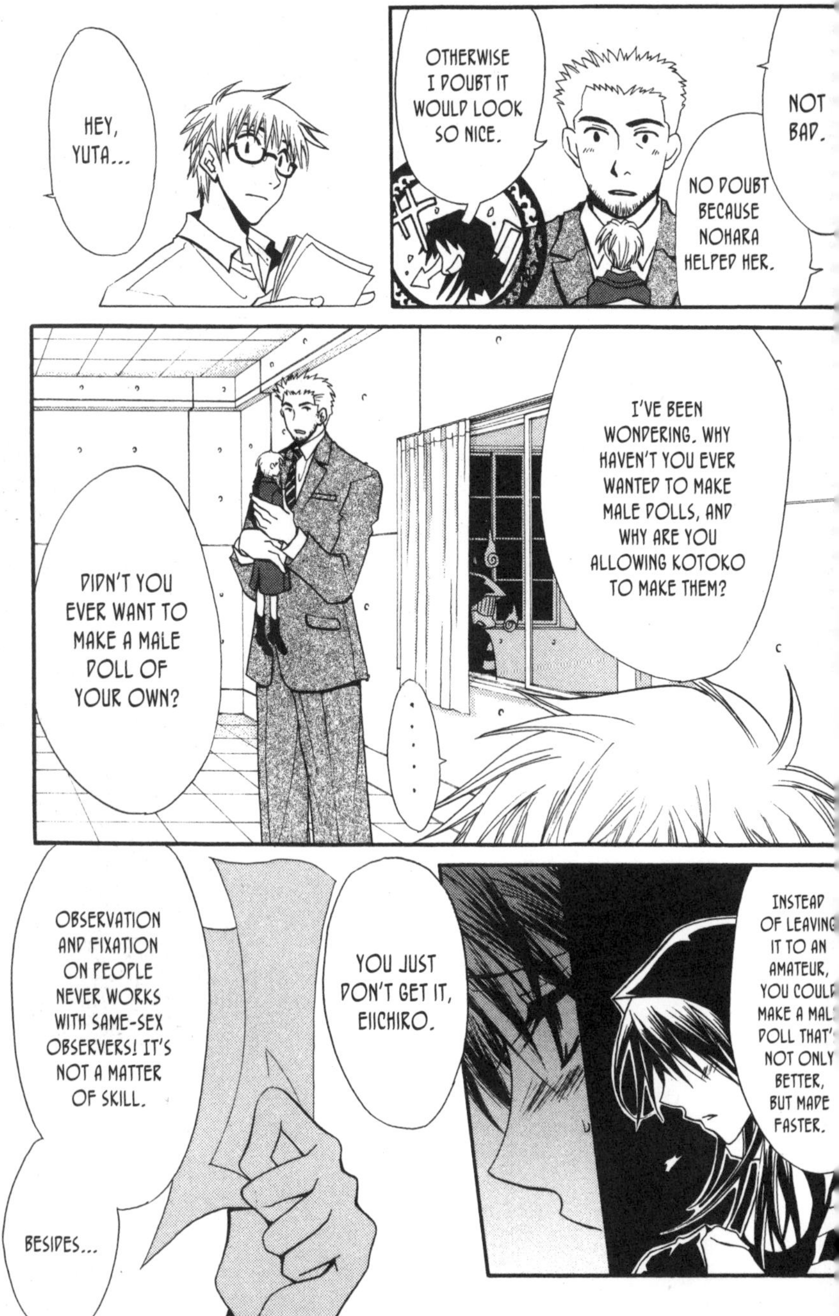
NOT BAD.
NO DOUBT BECAUSE NOHARA HELPED HER.
OTHERWISE I DOUBT IT WOULD LOOK SO NICE.
HEY, YUTA...
I'VE BEEN WONDERING. WHY HAVEN'T YOU EVER WANTED TO MAKE MALE DOLLS, AND WHY ARE YOU ALLOWING KOTOKO TO MAKE THEM?
......
DIDN'T YOU EVER WANT TO MAKE A MALE DOLL OF YOUR OWN?
INSTEAD OF LEAVIN IT TO AN AMATEUR, YOU COUL MAKE A MAL DOLL THAT' NOT ONLY BETTER, BUT MADE FASTER.
YOU JUST DON'T GET IT, EIICHIRO.
OBSERVATION AND FIXATION ON PEOPLE NEVER WORKS WITH SAME-SEX OBSERVERS! IT'S NOT A MATTER OF SKILL.
BESIDES...

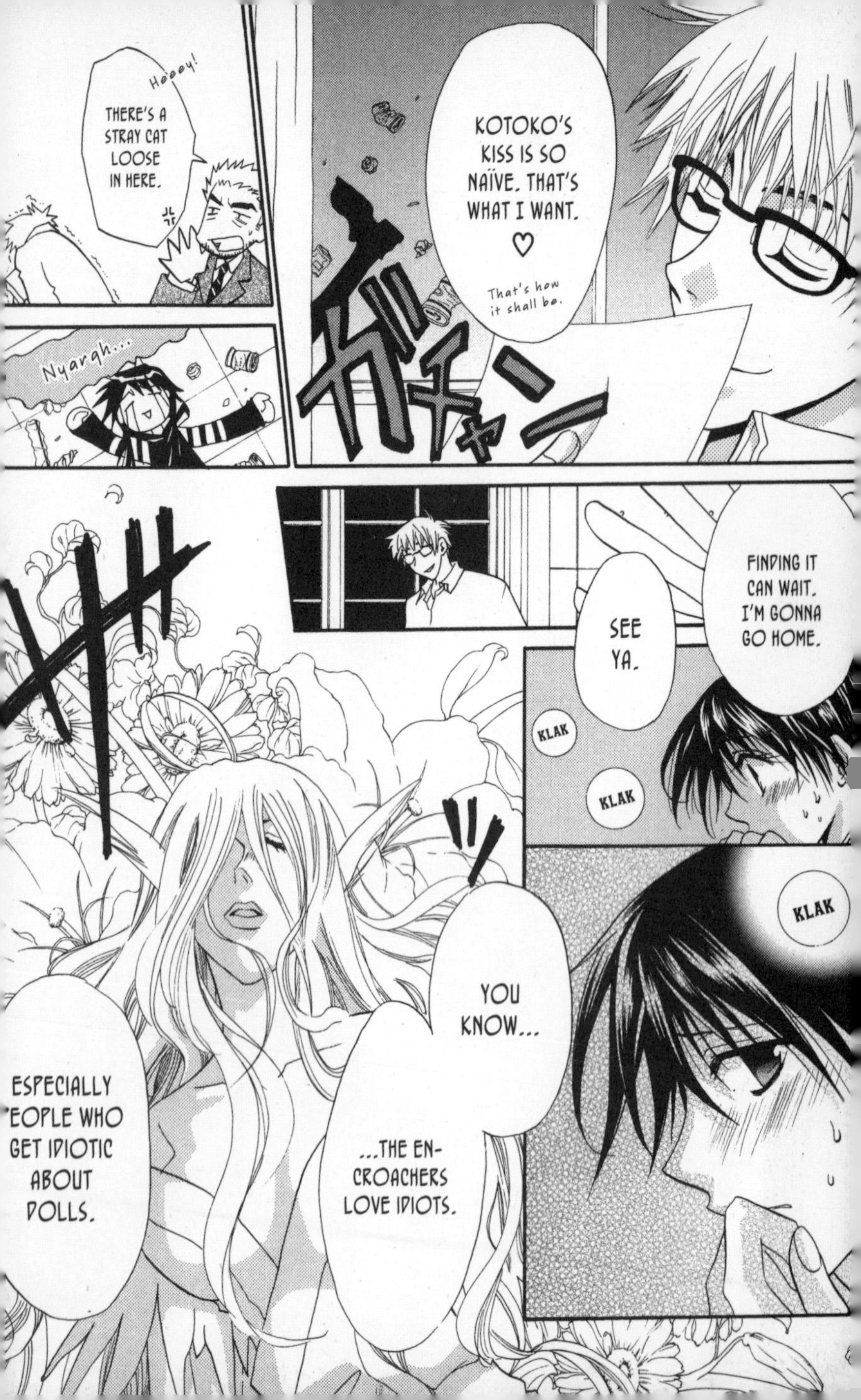
KOTOKO'S KISS IS SO NAÏVE. THAT'S WHAT I WANT. ♡
That's how it shall be.
ガチャーン
Heeey!
THERE'S A STRAY CAT LOOSE IN HERE.
Nyargh...
FINDING IT CAN WAIT. I'M GONNA GO HOME.
SEE YA.
KLAK
KLAK
KLAK
YOU KNOW...
...THE EN-CROACHERS LOVE IDIOTS.
ESPECIALLY
EOPLE WHO GET IDIOTIC ABOUT DOLLS.

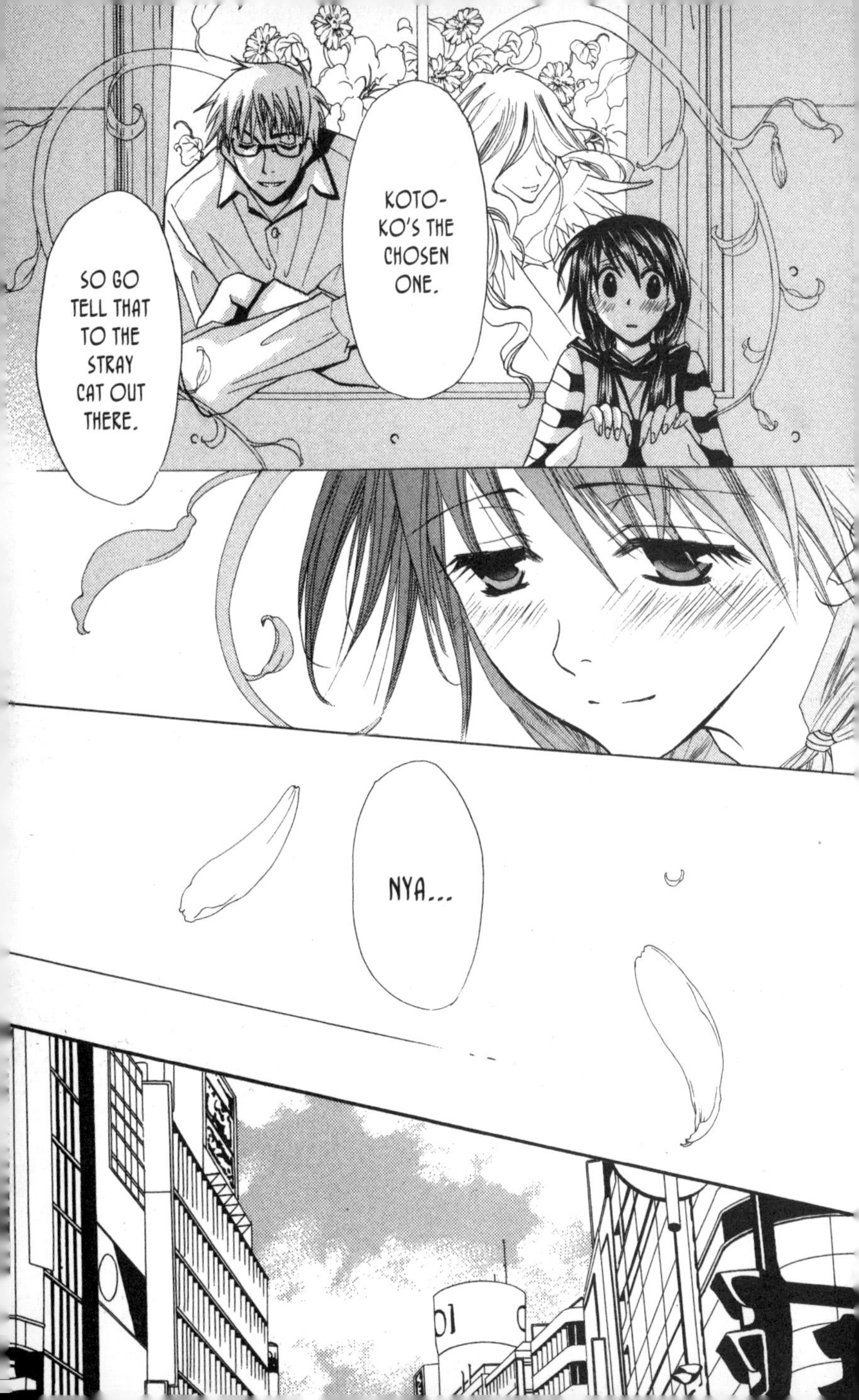
KOTO-KO'S THE CHOSEN ONE.
SO GO TELL THAT TO THE STRAY CAT OUT THERE.
NYA...

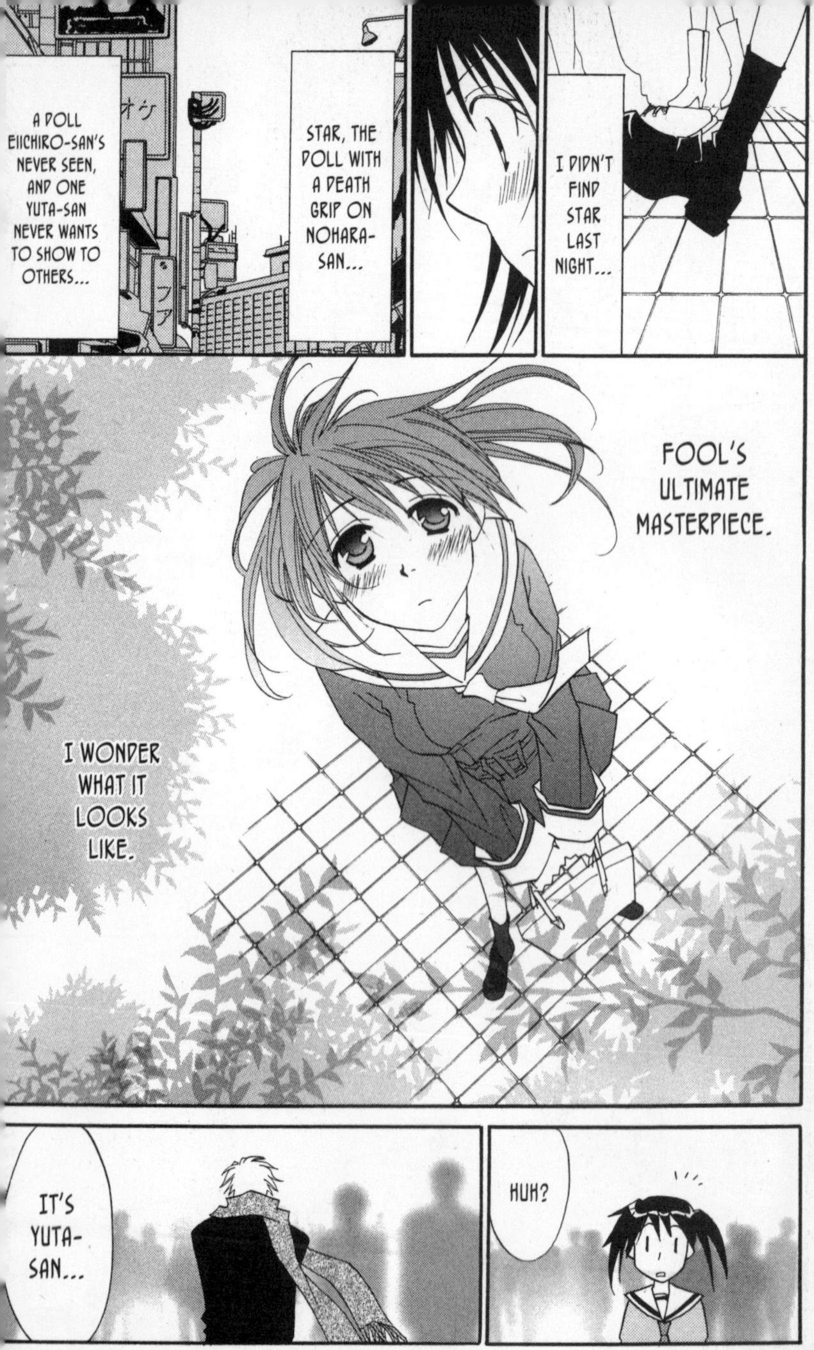
I DIDN'T FIND STAR LAST NIGHT...
STAR, THE DOLL WITH A DEATH GRIP ON NOHARA-SAN...
A DOLL EIICHIRO-SAN'S NEVER SEEN, AND ONE YUTA-SAN NEVER WANTS TO SHOW TO OTHERS...
FOOL'S ULTIMATE MASTERPIECE.
I WONDER WHAT IT LOOKS LIKE.
HUH?
IT'S YUTA-SAN...

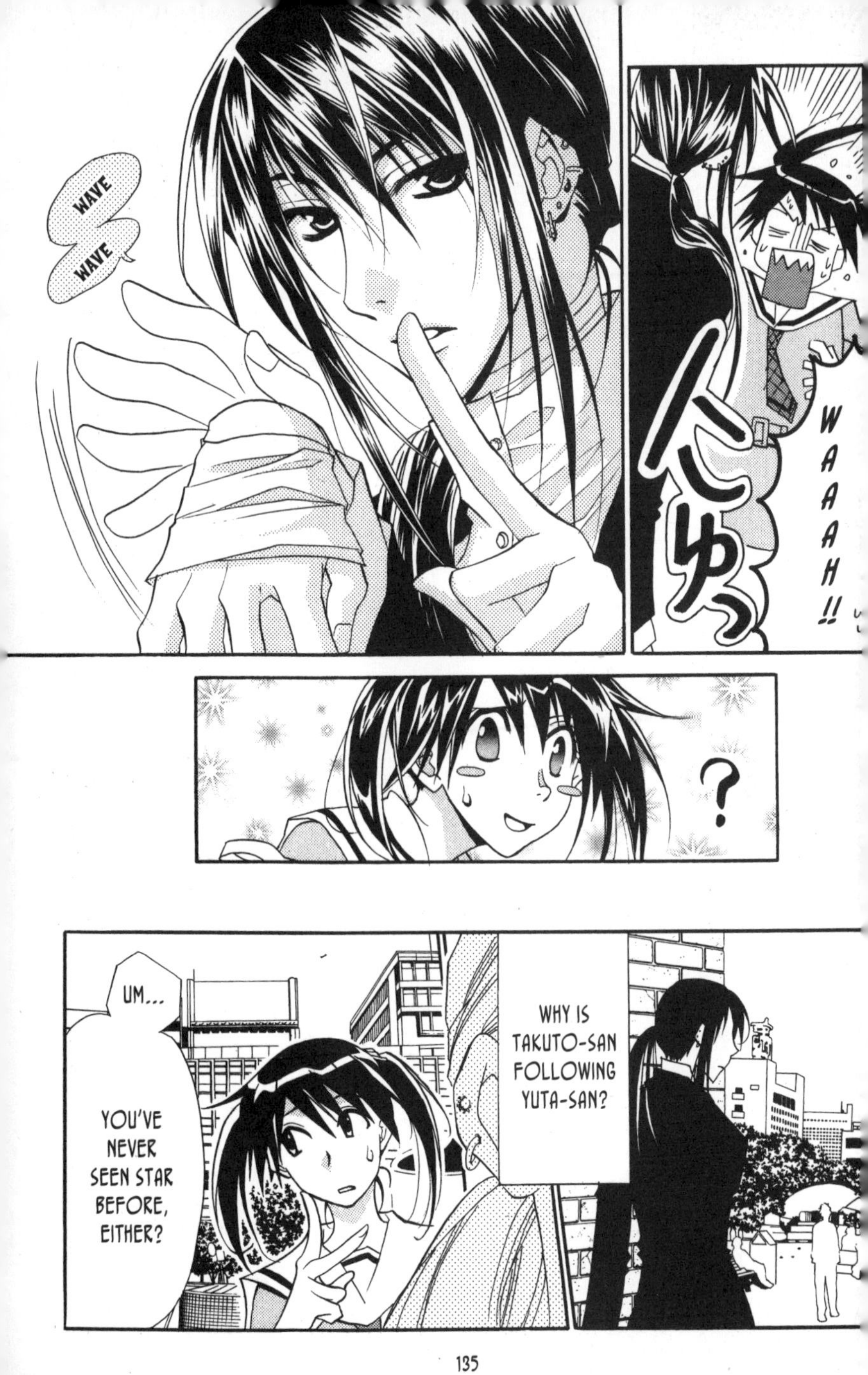
WAAAAH!!
しゅっ
WAVE WAVE
?
WHY IS TAKUTO-SAN FOLLOWING YUTA-SAN?
UM... YOU'VE NEVER SEEN STAR BEFORE, EITHER?

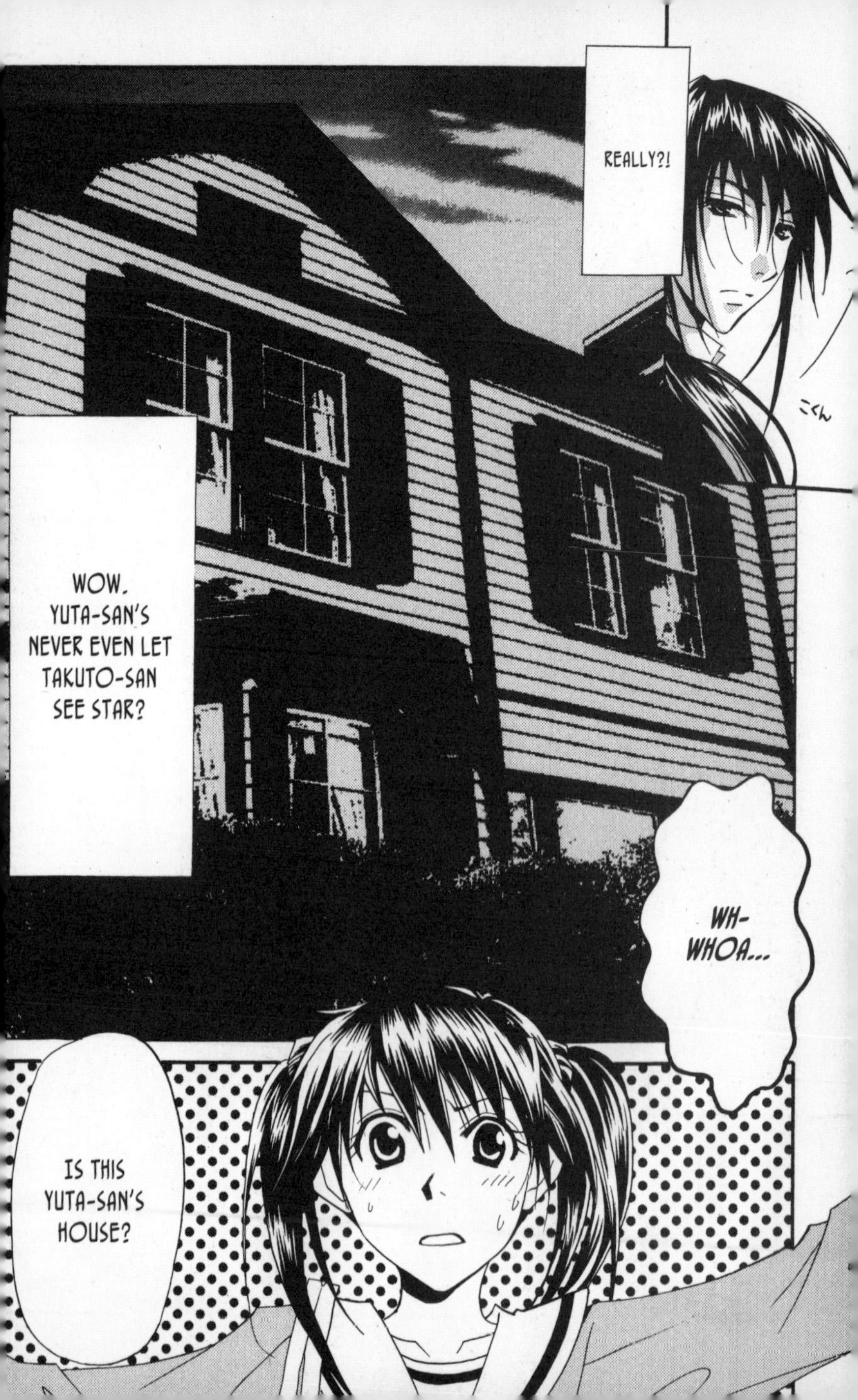
REALLY?!
こくん
WOW. YUTA-SAN'S NEVER EVEN LET TAKUTO-SAN SEE STAR?
WH- WHOA...
IS THIS YUTA-SAN'S HOUSE?

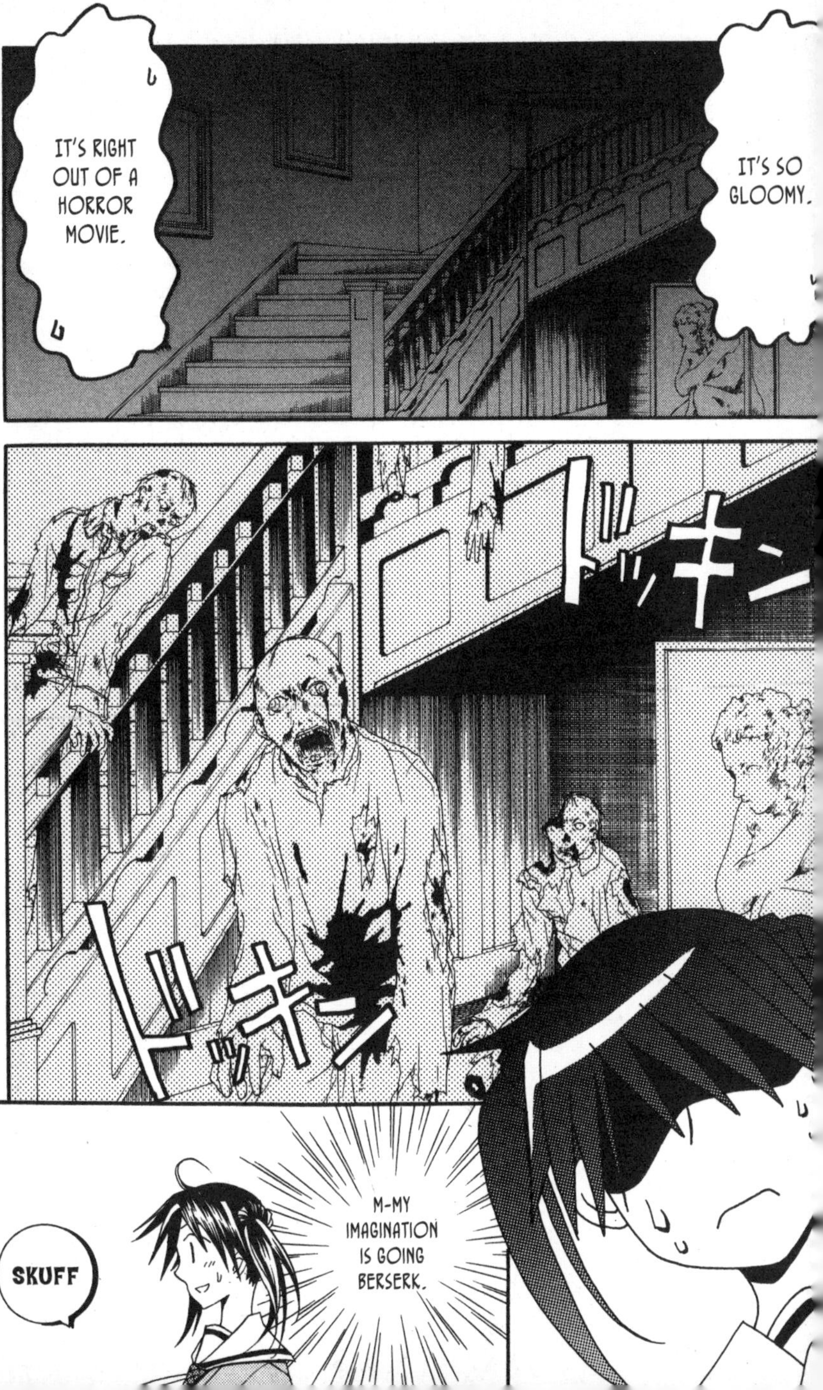
IT'S SO GLOOMY.
IT'S RIGHT OUT OF A HORROR MOVIE.
ドッキン
ドッキン
M-MY IMAGINATION IS GOING BERSERK.
SKUFF

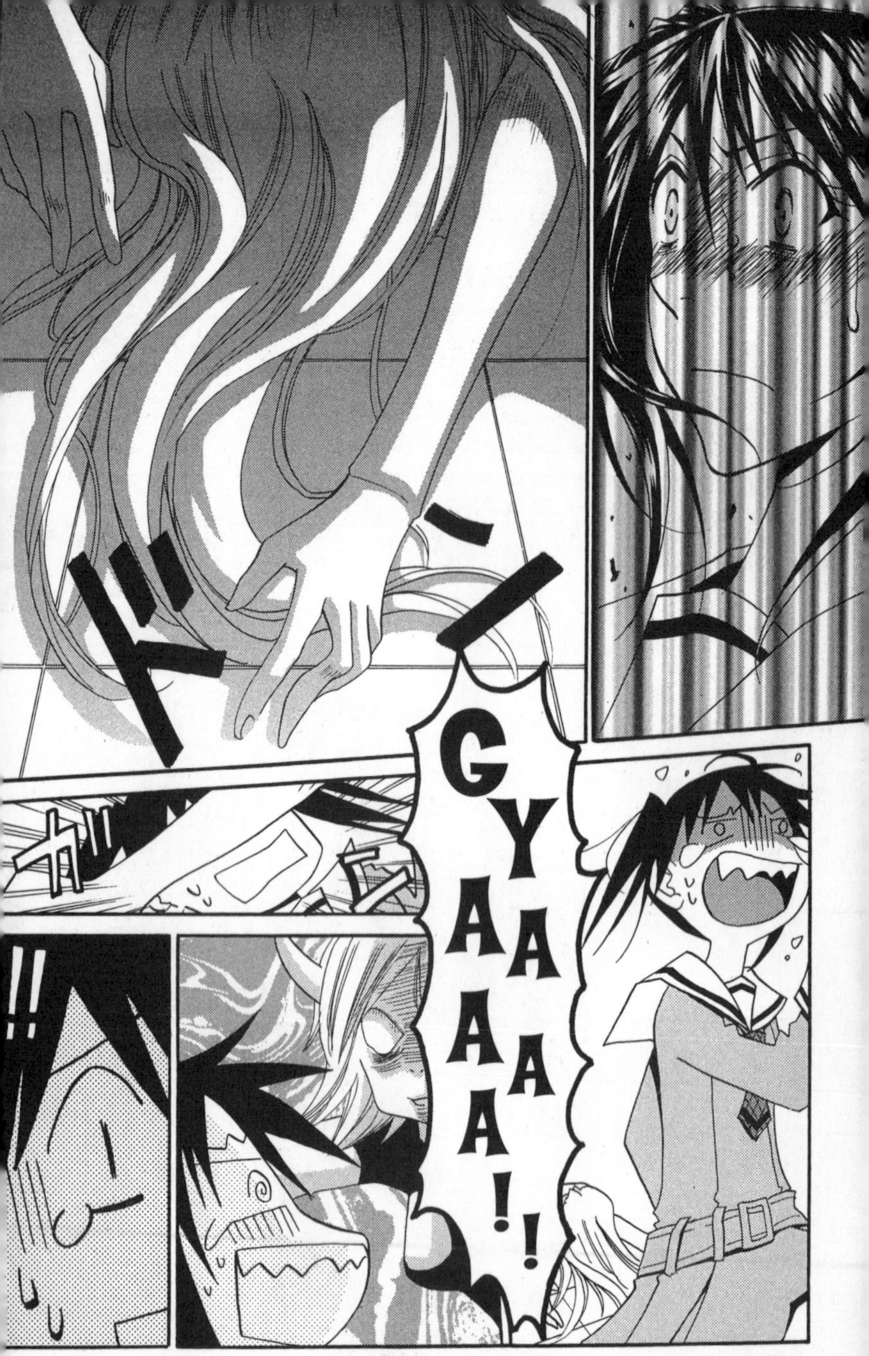
GYAAAAA!!

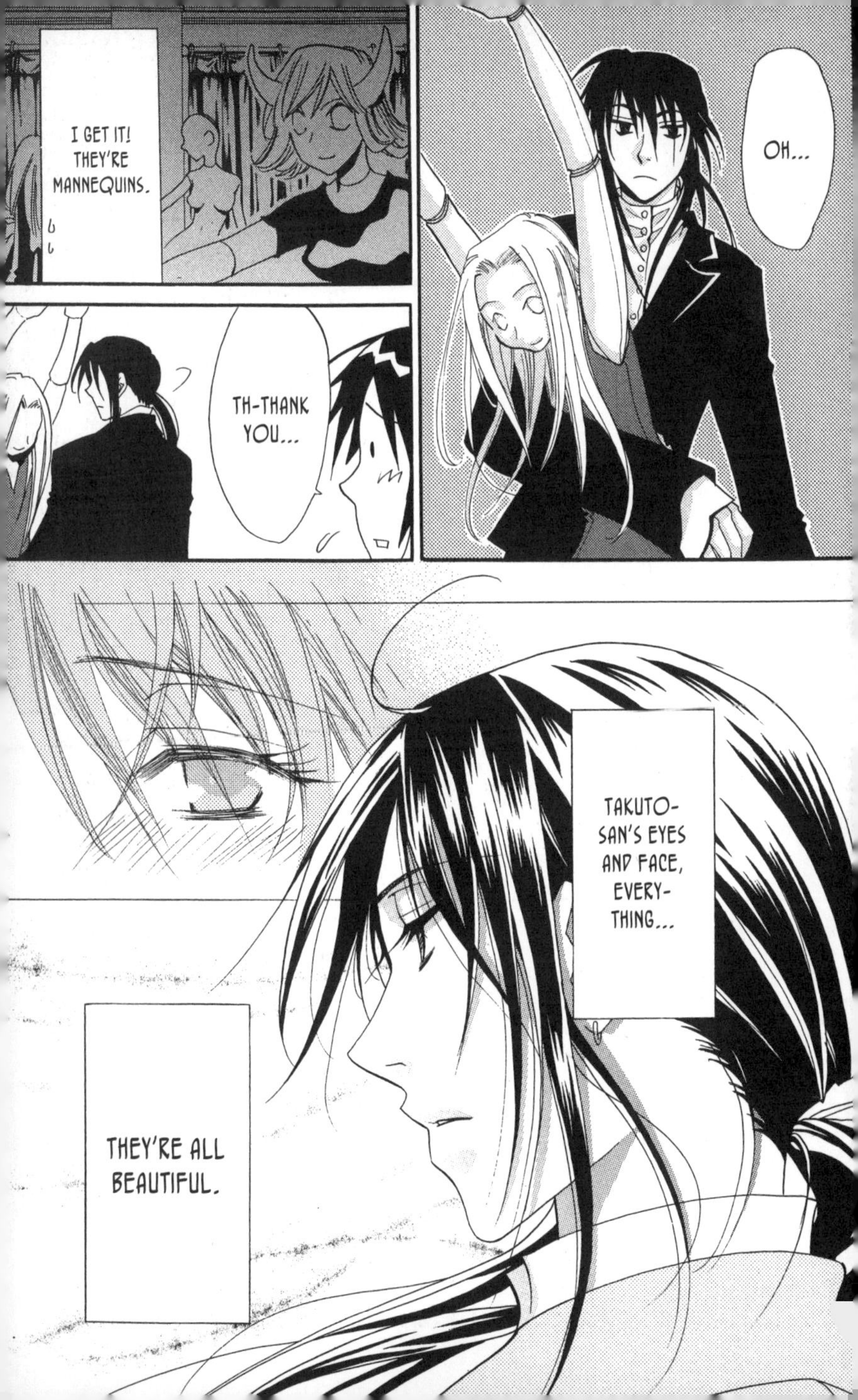
OH...
I GET IT! THEY'RE MANNEQUINS.
TH-THANK YOU...
TAKUTO-SAN'S EYES AND FACE, EVERY-THING...
THEY'RE ALL BEAUTIFUL.

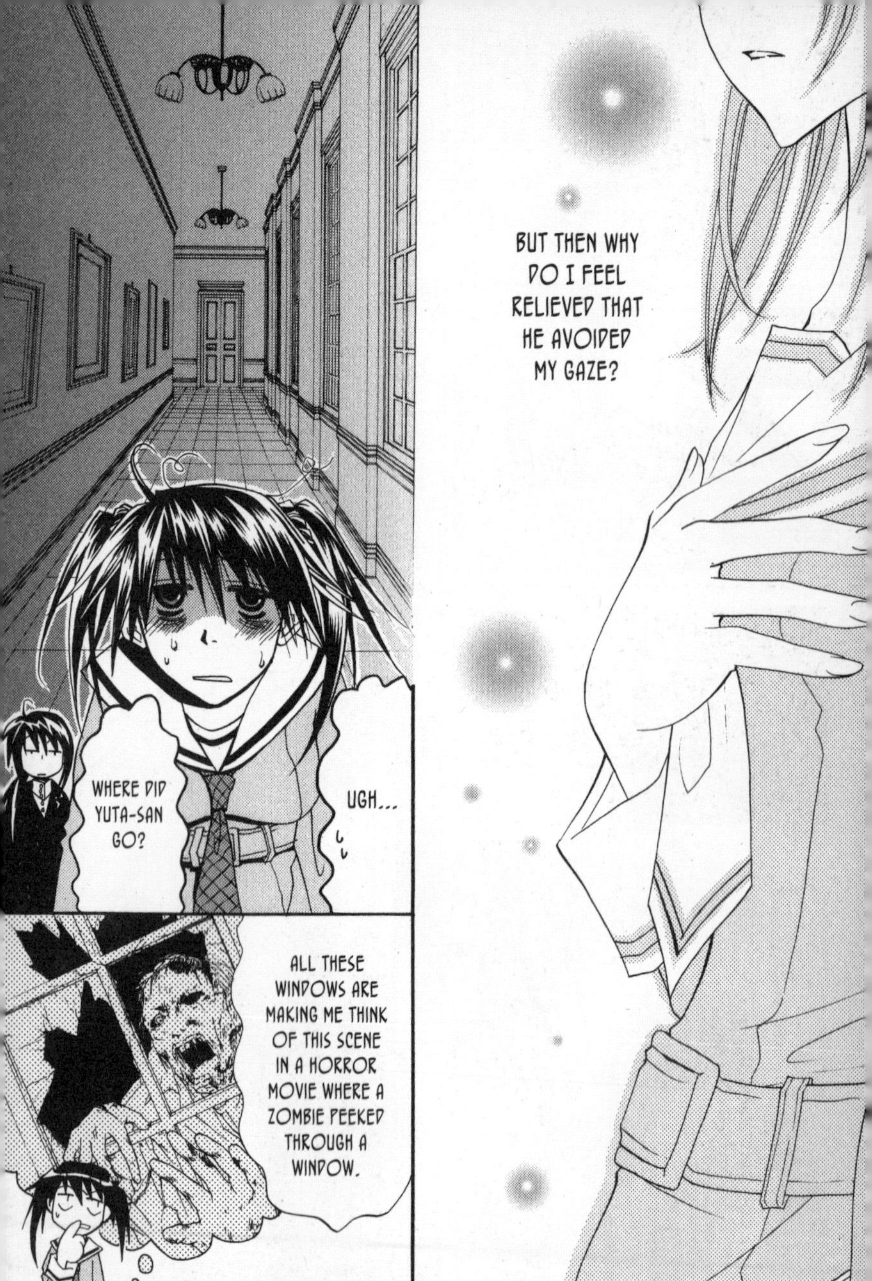
BUT THEN WHY DO I FEEL RELIEVED THAT HE AVOIDED MY GAZE?
UGH...
WHERE DID YUTA-SAN GO?
ALL THESE WINDOWS ARE MAKING ME THINK OF THIS SCENE IN A HORROR MOVIE WHERE A ZOMBIE PEEKED THROUGH A WINDOW.

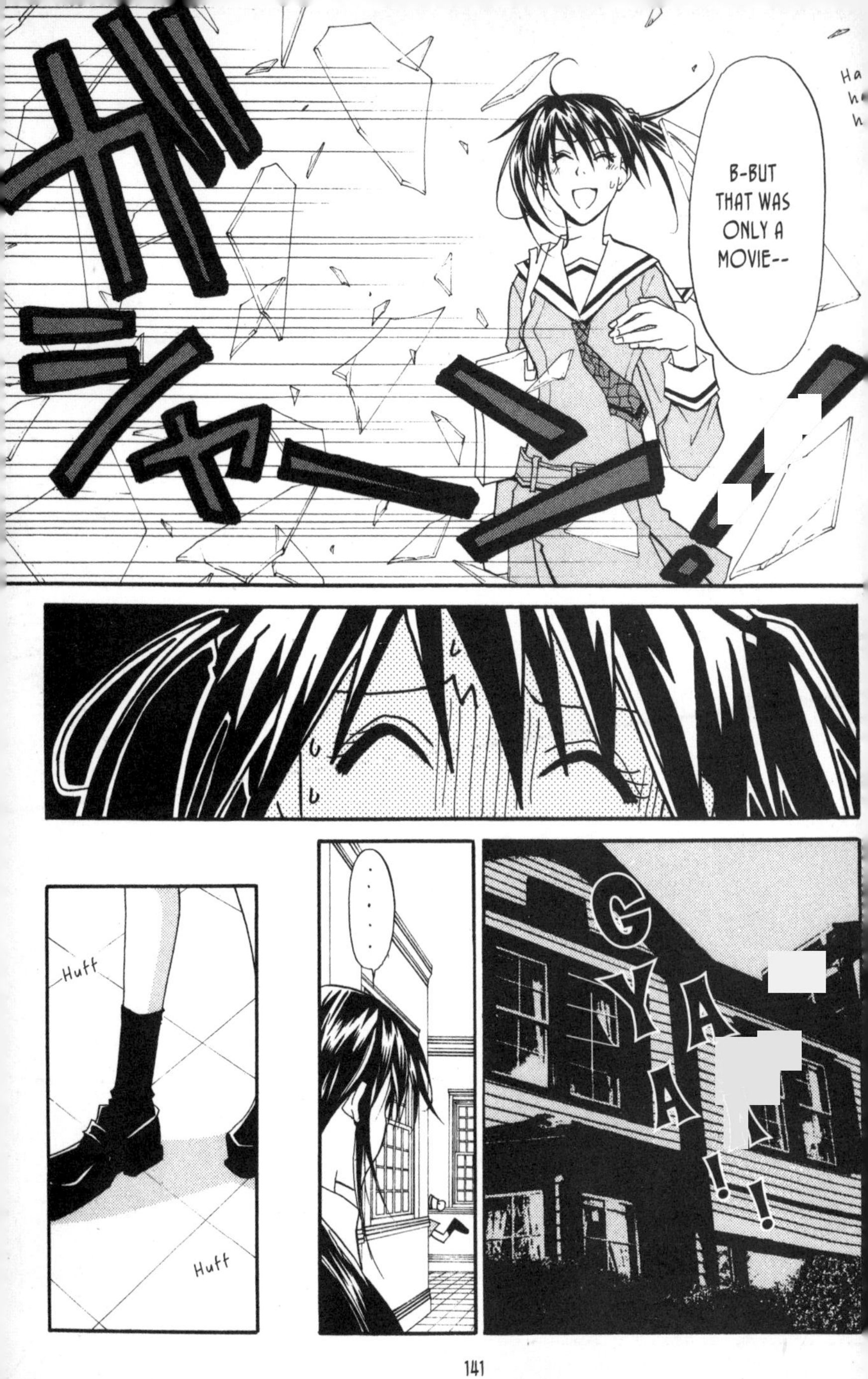
Ha ha h
B-BUT THAT WAS ONLY A MOVIE--
ガシャーン
GYAA!!
......
Huff
Huff

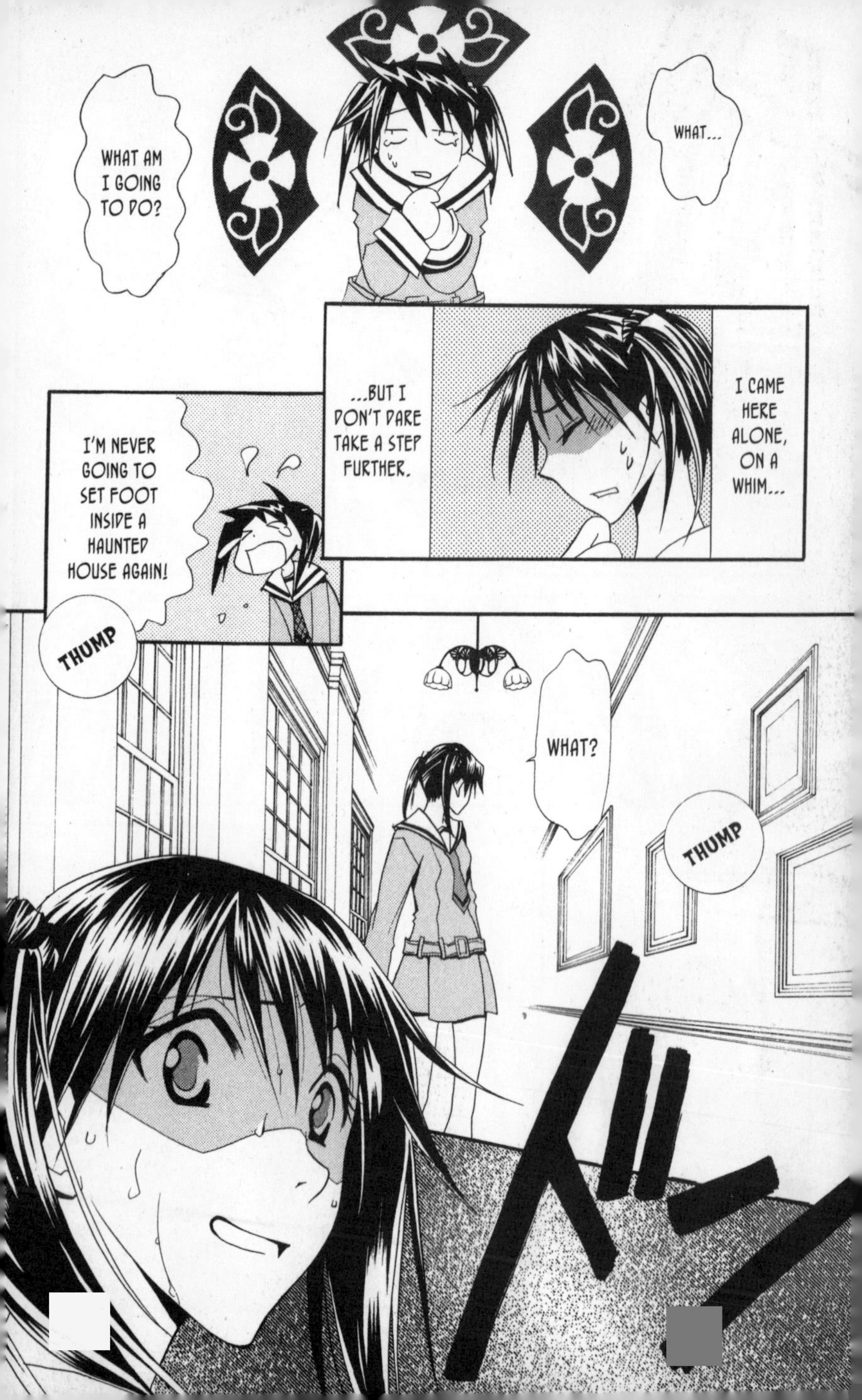
WHAT...
WHAT AM I GOING TO DO?
I CAME HERE ALONE, ON A WHIM...
...BUT I DON'T DARE TAKE A STEP FURTHER.
I'M NEVER GOING TO SET FOOT INSIDE A HAUNTED HOUSE AGAIN!
THUMP
WHAT?
THUMP

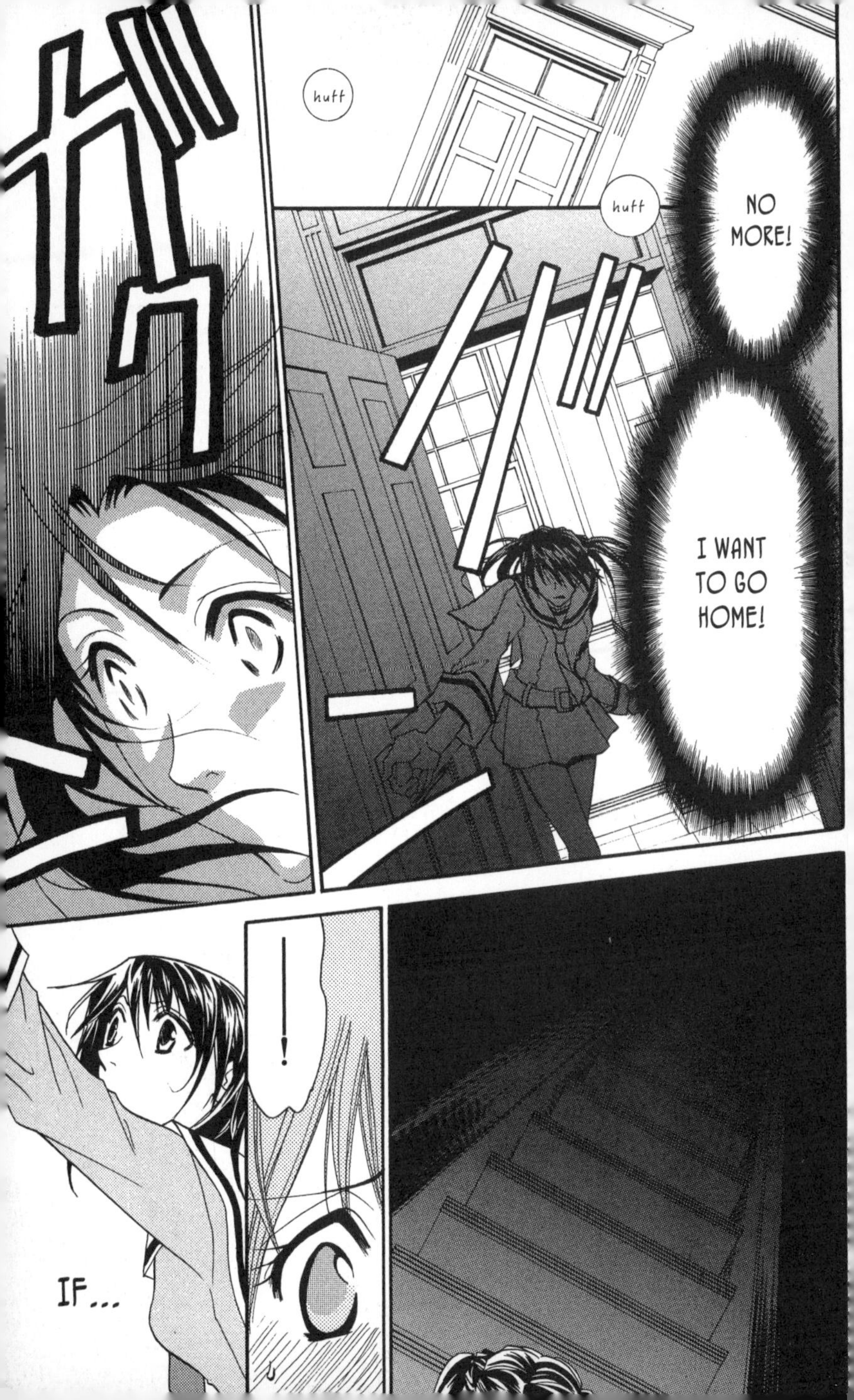
huff
huff
NO MORE!
I WANT TO GO HOME!
ガク
!
IF...

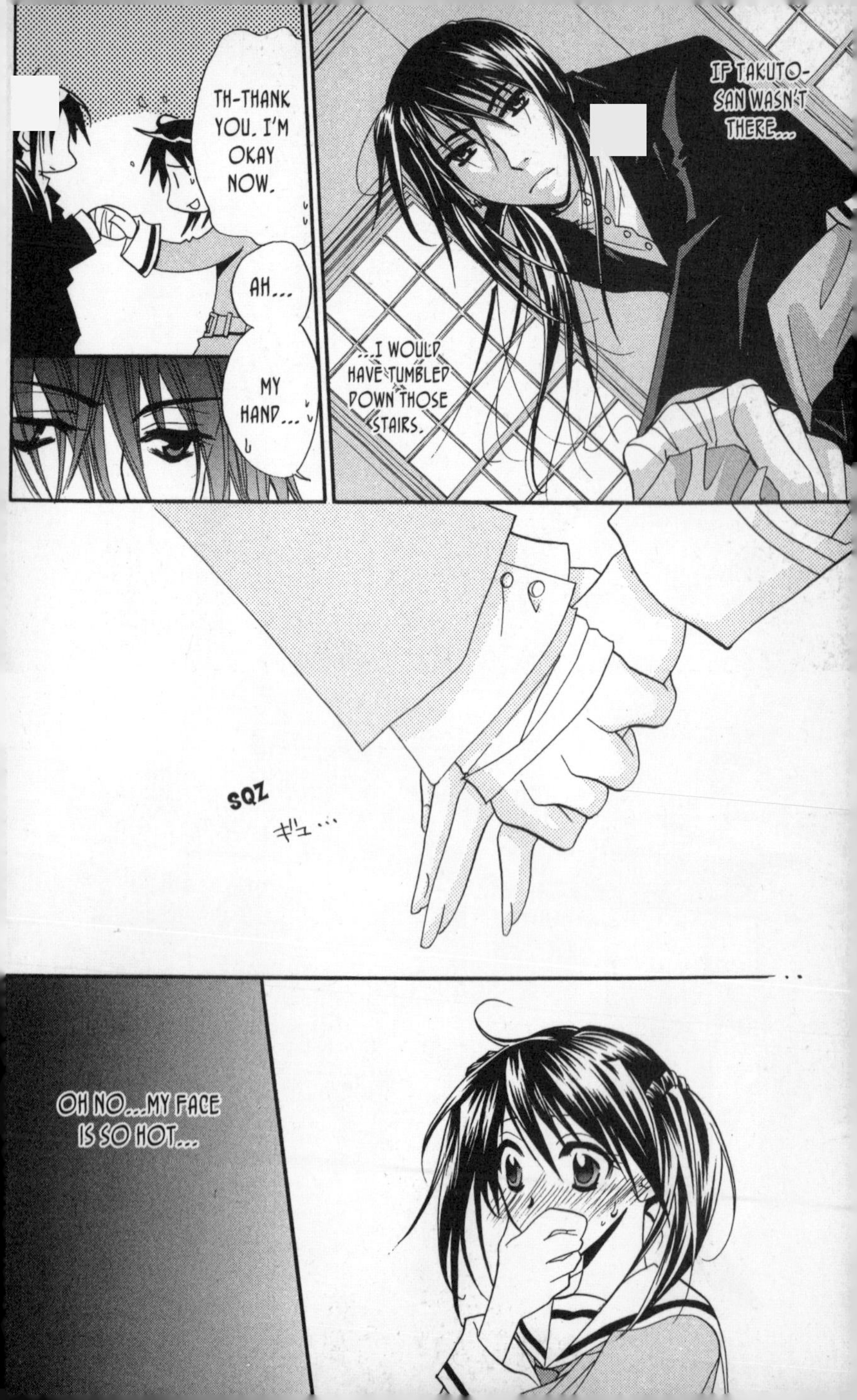
IF TAKUTO-SAN WASN'T THERE...
...I WOULD HAVE TUMBLED DOWN THOSE STAIRS.
TH-THANK YOU. I'M OKAY NOW.
AH...
MY HAND...
SQZ
ギュ…
OH NO...MY FACE IS SO HOT...

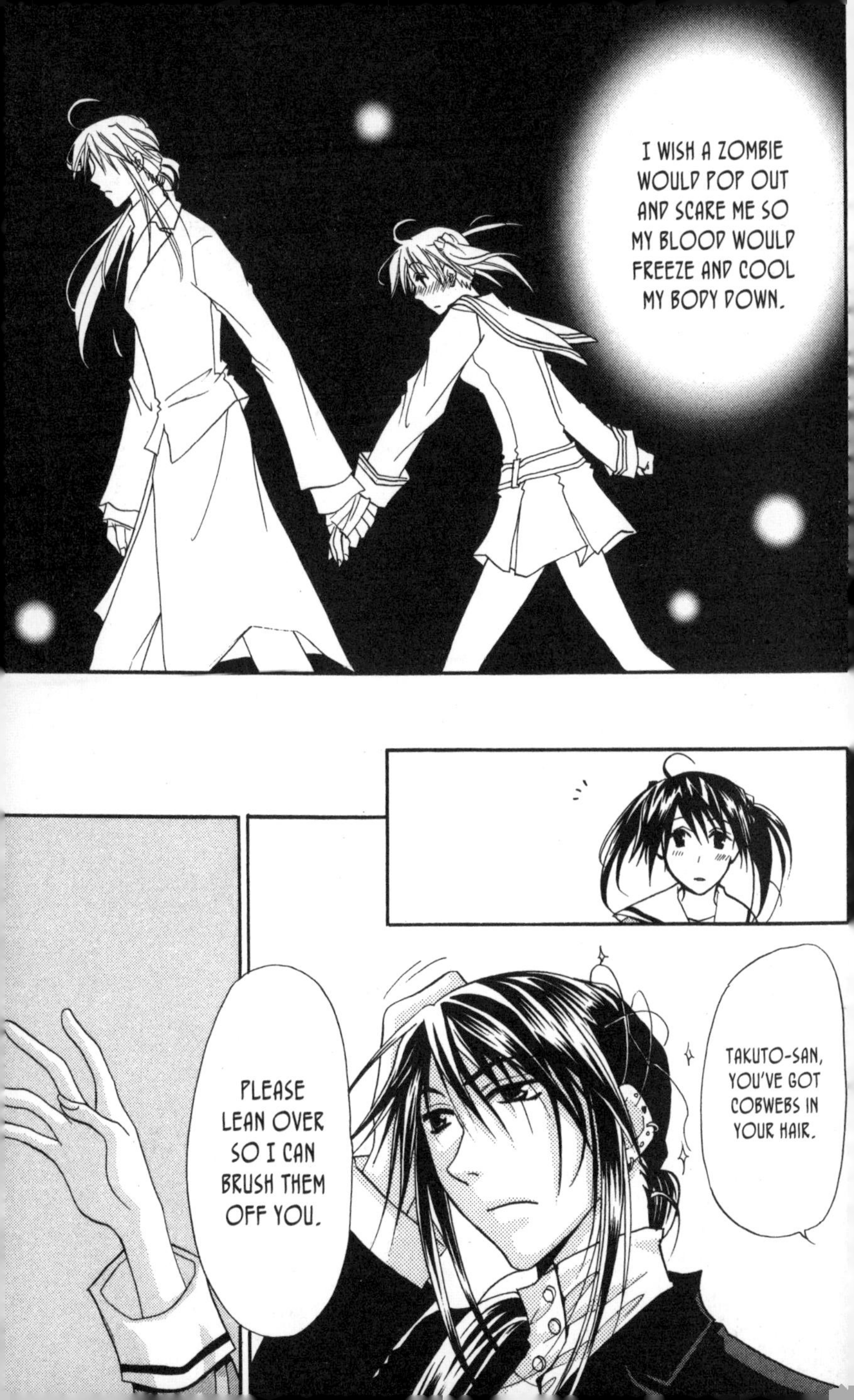
I WISH A ZOMBIE WOULD POP OUT AND SCARE ME SO MY BLOOD WOULD FREEZE AND COOL MY BODY DOWN.
TAKUTO-SAN, YOU'VE GOT COBWEBS IN YOUR HAIR.
PLEASE LEAN OVER SO I CAN BRUSH THEM OFF YOU.

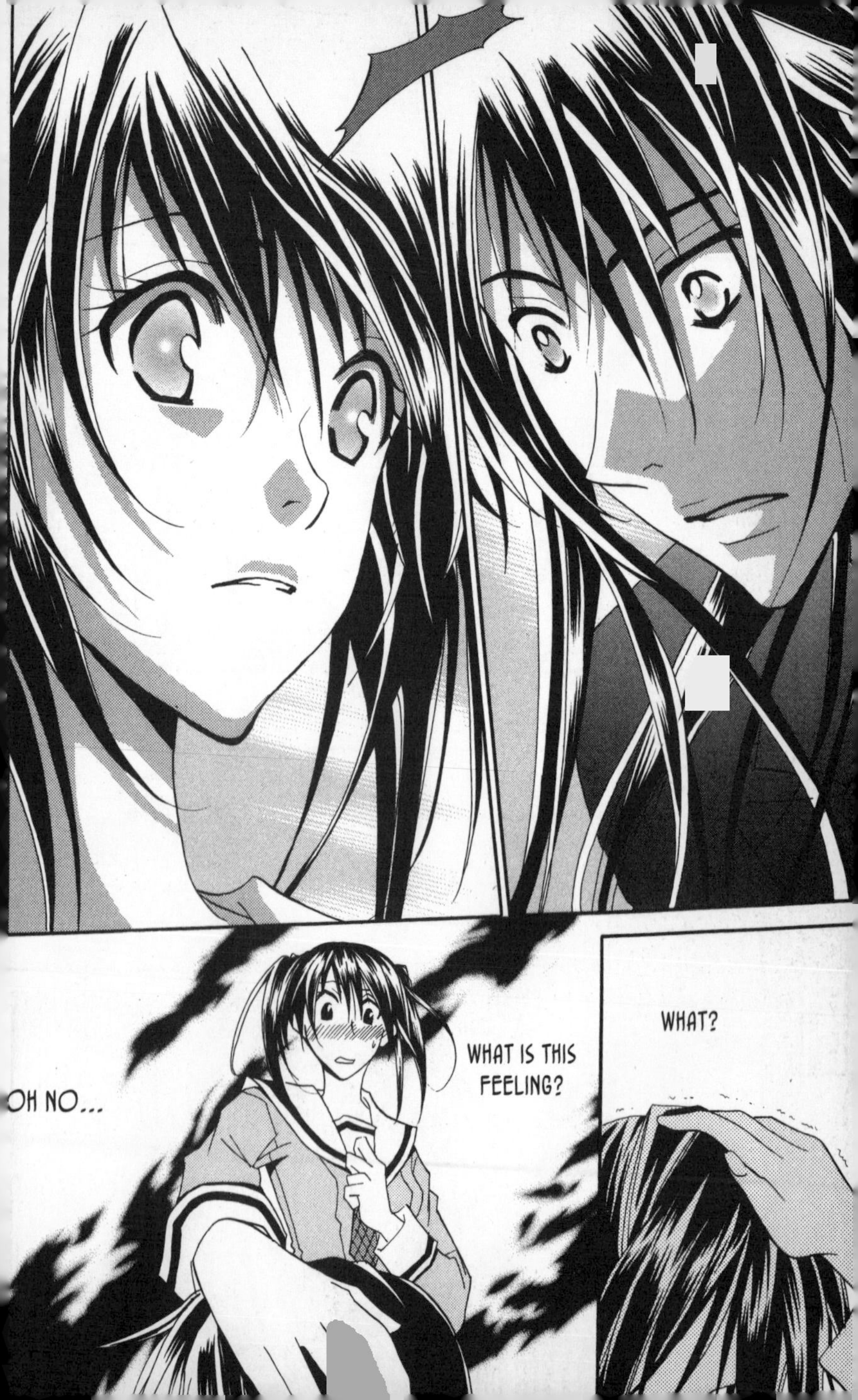
WHAT?
WHAT IS THIS FEELING?
OH NO...

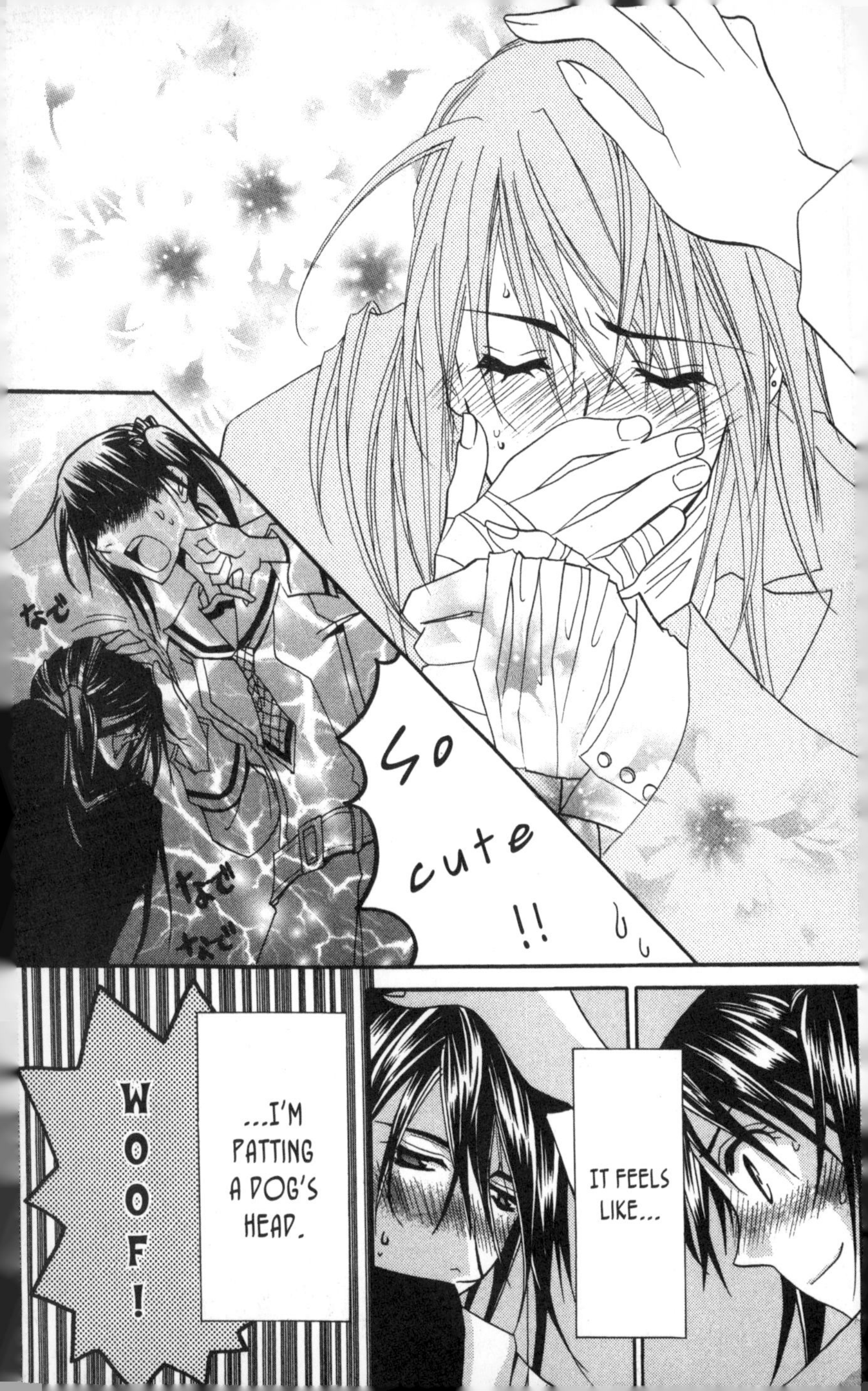

So cute !!
なで
なで
なで
IT FEELS LIKE...
...I'M PATTING A DOG'S HEAD.
WOOF!

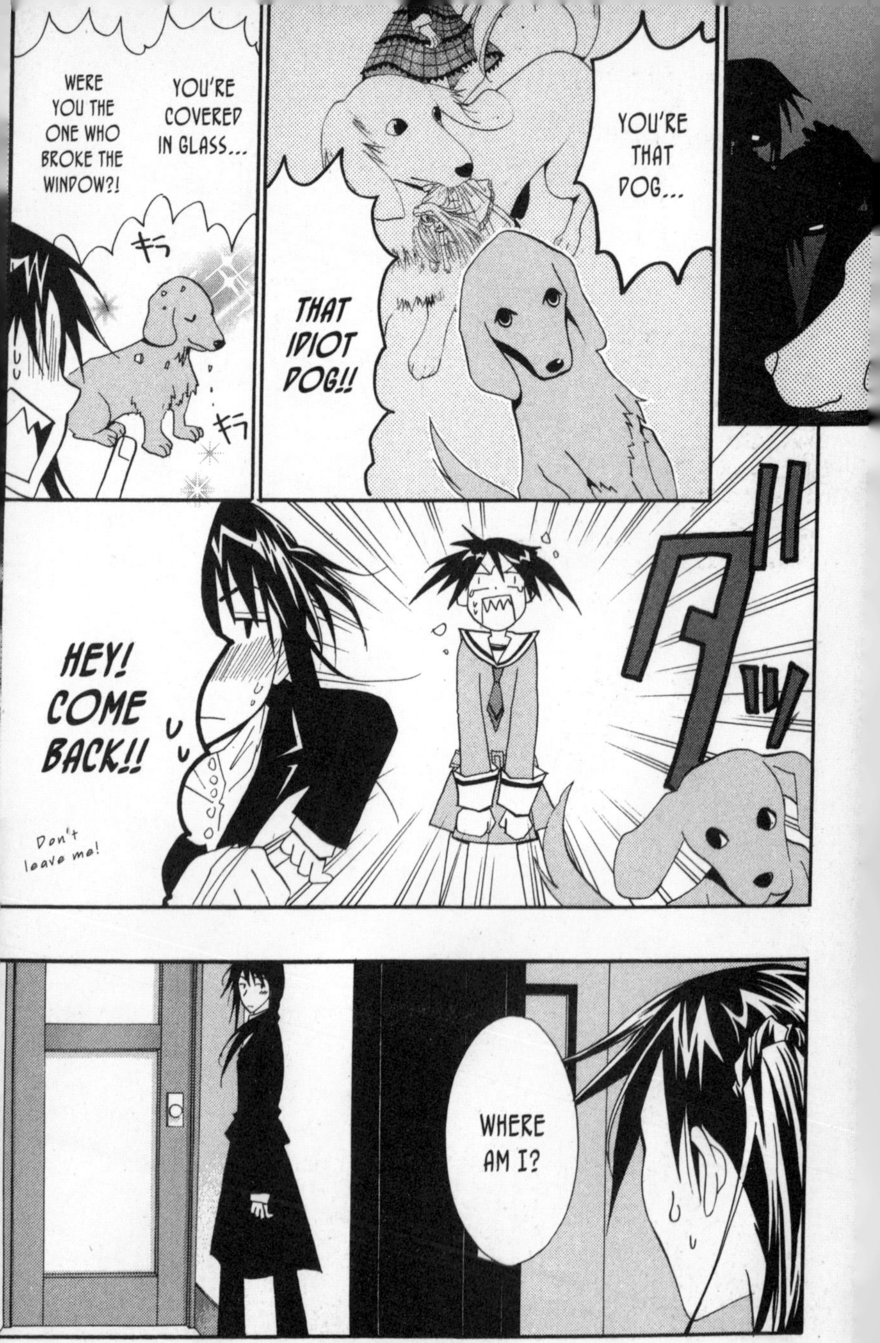
YOU'RE THAT DOG...
THAT IDIOT DOG!!
YOU'RE COVERED IN GLASS...
WERE YOU THE ONE WHO BROKE THE WINDOW?!
キラ
キラ
ダッ
HEY! COME BACK!!
Don't leave me!
WHERE AM I?

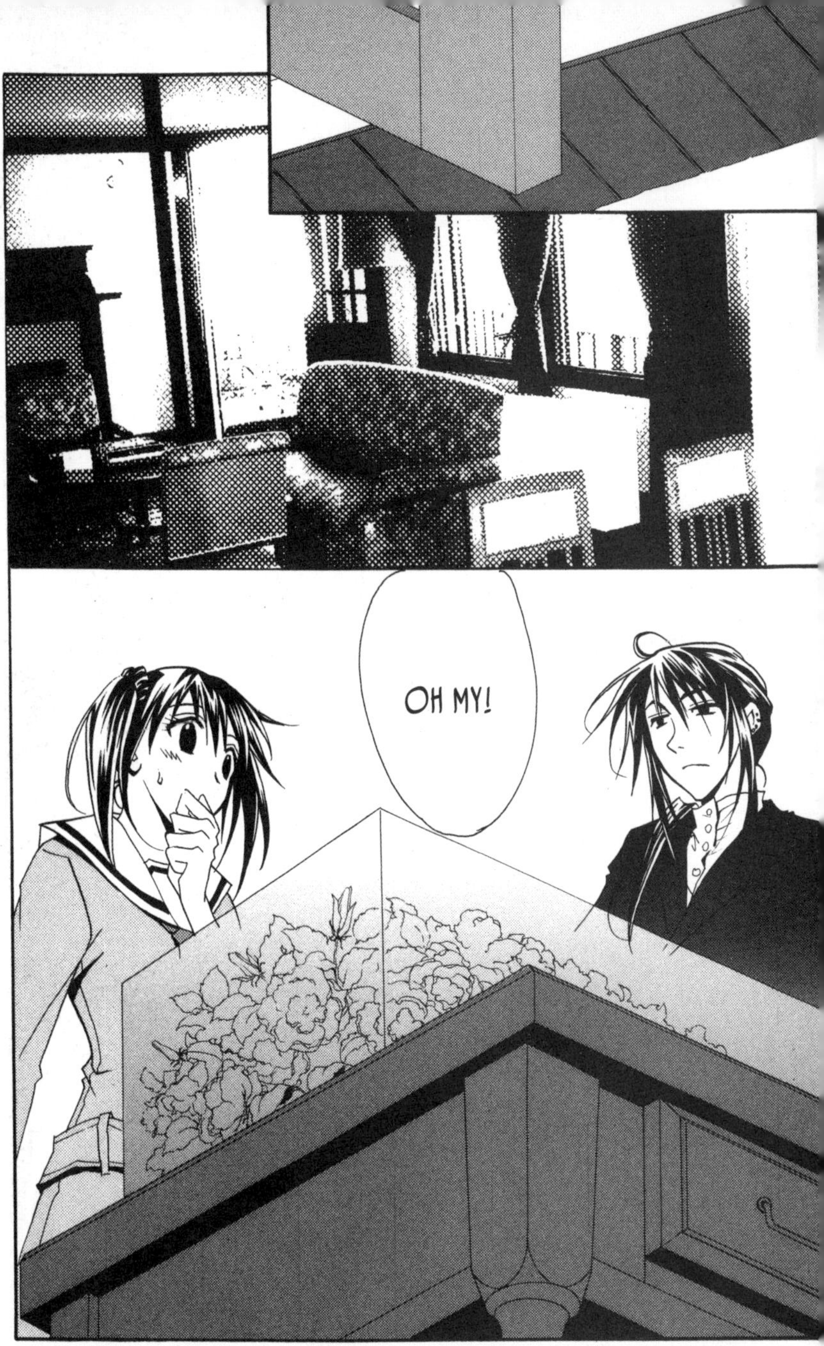
OH MY!

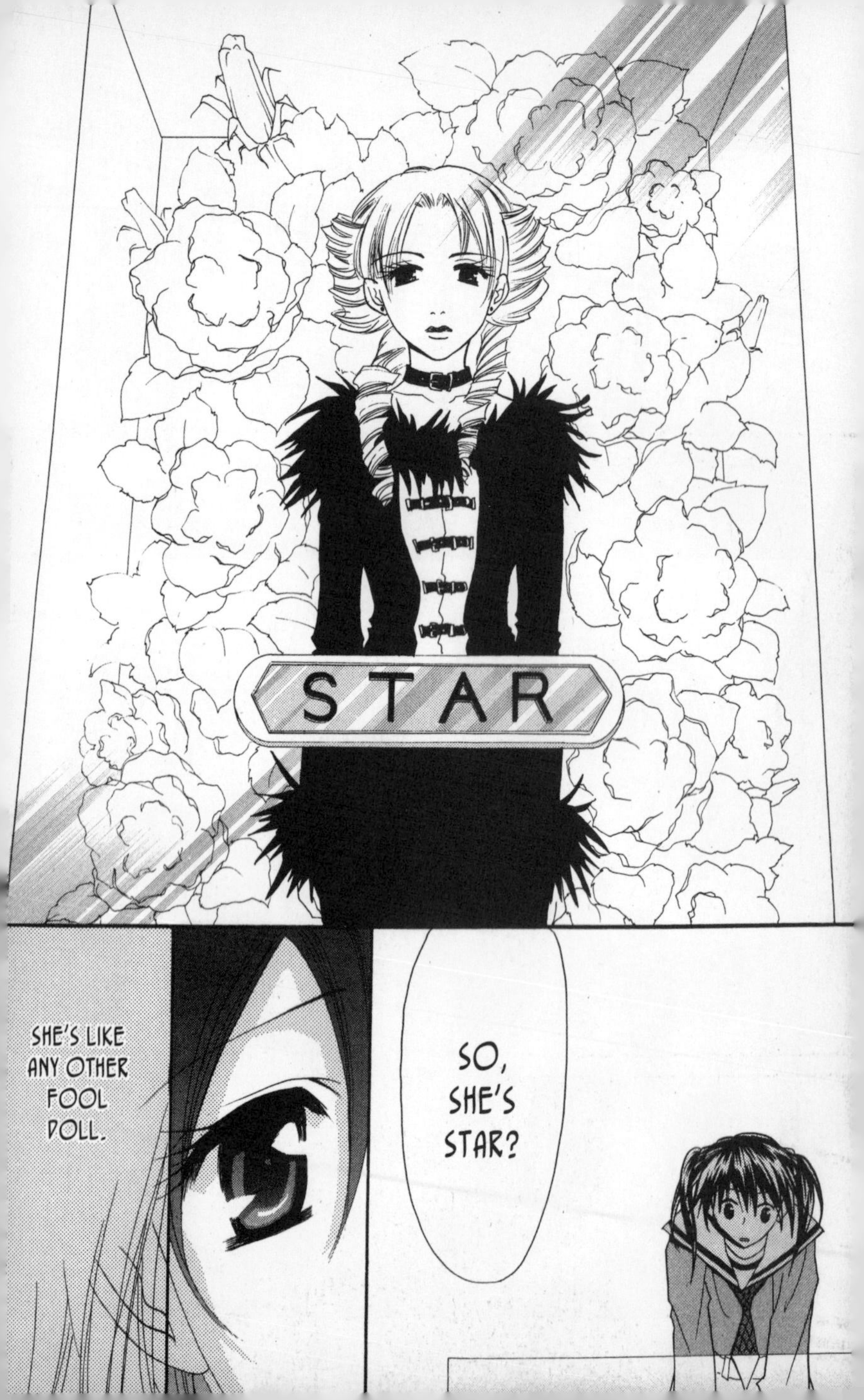
STAR
SO, SHE'S STAR?
SHE'S LIKE ANY OTHER FOOL DOLL.

I GUESS I THOUGHT IT WOULD BE SOMETHING MORE SPECIAL.

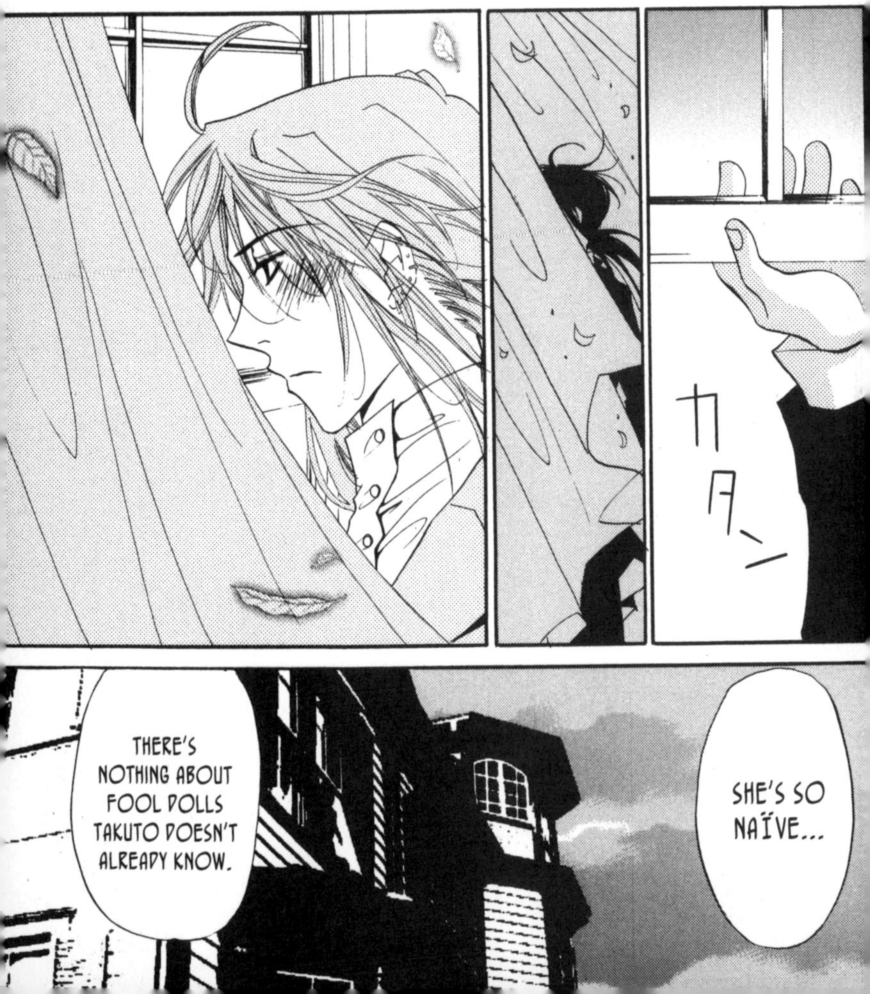
カタン
SHE'S SO NAÏVE...
THERE'S NOTHING ABOUT FOOL DOLLS TAKUTO DOESN'T ALREADY KNOW.

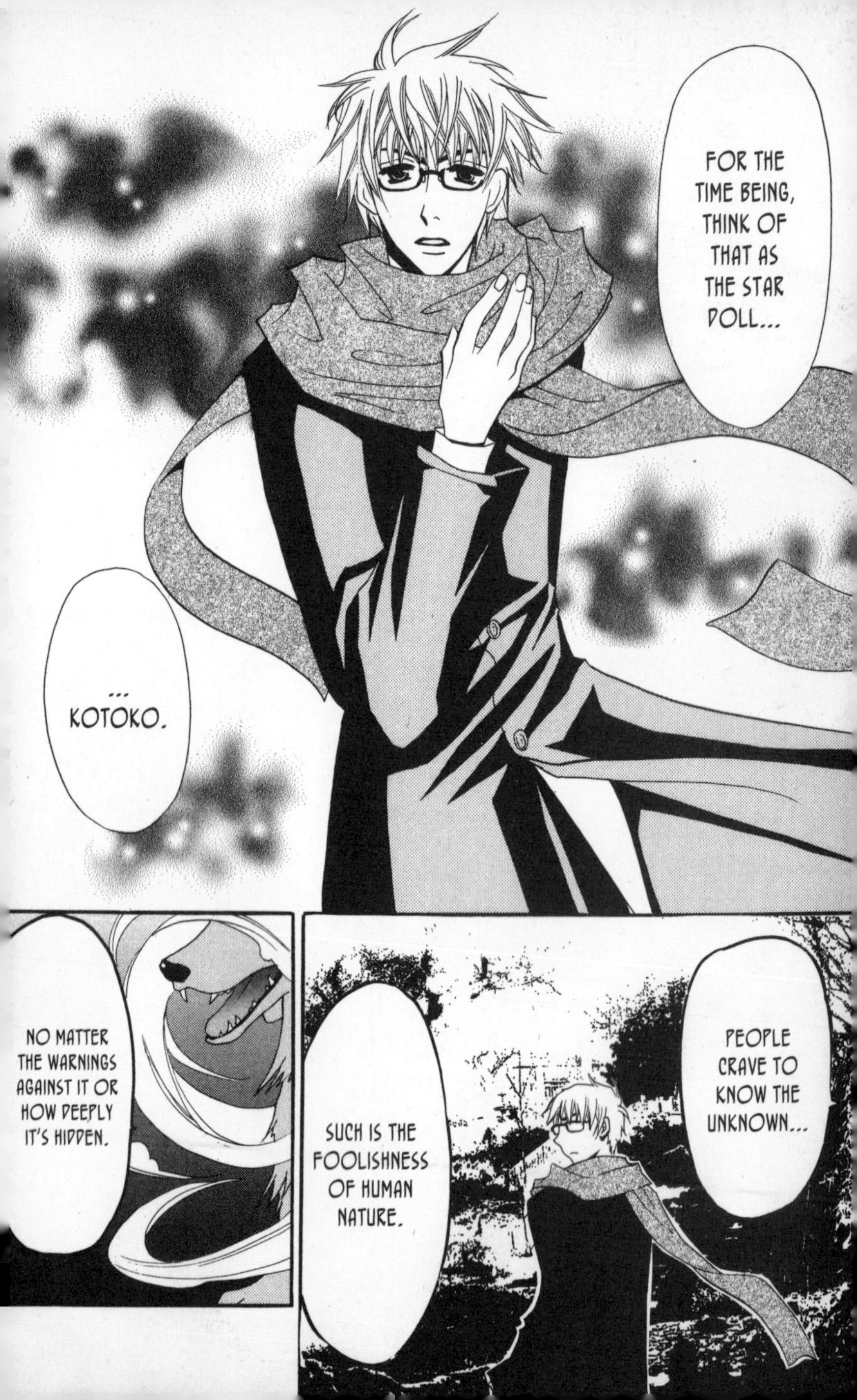
FOR THE TIME BEING, THINK OF THAT AS THE STAR DOLL...
...KOTOKO.
PEOPLE CRAVE TO KNOW THE UNKNOWN...
SUCH IS THE FOOLISHNESS OF HUMAN NATURE.
NO MATTER THE WARNINGS AGAINST IT OR HOW DEEPLY IT'S HIDDEN.

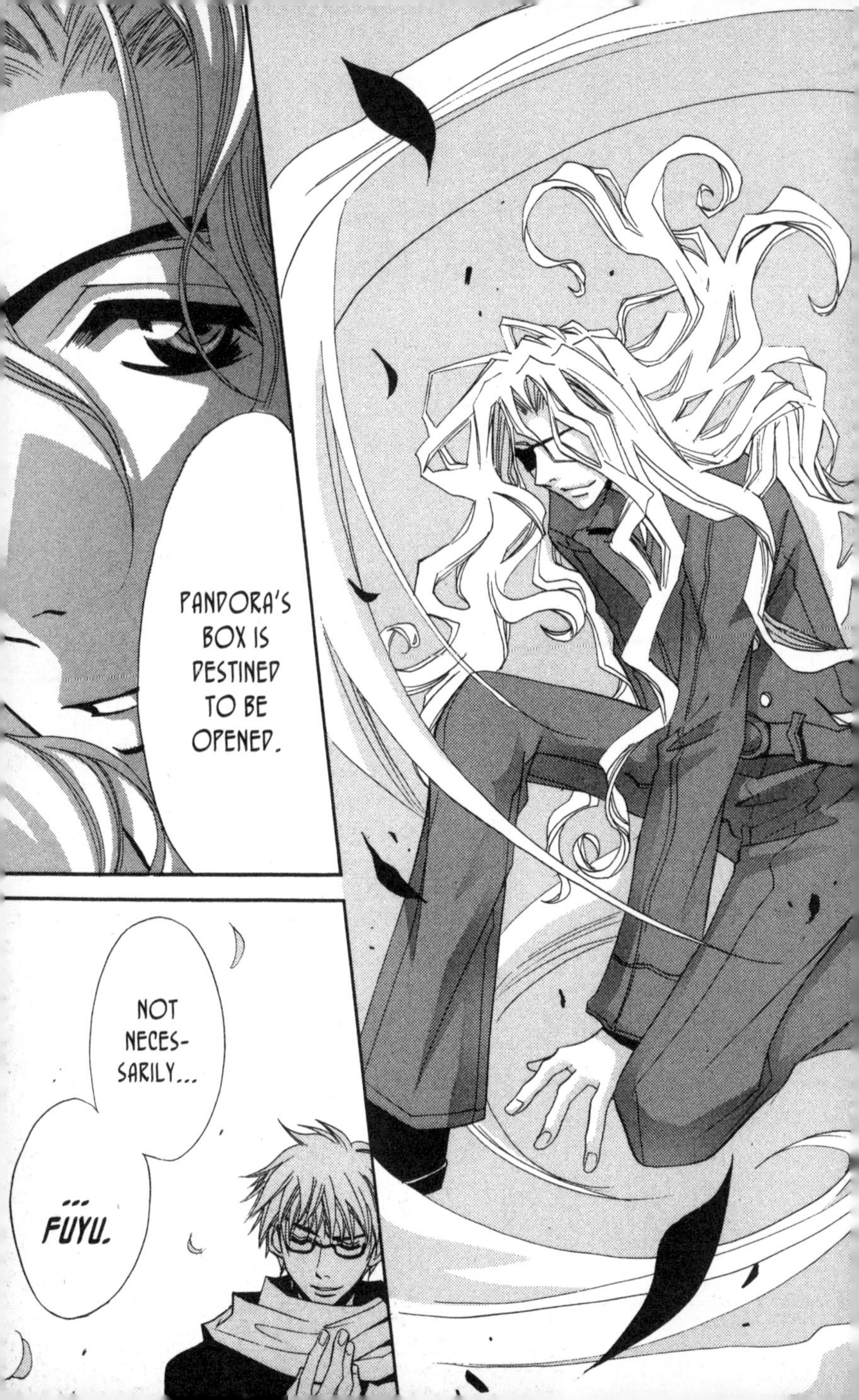
PANDORA'S BOX IS DESTINED TO BE OPENED.
NOT NECES-SARILY...
...FUYU.

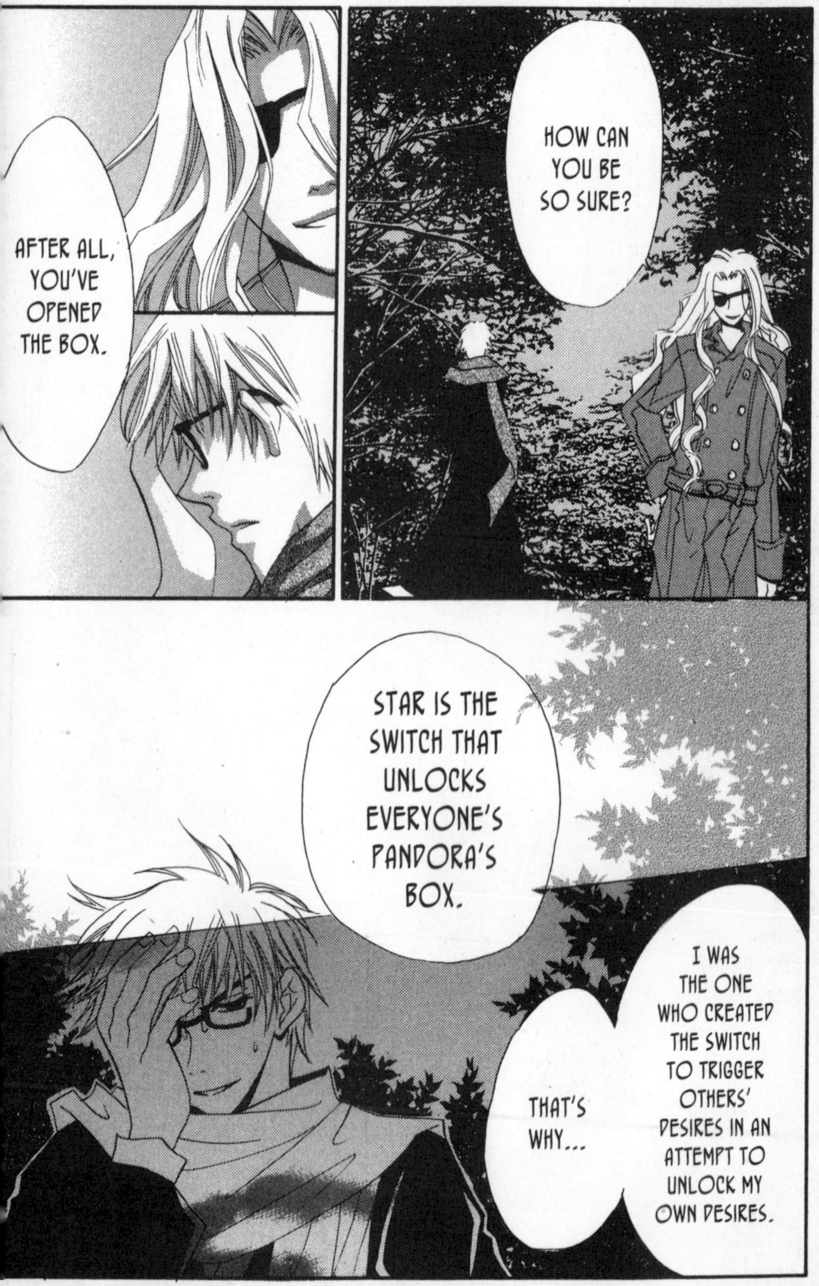
HOW CAN YOU BE SO SURE?
AFTER ALL, YOU'VE OPENED THE BOX.
STAR IS THE SWITCH THAT UNLOCKS EVERYONE'S PANDORA'S BOX.
I WAS THE ONE WHO CREATED THE SWITCH TO TRIGGER OTHERS' DESIRES IN AN ATTEMPT TO UNLOCK MY OWN DESIRES.
THAT'S WHY...

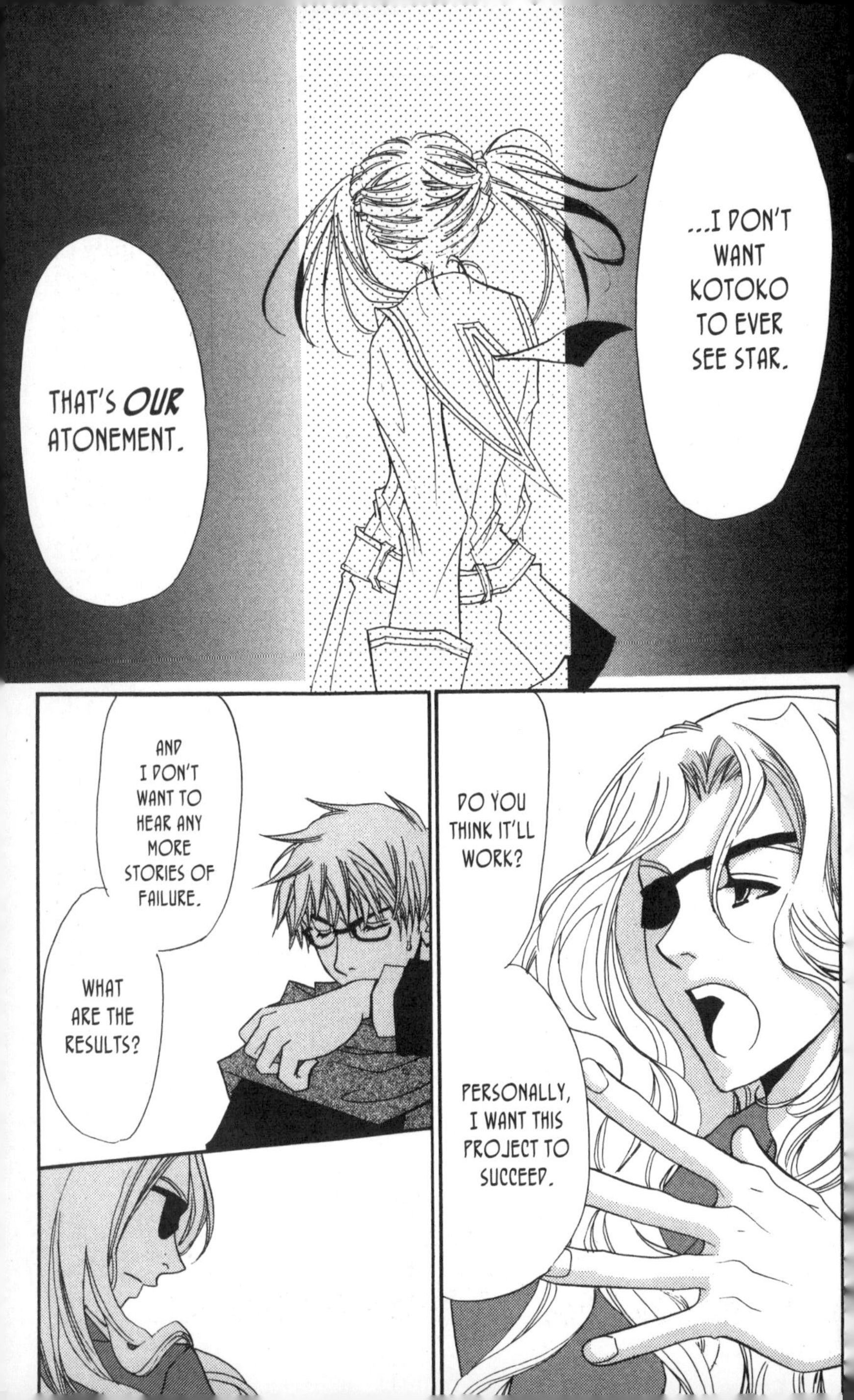
...I DON'T WANT KOTOKO TO EVER SEE STAR.
THAT'S *OUR* ATONEMENT.
DO YOU THINK IT'LL WORK?
PERSONALLY, I WANT THIS PROJECT TO SUCCEED.
AND I DON'T WANT TO HEAR ANY MORE STORIES OF FAILURE.
WHAT ARE THE RESULTS?

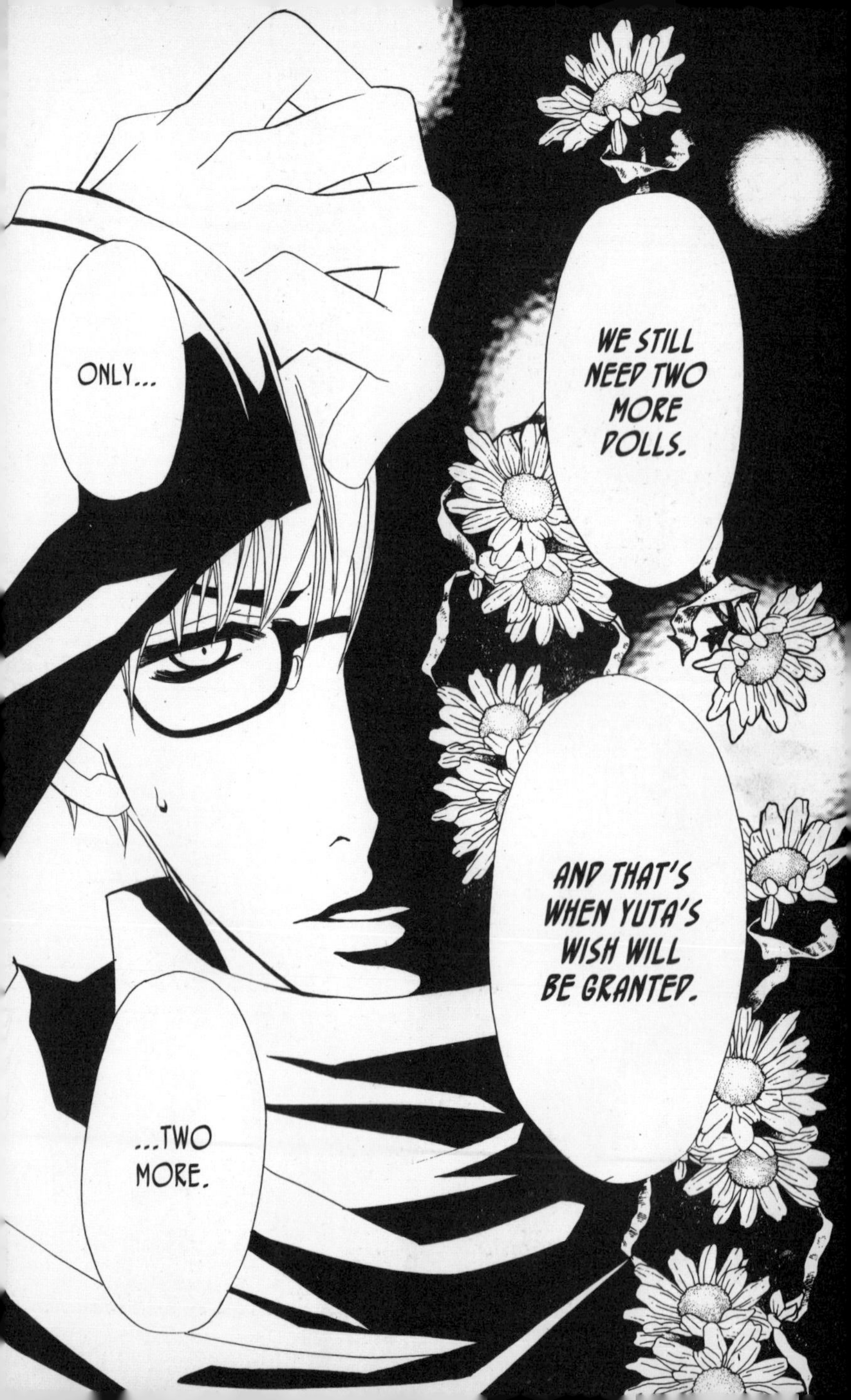
WE STILL NEED TWO MORE DOLLS.
AND THAT'S WHEN YUTA'S WISH WILL BE GRANTED.
ONLY...
...TWO MORE.

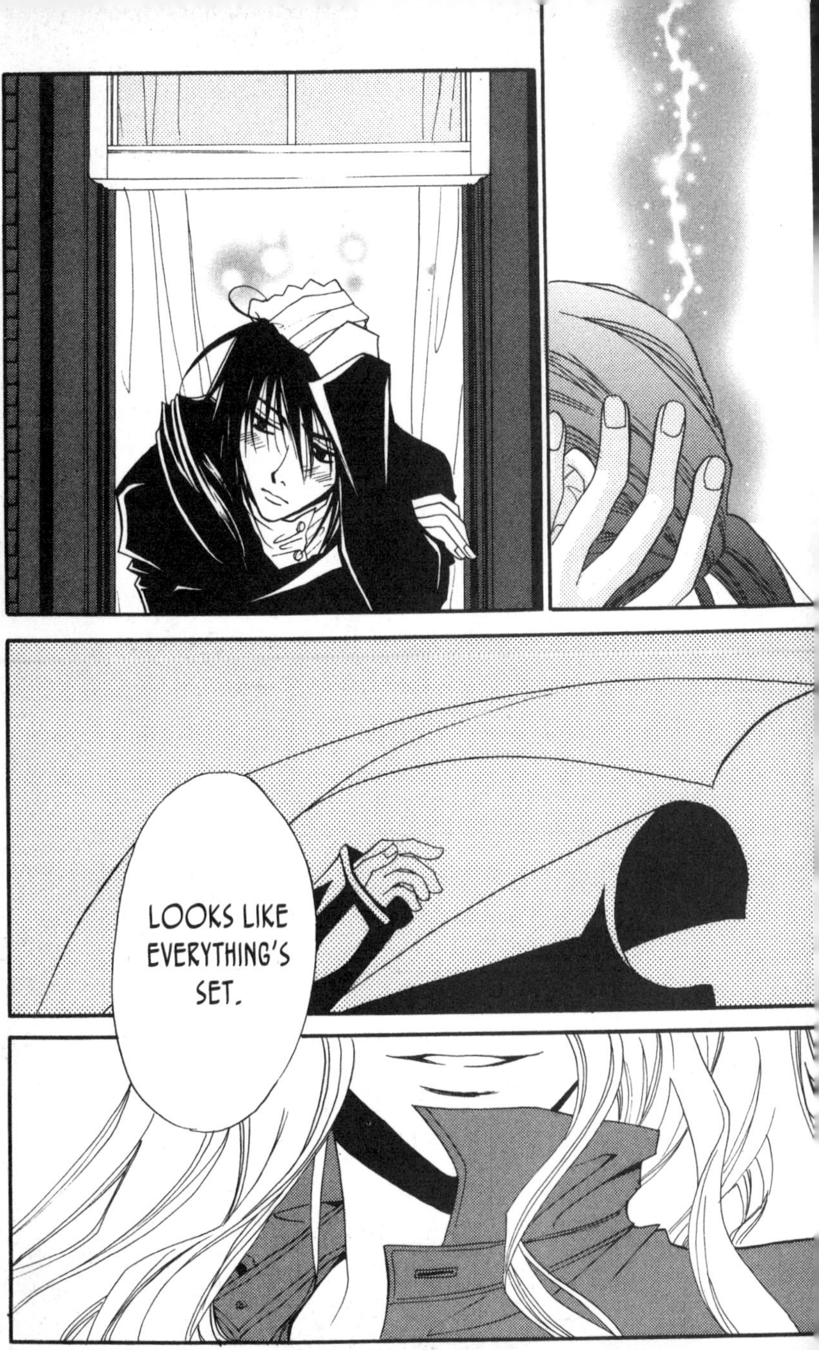
LOOKS LIKE EVERYTHING'S SET.

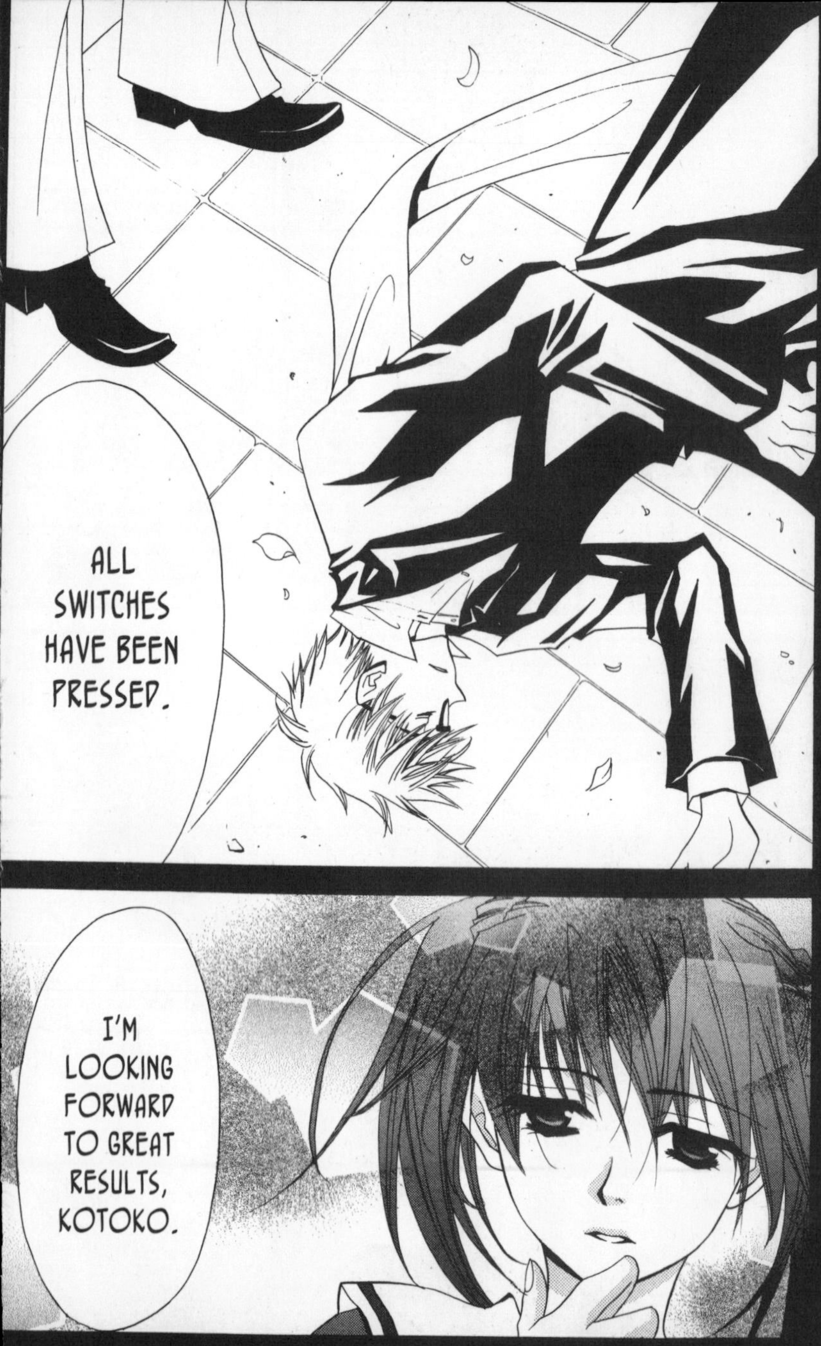
ALL SWITCHES HAVE BEEN PRESSED.
I'M LOOKING FORWARD TO GREAT RESULTS, KOTOKO.

4 End

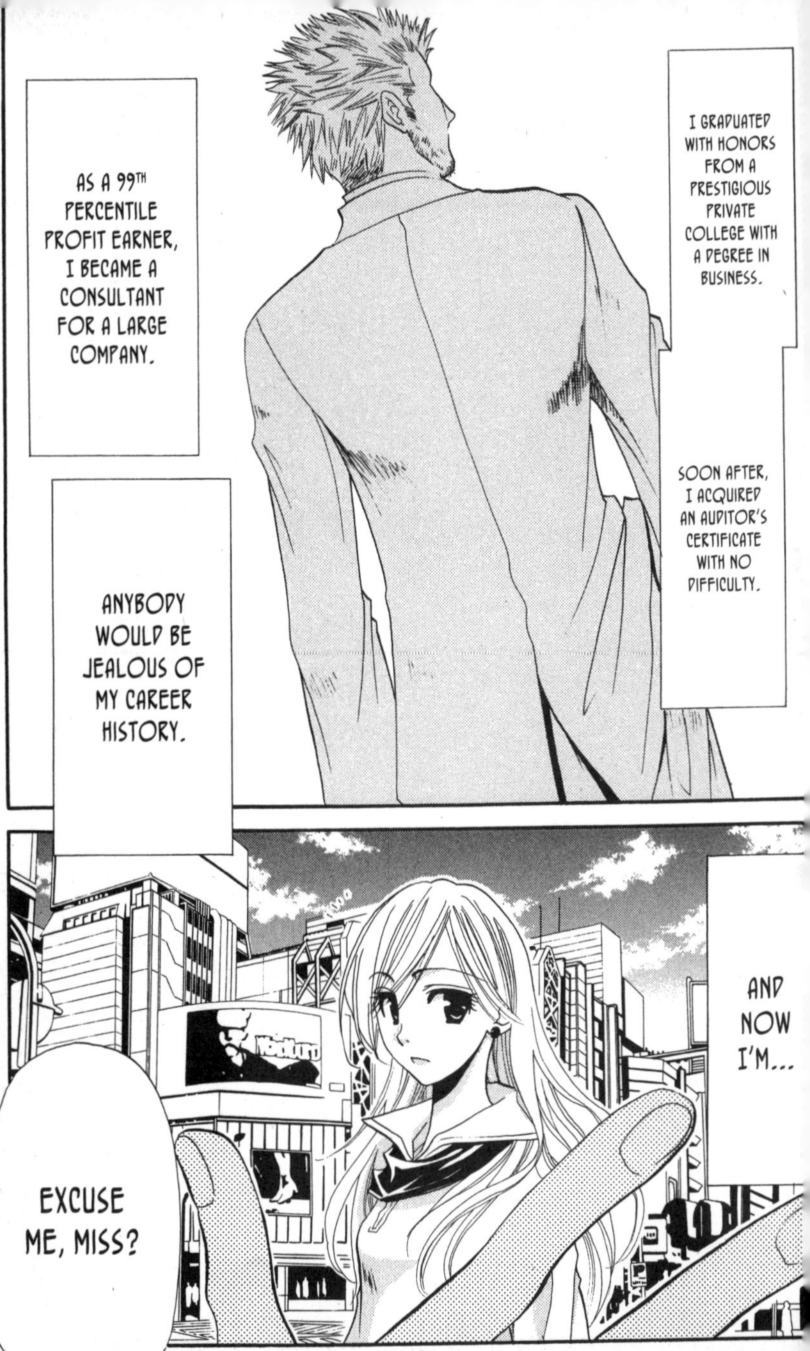
I GRADUATED WITH HONORS FROM A PRESTIGIOUS PRIVATE COLLEGE WITH A DEGREE IN BUSINESS.
AS A 99TH PERCENTILE PROFIT EARNER, I BECAME A CONSULTANT FOR A LARGE COMPANY.
SOON AFTER, I ACQUIRED AN AUDITOR'S CERTIFICATE WITH NO DIFFICULTY.
ANYBODY WOULD BE JEALOUS OF MY CAREER HISTORY.
AND NOW I'M...
EXCUSE ME, MISS?

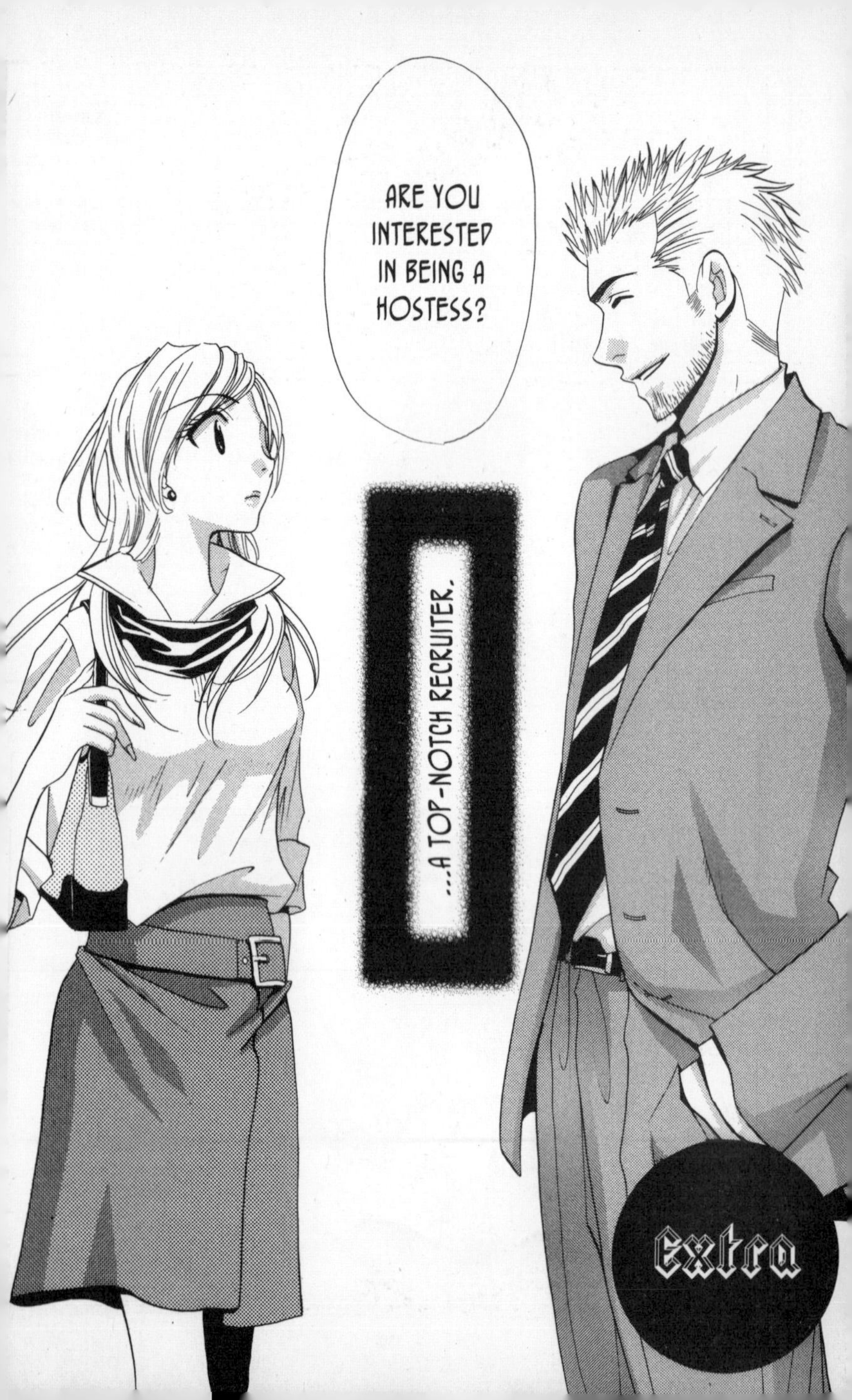
ARE YOU INTERESTED IN BEING A HOSTESS?
...A TOP-NOTCH RECRUITER.
extra

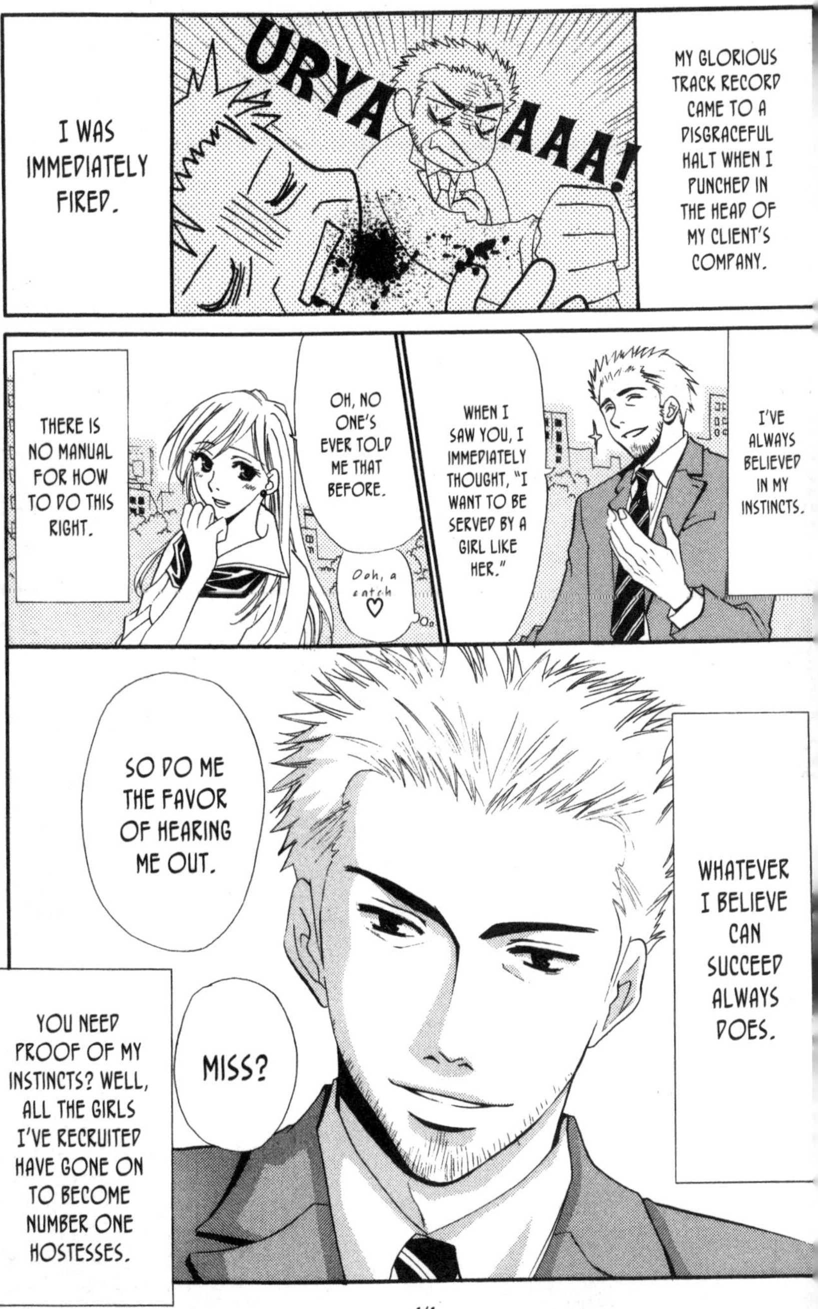
MY GLORIOUS TRACK RECORD CAME TO A DISGRACEFUL HALT WHEN I PUNCHED IN THE HEAD OF MY CLIENT'S COMPANY.
URYAAAA!
I WAS IMMEDIATELY FIRED.
I'VE ALWAYS BELIEVED IN MY INSTINCTS.
WHEN I SAW YOU, I IMMEDIATELY THOUGHT, "I WANT TO BE SERVED BY A GIRL LIKE HER."
OH, NO ONE'S EVER TOLD ME THAT BEFORE.
Ooh, a catch ♡
THERE IS NO MANUAL FOR HOW TO DO THIS RIGHT.
WHATEVER I BELIEVE CAN SUCCEED ALWAYS DOES.
SO DO ME THE FAVOR OF HEARING ME OUT.
MISS?
YOU NEED PROOF OF MY INSTINCTS? WELL, ALL THE GIRLS I'VE RECRUITED HAVE GONE ON TO BECOME NUMBER ONE HOSTESSES.

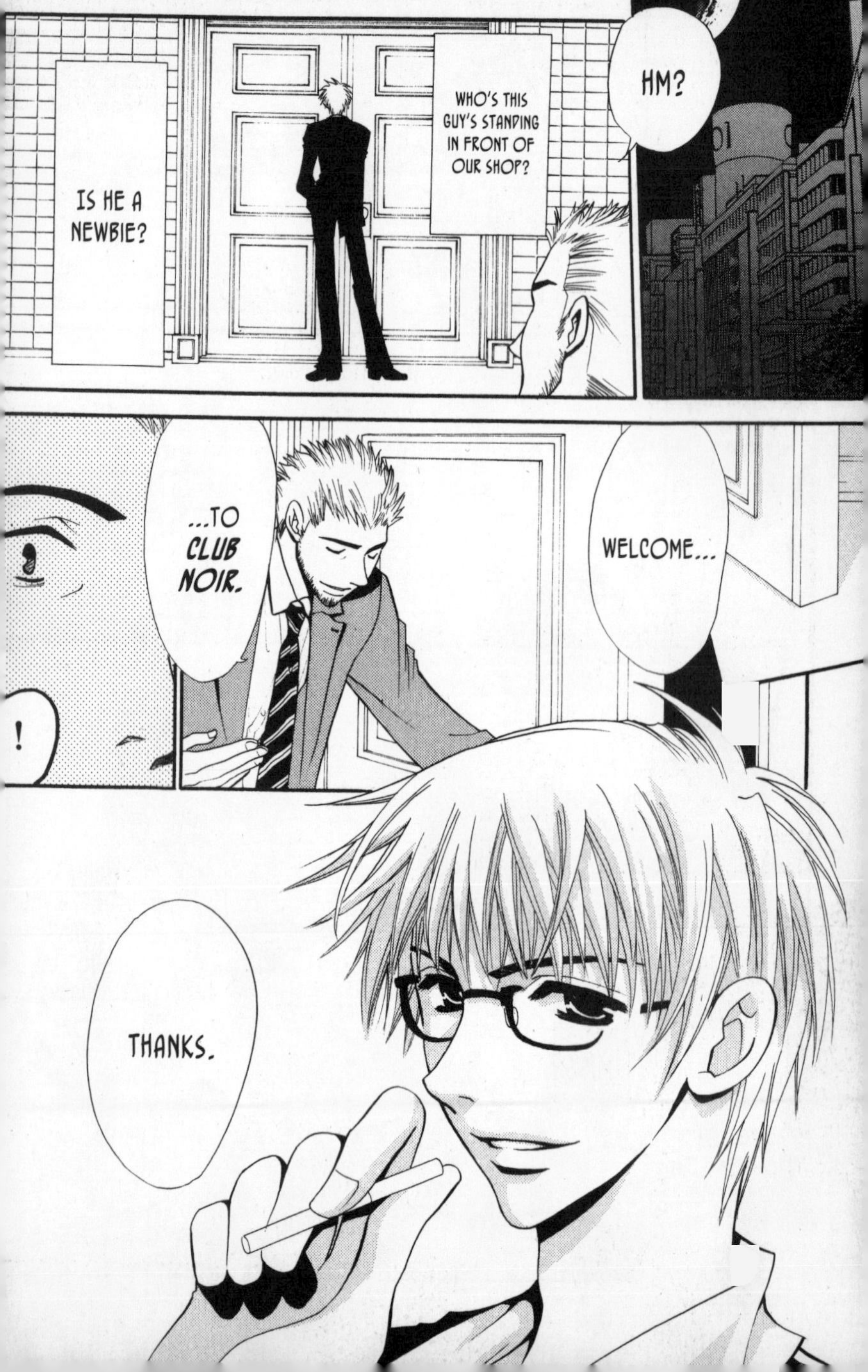

HM?
WHO'S THIS GUY'S STANDING IN FRONT OF OUR SHOP?
IS HE A NEWBIE?
WELCOME...
...TO CLUB NOIR.
!
THANKS.

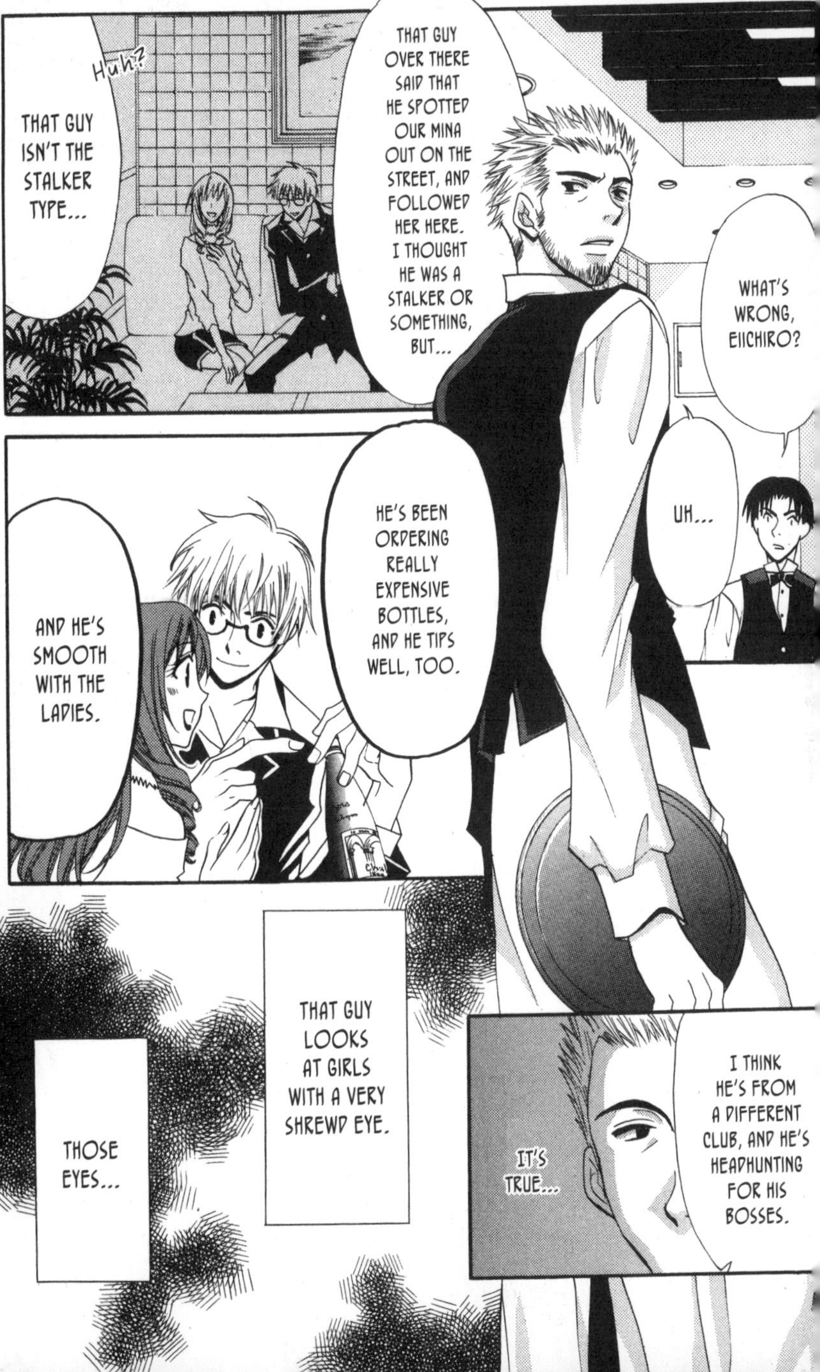
WHAT'S WRONG, EIICHIRO?
UH...
THAT GUY OVER THERE SAID THAT HE SPOTTED OUR MINA OUT ON THE STREET, AND FOLLOWED HER HERE. I THOUGHT HE WAS A STALKER OR SOMETHING, BUT...
Huh?
THAT GUY ISN'T THE STALKER TYPE...
HE'S BEEN ORDERING REALLY EXPENSIVE BOTTLES, AND HE TIPS WELL, TOO.
AND HE'S SMOOTH WITH THE LADIES.
I THINK HE'S FROM A DIFFERENT CLUB, AND HE'S HEADHUNTING FOR HIS BOSSES.
IT'S TRUE...
THAT GUY LOOKS AT GIRLS WITH A VERY SHREWD EYE.
THOSE EYES...

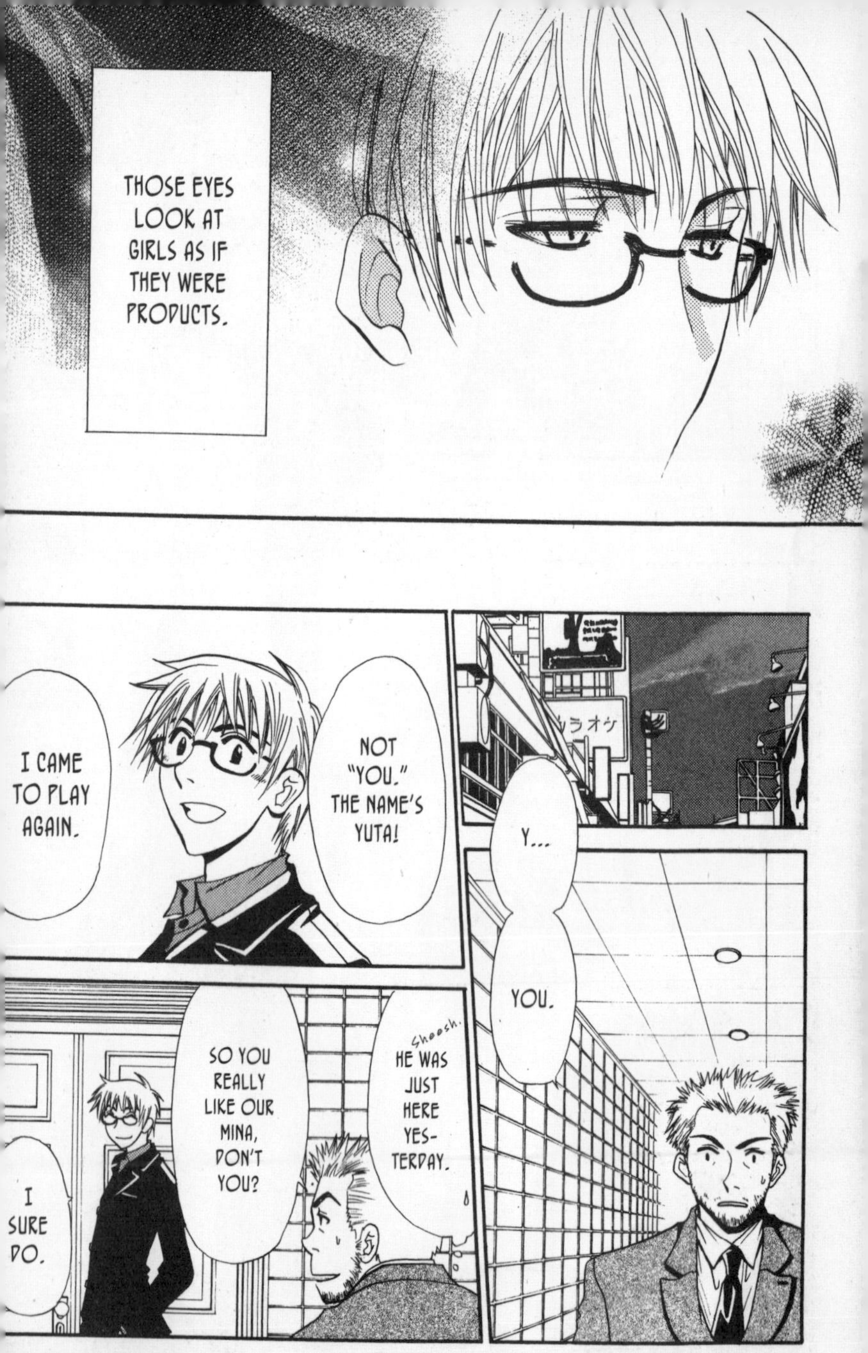
THOSE EYES LOOK AT GIRLS AS IF THEY WERE PRODUCTS.
Y...
YOU.
NOT "YOU." THE NAME'S YUTA!
I CAME TO PLAY AGAIN.
Shoosh.
HE WAS JUST HERE YES-TERDAY.
SO YOU REALLY LIKE OUR MINA, DON'T YOU?
I SURE DO.

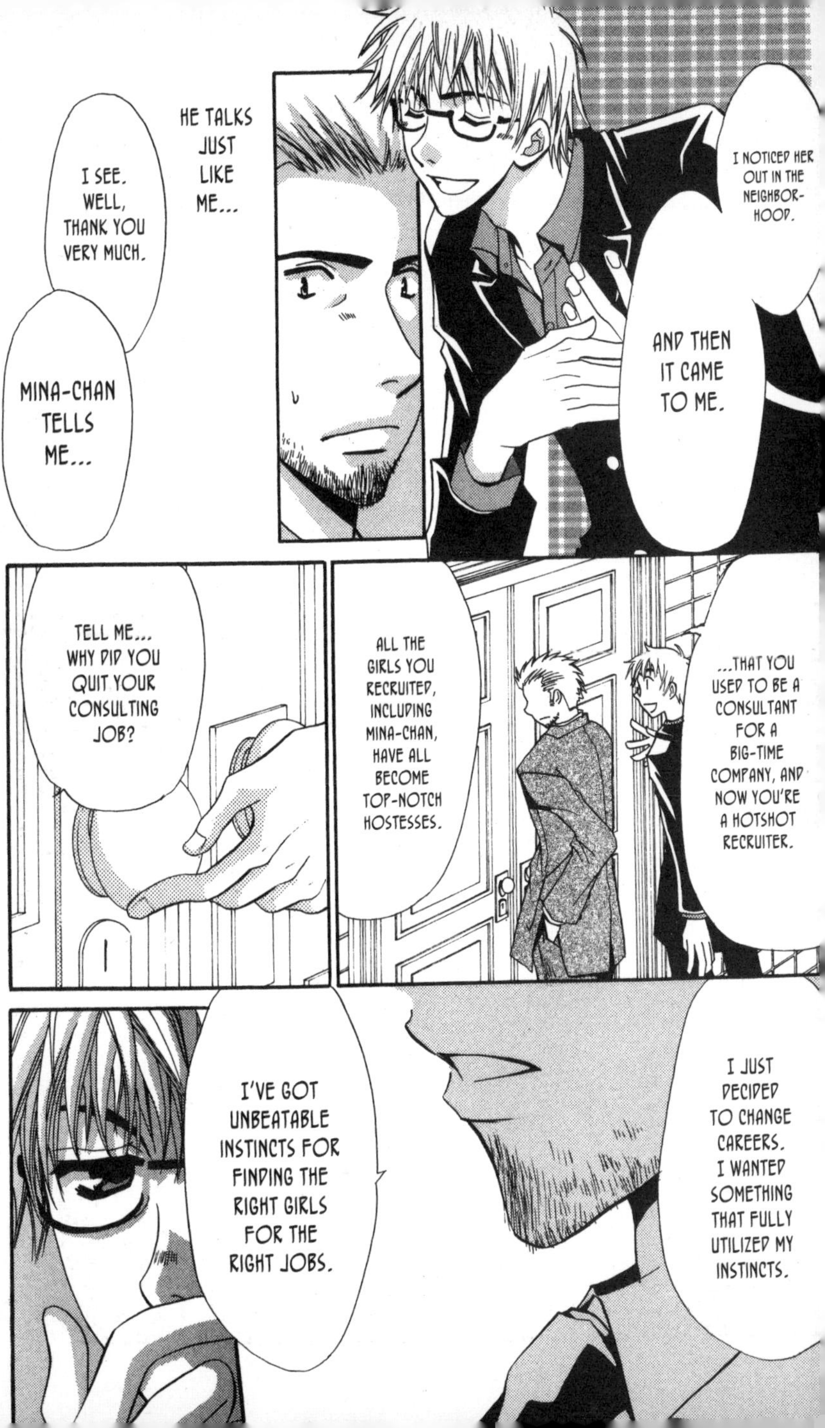
I NOTICED HER OUT IN THE NEIGHBOR-HOOD.
AND THEN IT CAME TO ME.
HE TALKS JUST LIKE ME...
I SEE. WELL, THANK YOU VERY MUCH.
MINA-CHAN TELLS ME...
...THAT YOU USED TO BE A CONSULTANT FOR A BIG-TIME COMPANY, AND NOW YOU'RE A HOTSHOT RECRUITER.
ALL THE GIRLS YOU RECRUITED, INCLUDING MINA-CHAN, HAVE ALL BECOME TOP-NOTCH HOSTESSES.
TELL ME... WHY DID YOU QUIT YOUR CONSULTING JOB?
I JUST DECIDED TO CHANGE CAREERS. I WANTED SOMETHING THAT FULLY UTILIZED MY INSTINCTS.
I'VE GOT UNBEATABLE INSTINCTS FOR FINDING THE RIGHT GIRLS FOR THE RIGHT JOBS.

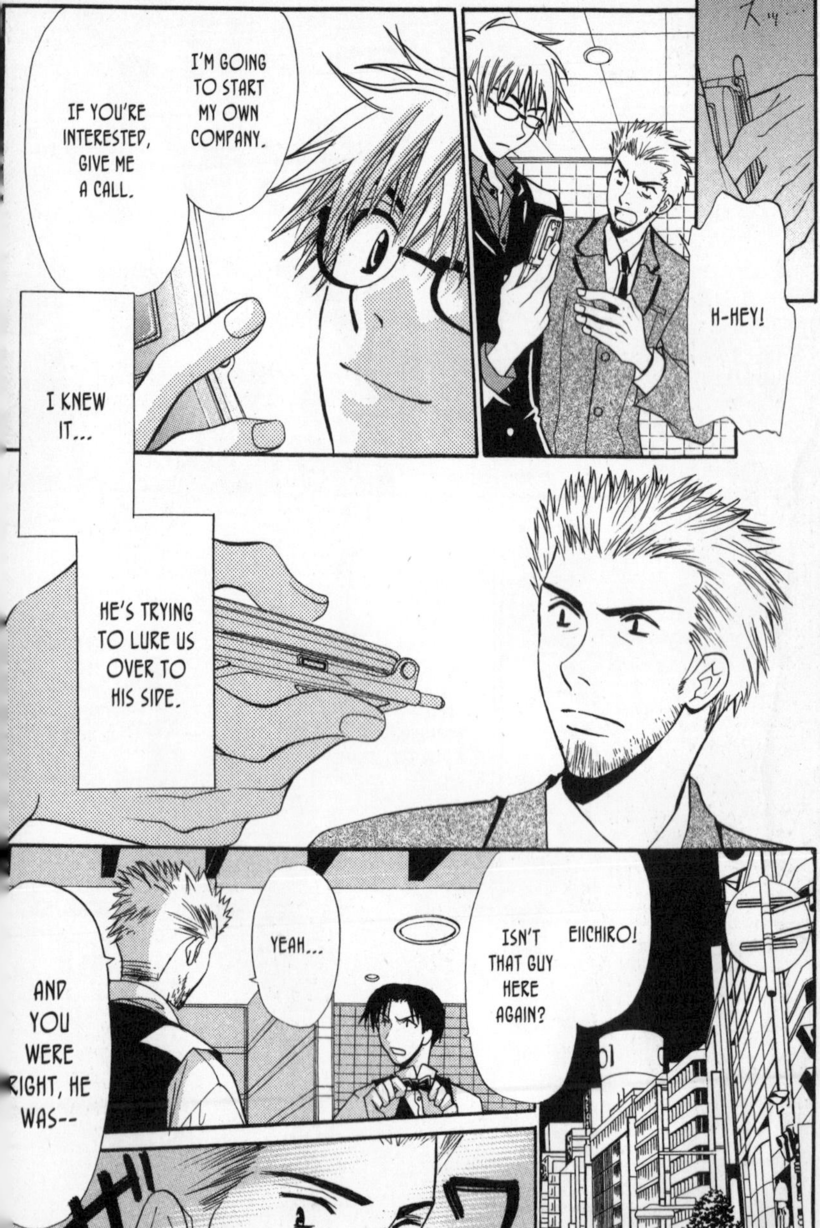
スッ…
H-HEY!
I'M GOING TO START MY OWN COMPANY.
IF YOU'RE INTERESTED, GIVE ME A CALL.
I KNEW IT...
HE'S TRYING TO LURE US OVER TO HIS SIDE.
EIICHIRO!
ISN'T THAT GUY HERE AGAIN?
YEAH...
AND YOU WERE RIGHT, HE WAS--

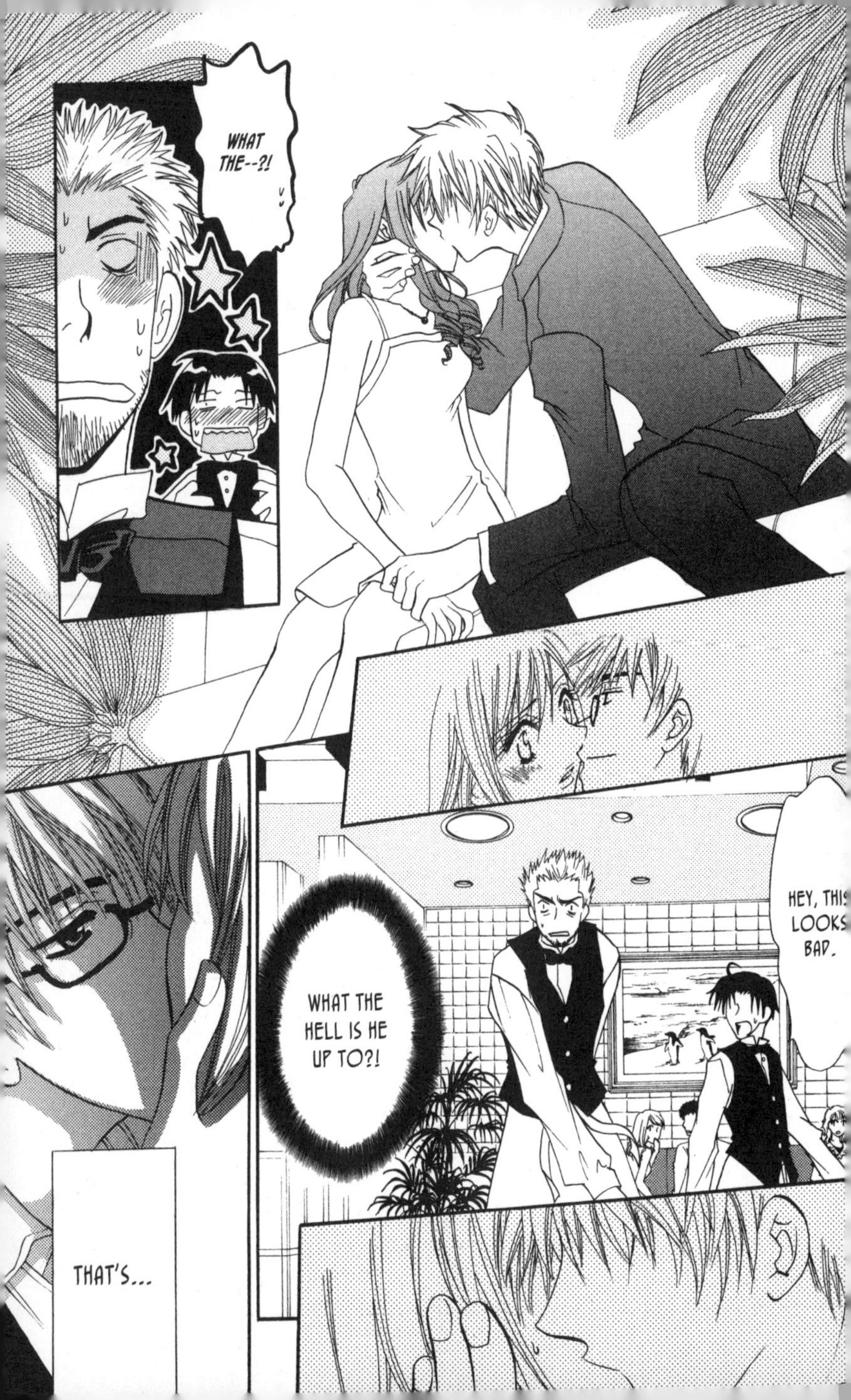
WHAT THE--?!
HEY, THIS LOOKS BAD.
WHAT THE HELL IS HE UP TO?!
THAT'S...

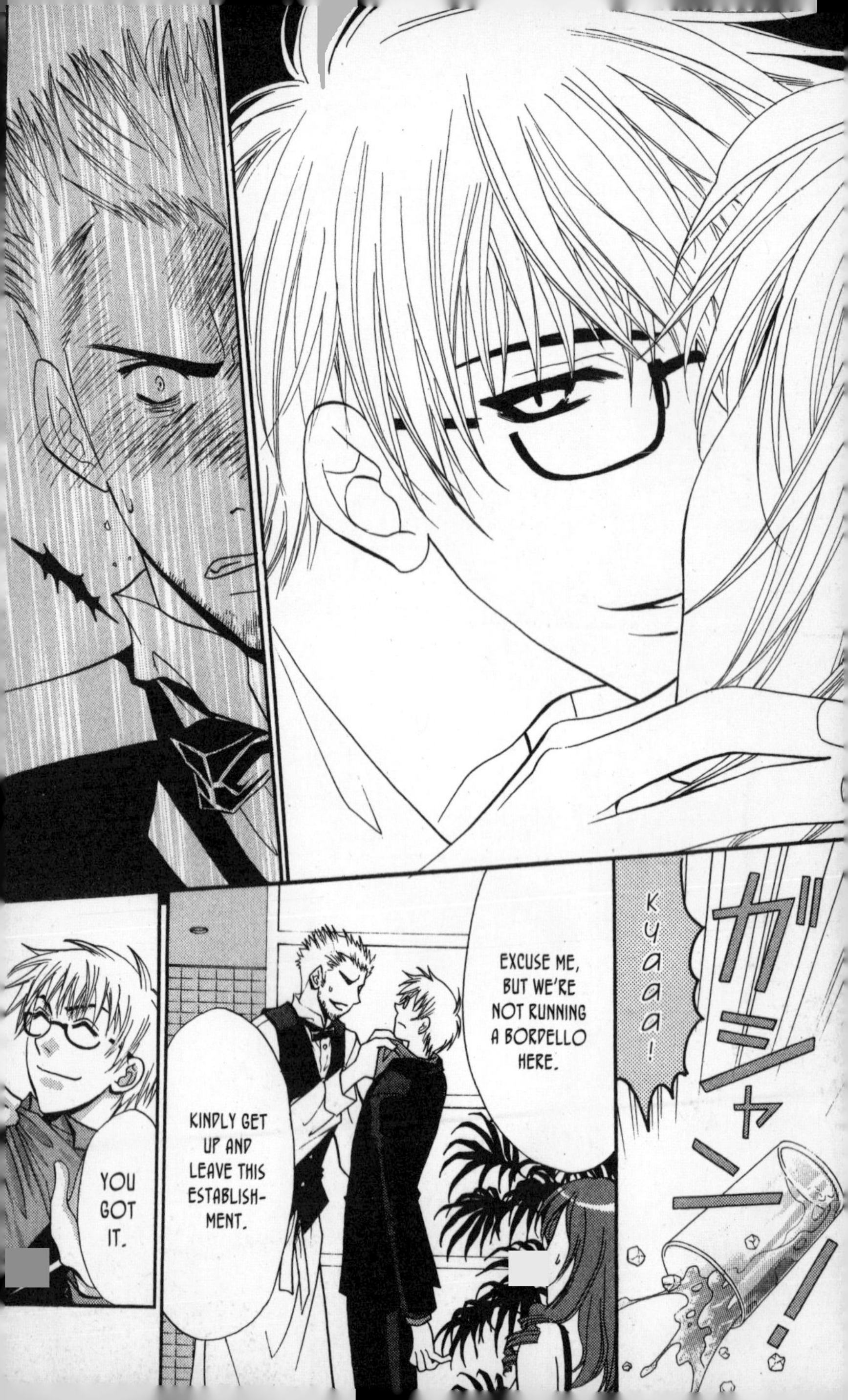
ガシャーン!!
Kyaaaa!
EXCUSE ME, BUT WE'RE NOT RUNNING A BORDELLO HERE.
KINDLY GET UP AND LEAVE THIS ESTABLISH-MENT.
YOU GOT IT.

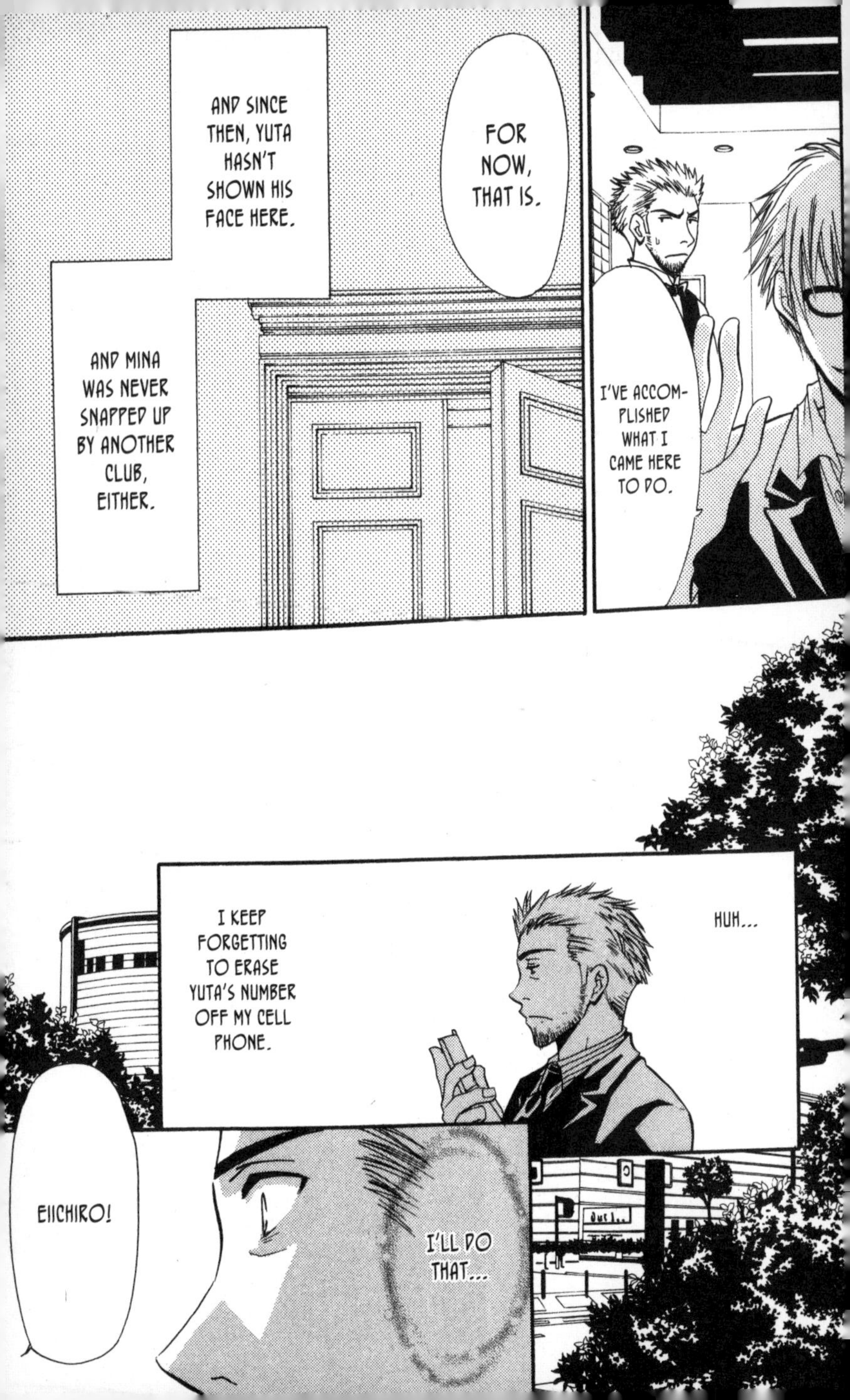
I'VE ACCOMPLISHED WHAT I CAME HERE TO DO.
FOR NOW, THAT IS.
AND SINCE THEN, YUTA HASN'T SHOWN HIS FACE HERE.
AND MINA WAS NEVER SNAPPED UP BY ANOTHER CLUB, EITHER.
HUH...
I KEEP FORGETTING TO ERASE YUTA'S NUMBER OFF MY CELL PHONE.
I'LL DO THAT...
EIICHIRO!

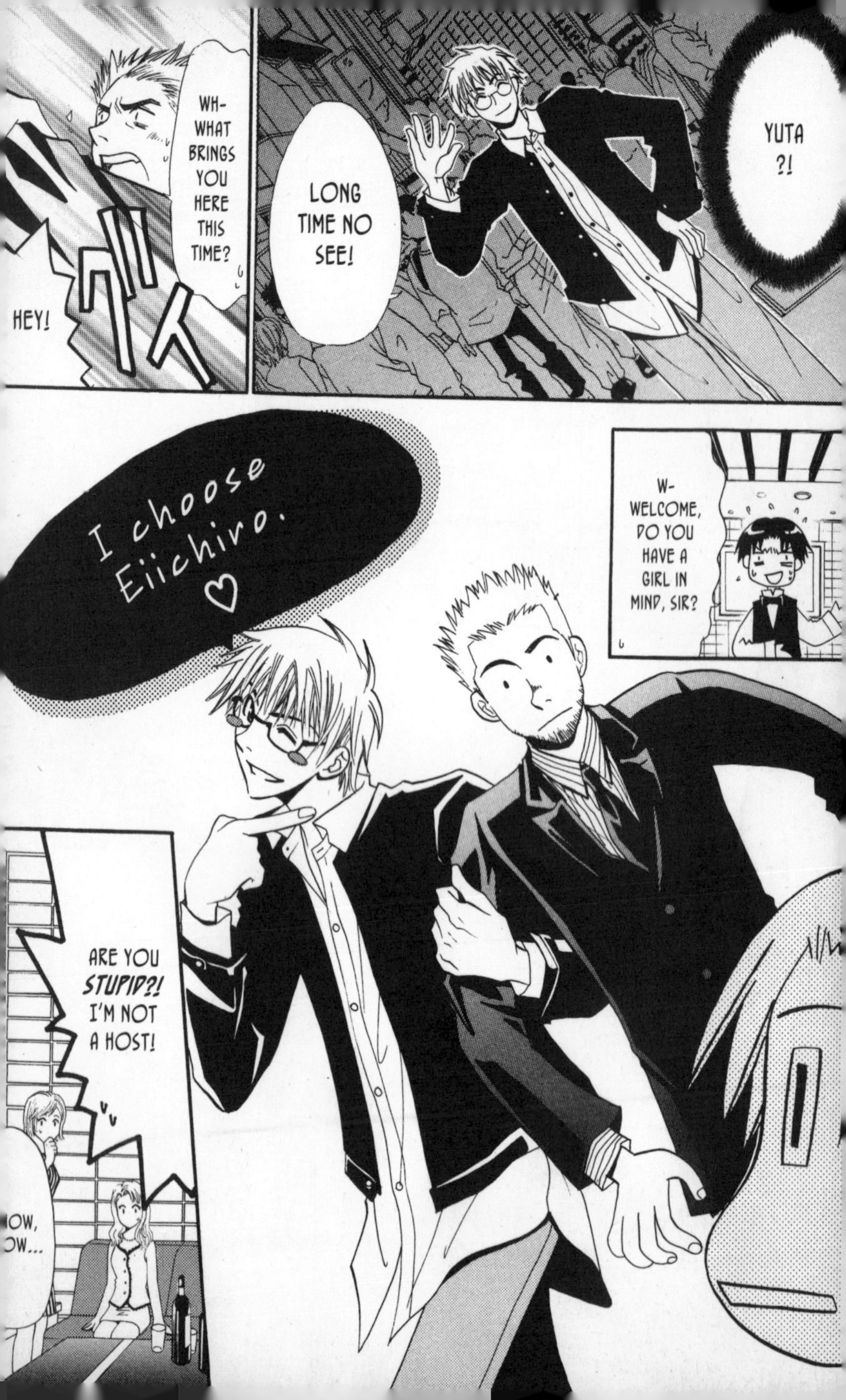
YUTA ?!
LONG TIME NO SEE!
WH- WHAT BRINGS YOU HERE THIS TIME?
HEY!
W- WELCOME, DO YOU HAVE A GIRL IN MIND, SIR?
I choose Eiichiro. ♥
ARE YOU STUPID?! I'M NOT A HOST!
OW, OW...

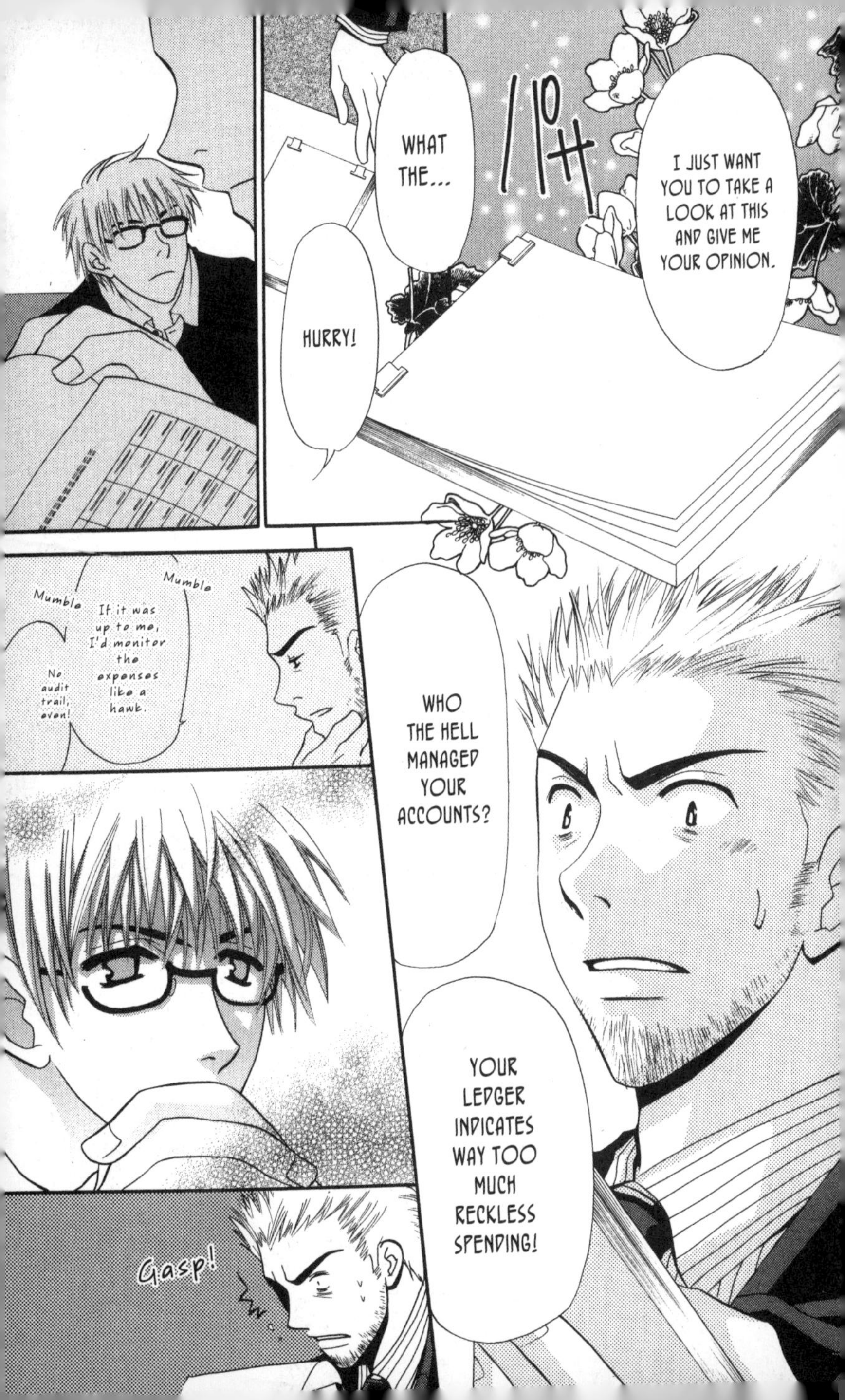
I JUST WANT YOU TO TAKE A LOOK AT THIS AND GIVE ME YOUR OPINION.
パサ
WHAT THE...
HURRY!
WHO THE HELL MANAGED YOUR ACCOUNTS?
YOUR LEDGER INDICATES WAY TOO MUCH RECKLESS SPENDING!
Mumble
Mumble
If it was up to me, I'd monitor the expenses like a hawk.
No audit trail, even!
Gasp!

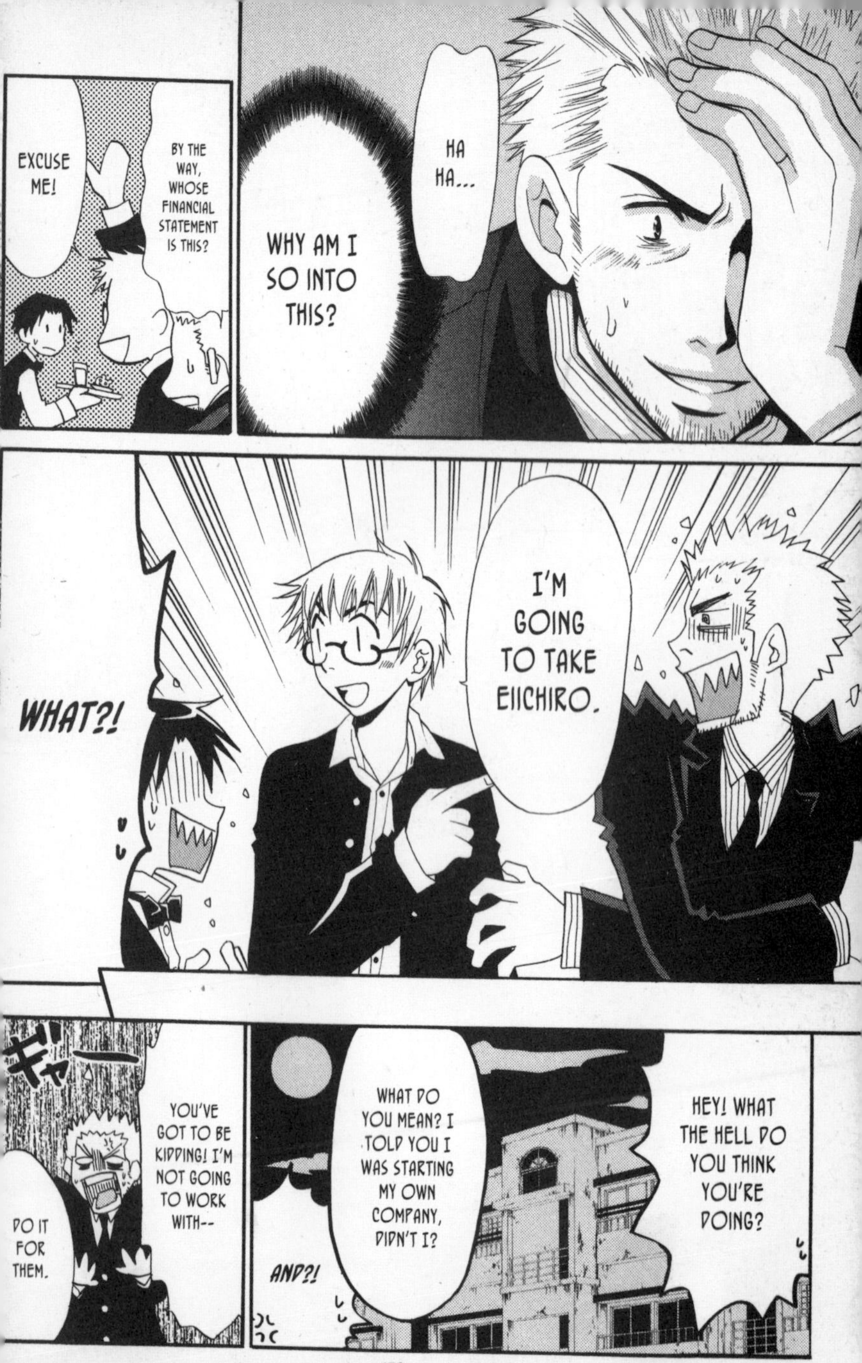
HA HA...
WHY AM I SO INTO THIS?
BY THE WAY, WHOSE FINANCIAL STATEMENT IS THIS?
EXCUSE ME!
I'M GOING TO TAKE EIICHIRO.
WHAT?!
HEY! WHAT THE HELL DO YOU THINK YOU'RE DOING?
WHAT DO YOU MEAN? I TOLD YOU I WAS STARTING MY OWN COMPANY, DIDN'T I?
AND?!
ギャー
YOU'VE GOT TO BE KIDDING! I'M NOT GOING TO WORK WITH--
DO IT FOR THEM.

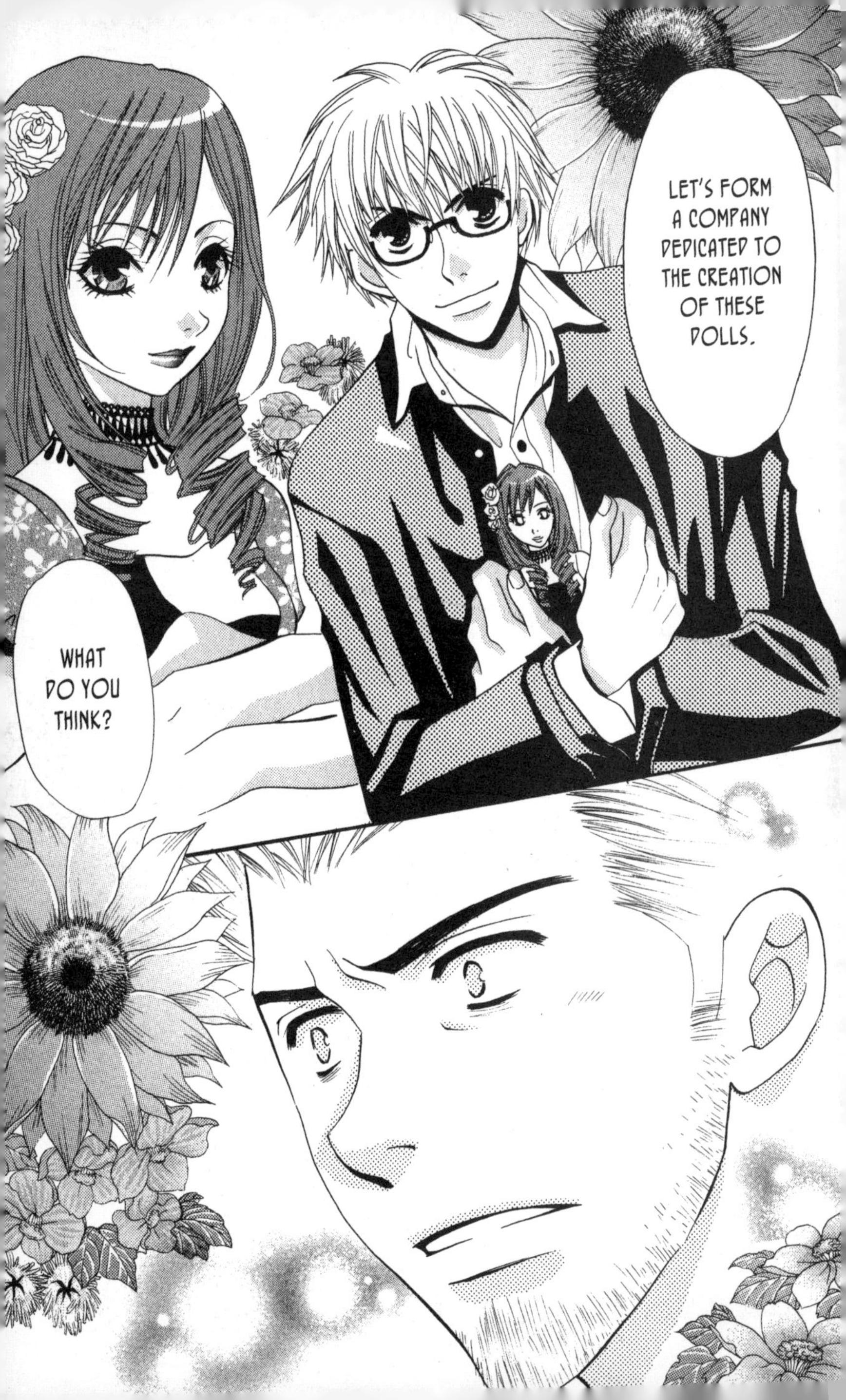
LET'S FORM A COMPANY DEDICATED TO THE CREATION OF THESE DOLLS.
WHAT DO YOU THINK?

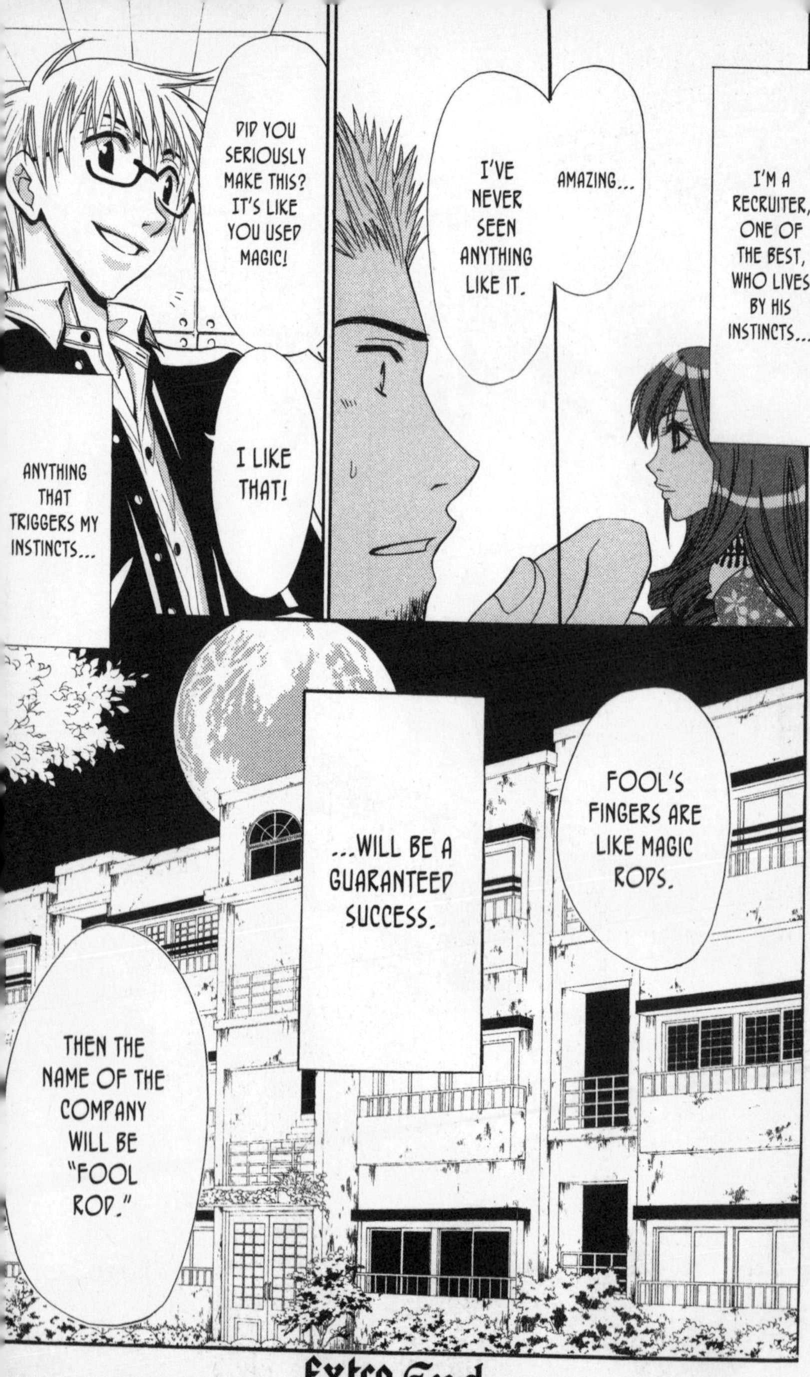
I'M A RECRUITER, ONE OF THE BEST, WHO LIVES BY HIS INSTINCTS...
AMAZING...
I'VE NEVER SEEN ANYTHING LIKE IT.
DID YOU SERIOUSLY MAKE THIS? IT'S LIKE YOU USED MAGIC!
I LIKE THAT!
ANYTHING THAT TRIGGERS MY INSTINCTS...
FOOL'S FINGERS ARE LIKE MAGIC RODS.
...WILL BE A GUARANTEED SUCCESS.
THEN THE NAME OF THE COMPANY WILL BE "FOOL ROD."

Extra End

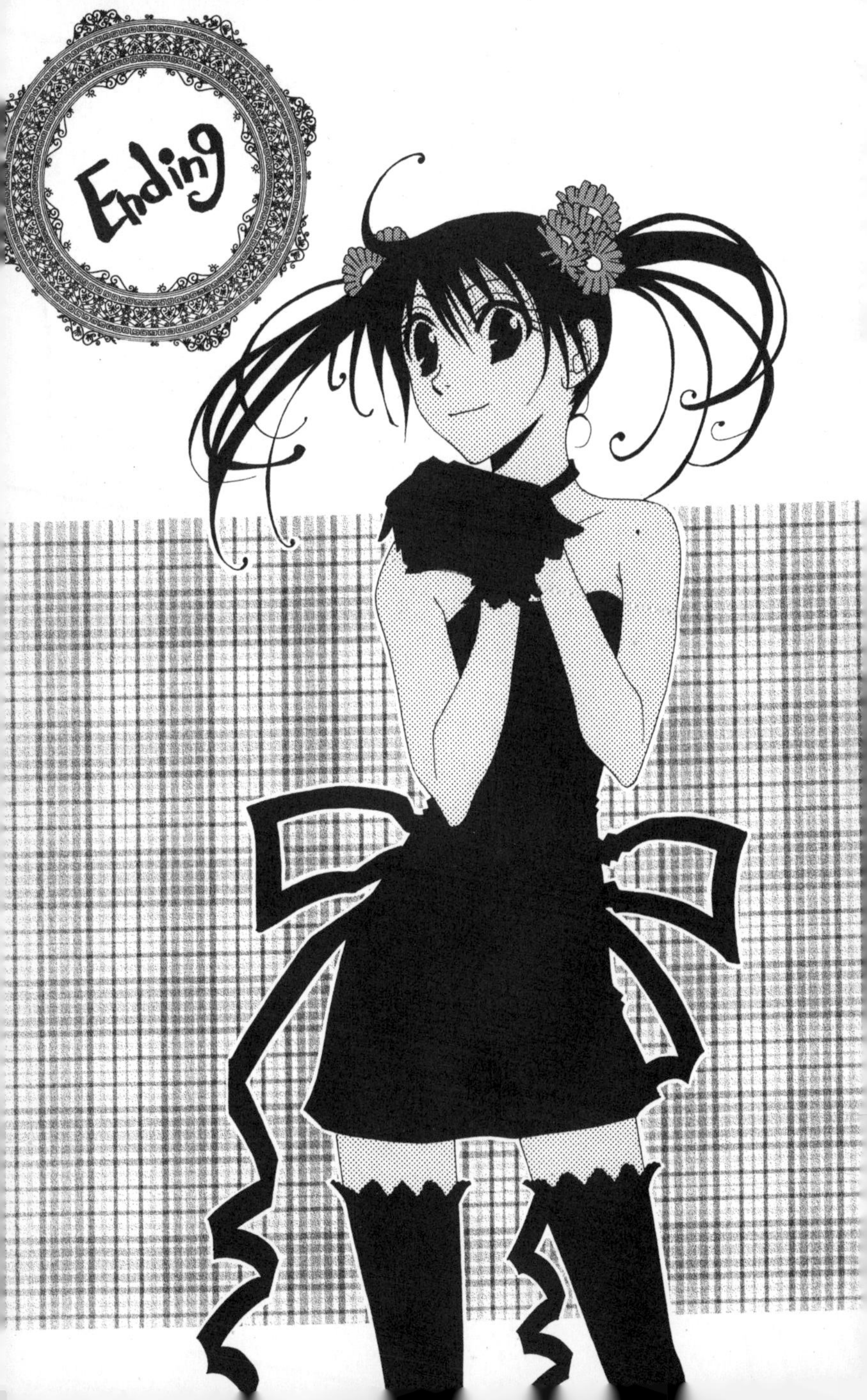
Ending

Hello! Long time no see! This is Kazuko Higashiyama!

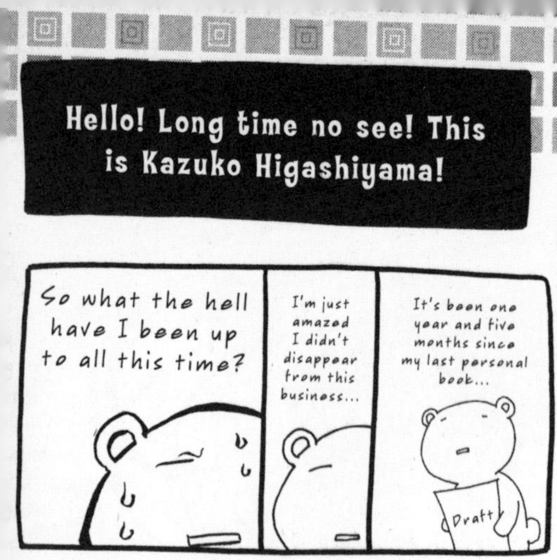
It's been one year and five months since my last personal book...
Draft
I'm just amazed I didn't disappear from this business...
So what the hell have I been up to all this time?

MY MEMORY'S BEEN REALLY, REALLY FOGGY RECENTLY. I SOMETIMES GET OUT OF MY CHAIR AND THEN FORGET WHY I GOT UP, AND I WILL STAND LIKE THAT FOR MINUTES.
THANK YOU FOR BUYING THE FIRST VOLUME OF "SHINSHOKU KISS." THIS IS MY FIRST MULTIPLE-VOLUME BOOK. AND THE MAIN CHARACTER IS A GIRL! AT FIRST, I WAS NERVOUS BECAUSE I DIDN'T KNOW WHAT TO DO WITH HER. AND MY FEAR STILL HASN'T COMPLETELY GONE AWAY. SORRY ABOUT THAT...

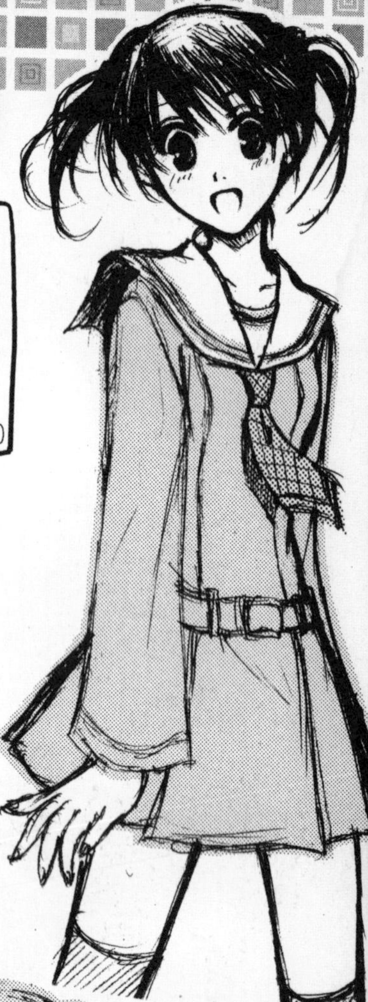

Kotoko in Uniform

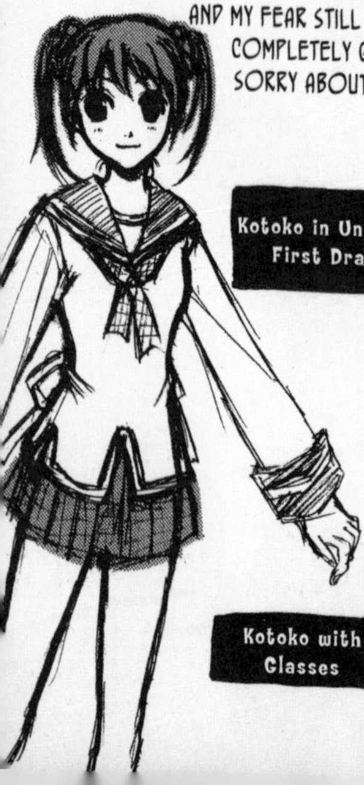

Kotoko in Uniform. First Draft

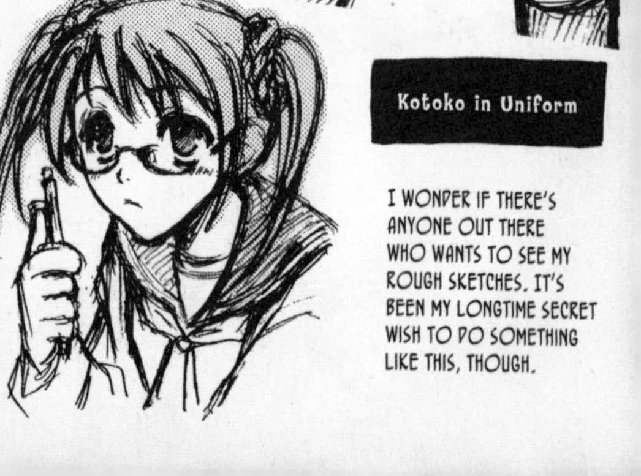

Kotoko with Glasses

I WONDER IF THERE'S ANYONE OUT THERE WHO WANTS TO SEE MY ROUGH SKETCHES. IT'S BEEN MY LONGTIME SECRET WISH TO DO SOMETHING LIKE THIS, THOUGH.

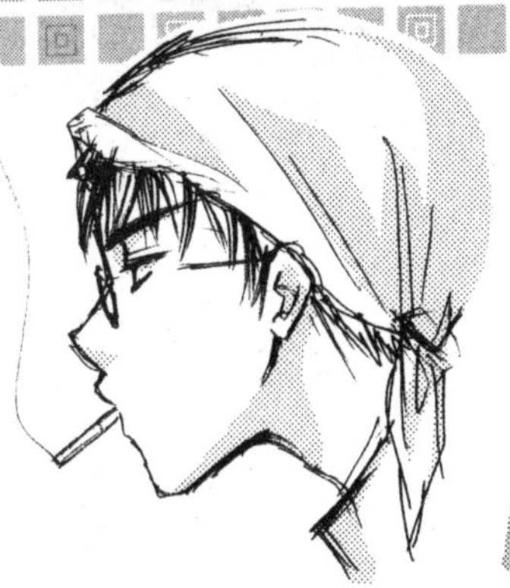

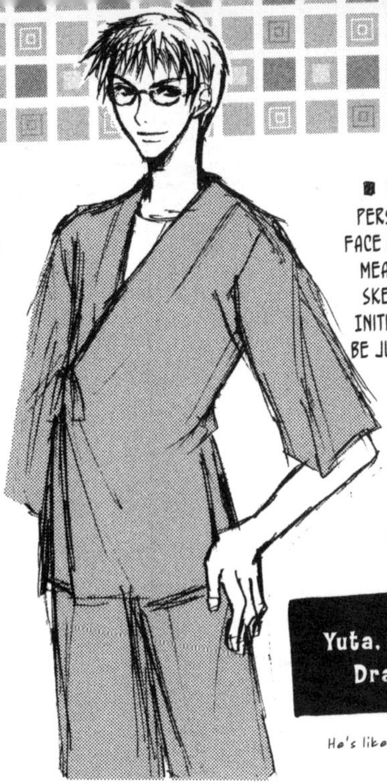

▪ THIS GUY'S PERSONALITY AND FACE ARE SOMEWHA MEANER THAN THIS SKETCH LETS ON. INITIALLY, I HAD HI BE JUST A PERVERTE ARTIST WITH A THING FOR WEARING KIMONOS. O I GUESS SOME PERVERSIONS NEVER REALLY CHANGE.

▪ I REALLY LIKE THIS "1 GIRL + 2 GUYS" COMBINATION. I REALLY DO. PLUS, I REALLY ENJOY THE FACT THAT THE GIRL IS REALLY SMALL AND SHORT, VERSUS THE GUYS, WHO'RE REALLY TALL AND OMINOUS. IF I WAS REALLY GOOD AT DRAWING CHILDREN, I WOULD'VE MADE KOTOKO A 12-YEAR-OLD GIRL...

Yuta, First Draft

He's like a snake.

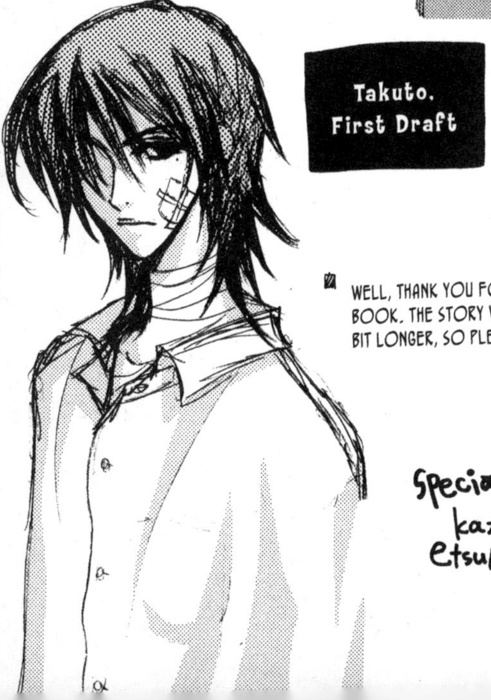

Takuto, First Draft

▪ HE'S TOTALLY DIFFERENT. I PREFER THE LENGTH OF HAIR SHORT AND PARTED ON THE LEFT, BUT I WANTED TO MAKE HIM DIFFERENT, SO I MADE HIS HAIR REALLY LONG. THE HARDEST PART IS INKING IN ALL HIS HAIR STRANDS. EVENTUALLY...PROBABLY... MOST LIKELY...MUMBLE MUMBLE...

▪ WELL, THANK YOU FOR PUTTING UP WITH THIS BOOK. THE STORY WILL CONTINUE FOR A BIT LONGER, SO PLEASE KEEP ON READING!

東山和子

Kazuko Higashiyama

Special thanx
kazuko.M sama / takako.W sama
etsuko.T sama / C sama
and You ♡

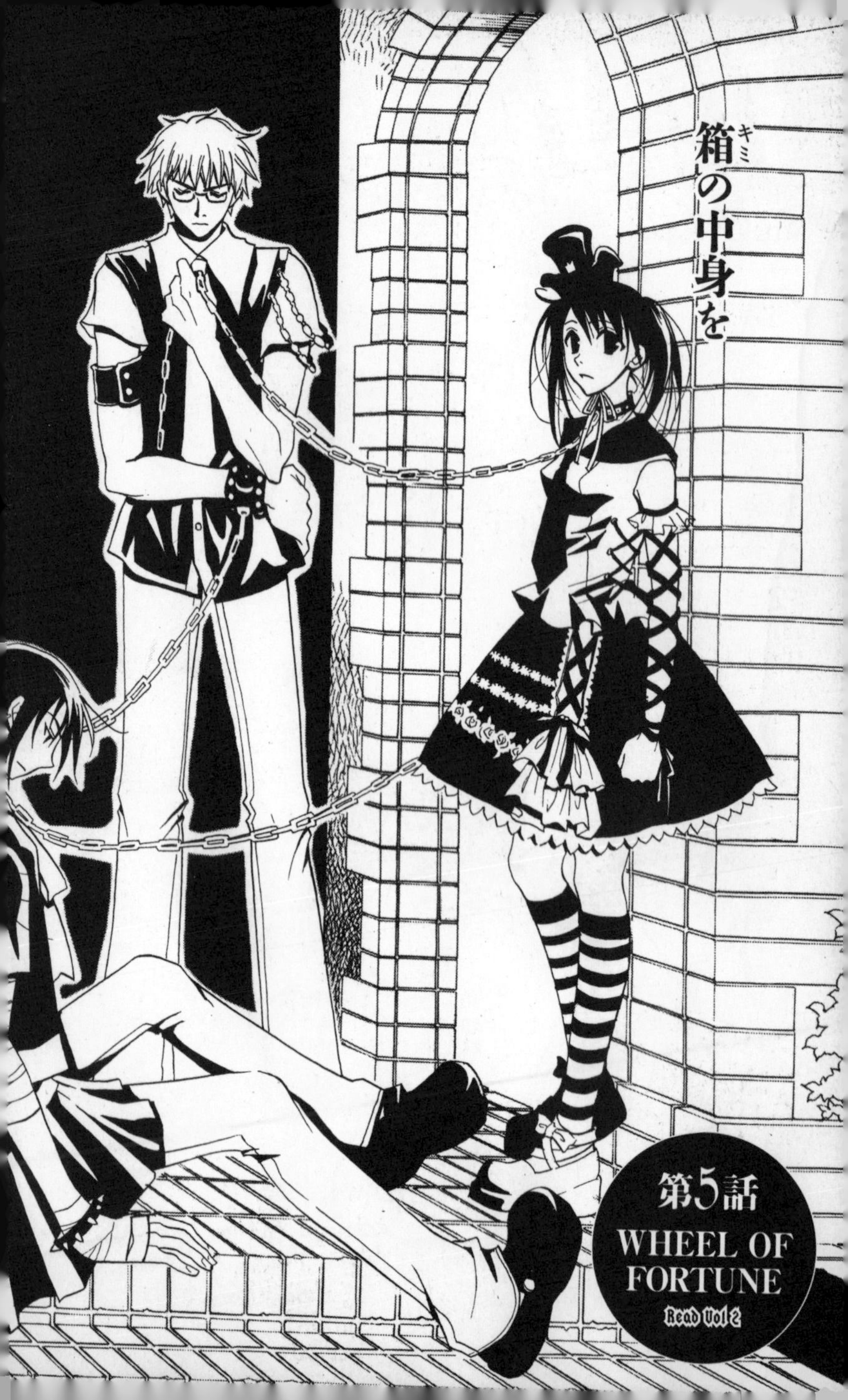
箱(キミ)の中身を
第5話
WHEEL OF FORTUNE
Read Vol 2

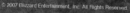

tactics

A collaboration from the creators
of *Detective Loki Ragnarok* and
Shinshoku Kiss!

Meet Kantarou, a folklore scholar living in
the Taisho period. Ever since he was a child,
he has been able to see and talk to various
spirits. But now that Kantarou's all grown up,
he moonlights as an exorcist solving
the problems of ghosts and demons...
all with the help of Haruka, the legendary
demon-eating tengu!

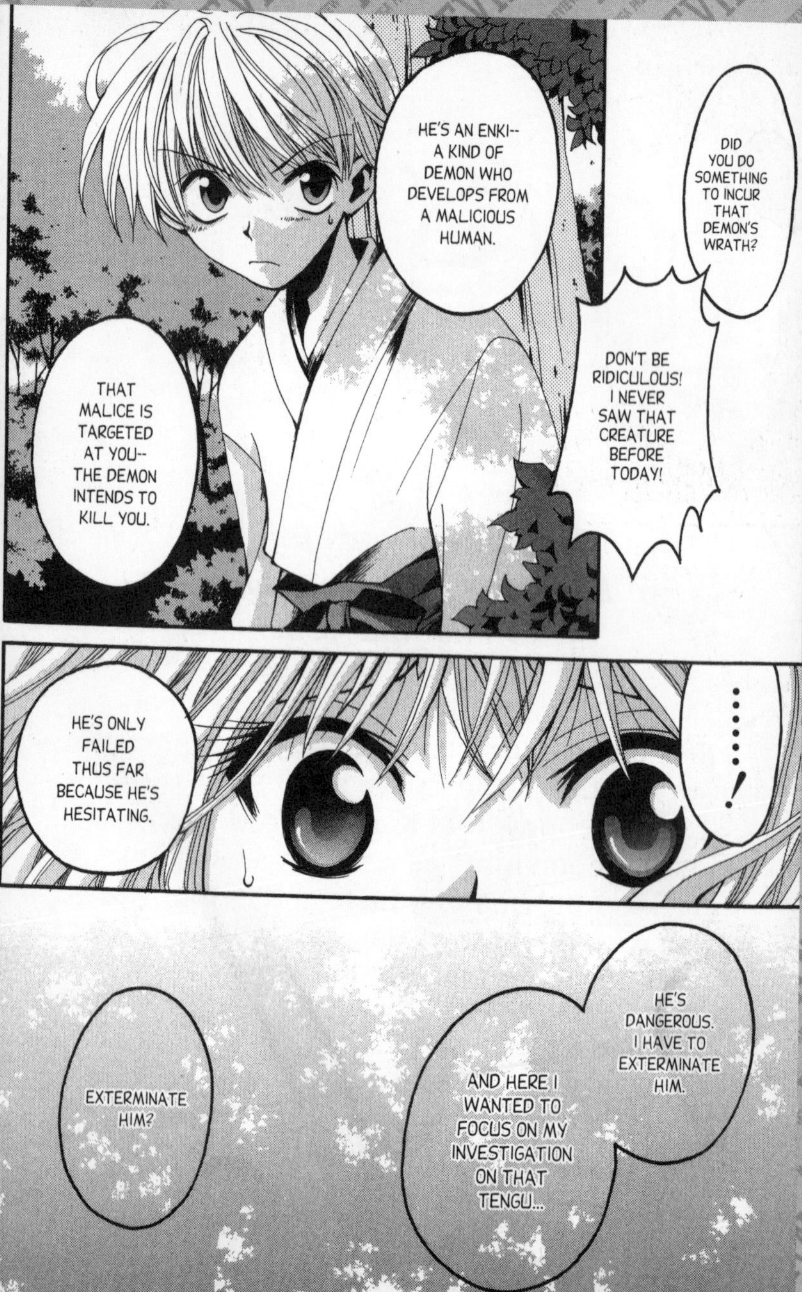
DID YOU DO SOMETHING TO INCUR THAT DEMON'S WRATH?
DON'T BE RIDICULOUS! I NEVER SAW THAT CREATURE BEFORE TODAY!
HE'S AN ENKI-- A KIND OF DEMON WHO DEVELOPS FROM A MALICIOUS HUMAN.
THAT MALICE IS TARGETED AT YOU-- THE DEMON INTENDS TO KILL YOU.
......!
HE'S ONLY FAILED THUS FAR BECAUSE HE'S HESITATING.
HE'S DANGEROUS. I HAVE TO EXTERMINATE HIM.
AND HERE I WANTED TO FOCUS ON MY INVESTIGATION ON THAT TENGU...
EXTERMINATE HIM?

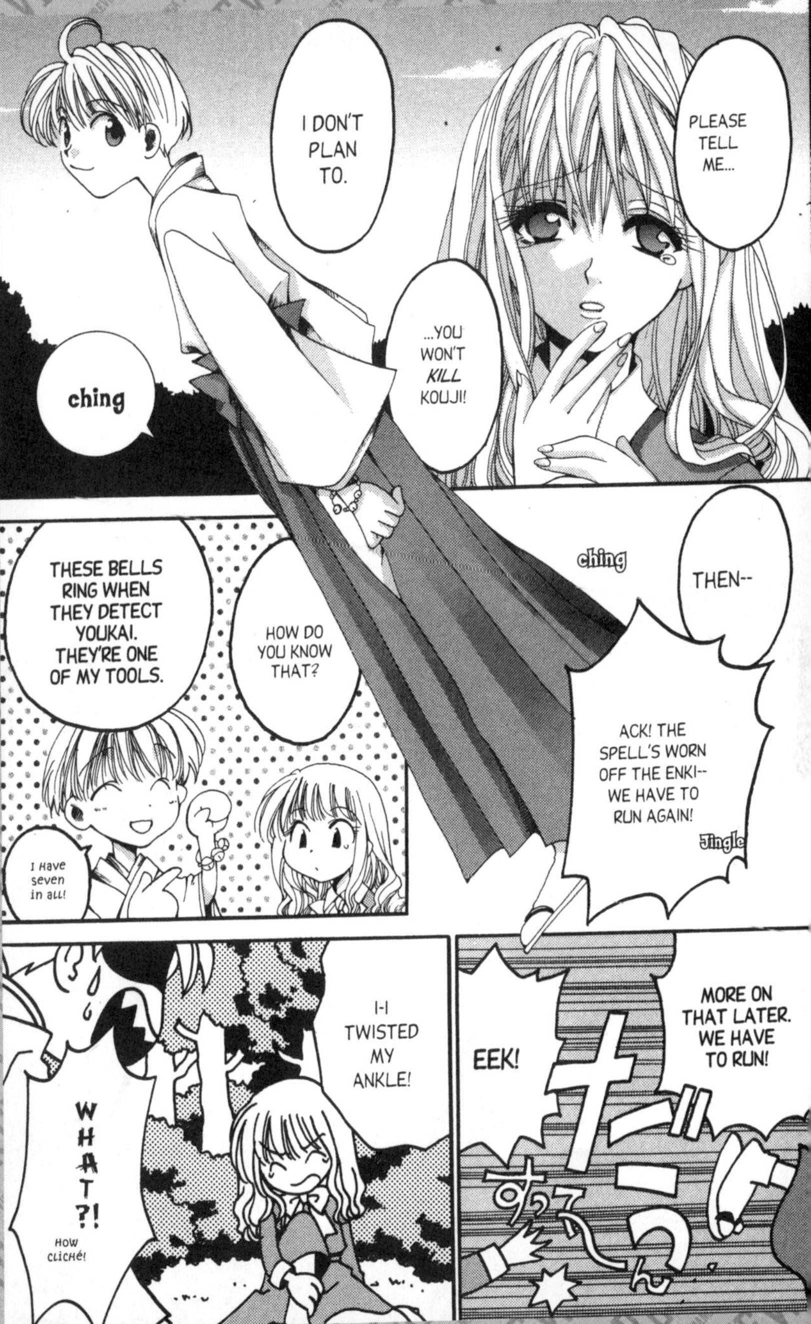
PLEASE TELL ME...
...YOU WON'T KILL KOUJI!
I DON'T PLAN TO.
ching
THEN--
ching
ACK! THE SPELL'S WORN OFF THE ENKI-- WE HAVE TO RUN AGAIN!
Jingle
HOW DO YOU KNOW THAT?
THESE BELLS RING WHEN THEY DETECT YOUKAI. THEY'RE ONE OF MY TOOLS.
I have seven in all!
MORE ON THAT LATER. WE HAVE TO RUN!
EEK!
I-I TWISTED MY ANKLE!
WHAT?!
How cliché!

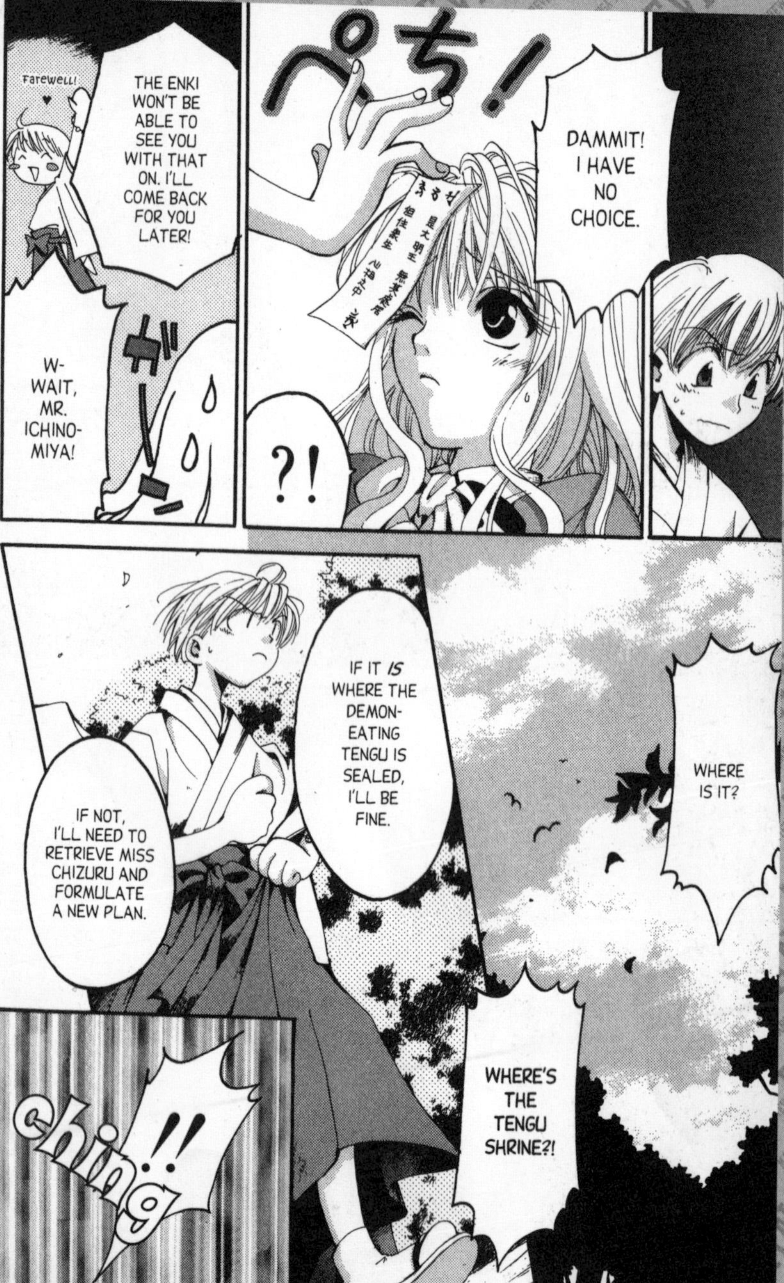
DAMMIT! I HAVE NO CHOICE.
ぺち!
?!
Farewell!
THE ENKI WON'T BE ABLE TO SEE YOU WITH THAT ON. I'LL COME BACK FOR YOU LATER!
W-WAIT, MR. ICHINO-MIYA!
ガー
WHERE IS IT?
WHERE'S THE TENGU SHRINE?!
IF IT *IS* WHERE THE DEMON-EATING TENGU IS SEALED, I'LL BE FINE.
IF NOT, I'LL NEED TO RETRIEVE MISS CHIZURU AND FORMULATE A NEW PLAN.
ching!!

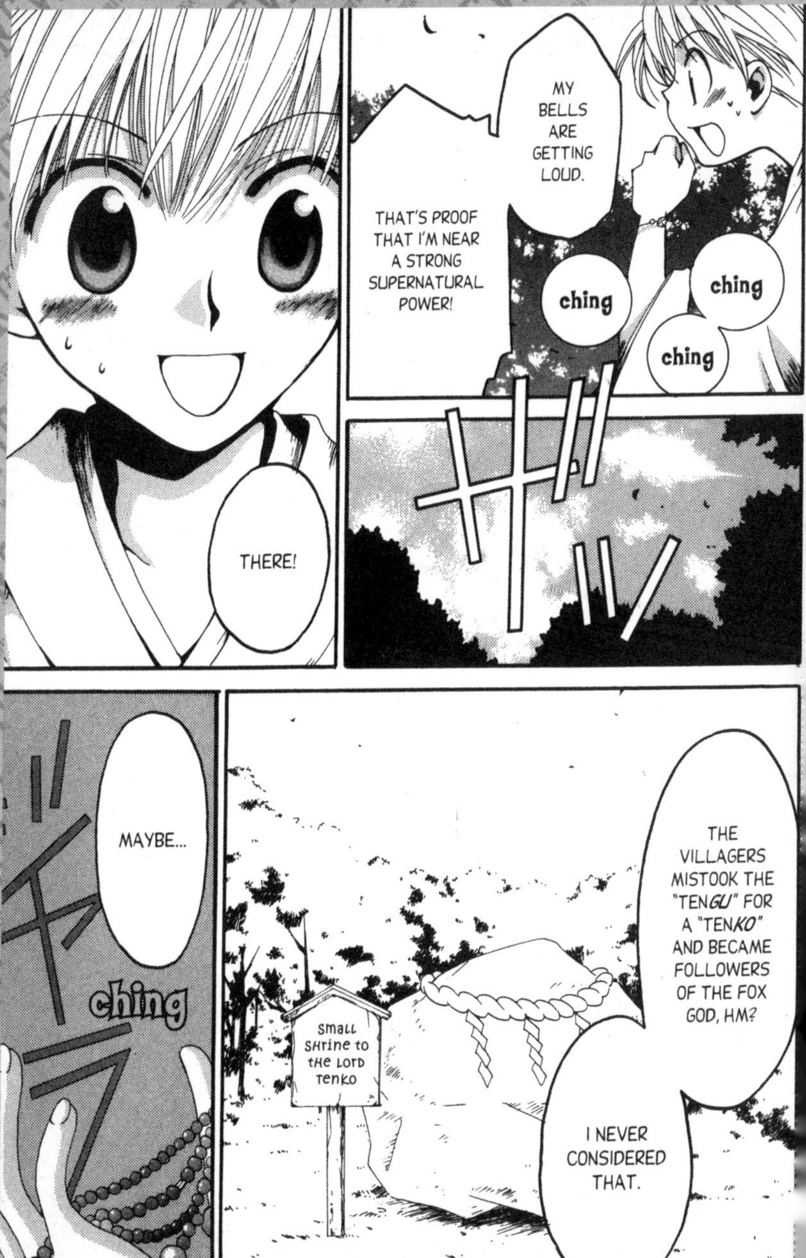
MY BELLS ARE GETTING LOUD.
THAT'S PROOF THAT I'M NEAR A STRONG SUPERNATURAL POWER!
ching
ching
ching
THERE!
THE VILLAGERS MISTOOK THE "TENGU" FOR A "TENKO" AND BECAME FOLLOWERS OF THE FOX GOD, HM?
Small Shrine to the Lord Tenko
I NEVER CONSIDERED THAT.
MAYBE...
ching

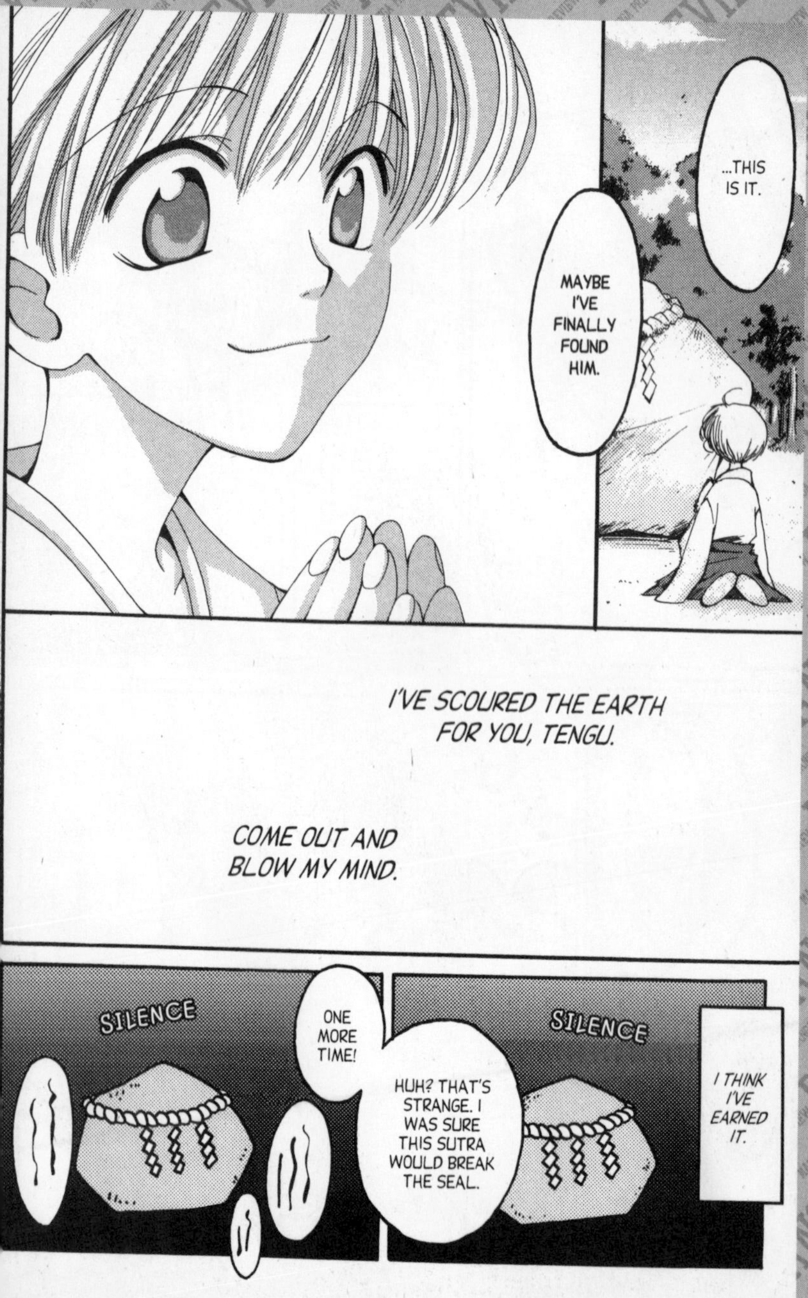
...THIS IS IT.
MAYBE I'VE FINALLY FOUND HIM.
I'VE SCOURED THE EARTH FOR YOU, TENGU.
COME OUT AND BLOW MY MIND.
I THINK I'VE EARNED IT.
SILENCE
HUH? THAT'S STRANGE. I WAS SURE THIS SUTRA WOULD BREAK THE SEAL.
ONE MORE TIME!
SILENCE

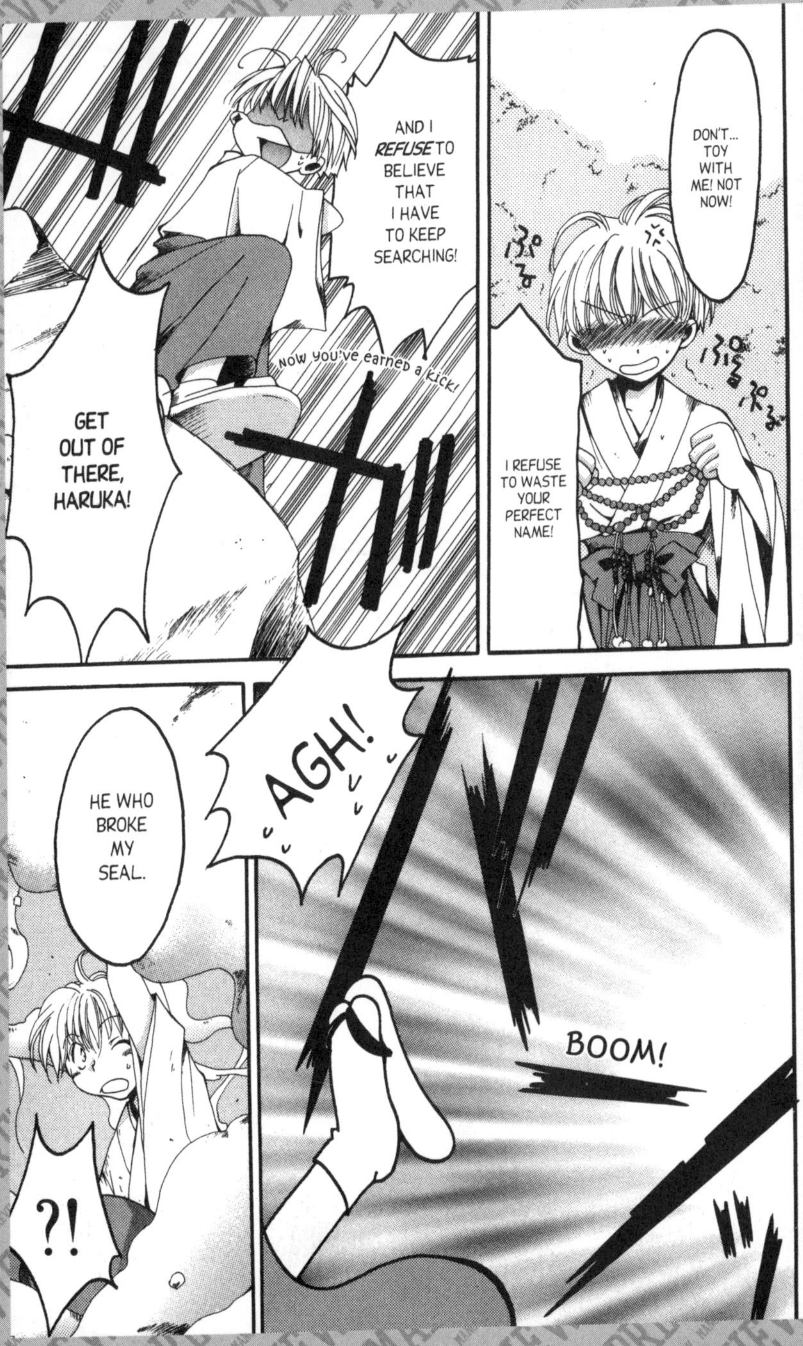
DON'T... TOY WITH ME! NOT NOW!
I REFUSE TO WASTE YOUR PERFECT NAME!
AND I *REFUSE* TO BELIEVE THAT I HAVE TO KEEP SEARCHING!
Now you've earned a kick!
GET OUT OF THERE, HARUKA!
AGH!
BOOM!
HE WHO BROKE MY SEAL.
?!

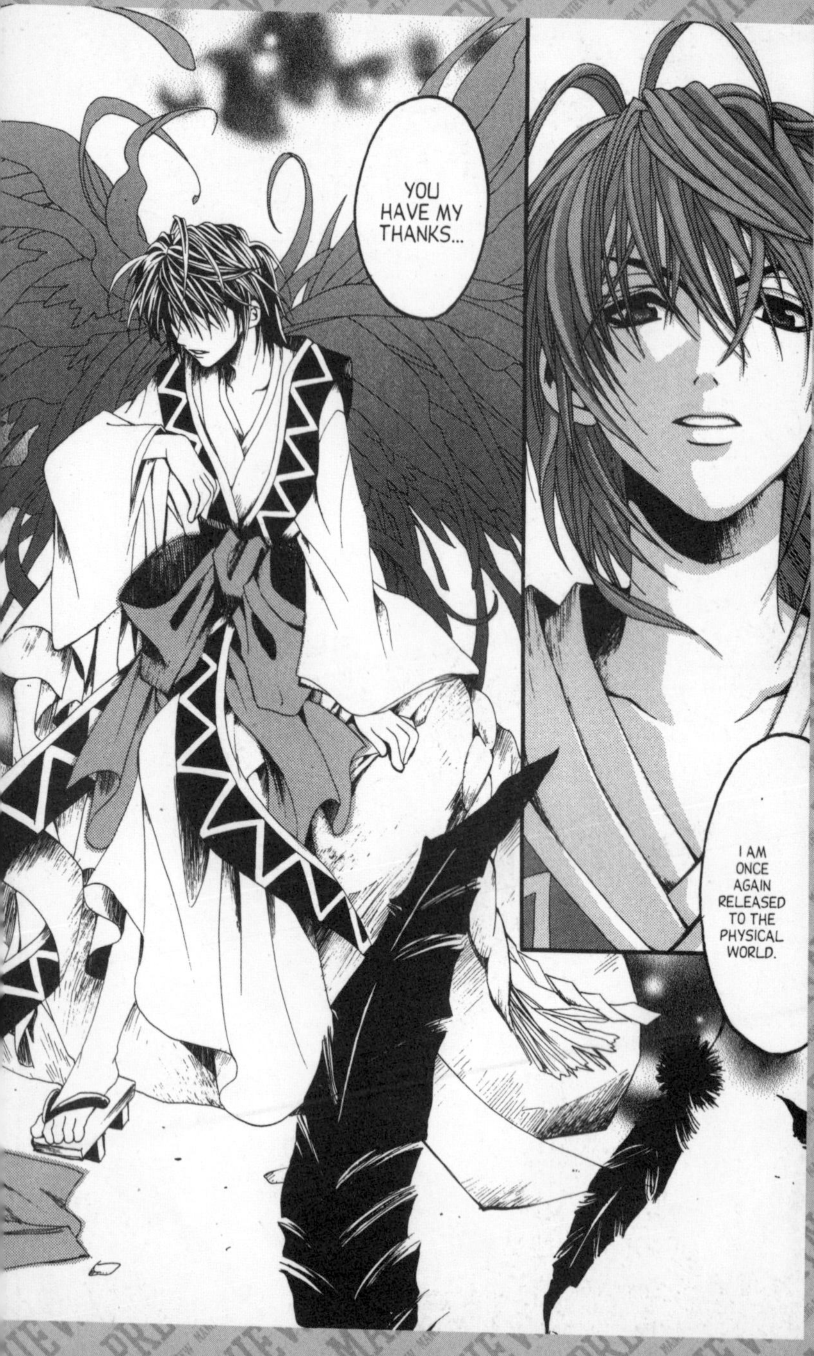
I AM ONCE AGAIN RELEASED TO THE PHYSICAL WORLD.
YOU HAVE MY THANKS...

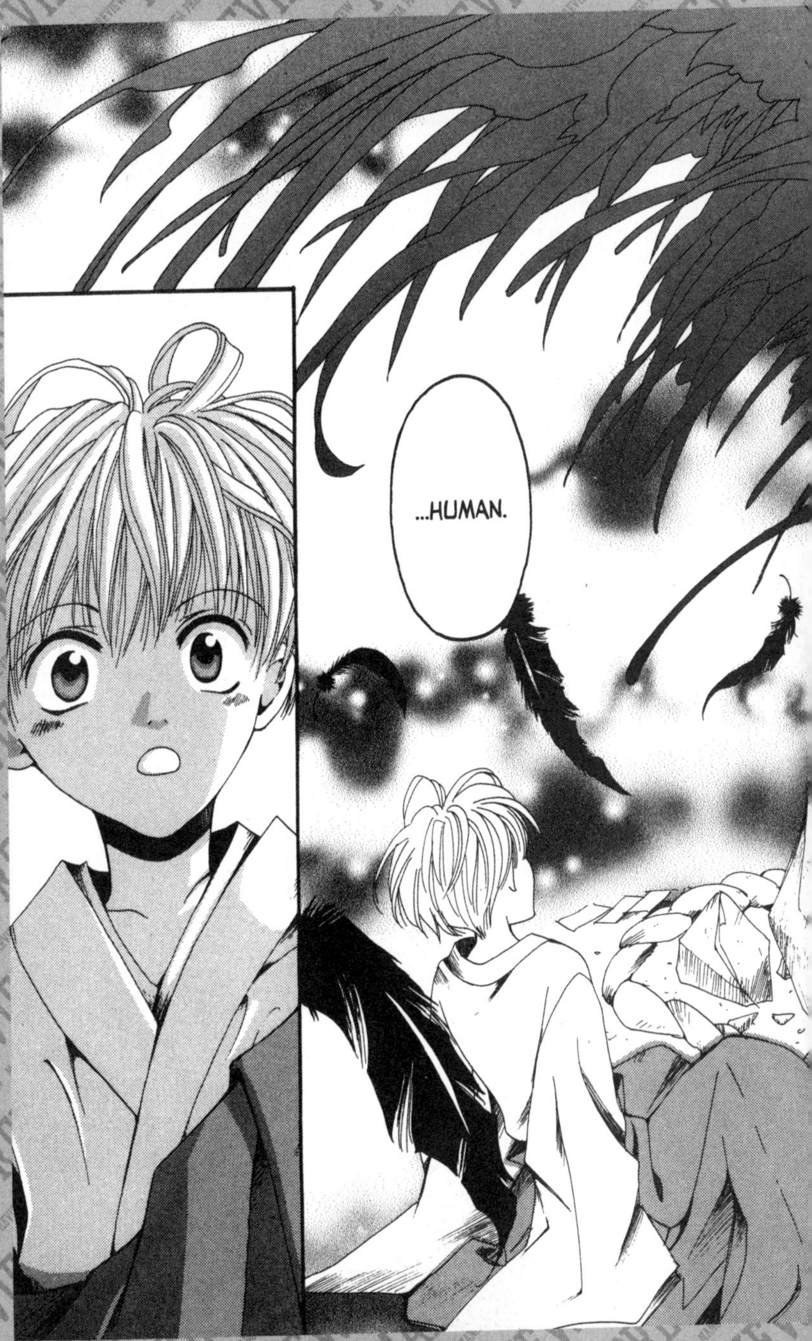
...HUMAN.

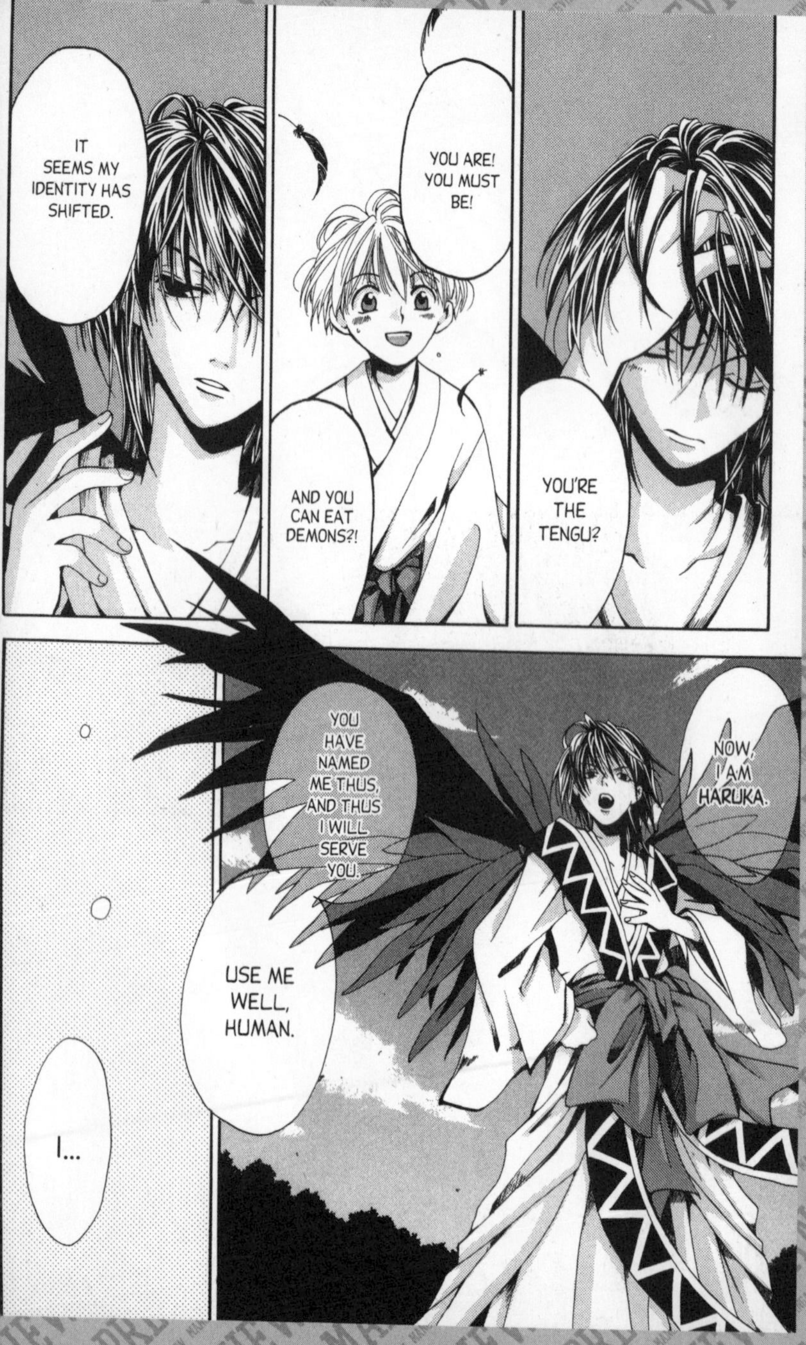
YOU'RE THE TENGU?
YOU ARE! YOU MUST BE!
AND YOU CAN EAT DEMONS?!
IT SEEMS MY IDENTITY HAS SHIFTED.
NOW, I AM HARUKA.
YOU HAVE NAMED ME THUS, AND THUS I WILL SERVE YOU.
USE ME WELL, HUMAN.
I...

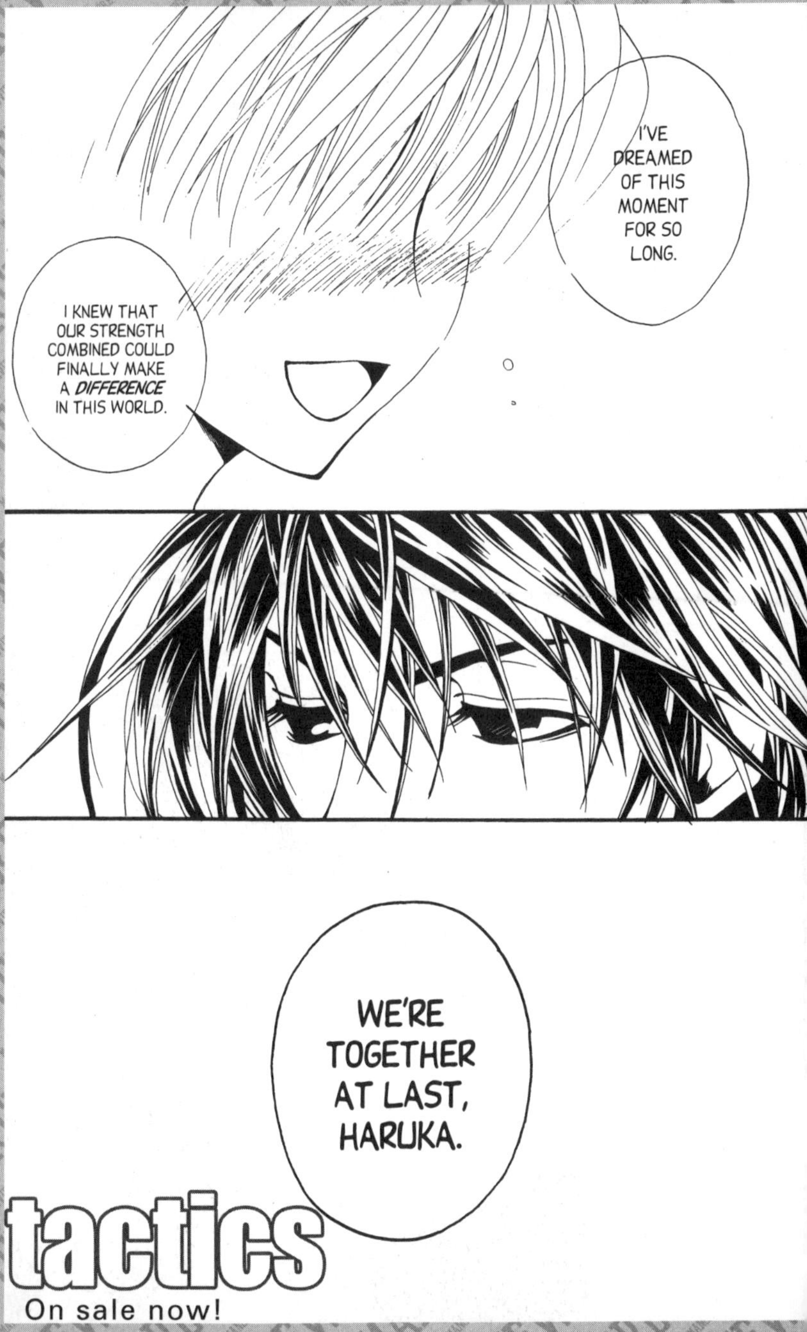
I'VE DREAMED OF THIS MOMENT FOR SO LONG.
I KNEW THAT OUR STRENGTH COMBINED COULD FINALLY MAKE A *DIFFERENCE* IN THIS WORLD.
WE'RE TOGETHER AT LAST, HARUKA.
tactics
On sale now!

STOP!

This is the back of the book.
You wouldn't want to spoil a great ending!

This book is printed "manga-style," in the authentic Japanese right-to-left format. Since none of the artwork has been flipped or altered, readers get to experience the story just as the creator intended. You've been asking for it, so TOKYOPOP® delivered: authentic, hot-off-the-press, and far more fun!

DIRECTIONS

1
2
3
4
5
6
7
8
9
10

If this is your first time reading manga-style, here's a quick guide to help you understand how it works.

It's easy... just start in the top right panel and follow the numbers. Have fun, and look for more 100% authentic manga from TOKYOPOP®!

THE MANGA REVOLUTION • LEADING
漫画革命